The Bare Essentials
Form A

Seventh Edition

Next Friday - Ch. 1-5
Sept. 10 online exercises

The Bare Essentials
Form A

Seventh Edition

Sarah Norton, Brian Green

NELSON EDUCATION

NELSON EDUCATION

The Bare Essentials, Form A, Seventh Edition

Sarah Norton and Brian Green

Vice-President and Editorial Director:
Evelyn Veitch

Editor-in-Chief:
Anne Williams

Executive Editor:
Laura Macleod

Marketing Manager:
Amanda Henry

Developmental Editor:
Theresa Fitzgerald

Permissions Coordinator:
Vicki Gould

Senior Content Production Manager:
Natalia Denesiuk Harris

Copy Editor:
June Trusty

Proofreader:
Wendy Thomas

Indexer:
Gillian Watts

Production Coordinator:
Ferial Suleman

Design Director:
Ken Phipps

Managing Designer:
Franca Amore

Illustrations:
JJ Rivera

Interior Design:
Greg Devitt

Cover Design:
Jennifer Leung

Cover Image:
JJ Rivera

Compositor:
Carol Magee

Printer:
Transcontinental

Library and Archives Canada Cataloguing in Publication Data

Norton, Sarah, date
    The bare essentials : form A / Sarah Norton, Brian Green.—7th ed.

Includes index.
ISBN 978-0-17-650034-4

1. English language—Grammar—Textbooks. 2. English language—Rhetoric—Textbooks. I. Green, Brian II. Title.

PE1408.N674 2009   808'.042
C2008-907771-7

ISBN-13: 978-0-17-650034-4
ISBN-10: 0-17-650034-0

CONTENTS

UNIT 6   READINGS

APPENDIXES

PREFACE

TO THE INSTRUCTOR

Welcome to the seventh edition of *The Bare Essentials, Form A*, a Canadian text designed for college and university students who need to learn to write correctly for academic and professional purposes. In addition to answering students' needs, the text meets the requirements of teachers who want simple explanations, Canadian examples, and plenty of practice for their classes.

The intended audience for this text is the *average* postsecondary student. Students who have a good understanding of syntax and grammar would be better served by the more advanced book in our series, *Essay Essentials*, which focuses on essay development and the art of research. *Essay Essentials* also contains a workbook section to meet the needs of those whose grasp of syntax, grammar, and punctuation is less than firm.

For students who would benefit from ESL support or for mixed classes containing both unilingual English speakers and second-language learners, we suggest *The Bare Essentials Plus*. This text combines concentrated versions of the best of both *Essentials* worlds: the basics from *Bare Essentials* and more challenging material from *Essay Essentials*, together with a separate unit devoted to topics of special interest to ESL students.

Below is a summary of the highlights of this new edition of *The Bare Essentials, Form A*.

- Units 1 through 4 begin with a "Quick Quiz" and conclude with a "Rapid Review." These tests preview and review the contents of each unit. They also provide practice in editing continuous prose passages.
- Chapter 1 focuses on audience-appropriate language. To help students find and use an appropriate register in their writing, we begin with an overview of the levels and kinds of language that are and are not appropriate in

written messages designed for specific audiences and purposes. In response to readers' requests, we have reinstated a short section on clichés.

- Chapter 21 now contains more examples of how to punctuate titles (including those from electronic sources), dialogue, and direct quotations.
- Unit 5, on paragraphs and essays, includes a more flexible treatment of thesis statements and a more comprehensive overview of outlines, ranging from the informal scratch outline to the detailed formal outline. Chapter 27, "Revising Your Paper," now includes exercises to give students practice in working through the three stages of a thorough revision.
- Chapter 28, "Using Research Resources Responsibly," is new to this edition. Our reviewers and readers asked for help in dealing with plagiarism and irresponsible use of Internet sources. This chapter uses examples to identify the difference between paraphrase and plagiarism, and then follows up with an exercise that gives students practice in distinguishing between the two.
- Unit 6 consists of six readings, two of them new to this edition. "Career Consciousness" appears first because it is the final product of the examples we use in Unit 5 to teach the process of essay writing. The remaining essays in this unit are arranged in order of difficulty: from the most basic to the most challenging. All reading selections are followed by discussion questions and writing suggestions. (Instructors will find suggested answers to the discussion questions on our website and in the *Instructor's Manual*.) Also, two essays in Unit 6 are examples of documented papers: one in the APA style and the other in the MLA style.
- Appendix A, "A Review of the Basics," has been included for the grammatically faithful. In it, you will find definitions and examples of the kinds and parts of sentences and the parts of speech.
- The "List of Grammatical Terms" (Appendix B) defines and illustrates terms that appear in bold print in the text, together with other grammatical terms with which you may want your students to be familiar.
- "Spelling Matters," which was an appendix in the previous version, is now on the Student Resources page of the website.
- On the inside back cover, in the left-hand column, is a list of commonly used correction abbreviations and symbols. The middle column identifies the meaning of each and indicates where to find an explanation and examples. The right-hand column has been left blank so that students can write in the correction symbols that you prefer.

This edition of *The Bare Essentials, Form A*, retains the features of all volumes in the *Essentials* series: clear, concise explanation of points, numerous examples, and plenty of practice exercises to reinforce learning. *The Bare Essentials* provides students with the knowledge they need in order to progress from basic sentence correctness through paragraph development to the organization and presentation of short college and university papers. We have tried to present these critical concepts clearly, in a friendly tone, and to motivate students with encouragement and humour.

The "essentials" are arranged from words (Unit 1) to syntax (Unit 2) to grammar (Unit 3) to punctuation (Unit 4) to paragraphs and essays (Unit 5) to readings that provide examples and inspiration (Unit 6). The units are independent of each other, so instructors can choose to present them in any order that suits the curriculum. The chapters within each unit, however, should be introduced in the order in which they appear. The exercises within each unit are cumulative: those in later chapters often include questions that assume mastery of skills covered in earlier chapters.

Almost all of the exercises can be completed in the text, and the answers (in Appendix C) are easy to find. The first exercise in each chapter refers students to the page on which the answers for that chapter begin, and all exercises are numbered by chapter as well as by exercise (e.g., Exercise 5.4 refers to the fourth exercise in Chapter 5). We instruct students to check their answers as soon as they have completed an exercise in order to get immediate feedback, learn from their mistakes, and avoid reinforcing their errors. **We urge instructors to emphasize the importance of this procedure**. Students who need more practice than the exercises in the text provide will find supplementary, self-scoring exercises on the website (www.barea. nelson.com). Web icons in each chapter identify when and where to find these additional exercises.

Answers to the chapter Mastery Tests are not included in this book. They are posted on the Instructor Resources page of the website and printed in the *Instructor's Manual*. Both resources also offer an alternative set of Mastery Tests that are equivalent to the ones in the book.

On the inside front cover is a quick revision guide that students can use as a checklist to guide them as they edit their work. Instructors can duplicate the guide, staple a copy to each student's paper, and mark ✔ or ✘ beside each point in the guide to identify the paper's strengths and weaknesses. This strategy provides students with clear and consistent feedback. Moreover, it saves hours of marking time.

INSTRUCTOR RESOURCES

WEBSITE (www.barea.nelson.com)

An outline of some of the features on our website is provided on the next page. On the Instructor Resources page, "Preventing Plagiarism: Why? What?

The Bare Essentials, Form A, Website

Instructor Resources Page	Student Resources Page

The Creative Classroom
Preventing Plagiarism: Why? What? How?
Answers to Mastery Tests
Alternative Mastery Tests & Answers
Suggested Answers to Discussion Questions (Unit 6)
Supplementary Readings
PowerPoint Slides & Transparencies
Essentials iTests
	Web Exercises (Chs. 2–27)
	Are You a Match for Guy Grammar?
	More Information
	• Additional Examples for Chapters 2–22
	• Spelling Matters
	• Formatting & Documentation
	  • MLA Style
	  • APA Style
	• InfoTrac/Research Skills
	• ESL Tips
	• Student Survival Skills
	More Practice
	• Practice Tests
	• Supplementary Readings
	Reading, Writing, & Reference Links
	Ask the Authors

How?" is new and offers helpful tips on dealing with this perennial problem. "The Creative Classroom" contains teaching tips and classroom activities based on game theory. An introductory essay explains the theory and the rationale behind these activities, which students find are fun to do.

The Student Resources page is divided into three major sections. The first, "Web Exercises," contains additional exercises, identified in Chapters 2 through 27, for students who need extra practice.

The second section of the Student Resources page, "More Information," contains additional examples of the principles explained in Chapters 2 through 22, instruction on MLA and APA formatting and documentation styles, and other useful information.

The third section, "More Practice," contains practice tests for Chapters 2 through 22, along with supplementary readings (posted on both the Instructor and the Student Resources pages), designed for students who need unambiguous examples of the five-paragraph essay structure. These essays are less sophisticated in language and structure than those in Unit 6.

INSTRUCTOR'S MANUAL

This print resource includes teaching tips, classroom activities, answers to the Mastery Tests for each chapter, an alternative set of Mastery Tests and answers, additional readings for analysis, and transparency masters that summarize chapter contents. The last 20 slides define and illustrate parts of speech and sentences and provide a quick review of major syntax, grammar, and punctuation errors.

ESSENTIALS iTESTS

The *Essentials iTests*, a self-scoring CD-ROM version of the *Essentials Test Manual*, is now available to support instructors who use any textbook in the *Essentials* series. This comprehensive test bank includes course diagnostic tests as well as pre- and post-tests for each unit and chapter. The tests address six principal points of composition: organization, syntax, grammar, punctuation, diction, and spelling. Instructors can select preformatted tests, revise them, or develop their own tests tailored specifically to their curriculum.

With its easy-to-use assessment and tutorial system, *Essentials iTests* enables you to create and deliver customized tests in minutes. You can choose either Quick Test Wizard or an Online Test Wizard to guide you step by step through the process of creating individualized tests. Each test appears on screen exactly as it will print or display online.

We have designed *The Bare Essentials, Form A,* not only for college and university students who need to learn how to write, but also for instructors who are dedicated to providing students with correct and effective writing skills as efficiently and painlessly as possible. While *The Bare Essentials* can successfully be used to support self-instruction and independent study, it works best for students lucky enough to have an instructor to guide them enthusiastically through its contents, adjust the pace and level of instruction to the needs of each class, and provide regular feedback and encouragement. We hope this new edition will fulfill these instructors' expectations and help them maintain their joy in teaching.

ACKNOWLEDGMENTS

We thank our reviewers, all of them generous with their time and suggestions. Their thoughtful responses helped shape this new edition: Veronica Abbass, Seneca College; Tim Chamberlain, Camosun College; Mary Gelinas, St. Lawrence College; and Don Stanley, Thompson Rivers University, Open Learning.

We are especially indebted to our illustrator, JJ Rivera, for bringing Guy Grammar and his war on solecisms so vividly to life. Together with Greg Devitt, the interior designer, JJ has created a new look that places *The Bare Essentials, Form A* firmly in the 21st century. Thanks are due to our executive editor, Laura Macleod, and our developmental editor, Theresa Fitzgerald, who enthusiastically supported our radical new look. We are once again humbled by the contributions of Natalia Denesiuk Harris, senior content production manager, and June Trusty, copy editor, for ensuring that our book reaches you as free of errors as is humanly possible.

Finally, we wish to thank the teachers across Canada whose encouragement and helpful criticism have kept *The Bare Essentials* alive for 30 years. We hope that the new design will not only please you, but also inspire you to approach teaching "the bare essentials" of our language with new enthusiasm.

Sarah Norton
Brian Green

INTRODUCTION

TO THE STUDENT:
WHY YOU NEED THIS BOOK

College and university composition courses have always had a public-relations problem. Writing skills is not a "core" course, and students often wonder why they are required to take it. The fact is that good writing skills will probably be as valuable to your career success as any subject you will take. That's why English composition is part of your curriculum: program advisory boards and curriculum committees know that graduates who can communicate well will get hired more quickly, advance more quickly, and climb higher in their professions than graduates with poor communication skills. Companies from Imperial Oil to IBM, from the CBC to Ford, from the Royal Bank to Bell Canada, not to mention all levels of government, hospitals, police forces, and the Canadian military, have gone on record as demanding superior communication skills as an essential hiring criterion.

To any employer, an employee is more valuable if he or she can write well. Fairly or unfairly, no matter what field you're in, employers, peers, and subordinates will judge your ability largely on the basis of your communication skills. In most careers, your ability to write well will be tested every day.

The good news is that writing skills can be learned. There is no reason you can't write clear and correct reports, memoranda, and even e-mails. This book is intended to help you do exactly that, just as it has helped hundreds of thousands of Canadian students since it was first published. All you need is the desire to improve. If you really want to succeed, you'll invest the time, effort, and care needed to make the concepts in this book work for you.

WHAT'S IN THIS BOOK

There is more to this text than meets the eye. In addition to the book you're holding in your hand, you have access to a comprehensive website that provides more exercises, information, and practice. Together, the book and the website give you the tools and resources you need to improve your writing.

If you turn to the table of contents (page v), you'll see that the book is divided into six units. Units 1 through 4 will help you identify and eliminate errors in your writing.

A writing error is a failure of communication. Miscommunication occurs when a message fails to meet the reader's expectations, or the writer's purpose, or both.

Unit 5 explains and illustrates how to organize and develop your ideas in effective paragraphs, essays, and reports. Unit 6 consists of six readings on a variety of topics we hope you will find interesting. These essays illustrate a number of common organizational patterns as well as the different levels of language, from informal to formal, that writers can use to suit their subject, audience, and purpose.

Three appendixes follow Unit 6: Appendix A covers basic grammatical points—the kinds and parts of sentences and the parts of speech—and B lists many of the grammatical terms used in the book. Whenever you find a **technical term** in bold type, you can turn to Appendix B to discover its definition and examples of its correct use. Appendix C contains answers to the exercises in the first five units (except for the Mastery Tests), and a comprehensive index concludes the book.

On the website, under "More Information," you'll find additional examples for every principle explained and illustrated in the book. A laptop icon tells you when and where exercises are available on the website for extra practice. The Web exercises are electronically scored, which means you can get immediate feedback about your progress. Also on the website are practice tests that check your knowledge of each rule or principle. (We suggest you do these practice tests before you try the chapter Mastery Tests.)

If you are required to write a research paper as part of your composition course, the "More Information" section of the website provides explanations and examples of both MLA and APA format and documentation styles. Since few of us have the courage (or common sense) to begin work on a major paper as soon as it is assigned, the website also provides a chapter on "Student Survival Skills," including topics that range from understanding course outlines to overcoming procrastination and writer's block.

A special feature of our website is the "Ask the Authors" button. Click on this button to send us questions that you don't want to raise in class: you may be afraid they'll sound "dumb"; your instructor is pressed for time and lets you know it; or you're too shy to ask questions in class. "Ask the Authors" questions are e-mailed to us, and one of us will get back to you and answer your questions. We believe there are few "dumb" questions about writing, so feel free to ask us about whatever is puzzling you. We also encourage you to tell us what you like and don't like about our book.

HOW TO USE THIS BOOK

In each chapter, we do three things: explain a point, illustrate the point with examples, and provide exercises to help you master it. The exercises are arranged in sets that become more challenging as you go along. After some of the exercises, you'll find a symbol directing you to the "Web Exercises" section on *The Bare Essentials* website (**www.barea.nelson.com**), where we have provided additional exercises for those who need extra practice. By the time you finish a chapter, you should have a good grasp of the skill. Then it's up to you to apply that skill every time you write. Competence in writing is no different from any other competence: it results from combining knowledge with practice.

Here's how to proceed:

1. Read the explanation. Do this even if you think you understand the point. Make sure you understand the concept, and get help from your instructor if it's not completely clear.
2. Study the highlighted rules and the examples that follow them.
3. If you find an explanation easy and think you have no problem with the skill, try the last set of exercises following the explanation. Then check your answers. If you've made no errors, go on to the next point.

   If you're less confident, don't skip anything. Start with the first set and work through all the exercises, including those on the website, until you are sure you understand the point. (As a general rule, getting three exercises in a row entirely correct demonstrates understanding and competence.)
4. **Always check your answers to one set of exercises before you go on to the next.** This step is crucial. Only by checking your results after

each set can you identify errors and correct them right away, instead of repeating and possibly reinforcing them.

5. When you find a mistake, go back to the explanation and examples. Study them again; then look up the additional examples for that point on the website. If you are truly stuck, check with your instructor. Your brain cannot learn anything as complex as the structure of language unless you clear up problems as you go. Continue with the exercises only when you are sure you understand where you went wrong and are confident that you won't repeat the error.

You can reinforce your understanding—and prepare for in-class tests—by doing the practice tests posted on the Student Resources page of *The Bare Essentials* website.

WHAT THE SYMBOLS MEAN

GO TO WEB EXERCISE

WWW.BAREA.NELSON.COM

When this symbol appears in the text, it means that you will find on *The Bare Essentials* website exercises that supplement the chapter you are working on. Once you've logged on to the website, click on "Web Exercises." The exercises are posted by chapter, so to get to the exercises for the apostrophe, for example, click on Chapter 3 in the list, then go to the numbered exercise(s) identified for you beside the icon in the textbook. Web exercises are marked automatically, so you will know instantly whether or not you have understood the material.

This symbol beside an exercise means the exercise is designed to be done by two or more students working together. Often you are instructed to begin work in a pair or group, then to work individually on a writing task, and finally to regroup and review your writing with your partner(s). (Of course, your instructor may choose to modify these exercises for students working independently.)

This symbol means "Note this." We've used it to highlight writing tips, helpful hints, hard-to-remember points, and information that you should apply whenever you write, not just when you are dealing with the principle covered in the paragraph marked by the icon.

When an exercise is marked with this icon, it means the activity is a Mastery Test—an exercise designed to check your level of understanding of the principles covered in the chapter you have just completed. The answers to these exercises are not in the back of the book; your instructor will provide them.

TWO FINAL SUGGESTIONS

Inside the front cover, you'll find a "Quick Revision Guide." Use it to help you revise your papers before handing them in. This book is meant to be a practical tool, not a theoretical reference. Apply the lessons in all of the writing you do. We can identify writing problems and show you how to solve them, and exercises can give you practice in eliminating errors, but only your own writing and revising can bring real and lasting improvement.

Inside the back cover, you'll find a list of the most common editing and proofreading symbols—the shorthand forms your instructor may use when grading your papers to signal where you've made mistakes. For each type of error, we explain and illustrate the standard symbols and also leave space for you to write in your instructor's preferred symbol or abbreviation. See Chapter 27 for suggestions about using this list to maximize your improvement from one essay to the next.

UNIT 1

Words

UNIT 1 QUICK QUIZ

This Quick Quiz is designed to test your competency in the writing skills covered in Unit 1. Your goal is to revise the paragraph below so that it contains no inappropriate language (e.g., slang and clichés), no redundancies (wordiness), and no misused words, apostrophes, capital letters, or numbers. Your results will show you which chapters in this unit you need to focus on.

When you've made your corrections, turn to page 382 in Appendix C to see how successful you've been at finding and correcting the 20 errors. For each error you miss, the "Answer Key" there directs you to the chapter(s) you need to work on.

[1]Yesterday I was in the city to do some shopping and enjoy an evening of fine dinning. [2]It was my girlfriend's Birthday, so I intended to score a pair of tickets to a play and then go for broke for dinner at an expensive restaurant. [3]First, I went to a stationary store to find a card, and when I came out, their was the heat, writing a parking ticket. [4]Suddenly I got what I thought was a great, utterly brilliant, out-of-this world idea. [5]I approached the Officer and asked that he except my apology and not write the ticket. [6]He ignored me and continued to write. [7]Determined to get a rise out of him, I called him a miserable swine. [8]He glared at me and began to write another ticket because the car had worn tires. [9]It was at this point in time that I insulted his ancestors and his ancestors ancestors. [10]He finished the 2nd ticket and began filling out a third, then a forth. [11]Even though he pretended not to hear me, I knew my

abuse was getting under his skin since he kept writing ticket's. [12]I didn't care,

because I had no idea who's car it was. [13]I always come into the city by public

transit, but I think its important to have a little fun every day.

1 Choosing the Right Words

> *The difference between the right word and the almost right word is the difference between lightning and the lightning bug.*
>
> **– Mark Twain**

Real estate salespeople say there are three things to consider when buying a property: location, location, location. Good writers know that there are three things to consider when sending a message: audience, audience, audience. Knowledge of your readers—what they need or want to know—and of what they expect from you, the writer, should be your constant focus.

We assume that, whenever and whatever you write, you want your reader (a) to understand your message and (b) to think well of you. To achieve these goals, your writing must be both accurate and appropriate. If your readers are to understand you, your message must consist of words that say what you mean, organized into grammatical sentences arranged in logical, well-developed paragraphs.

The notion of "correctness" in writing has been developed over hundreds of years—and is still changing—to help writers create messages that communicate what their authors intended. Error-filled writing does not meet the reader's minimum expectation that a message will be clearly and correctly communicated. Mistakes in grammar, sentence structure, spelling, and punctuation ensure that a message will not be easily understood. And there is a second, equally important, reason to ensure that your writing is accurate: our culture associates correct language with education and intelligence. Carelessly written, ungrammatical writing is often considered a sign of ignorance, or laziness, or both.

But that's not all. Accuracy alone will not get you to your goals. A message that is free of technical errors can still confuse or offend a reader if it contains inappropriate language. Slang; racist, sexist, obscene, or blasphemous language; pretentiousness; and even wordiness can interfere with your message. That's why we consider them "errors." They divert the reader's attention from what you're saying to how you're saying it. They also lower the reader's opinion of you.

In this chapter, we provide a brief introduction to choosing language that is accurate and appropriate for your message and your audience. Our assumption is that you are writing for readers in academic and professional environments. Our goals are to help you convey your message clearly and in a way that will leave your readers with a positive impression of you and your ideas.

Before you get started, you need to equip yourself with a few essential resources and some basic knowledge of what kind of language is appropriate when you write.

1. Buy and use a good dictionary.

A dictionary is a writer's best friend. You will need to use it every time you write, so if you don't already own a good dictionary, you need to buy one. For Canadian writers, a good dictionary is one that is Canadian, current, comprehensive (contains at least 75,000 entries), and reliable (published by an established, well-known firm).

A convenient reference is the *Collins Gage Canadian Paperback Dictionary*, available in an inexpensive paperback edition. Also recommended are the *Nelson Canadian Dictionary of the English Language* (Thomson Nelson, 1997) and, for those whose native language is not English, the *Oxford Advanced Learner's Dictionary*, 7th ed., paperback (Oxford, 2008). Unfortunately, no comprehensive Canadian dictionary is available on the Internet.

Unless you have already done so (and most people haven't), begin by reading the introduction or the guide provided in the front of the dictionary. This information may not be very entertaining, but it is essential if you want to understand how to read your dictionary accurately. No two dictionaries are alike. Only if you are familiar with your dictionary's symbols, abbreviations, and the format of its entries, will you be able to use it efficiently.

Knowing what is in the front matter of the dictionary will also save you time. For example, you may not need to memorize long lists of irregular plurals. Good dictionaries include irregular plurals in their entries. They also include irregular forms of verbs, adjectives, and adverbs. And if you've forgotten how regular plurals, verbs, adjectives, and adverbs are formed, you'll find that information in the front of the dictionary as well.

Take half an hour to read the front matter in your dictionary; then do the following sets of exercises. Be sure to check your answers to each set before going on to the next. Answers for exercises in this chapter begin on page 383.

EXERCISE **1.1**

1. What is another spelling of the word *humour*? Which spelling must you use when you add an ending such as *-ous* or *-ist* to the root word?
2. Is *harrassment* spelled correctly? Which syllable do you stress when you pronounce this word?
3. Is *tatoo* spelled correctly? Is the word a noun or a verb?
4. Are people who live in Saskatchewan more likely to experience a *tornado*, a *typhoon*, or a *tsunami*? Explain why.
5. Find alternative spellings for the words *programme*, *center*, *skillful*, *traveler*, and *judgement*. In each case, indicate the spelling most commonly used in Canada.

EXERCISE **1.2**

Write the plural form of each word.

1. basis
2. criterion
3. data
4. ratio
5. nucleus
6. appendix
7. formula
8. phenomenon
9. mother-in-law
10. syllabus

EXERCISE **1.3**

Combine each root word with the ending given.

1. delay + ed
2. journey + s
3. play + er
4. destroy + ing
5. repay + ment

6. lonely + ness
7. policy + s
8. easy + er
9. lazy + ness
10. necessary + ly

After you have checked your answers to this exercise, go back and look closely at the questions. What do the root words in questions 1 through 5 have in common? What do the root words in questions 6 through 10 have in common? How do these similarities affect the way they are spelled when an ending is added?

EXERCISE **1.4**

Using hyphens, show where each word could be divided at the end of a line. (Some words can be divided in two or more places: *def-ini-tion*, for example.) Good style requires that you never hyphenate a word if doing so means beginning the next line with fewer than three letters.

1. coffee
2. arrangement
3. precise
4. night
5. process

6. monitor
7. gradually
8. politics
9. dictionary
10. prenuptial

EXERCISE **1.5**

The following words are not pronounced the way you might expect if you've had no previous experience with them. Look them up in your dictionary and, in the space beside each word, write its pronunciation (the information given immediately after it in parentheses). Using your dictionary's pronunciation key to help you, practise sounding out each word, one syllable at a time. No answers are given for this exercise.

1. preferable
2. epitome
3. impotent

4. comparable
5. subtle
6. eulogy

7. indict   9. corps

8. irreparable   10. chassis

---

2. Use spelling and grammar checkers responsibly.

- Good spell-check programs can find typing errors and some common spelling mistakes. They have limitations, however; for example, they can't tell if you meant to write "your" or "you're" and will not flag either word, even if it's used incorrectly. (You'll learn more about such words in Chapter 2, "Hazardous Homonyms.") Also, since we use Canadian English, our spelling is sometimes different from American spelling, on which most word-processing programs are based. If your program can be set to Canadian spelling, make that adjustment. If it cannot, be aware that words such as *colour*, *honour*, and *metre*—all correct Canadian spellings—will be flagged as errors.
- Another useful tool is a hand-held spell checker. Conveniently pocket-sized and not expensive, these devices contain a large bank of words and can provide the correct spelling if the "guess" you type in is not too far off. Some checkers even pronounce the word for you. Ask your instructor if you can use this device (sound turned off, please) when you are writing in class and during exams.
- The best advice we can give you about grammar checkers (they announce their presence by producing wavy red and green lines under words or sentences as you write on your word processor) is to use them with caution. So far, no grammar checker has been able to account for most, let alone all, of the subtleties of English grammar. A grammar program is as likely to flag a perfectly good sentence, even to suggest a "fix" that is incorrect, as it is to ignore a sentence full of errors. "I done real good on my grammar test," for example, escapes the dreaded wavy green line.

3. Buy and use a good thesaurus.

If you use the same words over and over, you will bore your reader. A thesaurus is a dictionary of synonyms—words with similar meanings. For any word you need to use repeatedly in a document, a good thesaurus will provide a list of alternatives.

Please note that synonyms are not identical in meaning. Only you (or a knowledgeable friend) can decide which of the words listed in your thesaurus may be suitable for your message. Your dictionary will help you decide which terms are acceptable and which are not. We do not recommend that you rely

on the thesaurus in your word-processing program. For any given word, a word-processing thesaurus provides a list, in alphabetical order, of more-or-less synonyms, with no usage labels or examples. "More-or-less" is not good enough. The minimum information you need is whether the synonyms offered are nouns or verbs and whether they are in general use or are informal, technical, derogatory, or even obsolete. For this information, you need a book. Buy a good thesaurus and use it in conjunction with your dictionary.

Two thesauruses are available in inexpensive paperback editions: *The Oxford Thesaurus of English* (Oxford, 2006), and *Roget's Thesaurus* (Penguin, 2004).

Inexperienced writers sometimes assume that long, obscure words will impress their readers. In fact, the opposite is usually true. Most readers are annoyed by unnecessarily "fancy" language (see "Pretentious Language," page 18).

NEVER use a word whose meaning you do not know. When you find a possible but unfamiliar synonym, look it up in your dictionary to make sure that it means what you want to say.

LEVELS OF LANGUAGE

Good writing involves more than the meaning of words and sentences. It also requires the choice of appropriate language. No one would submit a book review that began, "This is an awesome book with, like, ideas that sort of make you think, you know?" You know instantly that the language is inappropriate. Similarly, if you were discussing the book with friends over a coffee and said, "This book contains provocative and stimulating ideas that engage and challenge the reader," your language would be equally inappropriate.

Written English (e-mail notwithstanding) is usually more formal than spoken English. Because writers have time to consider what they want to say and how best to say it, they can choose their words carefully, arrange them in meaningful sentences, and organize ideas into logical paragraphs. An appropriate level of language is an essential part of effective writing.

Choose a level that suits both your topic and your reader. There will be times when you need to compromise: when you send one message to a mixed audience, for example. In such cases, the safe bet is to aim at your highest-level reader and trust that the others will understand (or ask for clarification).

Sometimes it isn't clear what level you should be using. At such times, your reader's preference should determine your choice. Many colleges and universities expect students to write academic papers in formal English, which requires, among other things, third-person pronouns (*he, she, one, they*). Informal writing, with its first- and second-person pronouns (*I, me, you*), may not be acceptable. (See page 378 for an explanation of "person.") Ask your instructor about your school's policy and follow it.

Similarly, because employers tend to favour formal letters of application over casual ones, if you want to get the job, you will write a formal letter. For a talk you give to your class, an informal, conversational style may be appropriate. Most of what you read and write falls somewhere in the middle. Business documents, for example, are usually written in general-level Standard English.

There are no fixed divisions of English. The three levels we've identified often overlap. In this book, for example, we use a variety of styles, ranging from high-level informal through general (used for most of the text), with a few formal-level passages when they are appropriate. To help you choose the most appropriate level for your message and audience, the table on the next page outlines the basic features of informal, general, and formal written English.

No one level is "better" than another. Each has its place and function. Your message, your reader, and your purpose in writing should determine which level you choose.

Unless your instructor specifically says that you may use informal or colloquial language in your written work, use general-level English. The same rule applies to postings to online course discussion groups. Some instructors may be offended by colloquial voice-mail messages, too—especially if they are full of slang terms that teachers don't always "get"—and most will not be favourably impressed by cliché- and slang-riddled e-mails. You and your instructor are not BFFs. Your relationship is a professional one, and your language should reflect your understanding of that relationship.

> ?4U
> Do U TXT MSG?
> AFC DEGT

For the uninitiated, this message reads: "Question for you. Do you use text messaging? Away from the computer, don't even go there."

	Informal	General	Formal
Vocabulary and Style	Casual, everyday; usually concrete; some slang, colloquial expressions, contractions. Written in 1st and 2nd persons.	The language of educated persons; nonspecialized; balance of abstract and concrete; readily understood. Can use 1st, 2nd, and 3rd persons.	Often abstract, technical, or specialized; no contractions or colloquialisms. Written in 3rd person.
Sentence and Paragraph Structure	Sentences short, simple; some sentence fragments; paragraphs short.	Complete sentences of varying length; paragraphs vary, but are often fairly short.	Complete sentences, usually long, complex; paragraphs fully developed, often at length.
Tone	Conversational, casual; sounds like ordinary speech.	Varies to suit message and purpose of writer.	Impersonal, serious, often instructional.
Typical Uses	Personal letters, some fiction, some newspapers, much advertising.	Most of what we read: newspapers, magazines, novels, business correspondence.	Academic writing, some textbooks, scientific reports, journal articles, legal documents.

In the last few years, text-messaging short forms have been creeping into written assignments, reports, and even research papers and résumés. In these contexts, "text messagese" is so inappropriate and reflects so poorly on the writer that we urge you never to use it except on your cellphone. Why? Because these short forms are a code that some people may not understand, using short forms can hinder rather than help communication. Read "The Case against Quickspeak" in Unit 6 (page 346) for a fuller explanation of how and why short forms such as text-message code are not effective in professional writing.

The three paragraphs that follow, all on the same topic, illustrate informal, general, and formal written English.

INFORMAL LEVEL

So you're tired of paying through the nose at the pump! Well, the time has come to start paying attention to the alternatives out there. Everyone knows that our gas-guzzling cars and SUVs are responsible for a lot of the pollution that clogs the air, but not everyone knows that we can save money and feel good at the same time. The best bets to replace gas-powered cars are hybrid electric cars and fuel-cell electric cars. Hybrids use less gas than anything else on the road, and they are quickly becoming popular. But they are probably just a temporary fix until we move to fuel-cell cars that run on clean, plentiful hydrogen. The trouble is that we will have to change everything from refineries to fuel pumps before hydrogen-powered cars can become the standard. That's a big job!

GENERAL LEVEL

Gasoline prices are going up, but this news may not be all bad. The rise in gas prices has forced many of us to start looking at alternatives to our gas-guzzling vehicles. While our primary motivation is to save on fuel costs, we also know that reducing our use of fossil fuels will help clean up our environment. The two engines that are the current front-runner replacements for gasoline engines are the hybrid electric and the electric fuel cell. Hybrid cars use gas or diesel, but they are more efficient than anything now on the road, and they are already proving to be attractive to consumers. Hybrids, however, may be only a transition step to fuel-cell electric cars that run on clean, plentiful hydrogen. It's unlikely that this step will be taken soon, though, for we will have to transform our entire oil-based infrastructure—everything from refineries to fuel pumps—before we can all drive fuel-cell powered cars. That's an enormous undertaking!

FORMAL LEVEL

The higher gasoline prices rise, the more attention consumers and industry focus on alternatives to oil-based transportation. While the search for alternatives is driven primarily by the desire for cost savings, it has the additional appeal of being good for the environment. No one can be unaware of the atmospheric damage caused by CO_2 emissions, a large percentage of which are caused by burning fossil fuels in cars and trucks. Two alternative power plants compete for consumers' attention: hybrid electric vehicles and fuel-cell electric vehicles. The hybrid electrics, which do use gasoline or diesel but in significantly reduced amounts, are beginning to make an impact on consumers; however, many industrial observers see these cars as an interim step to fuel-cell electric vehicles that run on clean, plentiful hydrogen. Before the leap from gas-powered to hydrogen-powered cars can be made, however, the entire oil-based infrastructure must be redesigned, re-engineered, and replaced by a hydrogen-based infrastructure. A transformation of this magnitude is a daunting prospect.

ONLY ONE MAN, WITH HIS DEDICATED ORGANIZATION, G.S.I. (GRAMMAR STANDARDS INVESTIGATIONS), STANDS BETWEEN COMMUNICATION AND CHAOS: *GUY GRAMMAR.*

EXERCISE **1.6**

Using the chart on page 11, find some specific characteristics of vocabulary, sentence structure, and tone that identify the three paragraphs above as informal, general, and formal. Then turn to page 383 to compare your analysis with ours.

EXERCISE **1.7**

Working in pairs, study the following three sentences and identify the level of language of each.

1. The sport of professional cycling has been unfairly tarnished by revelations concerning the illicit use of performance-enhancing substances by some its most celebrated practitioners, despite the preponderance of evidence suggesting that every sport is riddled with those who augment their capabilities artificially, but who are seldom apprehended.
2. I don't think it's fair that bike racers get all the blame for using drugs just because their sport cracks down on doping, while other pro sports just ignore the problem or face up to it only when the media make a fuss.
3. While every professional sport has some participants who use performance-enhancing drugs, professional cycling seems to have been unfairly labelled as the worst offender, not because there are more cyclists who use drugs, but because the other sports organizations turn a blind eye to the problem.

Now, working alone, write three sentences of your own in different levels of language. (Choose topics with which you are familiar: e.g., music, sports, movies, fashion, fast food, work.)

- Finally, exchange papers with your partner and see if he or she can identify the level of language you were aiming for in each sentence.

So far, we've introduced you to the tools you'll need as a writer and to the levels of language you can choose from when writing a message for a particular audience. Let's turn now to the writing errors you must not commit, no matter what message you're sending or the audience to which you're sending it: wordiness, slang, pretentious language, clichés, offensive language, and "abusages."

WORDINESS

Wordiness—the use of words and phrases that are not essential to the communication of your message—is annoying to readers, no matter what topic you are writing about. Good writing communicates a message as concisely as possible. Wordy messages take up your reader's time and try your reader's patience. If you want to please your audience, be brief.

Sometimes wordiness results from the failure to revise carefully. In the edit stage of writing, you should be looking for the best words to express your meaning. Wordy expressions and awkward phrasing often pop into your mind when you are struggling to express an idea, and they often make their way into a first draft. There is no excuse for them to survive a careful edit and make their way into the second draft, however.

Here's an example of what can happen when a writer fails to prune his or her prose:

> In my personal opinion, the government of this country of ours needs an additional amount of meaningful input from the people of Canada.

This wordy sentence could be nicely condensed into "I think our government needs to hear more from the people." The writer has chosen impressive-sounding phrases (*meaningful input, this country of ours*) and has introduced unnecessary and meaningless words that should have been caught during editing (*personal opinion, an additional amount*). The result is a sentence that is so hard to read that it isn't worth the effort to decipher.

As you can see from the example above, one of the symptoms of wordiness is redundancy, or saying the same thing twice. Another is using several words where one or two would do.

The following list contains some of the worst offenders we've collected from student writing, corporate memoranda, form letters, and advertisements.

Wordy	Concise
a large number of	many
absolutely nothing/everything/ complete/perfect	nothing/everything/ complete/perfect
actual (*or* true) fact	fact
almost always	usually
at that point in time	then
at the present time	now
consensus of opinion	consensus
continue on	continue
could possibly (*or* may possibly, might possibly)	could (*or* may, might)
crisis (*or* emergency) situation	crisis (*or* emergency)
due to the fact that	because
end result	result
equally as good	as good
few and far between	rare
final conclusion	conclusion
for the reason that	because
free gift	gift
I myself (*or* you yourself, *etc.*)	I (*or* you, *etc.*)
I personally think/feel	I think/feel
in actual fact	in fact
in every instance	always
in my opinion, I think ...	I think
in the near future	soon
in today's society/in this day and age	now (*or* today)
is able to	can
many different kinds	many kinds
mutual agreement/cooperation	agreement/cooperation
my personal opinion	my opinion
no other alternative	no alternative
personal friend	friend
real, genuine leather (*or* real antique, *etc.*)	leather (*or* antique, *etc.*)
red in colour (*or* large in size, *etc.*)	red (*or* large, *etc.*)
repeat again	repeat

Wordy	Concise
return back	return (*or* go back)
really, very	*These words add nothing to your meaning. Leave them out.*
8:00 a.m. in the morning	8:00 a.m.
actual/real/true fact	fact
such as, for example ...	such as
take active steps	take steps
totally destroyed	destroyed
truly remarkable	remarkable
very (most, quite, almost, rather) unique	unique

EXERCISE **1.8**

Working with a partner, revise these sentences to make them as concise and clear as possible. Then compare your answers with our suggestions on page 384.

1. I myself personally feel that there is absolutely no basis in fact for the idea that UFOs exist.
2. Getting up at 5 a.m. in the morning and repeating the exact same daily routine every day for three weeks wore me out and exhausted me.
3. It has come to my attention that our competitor's products, although not equally as good as ours, are nevertheless, at this point in time, selling better than those that we produce.
4. In my opinion, I believe that my essay is equally as good as Jill's and deserves equally as good a mark, which it would have got if it weren't for the fact that the professor hates me.
5. There is absolutely nothing at the present time to suggest that this almost unique set of circumstances will ever again be repeated in the foreseeable future, so we can proceed ahead with real and genuine confidence.
6. Due to the fact that he is being transferred away from where he lives, Rowan plans to buy a brand-new car.
7. I personally think Alison is faking her illness and pretending to be sick so she can stay at home and not have to go to work.
8. Basically, I myself prefer modern contemporary furniture to old antiques.
9. Close personal friends almost always share tastes and opinions in common with each other.
10. In my opinion, I doubt that this particular new innovation will succeed in winning much in the way of market share.

WWW.BAREA.NELSON.COM

SLANG

Slang is "street talk": nonstandard words and phrases used by members of a group—people who share a culture, interest, or lifestyle. The group may be as large as a generation or as small as a high-school clique. Do you know what "amped," "badload," "busting," and "hodger" mean? The whole point of slang is its exclusivity. It's a private language and thus not appropriate for a message aimed at a general reader.

Another characteristic of slang is that it changes quickly. Terms that were "in" last month are "out" today. Except for a few expressions that manage to slip across the line that separates private language from mainstream English, most slang expressions are quickly outdated and sound silly. And finally, slang is an oral language. It is colloquial—that is, characteristic of casual speech—and not appropriate for use in professional or academic writing. There are thousands of slang expressions; in fact, there are whole dictionaries devoted to slang. Online dictionaries are the most current. For example, if you'd like to see examples of the latest rap/hip-hop slang, go to www.rapdict.org/Main_Page.

When you aren't sure if a word is appropriate for a written message, check your print dictionary. The notation *sl.* or *slang* appears after words that are slang or have a slang meaning. (In some dictionaries, some words, such as *house*, *cool*, and *bombed*, have both a general and a slang meaning.) If the word you're looking for isn't listed, chances are it's a recent slang term, and you should avoid using it in writing. Taking the time to choose words that are appropriate to written English increases your chances both of communicating clearly and of winning your readers' respect.

EXERCISE **1.9**

- Working in groups of three or four, list five slang expressions that are familiar to you but are no longer in current use.
- Now identify five current slang expressions that are used by everyone in your group.

- Explain each current slang term in a sentence or two, using language appropriate to a general reader. (If you don't have a clear picture of a "general reader," write the definitions in words your parents and teachers would understand.)

PRETENTIOUS LANGUAGE

One of the challenges writers face when trying to adapt their style from the familiar to the formal level is a tendency to overcompensate. Many beginning writers try so hard to impress their readers that they forget that the purpose of writing is to communicate. Writing filled with abstract nouns, multi-syllable words, and long, complicated sentences is **pretentious**. All readers hate pretentious writing because they have to take the time to "translate" it into language they can understand. (Most teachers and supervisors won't bother. They'll just return the piece to the student or employee for revision.)

Sometimes called "gobbledygook," pretentious language has sound but no meaning:

> Rupert's verbalization consisted of a declaration to the effect that he was profoundly moved by a self-actualizing emotion that was focused on Emilia and that he desired would, in time, be reciprocated by her.

Who knows what this means? More important, who cares? Few readers would have the patience to go through this passage, dictionary in hand, and translate its tortured message into what its writer intended to say: "Rupert told Emilia that he was in love with her and hoped she could learn to love him, too."

One symptom of pretentious writing is "buzz words." These are words and phrases that reflect new academic trends or psychological fads. They are often nouns with *-ize* added to them to make them into verbs: *utilize, verbalize, conceptualize*. What's wrong with "use," "say," and "think"?

Instead of impressing readers, pretentious writing makes them impatient and causes them to lose respect for the writer. If you really want to get your message across, write plainly and clearly in language your readers can understand.

EXERCISE **1.10**

With a partner, read through the following paragraph and highlight the pretentious words and phrases.

On our recent excursion to Montreal, in close proximity to Dorval, we detected the presence of storm clouds in advance of our position, which led us to the realization that precipitation was probably imminent. Within a short period of time, heavy precipitation began and our vehicle's windshield-clearing apparatus was inadequate to maintain visibility. When the rainfall began to descend in a congealed state due to falling temperatures, we repaired to the shelter of a hostelry in close proximity to the highway to bide our time until the storm should cease.

Now, working alone, revise this pretentious gobbledygook into a clear, concise statement. Then compare your revision with our suggestion on page 384.

CLICHÉS

While pretentious writing requires time and effort, clichéd writing requires neither. It is as easy and as thoughtless as casual talk. A **cliché** is a phrase that has been used so often it has lost its ability to communicate a meaningful idea.

> At this point in time, we have no choice but to focus all our efforts where it really counts: on the bottom line.

At this point in time, we have no choice but, focus all our efforts, where it really counts, on the bottom line: all of these phrases are clichés. They fail to create a picture in the reader's mind, and if your reader cannot "see" what you're saying, communication does not take place. After a few cliché-filled sentences, readers will conclude, "There's nothing new here. It's all been said before." And they will stop reading.

Spoken English is full of clichés—we often use them as shortcuts to put our thoughts into words, and if our listener doesn't "get the picture," we can always elaborate. Writers, on the other hand, have time to think through what they want to say. They also have the opportunity to revise and edit, so they are expected to communicate with more precision and more originality than speakers.

If you are a native speaker of English, clichés are easy to recognize. When you can read the first few words of a phrase and fill in the rest automatically, you know the phrase is a cliché: *Better late than* _____; *easier said than* _____; *when push comes to* _____.

The solution to a cliché problem involves time and thought, first to recognize the cliché and then to find a better way to express your idea. Think about what you want to say and then say it in your own words, not everyone else's.

As you go through the following exercise, notice how hard it is to form a mental picture of what each sentence means—how hard it is to remember what you have just read.

EXERCISE **1.11**

Working with a partner, identify the cliché(s) in each sentence and then rewrite the sentence, expressing the ideas in your own words.

1. The financial adviser told us there was a ~~window of~~ opportunity open to investors who could think outside the box. Then she gave us an eye-popping ballpark figure of what our bottom line would look like five years out if we put our money in her capable hands.

2. While you may want cutting-edge *[newest]* stereo and television equipment and a state-of-the-art computer and car, you need to understand that your lifestyle choices must depend on your income, not your desires. At the end of the day, your take-home pay doesn't make the grade.

3. Kayla knew that she was in over her head when the meeting ground to a halt because she had not done her homework. When she became office manager, she thought it would be child's play *[easy]* to get everyone on the same *[same level]* page, but she soon learned that careful preparation is a must. *[mandatory]*

4. Experts agree that meaningful relationships are important to mental health, even as divorce rates have reached epidemic proportions *[high levels]* and loneliness has become a fact of life. *[normal]*

5. ~~Last but not least~~, I want to thank George and Navika, my tried and true friends who have stood by me through thick and thin, *[everything]* even when there was no light at the end of the tunnel. The list of times when they have lent me a hand is endless.

GO TO WEB
EXERCISE 1.2

WWW.BAREA.NELSON.COM

OFFENSIVE LANGUAGE

The last thing you want to do when you write is to offend your reader, even if you are writing a complaint. As we've seen, some words occasionally used in speech are *always* inappropriate in writing. Swear words, for example, are unacceptable in a written message. So are obscene words, even mild ones. Offensive language appears much stronger in print than in speech. It can provoke, shock, or even outrage a reader. Racist language and blasphemy (the use of names or objects that are sacred to any religion) are always unacceptable and are deeply offensive.

Many writers have experienced the embarrassment of having a message read by people for whom it was not intended. What might have seemed at the time of composition to be an innocent joke or an emphatic expression may, if it is read by someone other than the intended audience, prove hateful to readers and mortifying to the writer. (This is why, before being sent, e-mails written in anger should always be saved as drafts and reviewed later.)

It is wise to avoid all questionable expressions in your writing. Language has power. As many linguists have observed, our language actually shapes as well as reflects our attitudes and values. Those who use racist, blasphemous, sexist, or profane terms not only reinforce the attitudes represented by those terms, but also project a profoundly negative image of themselves to their readers.

LANGUAGE ABUSAGES

Some words and phrases, even ones we hear in everyday speech, are *always* incorrect in written English. Technically, they are also incorrect in speech, but most people tolerate them as part of the casual standard that is common in informal conversation. If these expressions appear in your writing, your reader will assume you are uneducated, careless, or worse. Even in some conversations, particularly in academic and professional environments, these expressions make a poor impression on your listeners.

Carefully read through the following list and highlight any words or phrases that sound all right to you. These are the ones you need to find and fix when you revise.

Alot	There is no such word. Use *much* or *many*. ("A lot" is acceptable in informal usage.)
Anyways (anywheres)	The *s* on these words betrays the writer as uneducated.
Between you and I	A very common error. Use *between you and me*.
Can't hardly (couldn't hardly)	The correct expression is *can* (or *could*) *hardly*.
Could of (would of, should of)	Using the preposition *of* instead of the auxiliary verb *have* in these verb phrases is a common error. Write *could have*, *would have*, and *should have*.
Didn't do nothing	All double negatives are errors. Some familiar examples are "couldn't see nothing," "won't go nowhere," and "can't find nobody." Write *didn't do anything, couldn't see anything, won't go anywhere*, and *can't find anybody*.
Good **used as an adverb**	"How are you?" "I'm good." This all-too-common expression is incorrect (unless you mean to say that you are moral or ethical or saintly). If you want to say that you are healthy, then say, "I'm *well*."
Irregardless	There is no such word. *Regardless* is the word you may want, but check your thesaurus for other, possibly more appropriate, choices.
Media **used as singular**	The word *media* is plural. It is incorrect to say, "Television is a mass media." It is a mass *medium*. Newspapers, magazines, and the Internet are mass media. Radio is an electronic medium.
Off of	Use *off* by itself. "I fell *off* the wagon."

[handwritten annotation next to "Didn't do nothing": Did nothing or Didn't do anything]

Prejudice used as an adjective	It is incorrect to write "She is *prejudice* against blondes." Use *prejudiced*.
Prejudism	There is no such word. Use *prejudice* (a noun): "He showed *prejudice* in awarding the prize to his daughter."
Real used as an adverb	"Real good," "real bad," and "real nice" are not acceptable. You could use *really* or *very* and be correct, but such filler words add nothing to your meaning.
The reason is because	Write *the reason is that*: "The reason is that my dog ate my essay."
Sort of speak	If you *must* use this expression, get the words right: "So to speak."
Suppose to	Like "use to," this phrase is incorrect. Write *supposed to* and *used to*.
Themselfs	Also "ourselfs," "yourselfs." The plural of *self* is *selves*: *ourselves, yourselves,* and *themselves*. "Theirselves" is nonstandard English and is not used by educated speakers/writers.
Youse	There is no such word. *You* is both the singular and the plural form of the second-person pronoun. While occasionally heard in restaurants or retail stores, "Can I help youse?" labels the speaker as a high-school dropout.

EXERCISE **1.12**

Working with a partner, revise the following sentences to eliminate any abusages. Then compare your revisions with our suggestions on page 385.

1. I would be happy to meet youse any time, anywheres.
2. Don't be discouraged that Jessa's father can't hardly stand you; he's prejudice against alot of her friends.
3. Television is probably the best example of a media that remains popular irregardless of the quality of the programming.
4. This course was suppose to be real easy, but I could not of passed it without alot of help.
5. Between you and I, the reason our group got a C+ on our project is because Chris didn't do nothing to contribute to it.

EXERCISE **1.13**

Eliminate the 20 abusages from the following paragraph.

Dangerous sports are suppose to bring out the best in you, irregardless of your athleticism. The reason for this is because it is assumed you won't do nothing that will endanger you. I have a firm prejudism against high-risk activities because I hate the sight of blood—especially my own. Television is the mass media most responsible for promoting the idea that we should attempt death-defying stunts. Irregardless of the large number of people who seem to enjoy the phenomena of jumping off of a bridge or platform with a bungee cord tied around their feet, it's not my idea of a real good time. I used to think that I should be ashamed that I had never done nothing that involved physical risk, so I bought a motorcycle, even though I knew at the time I shouldn't of done it. Although I never had an accident, I sold it after a month anyways, and the reason is because I knew every time I returned home that I could ~~of~~ *have* been killed half a dozen times. My friends laughed ~~their~~ *them* selves silly,

but I could~~n't~~ hardly be blamed for trying to stay alive. I'm smart enough now

that I won't do ~~nothing~~ *anything* more dangerous than eating ~~alot~~ *lots* of butter and putting

cream in my coffee.

GUY CRAMER,
EXCEPT ARE ADVISE
AND QUITE, YOU
LOOSER!

2 Hazardous Homonyms

This chapter focuses on **homonyms**—words that sound alike or look alike and are easily confused: *accept* and *except*; *weather* and *whether*; *whose* and *who's*; *affect* and *effect*. A spell checker will not help you find spelling mistakes in these words because the "correct" spelling depends on the sentence in which you use the word. For example, if you write, "Meat me hear inn halve an our," no spell checker will find fault with your sentence—and no reader will understand what you're talking about.

Below is a list of the most common homonym hazards. Only some of the words in this list will cause you trouble. Careful pronunciation can sometimes help you tell the difference between words that are often confused. For example, if you pronounce the words *accept* and *except* differently, you'll be less likely to use the wrong one when you write. It's also useful to make up memory aids to help you remember the difference in meaning between words that sound or look alike. The list that follows includes several examples that we hope you will find helpful.

Make your own list of problem pairs and keep it where you can easily refer to it. Tape it inside the cover of your dictionary, or post it over your computer. Get into the habit of checking your document against your list every time you write.

accept
except

Accept means "take" or "receive." It is always a verb. *Except* means "**ex**cluding."

> I *accepted* the spelling award, and no one *except* my mother knew I cheated.

advice
advise

The difference in pronunciation makes the difference in meaning clear. *Advise* (rhymes with *wise*) is a verb. *Advice* (rhymes with *nice*) is a noun.

> I *advise* you not to listen to free *advice*.

affect
effect

Affect as a verb means "to ch**a**nge." Try substituting *change* for the word you've chosen in your sentence. If it makes sense, then *af-FECT* is the word you want. As a noun, *AF-fect* means "a strong feeling." *Effect* is a noun meaning "**re**sult." If you can substitute *result*, then *effect* is the word you need. Occasionally, *effect* is used as a verb meaning "to bring about."

> Learning about the *effects* (results) of caffeine *affected* (changed) my coffee-drinking habits.
> Depressed people often display an inappropriate *affect* (feeling).
> Antidepressant medications can *effect* (bring about) profound changes in mood.

a lot
allot

A lot (often misspelled *alot*) should be avoided in formal writing. Use *many* or *much* instead. *al-LOT* means "distribute" or "assign."

>   *many*   *much*
> He still has ~~a lot of~~ problems, but he is coping ~~a lot~~ better.
> The teacher will *allot* the marks according to the difficulty of the questions.

allusion
illusion

An *allusion* is an implied or indirect reference. An *illusion* is something that appears to be real or true but it is not what it seems. It can be a false impression, idea, or belief.

> Many literary *allusions* can be traced to the Bible or to Shakespeare.
> A good movie creates an *illusion* of reality.

are
our

Are is a verb. *Our* shows ownership. Confusion of these two words often results from careless pronunciation.

Where *are our* leaders?

beside
besides

Beside is a preposition meaning "by the side of" or "next to." *Besides* means "also," or "in addition to."

One evening with Mario was more than enough. *Besides* expecting me to buy the tickets, the popcorn, and the drinks, he insisted on sitting *beside* Lisa rather than me.

choose
chose

Pronunciation gives the clue here. *Choose* rhymes with *booze*, is a present tense verb, and means "select." *Chose* rhymes with *rose*, is a past tense verb, and means "selected."

Please *choose* a topic.
I *chose* to write about fuel-cell technology.

cite
sight
site

To *cite* means "to quote from" or "to refer to."

A lawyer *cites* precedents; writers *cite* their sources in articles or research papers; and my friends *cite* my e-mails as examples of comic writing.

Sight means "vision," the ability to see. It can also mean something that is visible or worth seeing.

She lost her *sight* as the result of an accident.
With his tattoos and piercings, Izzy was a *sight* to behold.

A *site* is the location of something: a building, a town, or a historic event.

The *site* of the battle was the Plains of Abraham, which lie west of Quebec City.

coarse
course

Coarse means "rough, unrefined." (The slang word ***arse*** is co**arse**.) For all other meanings, use course.

That sandpaper is too *coarse* to use on a lacquer finish.
Coarse language only weakens your argument.
Of *course* you'll do well in a *course* on the history of pop music.

complement
compliment

A *comple*ment comple*tes* something. A *compliment* is a gift of praise.

> A glass of wine would be the perfect *complement* to the meal.
> Some people are embarrassed by *compliments*.

conscience
conscious

Your *conscience* is your sense of right and wrong. *Conscious* means "aware" or "awake"—able to feel and think.

> After Ann cheated on the test, her *conscience* bothered her.
> Ann was *conscious* of having done wrong.
> The injured man was *unconscious*.

consul
council
counsel

A *consul* is a government official stationed in another country. A *council* is an assembly or official group. Members of a *council* are *councillors*. Counsel can be used to mean both "advice" and "to advise."

> The Canadian *consul* in Venice was very helpful.
> The Women's Advisory *Council* meets next month.
> Maria gave me good *counsel*.
> She *counselled* me to hire a lawyer.

desert
dessert

A *DE-sert* is a dry, barren place. As a verb, *de-SERT* means "to abandon" or "to leave behind." *Des-SERT* is the part of a meal you'd probably like an extra helping of, so give it an extra *s*.

> The tundra is Canada's only *desert* region.
> If you *desert* me, I'll be all alone.
> I can't resist any *dessert* made with chocolate.

dining
dinning

You'll spell *dining* correctly if you remember the phrase "wining and dining." You'll probably never use *dinning*, which means "making a loud noise."

> The dog is not supposed to be in the *dining* room.
> We are *dining* out tonight.
> The noise from the karaoke bar was *dinning* in our ears.

does
dose

Pronunciation provides the clue. *Does* rhymes with *buzz* and is a verb. *Dose* rhymes with *gross* and refers to a quantity of medicine.

Josef *does* drive fast, *doesn't* he?
My grandmother used to give me a *dose* of cod liver oil every spring.

forth
fourth

Forth means "**for**ward." *Fourth* contains the number **four**, which gives it its meaning.

Please stop pacing back and *forth.*
The Raptors lost their *fourth* game in a row.

hear
here

Hear is what you do with your **ear**s. *Here* is used for all other meanings.

Now *hear* this!
Ranjan isn't *here.*
Here is your assignment.

it's
its

It's is a shortened form of *it is*. The apostrophe takes the place of the *i* in *is*. If you can substitute *it is*, then *it's* is the form you need. If you can't substitute *it is*, then *its* is the correct word.

It's really not difficult. (*It is* really not difficult.)
The book has lost *its* cover. ("The book has lost it is cover" makes no sense, so you need *its*.)

It's is also commonly used as the shortened form of *it has*. In this case, the apostrophe takes the place of the *h* and the *a*.

It's been a bad month for new car sales.

knew
new

Knew is the past tense of *know*. *New* is an adjective meaning "having recently come into being," "fresh," or "original."

We *knew* our *new* pool would attract friends just as surely as fruit attracts flies.
Who would have thought that cropped pants, a style from the 1950s, would be considered a *new* fashion 60 years later?

know
no

Know is a verb meaning "to understand" or "recognize." *No* can be used as an adverb to express refusal or denial, or as an adjective to express a negative state or condition.

No, we do not *know* the results of the test yet.
Why are there *no* cookies left in the jar?

later
latter

Lāter refers to time and has the word **lāte** in it. *Latter* means "the second of two" and has two *ts*. It is the opposite of *former*.

It is *later* than you think.
You take the former, and I'll take the *latter*.

lead
led

Lead is pronounced to rhyme with *speed* and is the present tense of the verb *to lead*. (*Led* is the past tense of the same verb.) The only times you pronounce *lead* as "led" is when you are referring to the writing substance in a pencil or to the soft, heavy metal used to make bullets or leaded windows.

You *lead*, and I'll decide whether to follow.
Your suitcase is so heavy it must be filled with either gold or *lead*.

loose
lose

Pronunciation is the key to these words. *Loose* rhymes with *moose* and means "not tight" or "unrestricted." *Lose* rhymes with *ooze* and means "misplace" or "be defeated."

There's a screw *loose* somewhere.
When Moosehead beer is served, people say, "The moose is *loose*!"
Some are born to win, some to *lose*.
You can't *lose* on this deal.

miner
minor

A ***miner*** works in a **mine.** *Minor* means "lesser" or "not important," or a person who is not legally an adult.

Liquor can be served to *miners*, but not if they are *minors*.
For some people, spelling is a *minor* problem.

moral
morale

Again, pronunciation provides the clue you need. *MO-ral* refers to the understanding of what is right and wrong; *mo-RALE* refers to the spirit or mental condition of a person or group.

Most religions are based on a *moral* code of behaviour.
Despite his shortcomings, he is basically a *moral* man.
Low *morale* is the reason for our employees' absenteeism.

passed
past

Passed is the past tense of the verb *pass*, which has several meanings, most of which have to do with movement on land or water, but some of which have to do with sports or games. *Past* describes something that happened or existed in an earlier time. *Passed* is always a verb; *past* can be a noun, adjective, adverb, or preposition, but it is never a verb.

George *passed* the puck to Henry, who slammed it *past* the goalie to win the game.

peace
piece

Peace is what we want on **Ea**rth. *Piece* means a part or portion of something, as in "a **pie**ce of **pie**."

Everyone hopes for *peace* in the Middle East.
A *piece* of the puzzle is missing.

personal
personnel

PER-sonal means "priv**a**te." *person-NEL* refers to the group of people working for a particular employer or to the office responsible for maintaining employees' records.

The letter was marked "*Personal* and Confidential."
We are fortunate in having highly qualified *personnel*.
Yasmin works in the *Personnel* Office.

principal
principle

Principal means "m**a**in." A *princip**le*** is a ru**le**.

A *principal* is the main administrator of a school.
The federal government is the *principal* employer in Summerside, PEI.
The *principal* and the interest totalled more than I could pay. (In this case, the principal is the main amount of money.)
One of our instructor's *principles* is to refuse to accept late assignments.

quiet
quite

If you pronounce these words carefully, you won't confuse them. *Quiet* has two syllables (kwy-et); *quite* has only one.

The chairperson asked us to be *quiet*.
We had not *quite* finished our assignment.

stationary
stationery

Stationary means "fixed in place." *Stationery* is writing paper.

A *stationary* bicycle will give you a good cardio workout without stressing your knees.
Please order a new supply of *stationery*.

than
then

Than is used in comparisons: bigger than, better than, slower than, etc. Pronounce it to rhyme with *can*. *Then* refers to time and rhymes with *when*.

Kim is a better speller *than* I.
I'd rather be here *than* there.
Pay me first, *then* you can have my notes.

their
there
they're

Their indicates ownership. *There* points out something or indicates place. It includes the word **here**, which also indicates place. *They're* is a shortened form of *they are*. (The apostrophe replaces the *a* in *are*.)

It was *their* fault.
There are two weeks left in the term.
Let's walk over *there*.
They're late, as usual.

threw
through

Threw is the past tense of the verb *throw*. *Through* can be used as a preposition, adjective, or adverb, but never as a verb.

James *threw* the ball *through* the kitchen window. When he climbed *through* to fetch it, his mother angrily told him that his days of playing catch in the yard were *through*.

too
two
to

The *too* with an extra *o* in it means "more than enough" or "also." *Two* is the number after one. For all other meanings, use *to*.

It's *too* hot, and I'm *too* tired *to* go for another hike.
There are *two* sides *to* every argument.
The *two* women knew *too* much about each other *to* be friends.

wear
were
where
we're

If you pronounce these words carefully, you won't confuse them. *Wear* rhymes with *pear* and is a noun. *Were* rhymes with *purr* and is a verb. *Where* is pronounced "hwear," includes the word **here**, and indicates place. *We're* is a shortened form of *we are* and is pronounced "weer."

After 360,000 km, you shouldn't be surprised that your car is showing signs of *wear* and tear.
You *were* joking, *weren't* you?

Where did you want to meet?
We're on our way.

weather
whether

Weather refers to climatic conditions: temperature and humidity, for example. *Whether* means "if" and is used in indirect questions or to introduce two alternatives.

We're determined to go camping this weekend, no matter what the *weather* is like. We'll pack enough gear to be prepared *whether* it rains or shines.

who's
whose

Who's is a shortened form of *who is* or *who has*. If you can substitute *who is* or *who has* for the *who's* in your sentence, then you have the right spelling. Otherwise, use *whose*.

Who's coming to dinner? (*Who is* coming to dinner?)
Who's been sleeping in my bed? (*Who has* been sleeping in my bed?)
Whose paper is this? ("*Who is* paper" makes no sense, so you need *whose*.)

woman
women

Confusing these two is guaranteed to irritate your women readers. *Woman* is the singular form; compare **man**. *Women* is the plural form; compare **men**.

Only one *woman* responded to our ad.
Our company sponsors both a *women*'s team and a men's team.

you're
your

You're is a shortened form of *you are*. If you can substitute *you are* for the *you're* in your sentence, then you're using the correct form. If you can't substitute *you are*, use *your*.

You're welcome. (*You are* welcome.)
Unfortunately, *your* hamburger got burned. ("You are hamburger" makes no sense, so *your* is the word you want.)

In the exercises that follow, choose the correct word. If you don't know an answer, go back and re-read the explanation. Check your answers after each set. Answers for exercises in this chapter begin on page 385.

EXERCISE **2.1**

1. (~~You're~~/Your) (~~conscious~~/conscience) will guide you when you are tempted to tell fibs to the Canada Revenue Agency.
2. On my (fourth/~~forth~~) try, I (passed/~~past~~) the fitness test.
3. If a moral (principle/~~principal~~) is always a rule, does that mean that a school (~~principle~~/principal) is always a pal?
4. (~~Weather~~/Whether) we win or (~~loose~~/lose) this game, (we're/~~wear~~) planning a great end-of-season party.
5. (It's/~~Its~~) often thought that the feminist phrase "A (woman/~~women~~) needs a man like a fish needs a bicycle" is Gloria Steinem's, but it was actually coined by Irina Dunn.

EXERCISE **2.2**

1. His injuries are (~~quiet~~/quite) (~~miner~~/~~minor~~). _minor_
2. After the first class, Vincent realized that a (course/~~coarse~~) in the basics of bonsai would not prepare him to go (~~fourth~~/forth) and make millions.
3. Did you (know/~~no~~) that (~~you're~~/your) chances of being able to quit smoking without help are less than 25 percent?
4. On (~~who's~~/whose) (advice/~~advise~~) did you decide to buy bell-bottom pants?
5. In (~~passed~~/past) centuries, most people believed in God and followed (their/~~they're/there~~) religious leaders wherever they (led/~~lead~~).

EXERCISE **2.3**

1. "Football combines (~~to~~/two/~~too~~) of the worst aspects of American life: (~~Its~~/it's) nothing but violence punctuated by committee meetings." (George Will)
2. Although I was (~~conscience~~/conscious) that I shouldn't do it, I ordered (~~desert~~/dessert) anyway.
3. First, (~~loose~~/lose) 15 kg, (then/~~than~~) worry about (your/~~you're~~) bald spot.
4. When my fiancée broke (~~are~~/our) engagement, she destroyed the (~~allusions~~/illusions) I cherished about her and our relationship.
5. "Although golf was originally restricted to wealthy, overweight Protestants, today (~~its~~/it's) open to anyone (whose/~~who's~~) clothing is sufficiently hideous." (Dave Barry)

EXERCISE **2.4**

1. (~~Dose~~/Does) anyone (~~hear~~/here) remember the eighties?
2. The (coarse/~~course~~) fabric of my (~~knew~~/new) suit makes my skin itch.
3. "If you owe the bank $100, that's (~~you're~~/your) problem. If you owe the bank $100 million, (~~than/then~~) that's the bank's problem." (J. P. Getty)
4. My stuffing myself at (~~diner~~/dinner) (~~lead~~/led) to a sleepless night.
5. "If a (~~women~~/woman) has to (~~chose~~/choose) between catching a fly ball and saving an infant's life, she will (~~chose~~/choose) to save the infant's life without even considering if there are men on base." (Dave Barry)

GO TO WEB
EXERCISE 2.1

WWW.BAREA.NELSON.COM

EXERCISE **2.5**

1. She is the programmer (~~whose~~/who's) responsible for creating the visual (~~affects~~/effects) that so perfectly (~~compliment~~/complement) the action in this computer game.
2. An experienced manager (accepts/~~excepts~~) the fact that (~~a lot of/ allot of/~~ many) employees hate Mondays.
3. "I am returning this otherwise good (stationery/~~stationary~~) to you because someone has written gibberish all over it and put (~~you're~~/your) name at the top." (Comment by a professor at Ohio State University on a student's essay)
4. (~~Wear~~/Where) were you when our tour group assembled for the camel ride into the (desert/ ~~dessert~~)?
5. In old gangster films, people who (~~where~~/were/~~we're~~) shot were said to have received "a (~~does~~/dose) of (~~led~~/lead) poisoning."

EXERCISE **2.6**

Find and correct the 15 errors in the following sentences.

1. We certainly won't chose any candidate who's application was late.
2. Please check with the Personal Department before you hire legal council.
3. I bruise easily, and beside, I faint at the site of blood.

4. Whose the idiot who told us that our principle purpose in life was to serve as a warning to others?

5. You may think this is a miner point, but I think its important to chose a morale coarse of action rather then an unprincipaled one.

Find and correct the 15 errors in the following paragraph. Watch out for the one error we've included that is not on our list of hazardous homonyms.

Nothing causes more arguments between men and woman then money. Recently, my husband and I were driving threw the countryside and became involved in a miner disagreement about weather to treat ourselves to a vacation or buy a new refrigerator. I argued that if we bought the appliance, this would be the forth year in which we had not had a holiday. He countered that our fridge had past it's useful life, and a functioning refrigerator took precedents over having fun. What began as a spat quickly lead to a battle. Before we new it, our good sense desserted us, and we were having a serious fight. At this point, we past a farmyard containing several goats and pigs. Pointing to them, my husband asked if they were relatives of mine. "Of coarse," I replied. "There my in-laws."

Find and correct the 15 errors in this paragraph.

Many people today are chosing a quieter way of life, hoping to live longer and more happily by following the "slower is better" principal. Some, on the advise of they're doctors, have been forced to slow down. One heart surgeon,

for example, tells his patients to drive only in the slow lane rather then use the

passing lane. They may arrive a few minutes later, but their blood pressure will

not be effected. Others don't need to be prompted by their doctors. They

except that living at a slower pace doesn't mean loosing out in any way. In

fact, the opposite is true: choosing a healthy lifestyle benefits everyone. The

affect of increased piece and quite in your personnel life leads to increased pro-

ductivity, higher moral, and greater job satisfaction. Sometimes the improve-

ments are miner, but as anyone who has consciencely tried to slow the pace

of life can tell you, the slow lane is the fast lane to longevity.

GO TO WEB
EXERCISE 2.2

WWW.BAREA.NELSON.COM

EXERCISE **2.9**

Below is a list of word pairs that are often confused. Use each one in a sentence that clearly differentiates the word from the word or words that have the same sound. Use your dictionary to help you. When you are finished, exchange papers with another student and check each other's work.

1. altar, alter
2. breath, breathe
3. capital, capitol
4. stake, steak
5. waist, waste

6. cite, site
7. cloths, clothes
8. emigrate, immigrate
9. hoard, horde
10. precede, proceed

EXERCISE **2.10**

The English language includes many words that can be used as both nouns and verbs, although they are usually pronounced differently for each function. Working with a partner or small group, make up 10 sentences, each using the word we've provided as both a noun and a verb.

Example: tear

> I shed a tear when I saw the tear in my best blouse.

Hint: Use a dictionary if you are not familiar with both uses of the word.

1. wind
2. produce
3. dove
4. wound
5. present
6. refuse
7. object
8. lead
9. row
10. does

EXERCISE **2.11**

This exercise is more challenging. All of the words in the following paragraph are correctly spelled. The problem is that 20 of them are the wrong words—they don't mean what the writer intended. Can you solve the puzzle by supplying the right words?

So many studies and polls are conducted on North Americans that <u>its</u> often

hard to <u>chose</u> between those that could be important to us and those that have

<u>miner</u> or no significance. For example, one-sixth of us are fingernail biters.

Should we care? <u>Dose</u> this suggest insecurity or nervousness, perhaps brought

on by <u>to</u> much work—or the lack of work? It's probably a <u>waist</u> of time to

worry about such questions. A more revealing statistic comes from Louis

Harris, <u>who's</u> polls are famous for <u>there</u> accuracy. According to Harris's

research, only 53 percent of the population between the ages of 18 and 24 are satisfied with life. However, among those who are 50 or older, over 72 percent

express personnel satisfaction. The poll reports no significant variation

between men and woman. Its interesting to speculate why people's satisfac-

tion with life improves after 50. Does it mean that life's experiences are gen-

erally better latter then they are earlier? Or perhaps people in their middle

years don't expect as much from life and so tend to except things as they are.

Of coarse, statistics are subject to interpretation, so the morale is to chose

whichever numbers give you the affect you want. But remember: no matter

how much you prey, you're chance of getting a full house in a poker deal is

one in 693.

APOSTROPHE'S WILL TRIP UP THE UN-GRAMMATICAL'S EVERY TIME!

The Apostrophe 3

Never used for plural

What, you may ask, is a chapter on apostrophes doing in a unit on words? Why isn't it in Unit 4 with the other punctuation marks? Here's the reason: while all other punctuation marks show the intended relationship among parts of a sentence, apostrophes show the relationship between two words (in a possessive construction) or two parts of one word (in a contraction). Misused apostrophes change the meaning of words, and that is why we are discussing them here.

Can you spot how this one sentence from a letter of application revealed the applicant's poor writing skills?

I would like to be an active participant in you're companies [y's] success as it enters it's second decade of outstanding service to customer's.

Misused apostrophes show a writer's ignorance or carelessness. They also confuse, amuse, and sometimes annoy readers. The example above contains four apostrophe errors, which irritated the reader so much that the applicant didn't even make it to the interview stage.

Sometimes you need an apostrophe so that your reader can understand what you mean. For example, there's a world of difference between these two sentences:

The instructor began class by calling the students' names. — *Attendence*
The instructor began class by calling the students names. — *Disrespect*

In most cases, however, misused apostrophes either amuse or offend an alert reader:

The movie had it's moments.
He does a days work every week.
The Lion's thank you for your contribution.

It isn't difficult to avoid such mistakes. Correctly used, the apostrophe indicates either **contraction** or **possession**. It never makes a singular word plural. The following three sentences show where to use—and not use—apostrophes.

1. The *dog's* chasing cars again. (Contraction: dog's = dog is)
2. The *dog's* bark is more reliable than the doorbell. (Possessive: the bark belongs to the dog)
3. The *dogs* bark incessantly. (Plural, so no apostrophe)

CONTRACTION

Contraction is the combining of two words into one, as in *they're* or *can't*. Contractions are common in conversational, informal English. Unless you are quoting someone else's words, however, you should avoid them in the writing you do for school or work.

The rule about where to put an apostrophe in a contraction is one of the few rules to which there are no exceptions.

When two words are combined into one, and one or more letters are left out, the apostrophe goes in the place of the missing letter(s).

Here are some examples.

I am → I'm	they are → they're
we will → we'll	it is → it's
she is → she's	it has → it's
do not → don't	who has → who's
	who is → "

EXERCISE **3.1**

Place apostrophes correctly in these words, which are intended to be contractions. Notice that when the apostrophe is missing, the word often has a different meaning. Answers for exercises in this chapter begin on page 387.

1. can't

2. she'd

3. he'll

4. we'd

5. let's

6. hasn't

7. you're

8. won't

9. she'll

10. we'll

EXERCISE **3.2**

Make these sets of words into contractions.

1. they are they're

2. I will I'll

3. it has it's

4. would not wouldn't

5. everyone is everyone's

6. could not couldn't

7. who has who's

8. you are you're

9. we would we'd

10. will not won't

GO TO WEB
EXERCISE 3.1

WWW.BAREA.NELSON.COM

EXERCISE **3.3**

Correct these sentences by placing apostrophes where they are needed.

1. I'm sure shed help us if we asked her.

2. There wont be any problem if youve got an invitation.

3. Im positive that contractions shouldnt be used in formal writing.

4. We cant leave until the shows over.

5. Dont worry about your heart; itll last as long as you do.

6. Its best to get started on your paper early unless youre sure you can get an extension.

7. If you cant be a good example, maybe youll be able to serve as a horrible warning.

8. Wouldnt it be great if everyone whos celebrating a birthday today could get together for a big party?

9. Id support the idea only if the party wasnt held anywhere near my apartment.

10. A mans got to do what a mans got to do. A womans got to do what he cant. (Rhonda Hansome)

EXERCISE **3.4**

In some formal kinds of writing—academic, legal, and technical, for example—contractions are not acceptable. A good writer is able not only to contract two words into one, but also to expand any contraction into its original form: a two-word phrase. In the following paragraph, find and expand the contractions into their original form.

I'm writing to apply for the position of webmaster for BrilloVision.com that you've advertised in the *Daily News*. I have the talent and background you're looking for. Currently, I work as a web designer for an online publication, Vexed.com, where they're very pleased with my work. If you click on their website, I think you'll like what you see. There's little in the way of web design and application that I haven't been involved in during the past two years. But it's time for me to move on to a new challenge, and BrilloVision.com promises the kind of opportunity I'm looking for. I guarantee you won't be disappointed if I join your team!

POSSESSION

The apostrophe is also used to show ownership or possession. The following rule applies in most cases.

> Add 's to the word that names the *owner*.
> If the resulting word ends in a double or triple *s*, delete the last *s*, leaving the apostrophe in place.[1]

Here are some examples that illustrate the rule.

singer + 's = singer's voice   women + 's = women's voices
band + 's = band's instruments   student + 's = student's report card
players + 's = players's uniforms   students + 's = students's report cards
ships + 's = ships's sails   colleges + 's = colleges's teams

To form a possessive correctly, you must first identify the word in the sentence that identifies the "owner." Then decide if the "owner" is singular or plural. For example, "the managers duties" can have two meanings, depending on where you put the apostrophe:

the manager's duties (the duties belong to one *manager*)
the managers' duties (the duties belong to two or more *managers*)

---

[1] Many writers today prefer to keep the final *s* when it represents a sound that is pronounced, as it is in one-syllable words such as *boss* and *class*, and in some names such as *Harris* and *Brutus*.

To solve an apostrophe problem, follow this two-step process:
1. Find the owner word.
2. Apply the possession rule.

Problem: Julias hair is a mess.
Solution: 1. The owner word is *Julia* (singular).
      2. Add *'s* to *Julia*.

Julia's hair is a mess.

Problem: The technicians strike halted the production.
Solution: 1. The owner word is *technicians* (plural).
      2. Add *'s* to *technicians*, then delete the second *s*, leaving the apostrophe.

The *technicians'* strike halted the production.

Sometimes the meaning of your sentence is determined by where you put the apostrophe.

Problem: The writer was delighted by the critics response to her book.

Now you have two possibilities to choose from, depending on your meaning.

Solution A: 1. The owner word is *critic* (singular).
      2. Add *'s* to *critic*.

The writer was delighted by the *critic's* response to her book.

Solution B: 1. The owner word is *critics* (plural).
      2. Add *'s* to *critics*, then drop the second *s*, leaving the apostrophe.

The writer was delighted by the *critics'* response to her book.

Both solutions are correct, depending on whether the book was reviewed by one critic (A) or by more than one critic (B).

Possession does not have to be literal. It can be used to express the notion of "belonging to" or "associated with." That is, the owner word need not refer to a person or group of people. Ideas or concepts (abstract nouns) can be "owners" too.

today's news = the news of today
a month's vacation = a vacation of one month
a year's salary = the salary of one year

EXERCISE **3.5**

In each of the following phrases, make the owner word possessive.

1. Cass voice

2. heaven gate

3. families budgets

4. crew mutiny

5. soldiers uniforms

6. everyone choice

7. the all-candidates debate

8. Britney Spears children

9. teacher attitude

10. Marge Simpson blue hair

GO TO WEB
EXERCISE 3.2

WWW.BAREA.NELSON.COM

A few words, called **possessive pronouns**, are already possessive in form, so they don't have apostrophes.

yours	ours
hers	theirs
its	whose

The decision is *hers,* not *yours.*
Whose version do you prefer, *theirs* or *ours*?
The dog has lost *its* bone.

Four possessive words (*its, theirs, whose,* and *your*) are often confused with the contractions that sound like them. When you are trying to decide which spelling to use, expand the contraction into its original two words and try those words in your sentence. If the sentence still makes sense, use the contraction. If it doesn't, use the possessive.

Possessive	**Contraction**
its = *it* owns something	it's = it is/it has
their = *they* own something	they're = they are
whose = *who* owns something	who's = who is/who has
your = *you* own something	you're = you are

Error: They're (they are) going to sing they're (~~they are~~) latest song.
Revision: They're going to sing *their* latest song.

Error: It's (it is) you're (~~you are~~) favourite song.
Revision: It's *your* favourite song.

Error: Who's (~~who is~~) CD are you listening to?
Revision: *Whose* CD are you listening to?

Error: That car has a hole in it's (~~it is~~) muffler.
Revision: That car has a hole in *its* muffler.

EXERCISE **3.6**

Make the words in parentheses possessive. This exercise will help you discover how well you understand the difference between possessive pronouns and their sound-alike contractions.

1. (Bikers) equipment is on sale this week at (Larry) Leather Boutique.

2. My parents would like to know (who) yogurt was left in (they) fridge for two months.

3. The (dogs) owners can't seem to control them when they run in the (city) parks.

4. After only a (month) wear, my (son) jacket fell apart.

5. (Texas) record of executing people is one of the (United States) most notorious statistics.

6. This (week) *Fashion* magazine devotes two pages to (men) clothing and forty pages to (women).

7. WD-40 is a product (who) name comes from the fact that it was the fortieth formula attempted by San Diego Rocket Chemical for the (company) new "water displacement compound" in 1953.

8. According to (consumers) testimonials on the Internet, one of (WD-40) unexpected uses is to remove ketchup stains from clothing.

9. If you spray WD-40 on your balcony railing, (it) smell is supposed to keep pigeons away, while if you spray it on (you) fishing lures, fish will find them more attractive.

10. Other users testify that WD-40 takes lipstick stains out of (they) clothing, prevents water spots from forming on shower doors, and drives flies away from (cows) hides.

In the two exercises that follow, correct the sentences by placing apostrophes where they are needed in contractions and possessive constructions. Delete any misused apostrophes. There are 10 errors in each exercise.

EXERCISE **3.7**

1. The festivals opening act was my little brothers punk band.

2. Who says nobodys perfect? In my mothers opinion, I am.

3. Most mothers beliefs about their childrens characters are unrealistically positive.

4. Most fathers opinions are negative when they first meet their daughters boyfriends.

5. Did you ever notice that when you blow in a dogs face, he gets mad at you, but when you take him on a car ride, he stick's his head out the window?

EXERCISE **3.8**

1. This years hockey schedule puts the Stanley Cup final's halfway through baseball season.

2. The candidates debate was deadly boring until the heckler's in the audience started a fistfight.

3. Todays styles and tomorrows trends are featured in every issue of our magazine.

4. My in-laws home is about four hours drive north of Red Lake.

5. Have you noticed that since everyones got a cellphone camera or a handheld camcorder, theres been a drop in the number of UFO sightings?

PLURALS

The third apostrophe rule is very simple. Memorize it, apply it, and you will instantly correct many of your apostrophe errors.

> Never use an apostrophe to make a word plural.

The plural of most English words is formed by adding *s* to the root word, not *'s*. The *s* alone tells the reader that the word is plural: e.g., *memos, letters, files, broadcasts, newspapers, journalists.* If you add an apostrophe + *s*, you are telling your reader that the word is either a contraction or a possessive.

Incorrect:　Never use apostrophe's to make word's plural.
Correct:　Never use apostrophes to make words plural.

EXERCISE **3.9**

Correct the misused and missing apostrophes in the following sentences, and correct the spelling if necessary. There are 10 errors in this exercise.

1. Instead of a cake, Caro made both chocolate and vanilla cupcake's for the childrens party.

2. My iPods playlists need editing; they're full of song's that I no longer want to listen to.

3. Golf requires different club's for different shots: woods for long shots, irons for short one's, and a putter for character development.

4. Good writing skill's may not guarantee success in you're career, but their lack will certainly contribute to failure.

5. Forming plural nouns by using apostrophe's is one way to ensure that your writing attract's attention.

GO TO WEB
EXERCISE 3.4

WWW.BAREA.NELSON.COM

Correct the misused and missing apostrophes in the two exercises that follow, and correct the spelling if necessary. There are 10 errors in each exercise.

EXERCISE **3.10**

1. When your cars warranty expires, prepare yourself for some major repair's.

2. Ive posted a sign on my front lawn: "Salespeoples visits are always welcome. Dog foods expensive."

3. Won't our employee's be disappointed to hear that your cancelling the companies annual picnic?

4. In Canada, as soon as its warm enough to take off you're shirt, you know it's mosquito season.

EXERCISE **3.11**

1. One of Ogden Nashs most famous poems is both short and sweet: "Candy is dandy, but liquors quicker." (Ogden Nash)

2. We very much appreciated the flower's you sent for our mothers memorial service.

3. Four months work was wasted by a few minutes carelessness.

4. We will need everybodies maximum effort if we are to meet tomorrows deadline.

5. Geoff devoted his two year's at Queens University to hard partying.

EXERCISE **3.12**

This exercise will test your ability to use apostrophes correctly in contractions and possessive constructions—but *not* to form plurals. Find and correct the 15 errors in the following sentences.

1. Brain cell's come and brain cell's go, but fat cell's live forever.

2. One of our colleges objectives is to meet our students social needs as well as their academic goals.

3. Anyone whose able to swallow pill's at a drinking fountain deserves to get well.

4. The three tenors most spectacular concert was held in Romes ancient Coliseum.

5. The health of Canadas economy depends not only on its abundant natural resources, but also on its pool of skilled labourers and well-educated professional's.

6. What do I think of computer dating? Its terrific if your a computer. (Rita
Mae Brown)

SUMMARY

- When contracting two words into one, put an apostrophe in the place
  of the missing letters.
- Watch for owner words: they need apostrophes.
- To indicate possession, add 's to the owner word. (In most cases, if the
  owner word already ends in s, just add the apostrophe.)
- Possessive pronouns (e.g., *yours, its, ours*) do not take apostrophes.
- Never use an apostrophe to form the plural of a word.

Before you do the final exercise in this chapter, carefully review the information in the summary box above.

EXERCISE **3.13**

This exercise will test your ability to use apostrophes correctly: in contractions,
in possessive constructions, but *not* to form plurals. Find and correct the 15
errors in the following sentences.

1. Researcher's tell us that persons from different backgrounds encourage
   creativity in one another: one persons problem is anothers challenge.

2. In todays competitive global markets, we need strategic thinkers who can
   analyze problems from a variety of cultural viewpoint's.

3. As Canadian's, we've long been proud of our countries commitment to
   multiculturalism, and our citizens economic well-being justifies our pride.

4. If company's want to improve their ability to find innovative solutions to
   complex business problems, then they should hire employee's from various cultural and racial groups.

5. If the Canadian government is serious about improving Canada's ability to function in the knowledge economy, then it's immigration policy's need to encourage even more diversity.

6. As knowledge worker's replace industrial worker's, the challenge of the 21st century will be to stimulate diversity in order to ensure our nations economic survival.

THEY DESERVE CAPITALIZATION PUNISHMENT.

canadians demand more sundays, fewer mondays!

ungrammatical are people

Capital Letters | 4

Capital letters belong in a few specific places and nowhere else. Some writers suffer from "capitalitis." They put capital letters on words without thinking about their position or function in a sentence.

Not many people have this problem. If you are in the majority who generally use capitals correctly, skip this chapter and go on to something else. If you are puzzled about capital letters, though, or have readers who are puzzled by your use of them, read on.

Capitalize the first letter of a word that fits into one of the six categories listed below:

1. The first word of a sentence, a direct quotation, or a sentence from a quoted source.

Are you illiterate? Write to us today for free help.
The supermodel cooed, "I just love the confidence makeup gives me."

Lister Sinclair once said, "The only thing Canadians have in common is that we all hate Toronto."

EXERCISE **4.1**

Revise the following sentences by adding the missing capital letters and deleting the incorrect ones. Answers for exercises in this chapter begin on page 389.

1. time is nature's way of keeping everything from happening at once.

2. Dana called, "you left the light on in the garage."

3. On the first day of term, our teacher told us, "learning Standard English is, for many people, like learning another Language."

4. Richard Harkness summed up my feeling about committees when he wrote, "a committee is a group of the unwilling, picked from the unfit, to do the unnecessary."

5. in conclusion, I want you to consider the words of Wendell Johnson: "*always* and *never* are two words you should always remember never to use."

 2. The names of specific people, places, and things.

Names of people (and their titles):

Avril Lavigne, Governor General Michaëlle Jean, the Reverend Henry Jones, Dr. Norman Bethune, Senator Hugh Segal

Names of places, regions, and astronomical bodies (but not general geographic directions):

Stanley Park, Lake Superior, Cape Breton Island; Nunavut, the Badlands; Saturn, Earth, the Moon, the Asteroid Belt; south, north

Names of buildings, institutions, organizations, companies, departments, products, etc.:

> the National Art Gallery, the Museum of Civilization; McGill University, Red Deer College; the Liberal Party, the Kiwanis Club; Petro-Canada, Rogers; the Department of English, the Human Resources Department; Kleenex, Volvo, Labatt Blue

EXERCISE 4.2

Add capital letters where necessary in the following sentences. There are 30 errors in this exercise.

1. After a brief stay in the maritimes, captain tallman and his crew sailed west up the st. lawrence.

2. The broadcast department of niagara college has ordered six sony cameras for their studios in welland, ontario.

3. Do you find that visa is more popular than American express when you travel to faraway places such as mexico, france, or jupiter?

4. Our stay at the seaview hotel, overlooking the pacific ocean, certainly beat our last vacation at the bates motel, where we faced west, overlooking the city dump.

5. As a member of the alumni association I am trying to raise funds from companies like disney, general motors, bell Canada, and the cbc, where our graduates have positions.

---

3. Names of major historical events, historical periods, religions, holy texts, and holy days.

> World War II, the Depression, the Renaissance; Islam, Judaism, Christianity, Buddhism, Hinduism; the Torah, the Koran, the Bible, the Upanishads; Ramadan, Yom Kippur, Easter

EXERCISE **4.3**

Add the 20 capital letters that are missing from the following sentences.

1. Many of the celebrations we think of as originating in the last 2,000 years have much older roots; halloween and easter are two such festivals.

2. The celebration of christmas has its origins in ancient babylon, where the birth of the son of isis was marked by feasting and gift-giving.

3. The romans, too, had a traditional celebration called saturnalia, held at the end of December. The tradition of seasonal songs, known to us as carols, began in roman times.

4. The Christmas tree and mistletoe date from pagan celebrations called yule, which were held in northern europe on the shortest day of the year.

5. The observance of ramadan is one of the five pillars of the islamic faith, and is a month when muslims show obedience and submission by fasting.

6. At the end of ramadan, a huge feast called eid lasts the entire night.

7. In the jewish faith, the festival of hanukkah often occurs at the same time that christians are observing christmas.

8. The celebration of hanukkah involves the lighting of one candle each day on a seven-branched candelabrum.

GO TO WEB
EXERCISE 4.1

WWW.BAREA.NELSON.COM

4. The days of the week, months of the year, and specific holidays (but not the seasons).

Wednesday; January; Remembrance Day, Canada Day; spring, autumn

EXERCISE **4.4**

The following sentences contain both missing and unnecessary capitals. Find and correct the 15 errors.

1. My favourite months are january and february because I love all Winter sports.

2. This monday is valentine's day, when messages of love are exchanged.

3. In the summer, big meals seem to be too much trouble; however, after thanksgiving, we need lots of food to survive the winter cold.

4. In curaçao, people celebrate new year's day with elaborate firework displays.

5. By thursday, I'll have finished my st. patrick's day costume.

5. The major words in titles of published works (books, magazines, films; essays, poems, songs; works of art; etc.). Do not capitalize minor words (articles, prepositions, conjunctions) in titles unless the word is the first or last word in the title.

Eats, Shoots, and Leaves   *The Thinker*
Of Mice and Men   "An Immigrant's Split Personality"
Maclean's   "In Flanders Fields"
A Room with a View   "Lucy in the Sky with Diamonds"

EXERCISE **4.5**

Add the 20 capital letters that are missing from the following sentences.

1. I agreed to go out and see the movie *basic instinct 2*, but I should have stayed home, made some popcorn, and watched TV.

2. The 2007 movie with the longest title was *the assassination of Jesse James by the coward Robert Ford*, based on Ron Hansen's book of the same name.

3. Botticelli's famous painting, *birth of venus* was the inspiration for my poem "woman on the half-shell."

4. *all the king's men* was a great film when it was made in 1949, but the 2006 remake was one of that year's worst movies.

5. Most reviewers found Conrad Black's memoir, *A life in progress*, to be well written but wordy.

6. Did you know that the great Francis Ford Coppola film *Apocalypse now* was based on Joseph Conrad's novel *Heart of darkness*?

7. The Cowboy junkies have issued a new CD that is a remake of their most famous album, *The trinity sessions*.

Pay special attention to this next category. It is one that causes everybody trouble.

6. The names of specific school courses.

Marketing 101, Psychology 100, Mathematics 220, English 110,

but

a) not the names of general school subjects

e.g., marketing, sociology, mathematics

b) *unless* the subjects are languages or pertain to specific geographical areas whose names are capitalized

e.g., English, Greek, the study of Chinese history, modern Caribbean literature, Latin American poetry

(Names of languages, countries, and geographical regions are always capitalized.)

In the space below, list the subjects you are taking this term, together with their specific course numbers and names. An example has been provided.

Subject	Course Number and Name
marketing	MA 101: Introduction to Marketing
English	_____
_____	_____
_____	_____
_____	_____

EXERCISE **4.6**

Add capital letters where necessary in the following sentences. There are 10 errors in this exercise.

1. We began our study of Sociology with the concept of relationships.

2. After studying geography for two years, I began taking courses in spanish and modern european history.

3. Math is her strong subject, but Laurie struggles with english and conversational french.

4. By taking Professor Subden's non-credit course, introduction to Wine, I qualified to register for winemaking 101 the next semester.

5. The prerequisite for Buddhism through the ages is Introduction to world religions.

GO TO WEB
EXERCISE 4.2

WWW.BAREA.NELSON.COM

EXERCISE **4.7**

In the two exercises that follow, correct the spelling by adding or deleting capital letters as necessary. There are 25 errors in each exercise.

1. You must take some Science courses, or you'll never get into the program you want at malaspina college in the Fall.

2. Gore Vidal, author of *the best man*, once said, "it is not enough to succeed; others must fail."

3. After the Game, we went to the burger palace for a late snack and then went home to watch *this Hour Has 22 minutes* on television.

4. Next thursday evening, the anglican church on birch avenue will hold a fund-raising dinner to support people in darfur.

5. We've been assigned to read *the englishman's boy*, a novel about life among the settlers of the american and canadian west, by the end of march break.

EXERCISE **4.8**

1. I wonder how our College gets away with requiring students to take english and Mathematics courses in addition to our Major subjects.

2. Leonard Cohen first became famous as a novelist when he published *the favourite game* and *beautiful losers*.

3. Years later, cohen's career was spectacularly revived with the release of albums such as *I'm your man* in 1988 and *the future* in 1992.

4. Marg Delahunty's campaign to be elected mayor ran into trouble on friday when she was quoted as saying, "our political system is nothing but mob rule with taxes."

5. I was raised a baptist, but since taking professor Chan's course, introduction to world religions, I've been interested in hinduism and buddhism.

6. I plan to travel to asia next Summer to learn more about these religions.

EXERCISE **4.9**

The following exercise is the mastery test and contains 30 errors. Before you begin, it would be a good idea to review the six capitalization rules, which are highlighted on pages 55–60.

1. Have you ever been to thorold, ontario, where ships bypass Niagara falls on their way East to the atlantic or West to lake superior?

2. The religion of buddhism originated in india more than 2,500 years ago and, like other religions, has its own set of teachings and practices; unlike in other faiths, however, buddhists do not worship a deity.

3. This term I am enjoying two Sociology classes: on tuesdays I have society and competition and on thursdays I have social behaviour.

4. Have you seen the may edition of *Canadian geographic*? It has an article about how a series of Lakes in ontario were named after characters from a. a. milne's book *winnie the pooh*.

5. A National Holiday to be called flag day was once proposed, but it was never officially approved.

5 Numbers

Numbers may be expressed as words (*one, four, nine*) or as figures (*1, 4, 9*), depending on the kind of assignment you are writing and what the numbers refer to. In a few circumstances, a combination of words and figures is required. In scientific and technical papers, numbers are normally given in figures; in humanities papers, numbers that can be expressed in one or two words are spelled out. For college and university papers, ask your instructor which style he or she prefers. For general purposes, including most business writing, follow the four guidelines given in this chapter.

WHEN TO USE WORDS

1. Use words to express whole numbers one through nine and simple fractions. Use figures for numbers 10 and above.

The novel's *three* parts chronicle the *nine*-week journey of the *five* Acadian teenagers.

China and India together account for more than *one-third* of the Earth's population.

Approximately *35* years ago, Paul Henderson scored the most famous goal in the history of Canadian hockey.

There are two exceptions to this general rule.

A. Spell out any number that begins a sentence, or rewrite the sentence so that the number does not come first.

Incorrect: 157 students submitted essays to the awards committee.

Correct: *One hundred and fifty-seven* students submitted essays to the awards committee.

Preferable: The awards committee received essays from *157* students.

B. Use either figures *or* words to express numbers that modify the same or similar items in one sentence. (That is, be consistent within a sentence.)

Canada has *ten* provinces and *three* territories. (Not *10* and *three*)

Only *9* of the *55* applicants had both the qualifications and the experience we required. (Not *nine of the 55 applicants*)

2. Treat ordinal numbers (first, second, etc.) as you would cardinal numbers (one, two, etc.).

Up to its *sixth* or *seventh* month, an infant can breathe and swallow at the same time.

In 1904, Sir Wilfrid Laurier declared that the *20th* century would belong to Canada. Canadians in the *21st* century are still waiting.

EXERCISE **5.1**

Applying the two highlighted rules on page 65, correct any errors in the following sentences. Answers begin on page 391.

1. After listening to 4 of the songs on your demo tape, I urge you not to give up your day job.

2. This is the 3rd time you have been late this week.

3. The 1st six of the twenty contestants were simply awful, and the next 6 were awfully simple, as the *Idol* show limped along to its dreadful conclusion.

4. Did you know that with 1 ostrich egg you can make 9 omelettes?

5. Third, and most important, always have a backup plan in case your 1st and 2nd plans don't work out.

6. It takes 43 muscles to frown, but only seventeen muscles to smile.

7. Jenn's grade was in the top $1/3$ of her class, an excellent result, considering that almost $1/2$ of the students failed.

8. When I was between five and 12 years old, my parents home-schooled me.

9. If we order a large pizza with 4 toppings, we get 2 bottles of cola and 9 chicken wings for $1/2$-price.

10. On the 5th day, she received 5 gold rings, but by then she was pretty fed up with the mess made by the 4 calling birds, 3 French hens, 2 turtle-doves, and the partridge in the pear tree.

GO TO WEB
EXERCISE 5.1

WWW.BAREA.NELSON.COM

WHEN TO USE FIGURES

As a general rule, you should use figures when you are presenting technical or precise numerical information or when your sentence or paragraph contains several numbers.

3. Use figures to express dates, specific times, addresses, and percentages; with abbreviations or symbols; and with units of currency.

Dates	April 1, 2009, *or* 1 April 2009
Times	8:45 a.m. *or* 08:45, 7:10 p.m. *or* 19:10 (Use words with *o'clock*: e.g., *nine o'clock*.)
Addresses *Priminister*	24 Sussex Drive, 2175 West 8th Street
Percentages	19 percent, a 6.5 percent interest rate (Use the % sign only with figures in tables and diagrams.)
With abbreviations or symbols	7 mm, 293 km, 60 km/h, 40 g, 54 kg, 18°C, 0.005 cm, 1.5 L, 8½", p. 3
Amounts of money	79 cents *or* $0.79, $2, $100, $30,000, $20 million, $65 billion (Use words if the unit of currency follows whole numbers one through nine: e.g., *two dollars, seven euro*s, unless the number includes a decimal: e.g., *1.5 trillion dollars*.)

EXERCISE **5.2**

With Rule 3 in mind, correct the errors in the following sentences.

1. I was born on August fifteenth, 1983, and my horoscope for the day predicted a happy and eventful life. So far, so good.

2. The power went off in my building at four-fifteen a.m., causing my clock radio to fail, which is why I slept through my eight-thirty exam.

3. A fire at six-ten East forty-fourth Street brought traffic to a standstill until firefighters put it out 4 hours later.

4. While seven % of men suffer from colour blindness, only one % of women have it. Isn't that discriminatory?

5. After spending thirty dollars for a bottle of wine and twenty-six dollars for flowers, I didn't expect my date to spend the evening complaining that I was cheap!

6. If your skin gets dry in the winter, it may be because the humidity in the average Canadian home during the winter months is thirteen percent. The Sahara Desert, by comparison, has a humidity level of 25%.

7. At eight a.m., I was awakened by my roommate zooming up the driveway at thirty km/h on her motorcycle.

8. Driving a car at ninety km/h uses about twenty percent less fuel than driving it at 105 km/h.

9. My salary was raised on May fifteenth by 7 percent; however, I calculate that my expenses have risen at least eleven % over the past year.

10. To prepare prospective mothers for the effect having a baby might have on their bodies, a creative doctor urged his patients to strap a four kg beanbag to their stomachs, wear it for 9 months, and then remove about 1/3 of the beans.

GO TO WEB
EXERCISE 5.2

WWW.BAREA.NELSON.COM

WHEN TO USE BOTH WORDS AND FIGURES

4. When one number immediately follows another, spell out the one that makes the shorter word.
5. For numbers over a million, express the introductory numbers in figures and the quantity (e.g., billion, trillion) in words.

The Grey Cup is contested by *two 12-man* teams of heavily padded and helmeted warriors.

Our local car dealers sold more than *200 four-wheel*-drive vehicles the day after our first big storm.

The human stomach contains more than *35 million* digestive glands.

Light from the most distant stars in our galaxy takes *4 billion* years to reach Earth.

The following exercises will test your ability to apply all of the rules and exceptions presented in this chapter.

EXERCISE **5.3**

Correct any errors in the expression of numbers in the following sentences.

1. We need three cases of 12 1.5-L bottles.

2. A blue whale weighs as much as thirty elephants and is as long as three Greyhound buses.

3. The budget surplus of five billion dollars was more than expected and allowed the government to pay off a tiny fraction (less than 1%) of the national debt.

4. Almost 60% of students in my survey say they would rather be teachers, but more than ninety percent of teachers would rather be students.

5. I've told you 1,000,000 times not to exaggerate!

6. In the <u>fourteenth</u> century, the Black Plague killed $\frac{1}{2}$ the population of Europe.

7. The Earth now supports more than six billion people, and two countries, India and China, account for more than 1,000,000,000 each.

8. Although I was travelling at <u>eighty</u> km/h, which is what I thought the speed limit to be, the officer told me that I was <u>two</u> km inside the city limits, so the speed limit was 50 km/h. My fine was <u>one hundred and eight</u> <u>dollars.</u>

9. 1 8-cylinder SUV puts more pollution into the atmosphere than two <u>four-cylinder</u> diesel Volkswagens or 3 Toyota gas-electric hybrids.

10. The total population of Earth in <u>five thousand</u> B.C. is estimated to have been about 5,000,000 people, about $\frac{1}{6}$ the number who now live in Canada.

GO TO WEB
EXERCISE 5.3

WWW.BAREA.NELSON.COM

EXERCISE **5.4**

Before you tackle this exercise, review the five highlighted rules in this chapter. It would be a good idea to write them on a single sheet of paper and keep them in front of you as you find the 15 errors in this exercise.

Trivial Pursuit is the ultimate board game for people from 9 to 99 who either know or love to learn 1000s of miscellaneous, little-known facts. One interesting piece of trivia is that the game itself was invented by 2 enterprising Canadian journalists: Chris Haney, a photo editor for the *Montreal Gazette,* and Scott Abbott, a sports editor for the Canadian Press. The friends started with a simple prototype in nineteen seventy-nine and scrambled and scraped to raise enough money to produce one thousand games 2 years later. The production budget was so tight that the initial artwork was created by an eighteen-year-old artist who agreed to work for company shares instead of cash (in 1986, his 5 shares were worth $2.5 million).

When the 1st-edition sets were finally ready in 1981, they retailed in the American market at approximately thirty dollars each. This was a high price for a board game, but Trivial Pursuit rapidly became a success in spite of its price tag, selling more than three-and-one-half million copies in its first 5 years. The eighteenth-century poet Alexander Pope seems to have been prophetic when he wrote, "What mighty contests arise from trivial things."

In 1988, Parker Brothers, now Hasbro Inc., secured the rights to the game. By 2000, 19 years after the initial production run, Trivial Pursuit contests had become such a popular form of amusement worldwide that the game's cumulative sales totalled more than $1,000,000,000. Today, the game has spun off dozens of clones, including DVD-based games, a cellphone version, and even a *Lord of the Rings* edition. The 2 inventors, whose 22% of the game made them very wealthy, remain good friends.

UNIT 1 RAPID REVIEW

As a final check of your mastery of the information you have worked on in Unit 1, correct the 20 errors in the following passage. Then check the answers on page 393 to see if you need to review any of the material you've covered.

[1]Irregardless of any negative attitudes, feelings, or thoughts you may have about working in retail sales, this kind of work does, in actual fact, provide employee's with alot of amusing moments. [2]During our last boxing day sale, for example, I was serving a women who wanted to buy 3 pairs of shoes to compliment the brand-new outfits she had just purchased. [3]As she opened her humongous, real leather designer purse, she asked if we excepted american express. I assured her that her credit card would be fine. [4]She rummaged around for her wallet, then turned her purse upside down, dumping its contents all over the counter right beside the cash register. [5]I could not help noticing a television remote control among the items scattered over our counter. [6]Curious, I asked if their was a reason she carried a remote control when she went on a purchasing expedition. [7]Her answer gave me one of the best laughs I've had in my job. [8]She told me that her husband said he wanted to watch football rather than go shopping with her. [9]She was so ticked off that she took the remote control because she thought that was the most evil thing she could legally do to him.

UNIT 2

Sentences

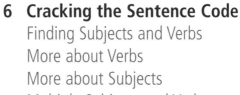

Sentences

UNIT 2 QUICK QUIZ

This Quick Quiz will show you which chapters of Unit 2 you need to focus on. The passage below contains a total of 15 errors in sentence structure. You will find one or more examples of sentence fragments, run-ons, misplaced and dangling modifiers, and unparallel constructions. When you've made your corrections, turn to page 394 and compare your revisions with ours. For each error you miss, the "Answer Key" there directs you to the chapter you need to work on.

[1]The 100-kilometre diet is not a way to lose weight. [2]A plan to encourage consumers to buy and have an appreciation of locally grown food. [3]The idea is to only buy those meats and vegetables that have been produced within 100 km of where we live. [4]As consumers, it's a way to spend our dollars and at the same time help ourselves, our community, and is good for the planet. [5]By insisting that we want to buy only meats and vegetables that have been grown in our region, local farmers are supported, we put pressure on merchants to stock local products, and minimize the amount of petroleum used to transport foods from producer to market. [6]A distance that is often half a continent or more. [7]Besides, when we buy fruits and vegetables fresh from the farm, we get better food, produce that was harvested green and allowed to ripen often during the long journey to our stores has less colour, is not as flavourful, and has fewer nutrients.

[8]Of course, not all foods can be found year-round in every locality, sometimes if we simply must have a certain fruit or vegetable to satisfy a craving or for the preparation of a special meal, we have no choice but to buy from outside our region. [9]With new growing and preserving techniques, however, it is becoming increasingly possible to stock up on local produce in season and enjoy it year-round. [10]Healthier consumers, decreased pollution, and profitable farms. [11]These benefits make the 100-kilometre diet a wise consumer choice.

Sentences

6 | Cracking the Sentence Code

A baby's first word is a big step, one that all parents mark as a significant stage of development. Not all parents recognize that an even more significant step in a baby's progress is the first time he or she puts together the two elements of a complete sentence: a subject and a verb. *Words* enable us to communicate images; *sentences* are the tools with which we communicate ideas.

There is nothing really mysterious or difficult about sentences. You've been speaking them successfully since you were a toddler. The difficulty arises when you write—not sentences, oddly enough, but paragraphs. Most university and college students, if asked to write 10 sentences on 10 different topics, could do so without errors. But when those same students write paragraphs, errors such as fragments and run-ons appear. Sometimes these errors cause a failure of communication; at other times, they simply give the reader a poor impression of the writer.

Sentences

The solution to sentence-structure problems has two parts.

Be sure every sentence you write
1. has both a subject and a verb
   and
2. expresses a complete thought.

Your ear may be the best instrument with which to test your sentences. If you read your sentences aloud, you may be able to tell by the sound whether they are complete and clear. Sometimes, however, your ear may mislead you, so this chapter will show you, step by step, how to decode your sentences to find their subjects and verbs. When you know how to decode sentences, you can make sure that every sentence you write is complete.

Read these sentences aloud.

Yak skiing is one of Asia's newest sports.
Although yak skiing is still a young sport.

The second "sentence" doesn't sound right, does it? It does not make sense on its own and is in fact a sentence fragment.

Testing your sentences by reading them aloud won't work if you read your paragraphs straight through from beginning to end. The trick is to read from end to beginning. That is, read your last sentence aloud and *listen* to it. If it sounds all right, then read aloud the next-to-last sentence, and so on, until you have worked your way back to the first sentence you wrote.

Now, what do you do with the ones that don't sound correct? Before you can fix them, you need to decode each sentence to find out if it has both a subject and a verb. The subject and the verb are the bare essentials of a sentence. Every sentence you write must contain both. There is one exception:

In a **command**, the subject is suggested rather than stated.

Consider these examples.

Sign here. = [You] sign here. (The subject you is implied or understood.)
Charge it. = [You] charge it.
Play ball! = [You] play ball!

FINDING SUBJECTS AND VERBS

A sentence is about *someone* or *something*. That someone or something is the **subject**. The word (or words) that tells what the subject *is* or *does* is the **verb**. In the following sentences, the subject is underlined once and the verb twice.

Snow falls.
Toshiki dislikes winter.
We love snowboarding.
Mt. Whistler offers excellent opportunities for winter sports.
In Canada, winter is six months long.
Some people feel the cold severely.

The subject of a sentence is always a **noun** (the name of a person, place, thing, or concept) or a **pronoun** (a word such as *I, you, he, she, it, we,* or *they* used in place of a noun). In the examples above, the subjects include persons (*Toshiki, we, people*); a place (*Mt. Whistler*); a thing (*snow*); and a concept (*winter*). In one sentence, a pronoun (*we*) is the subject.

> Find the verb first.

One way to find the verb in a sentence is to ask what the sentence says about the subject. There are two kinds of verbs:

- **action verbs**, which tell you what the subject is doing. In the examples above, *falls, dislikes, love,* and *offers* are action verbs.
- **linking verbs**, which link or connect a subject to a noun or adjective describing that subject. In the examples above, *is* and *feel* are linking verbs. Linking verbs tell you the subject's condition or state of being. (For example, "Tadpoles *become* frogs," "Frogs *feel* slimy.") The most common linking verbs are forms of *to be* (*am, is, are, was, were, have been,* etc.) and verbs such as *look, taste, feel, sound, appear, remain, seem,* and *become.*

Another way to find the verb in a sentence is to put a pronoun (*I, you, he, she, it,* or *they*) in front of the word you think is the verb. If the result makes sense, it is a verb. For example, you could put *she* in front of *falls* in the first sentence listed above: "she falls" makes sense, so you know *falls* is the verb in this sentence. Try this test with the other five example sentences.

Keep this guideline in mind as you work through the exercises below.

To find the subject, ask <u>who</u> or <u>what</u> the sentence is about.
To find the verb, ask what the subject <u>is</u> or <u>is doing</u>.

EXERCISE **6.1**

In each of the following sentences, underline the <u>subject</u> with one line and the <u>verb</u> with two. Answers for exercises in this chapter begin on page 394. If you make even one mistake, go to the website and do the exercise identified beside the Web icon that follows this exercise. Be sure you understand this material thoroughly before you go on.

1. <u>Canadians</u> <u>love</u> doughnuts.

2. <u>They</u> <u>eat</u> more doughnuts than any other nation.

3. Most <u>malls</u> <u>contain</u> a doughnut shop.

4. <u>Doughnuts</u> <u>taste</u> sweet.

5. Glazed <u>doughnuts</u> <u>are</u> my favourite.

6. <u>Hot chocolate</u> <u>is</u> good with doughnuts.

7. <u>Try</u> a bran doughnut for breakfast. *You is subject (command)*

8. <u>It</u> <u>is</u> good for your health.

9. Doughnut <u>jokes</u> <u>are</u> common on television.

10. <u>Dentists</u> <u>like</u> doughnuts too, but for different reasons.

GO TO WEB
EXERCISE 6.1

WWW.BAREA.NELSON.COM

EXERCISE **6.2**

Underline the subject with one line and the verb with two.

1. I hate cellphones.

2. Today, however, cellphones are practically a necessity.

3. Turn your cellphone off, please. *Command*

4. My cellphone takes pictures.

5. Alissa's cellphone is an expensive model.

6. She is on a very strict diet.

7. The cellphone's memory contains information about her diet.

8. Now she checks her cellphone before every meal.

9. Alissa is happy about her weight loss.

10. Her telephone bills, though, infuriate her.

GO TO WEB
EXERCISE 6.2

WWW.BAREA.NELSON.COM

Usually, but not always, the subject comes before the verb in a sentence.

Occasionally, we find the subject after the verb:

* In sentences beginning with *Here* + a form of *to be* or with *There* + a form of *to be (here* and *there* are never the subject of a sentence):

Here are the test results. (Who or what are? Results.)
There is a fly in my soup. (Who or what is? A fly.)

* In sentences that are inverted for emphasis:

Finally, at the end of the long, boring joke, came the pathetic punch line.
Out of the stadium and into the rain marched the demonstrators.

- In questions:

  Are we there yet?
  Is she the one?

  But notice that in questions beginning with *who, whose, what,* or *which,* the subject and verb are in "normal" order: subject followed by verb.

  Who ate my sandwich?   Whose horse came first?
  What caused the accident?   Which car uses less gas?

Sentences

EXERCISE **6.3**

Underline the subject with one line and the verb with two. Watch out for inverted-order sentences. Check your answers before going on. If you made even one mistake, do the Web exercise indicated at the end of this exercise.

1. Whose homework is missing?

2. Drive carefully. *You (command)*

3. Slowly down the spiral staircase came the bride.

4. Have you no heart?

5. Then give me a kilogram of liver and a couple of kidneys instead. *(command) You*

6. Into the pool leaped the terrified cat.

7. There are two electives to choose from.

8. Which one is more interesting?

9. Here is just the person to answer your question.

10. Were you happy with the answer?

GO TO WEB
EXERCISE 6.3

WWW.BAREA.NELSON.COM

MORE ABOUT VERBS

The verb in a sentence may be a single word, as in the exercises you've just completed, or it may be a group of words. When you are considering whether or not a word group is a verb, there are two points you should remember.

1. No verb form preceded by *to* is ever the verb of a sentence.[1]
2. **Helping verbs**[2] are often added to main verbs.

The list below contains the most common helping verbs.

be (all forms of *to be* can act as helping verbs: e.g., *am, are, is, was, were, will be, have/had been*, etc.)	can could/could have do/did have/had may/may have might/might have	must/must have ought shall/shall have should/should have will/will have would/would have

The complete verb in a sentence consists of the **main verb** + any **helping verbs**.

Below are a few of the forms of the verb *to take*. Study this list carefully, and note that when the sentence is in question form, the subject comes between the helping verb and the main verb.

We are taking a required English course.
You can take it with you.
Could Ray have taken it?
Did you take your turn?
The money has been taken.
We have taken too much time.
You may take a break now.

We might have taken your advice.
You must take the bus.
Lucy ought to have taken a course in stress management.
Shall we take his offer?
I should take more time.
We will take the championship.
We should have taken the gold medal.

---

[1] The form *to + verb*—e.g., *to speak, to write, to help*—is an infinitive. Infinitives can act as subjects or objects, but they are never verbs.

[2] If you are familiar with technical grammatical terms, you will know these verbs as **auxiliary verbs**.

One verb form always requires a helping verb. Here's the rule.

A verb ending in *-ing* MUST have a helping verb (or verbs) before it.

Sentences

Here are a few of the forms that a verb ending in *-ing* can take.

Ralph <u>is taking</u> the test.
<u>Am</u> I <u>taking</u> your place?
You <u>are taking</u> an awfully long time.
These new computers <u>will be taking</u> over our jobs.
<u>Have</u> you <u>been taking</u> French lessons?

EXERCISE **6.4**

Underline the complete verb with a double line.

1. We <u>are finding</u> most of the verbs.

2. Someday my prince <u>will come</u>.

3. <u>Have</u> you <u>planned</u> a party to celebrate his arrival?

4. This book <u>must have been written</u> by a genius.

5. The verbs <u>must be underlined</u> twice.

6. Keith <u>will have</u> another coffee and a doughnut.

7. <u>Do</u> you <u>know</u> anything about grammar?

8. We <u>have knocked</u> on the door several times.

9. I <u>will be looking</u> for verbs in my sleep.

10. We <u>must have practised</u> enough by now.

GO TO WEB
EXERCISE 6.4

WWW.BAREA.NELSON.COM

Beware of certain words that are often confused with helping verbs.

> Words such as *always, ever, just, never, not, often, only,* and *sometimes* are NOT part of the verb.

These words usually appear in the middle of a complete verb, but they are modifiers, not verbs. Do not underline them.

Sophie is always chosen first.
They have just been married.
The question has not often been asked.

Do you ever have doubts about your ability?
Will you never learn?
I have often wondered about that.

In the following two exercises, underline the subject with one line and the verb with two. Check your answers to the first set before going on to the next.

EXERCISE **6.5**

1. I am making a nutritious breakfast.

2. It does not include pop.

3. You can add fresh fruit to the cereal.

4. The toast should be ready now.

5. My doctor has often recommended yogurt for breakfast.

6. I could never eat yogurt without fruit.

7. With breakfast, I will drink at least two cups of coffee.

8. I don't like tea.

9. I simply cannot begin my day without coffee.

10. I should probably switch to decaf.

EXERCISE **6.6**

1. The security guard is sleeping again.

2. The security guard is often found asleep.

3. Have you ever been lonely?

4. There has never been a better time to invest.

5. Marie is carefully considering her options.

6. Where and when are we meeting?

7. Teenagers are sometimes embarrassed by their parents' behaviour.

8. Could you please explain one more time.

9. "Ladies are requested not to have children in the bar." (Sign in a Norwegian club)

10. "The manager has personally passed all our water." (Sign in an Acapulco hotel)

GO TO WEB
EXERCISE 6.5

WWW.BAREA.NELSON.COM

MORE ABOUT SUBJECTS

Groups of words called **prepositional phrases** often come before the subject in a sentence or between the subject and the verb. When you're looking for the subject in a sentence, prepositional phrases can trip you up unless you know the following rule.

The subject of a sentence is NEVER in a prepositional phrase.

You must be able to identify prepositional phrases so that you will know where *not* to look for the subject.

> A prepositional phrase is a group of words that begins with a preposition and ends with a noun or pronoun.

The noun or pronoun is called the object of the preposition. It is this word that, if you're not careful, you might think is the subject of the sentence.

Below is a list of prepositional phrases. The italicized words are prepositions; the words in regular type are their objects.

about your message	*between* them	*near* the wall
above the door	*by* the way	*of* the memo
according to the book	*concerning* your request	*on* the following day
after the meeting	*despite* the shortfall	*onto* the floor
against the wall	*down* the corridor	*over* the page
along the hall	*except* the contract	*through* the window
among the staff	workers	*to* the staff
around the office	*for* the manager	*under* the table
before lunch	*from* the office	*until* the meeting
behind my back	*in* the afternoon	*up* the corridor
below the window	*inside* the office	*with* permission
beside my computer	*into* the elevator	*without* the software

Before you look for the subject in a sentence, lightly cross out all prepositional phrases and identify the verb.

A bird ~~in the hand~~ is messy.   (What is messy? The bird, not the hand.)

This deck ~~of cards~~ is unlucky.   (What is unlucky? The deck, not the cards.)

Many houses ~~in our neighbourhood~~ need painting.   (What need painting? The houses, not the neighbourhood.)

In the following exercises, first cross out the prepositional phrase(s) in each sentence. Then underline the subject with one line and the verb with two. Check your answers to Exercise 6.7 on page 396, and if you make even one error, do Web Exercise 6.6 before going on to Exercise 6.8.

EXERCISE **6.7**

1. A couple ~~of hamburgers~~ should be enough ~~for each of us~~.

2. Only a few ~~of us~~ save money ~~in an RRSP~~.

3. One-seventh ~~of your life~~ is spent ~~on Mondays~~.

4. Exaggeration ~~in your writing~~ is a million times worse than understatement.

5. Your flu, ~~despite your precautions~~, has infected everyone ~~in the office~~.

6. ~~In their secret dreams~~, many grown men would still like to own a train set.

7. Nothing ~~in the known universe~~ travels faster than a bad cheque.

8. ~~During the trial, before the decision~~, you must have been nervous.

9. Ninety-eight percent ~~of all statistics~~ are made up.

10. A day ~~without sunshine~~ is, ~~in most respects~~, just like night.

GO TO WEB
EXERCISE 6.6

WWW.BAREA.NELSON.COM

EXERCISE **6.8**

1. ~~According to my financial adviser, my earliest possible~~ retirement date is 2052.

2. ~~By waiting on tables, baby-sitting, and borrowing~~ from friends, I manage to make ends meet.

3. ~~Except for me~~, everyone understands prepositions.

4. ~~With the permission of the professor~~, I will demonstrate my mastery ~~of verb identification~~.

5. No book ~~of Canadian humour~~ would be complete ~~without some shots at American tourists~~.

6. ~~Despite its strong taste~~, espresso contains no more caffeine ~~than regular coffee~~.

7. A daily intake ~~of more than 600 mg of caffeine~~ can result ~~in headaches, insomnia, and heart palpitations~~.

8. Six to ten cups of coffee will usually contain about 600 mg of caffeine.

9. One of the network's foreign correspondents will speak at noon in the auditorium about her experiences in Afghanistan.

10. Our teacher's uncertainty about the date of the War of 1812 made us curious about his knowledge of Canadian history.

EXERCISE **6.9**

1. In my opinion, fear of flying is entirely justifiable.

2. In our basement are stacks of magazines dating from the 1950s.

3. The rats in our building have written letters of complaint to the Board of Health.

4. When did the president of your company decide on this policy?

5. For reasons of privacy, I am listed in the telephone book under my dog's name.

6. Into the classroom and up to the front marched a tall, grey-haired woman with a determined look in her eyes.

7. After eight hours of classes, the thought of collapsing in front of the TV is very appealing.

8. In future, be sure to read through your notes before the exam. You

9. In your brochure, you advertise a "semiannual after-Christmas sale" of quality items.

10. According to my dictionary, the word "semiannual" means twice a year.

GO TO WEB
EXERCISE 6.7

WWW.BAREA.NELSON.COM

MULTIPLE SUBJECTS AND VERBS

Until now, you have been decoding sentences containing a single subject and a single verb, even though the verb may have consisted of more than one word. Sentences can, however, have a multiple (or **compound**) subject and/or a multiple (or compound) verb.

Here is a sentence with a multiple subject:

French fries and onion rings are Brian's idea of a balanced diet.

This sentence has a multiple verb:

Selena walks and dresses like a supermodel.

And this sentence contains both a multiple subject and a multiple verb:

Alan and Dave drove to the mall and shopped for hours.

The parts of a multiple subject are usually joined by *and* or *or,* sometimes by *but* or *nor.* A multiple subject or a multiple verb may contain more than two elements. Look at the following examples.

Clarity, brevity, and simplicity are the basic qualities of good writing.

Raj deleted his work, shut down the computer, unplugged it, and dropped it out of the window.

Identify the subjects and verbs in the three exercises that follow. First, cross out any prepositional phrases. Then underline the subjects with one line and the verbs with two. Be sure to underline all elements of a multiple subject or verb (there may be more than two). Check your answers to each set, and if you've made any errors, do Web Exercises 6.8, 6.9, and 6.10 before you go on to the next exercise.

EXERCISE **6.10**

1. Maple sugar and wild rice are native Canadian products.

2. Professor Dasgupta handed out the tests and wished us luck.

Sentences

3. The screen blinked twice and then went blank.

4. Elgar and Grieg are the names of my two unfortunate nephews.

5. My weird brother and his equally weird wife chose the names in honour of their favourite composers.

6. They could have done worse and chosen Humperdinck and Shostakovich.

7. A good sermon writer creates a brilliant opening, develops a stirring conclusion, and puts the two as close together as possible. (George Burns)

8. Today my neighbour and I raked the leaves, dug up our gardens, and put away the lawn furniture.

9. Students with good time-management skills can research, organize, draft, and revise a first-class paper by the deadline.

10. Those with excellent time-management skills can keep on top of their schoolwork, hold a part-time job, volunteer at a local charity, and still find time for a social life.

GO TO WEB
EXERCISE 6.8

WWW.BAREA.NELSON.COM

EXERCISE **6.11**

1. Food and drink are the most reliable sources of pleasure.

2. According to Angelo, Werner, and Vijay, Italy, Germany, and India produce and eat the best food in the world.

3. Question, disagree, and argue with them at your own risk!

4. When can the three chefs and their guests gather for a demonstration?

5. Angelo, Werner, and Vijay discussed and debated recipes all night.

6. During the following week, each one chose and prepared a meal for the other two.

7. Werner's sauerbraten with rösti and Black Forest cake amazed and delighted his friends.

8. Angelo chopped, sliced, simmered, and baked a magnificent Italian four-course meal.

9. Vijay and his sister worked in the kitchen for two days and prepared a delicious Indian feast.

10. By the end of the week, Vijay, Angelo, and Werner were ready for a fast.

GO TO WEB
EXERCISE 6.9

WWW.BAREA.NELSON.COM

EXERCISE **6.12**

I have news for all you short people out there. Being tall is not an enviable condition. First of all, tall people are the butt of constant jokes: "How's the weather up there?" "What great kneecaps you have!" The humour is pretty lame. Next, there is the risk of serious head injury. I have been bashed by cupboard doors and concussed by signboards. On one memorable occasion, I was knocked senseless by a chandelier. Clothes present another problem. Finding anything to fit is a challenge. Finding anything remotely fashionable is next to impossible. Clerks in men's clothing departments are apparently hired for their ability to humiliate outsized men. They seem to be genuinely surprised at one's reluctance to appear in public wearing pants that end at midcalf. And finally, there is basketball. Like many tall people, I detest the game. Despite popular belief, not all people more than 2 m tall have been blessed with the natural ability to dribble, jump-shoot, and slam-dunk. Many of us would rather join a chain gang than a basketball team. To be honest, though, for the most part, I do like being tall. But I wouldn't mind fewer jokes, more sympathy, and less basketball.

Sentences

WWW.BAREA.NELSON.COM

Here's a summary of what you've learned in this chapter. Keep it in mind as you write Exercise 6.13, the Mastery Test.

SUMMARY

- The subject is *who* or *what* the sentence is about.
- The verb tells what the subject *is* or *does*.
- The subject normally comes before the verb (exceptions are questions, sentences that begin with *here* or *there*, and sentences that begin with prepositional phrases).
- An infinitive (a phrase consisting of *to* + verb) is never the verb of a sentence.
- The complete verb consists of a main verb + any helping verbs.
- A word ending in *-ing* is not, by itself, a verb.
- The subject of a sentence is never in a prepositional phrase.
- A sentence can have more than one subject and verb.

EXERCISE **6.13**

Before you do this exercise, review the information in the "Summary" box above. This exercise will test your ability to identify subjects and verbs in different kinds of sentences. First, lightly cross out any prepositional phrases. Next, underline the subject(s) with one line and the verb(s) with two. Be sure to underline all elements in a multiple subject or verb.

1. Turn the corner, put the past behind you, and get on with life.

2. Of all the emotions, sincerity is the most difficult to fake.

3. The difference between the right word and almost the right word is the difference between lightning and the lightning bug. (Mark Twain)

4. Out of the pages of an illustrated history book stepped a courier du bois and an Iroquois warrior.

5. After a huge argument with Brad, Marita threw his clothes out of the window, changed the locks on the doors to the house and the garage, and checked in at her favourite spa for a week.

6. Old age may be difficult, but it is better than the alternative.

7. According to Mame's obituary, clubs, all-night parties, and martinis for breakfast were her favourite pleasures during her short life.

8. Her lawyer, my lawyer, the accountant, and the mediator picked up the pen in turn, signed the document, and shook my hand.

9. The floors are cold, the windows are drafty, and the roof leaks in my newly purchased dream home.

10. Among the students in Irena's singing class are a grandmother of 12, a student chef with a nose ring, and an aspiring actor with a huge ego.

7 Solving Sentence-Fragment Problems

Every complete sentence has two characteristics: it contains a subject and a verb, and it expresses a complete thought. Any group of words that is punctuated as a sentence but lacks one of these characteristics is a **sentence fragment**. Fragments are appropriate in conversation and in some kinds of writing, but normally they are not acceptable in academic, technical, or business writing.

There are two kinds of fragments you should watch out for: the "missing piece" fragment and the dependent clause fragment.

"MISSING PIECE" FRAGMENTS

Sometimes a group of words is punctuated as a sentence but is missing one or both of the essential parts of a sentence: the subject and the verb. Consider these examples.

Won an award for creativity.
(<u>Who</u> or <u>what</u> won an award? The sentence doesn't tell you. The subject is missing.)

The hamster under the bed.
(The sentence doesn't tell you what the hamster <u><u>was</u></u> or <u><u>did</u></u>. The verb is missing.)

During their lunch break.
(<u>Who</u> or <u>what</u> <u><u>was</u></u> or <u><u>did</u></u> something? Both subject and verb are missing.)

The team missing two of its best players.
(Part of the verb is missing. Remember that a verb ending in *-ing* needs a helping verb to be complete.)

Finding fragments like these in your work is the hard part. Fixing them is easy. There are two ways to correct sentence fragments. Here's the first one.

> To change a "missing piece" fragment into a complete sentence, add whatever is missing: a subject, a verb, or both.

You may need to add a subject:

Her <u>essay</u> won an award for creativity.

You may need to add a verb:

The hamster <u><u>was</u></u> under the bed. (linking verb)
The hamster under the bed <u>chewed</u> my socks. (action verb)

You may need to add both a subject and a verb:

Many desk-bound <u>workers</u> <u>enjoy</u> running in the park during the lunch break.

Or you may need to add a helping verb:

The team <u>was missing</u> two of its best players.

Don't let the length of a fragment fool you. Students sometimes think that if a string of words is long, it must be a sentence. Not so. No matter how long the string of words, if it doesn't contain both a subject and a verb, it is not a sentence. For example, here's a description of a woman paddling a canoe on a lake in summertime:

The paddle dipping into the lake, sliding beneath the surface, and emerging at the end of the stroke, the face of the paddle glistening in the sun and droplets from its edge making a trail in the water as she reaches forward to dip again just as before, repeating the movement hundreds of times, thousands of times, in a hypnotic rhythm that becomes as natural as breathing, as calming as meditation.

At 71 words, this "sentence" is long, but it is a fragment. It lacks both a subject and a verb. If you add "<u>She</u> <u>watches</u>" at the beginning of the fragment, it becomes a complete sentence.

EXERCISE **7.1**

In the following exercise, decide whether each group of words is a complete sentence or a "missing piece" fragment. Write "S" in the space before each complete sentence and "F" before each fragment. Make each fragment into a complete sentence by adding whatever is missing: the subject, the verb, or both. Then compare your answers with our suggestions. Answers for exercises in this chapter begin on page 398.

1. _____ According to the government.

2. _____ Exhausted, I slept.

3. _____ Happy to help.

4. _____ Hoping to hear from you soon.

5. _____ Take another.

6. _____ In case you were wondering.

7. _____ Sentence fragments such as these.

8. _____ Close the door quietly on your way out.

9. _____ Pausing to think of an appropriate reply.

10. _____ Working as a server in a cheap restaurant is not rewarding.

GO TO WEB
EXERCISE 7.1

WWW.BAREA.NELSON.COM

Most of us can identify a fragment when it stands alone. But when we write, of course, we write in paragraphs, not in single sentences. Fragments are harder to identify when they occur in a context, as you'll see in the next exercise.

EXERCISE **7.2**

Read the following selections carefully and decide whether each question contains only complete sentences or whether it contains one or more sentence fragments. Put "S" beside the questions that contain only sentences. Put "F" beside those that contain fragments. Then check your answers.

1. _____ I wanted to stay home, but my girlfriend wanted to go to the movies. To see the Coen brothers' new film.

2. _____ In volleyball, our college is well respected. Our team won the provincial championship last year. Placing three players on the All-Star team.

3. _____ Whenever I go fishing, the fish aren't biting, but the mosquitoes are. Maybe I should give up fishing. And start collecting insects instead.

4. _____ My son is a genius. On his last birthday, he was given a toy that was guaranteed to be unbreakable. Guess what? Used it to break all his other toys.

5. _____ We weren't lost, but we certainly were confused. I realized this when we drove past City Hall. For the third time.

6. _____ Place the paper in the feed tray. Select the quality of copy that you want. Print.

7. _____ My friends and I often go to the hockey arena during the winter. Not to watch sports, but to hear concerts by some of the best local bands. These concerts give new meaning to the word "cool."

8. _____ According to the weather report on our college radio station, a storm with high winds and heavy rain is approaching our region. Yesterday, when the temperature hit 10°C, the reporter predicted light snow.

9. _____ I enjoy reading travel blogs. Faraway places that I have never visited and will probably never get to see. The fun is in the dreaming, not the doing.

10. _____ Spending my days skiing and boarding and my nights dancing and clubbing. That's how I plan to spend my retirement.

Once you have learned to identify fragments that occur within a paragraph, it's time to consider the best way to correct them. You could fix all of them the way you did in Exercise 7.1, by adding the missing piece or pieces to each one, and in some cases, that is your only choice. However, there is another, shorter, way that can often be used to correct fragments in a paragraph.

> You can sometimes correct a "missing piece" fragment by attaching it to a complete sentence that comes before or after it—whichever one makes sense.

 Sometimes you need to put a comma between a "missing piece" fragment and the complete sentence to which you attach it. (See Chapter 18, "The Comma," Rule 3, page 218, and Rule 4, page 219.)

EXERCISE **7.3**

Now go back to the sentences in Exercise 7.2 and correct the fragments. As you go through the exercise, try to use both techniques we've identified for fixing fragments:

- Add the missing piece(s).
- Join the fragment to a complete sentence next to it.

When you've finished, compare your answers with ours on pages 398–99.

EXERCISE **7.4**

Read through the following paragraph, and put "S" before each complete sentence and "F" before each fragment. Then check your answers.

(1) _S_ Ed forgot his wife's birthday. (2) _F_ Knowing he was in trouble from the moment he got home from work and saw her angry face, (3) _F_ _he_ Apologiz~~ing~~ _ed_ and ask~~ing~~ _ed_ how he could make it up to her. (4) _S_ She replied that she wanted to find something in the driveway that would go from zero to 100 in less than five seconds, (5) _F_ No later than tomorrow morning. (6) _S_ The next day, Ed left for work early, (7) _F_ Leaving a colourful package tied with a large bow in the middle of the driveway. (8) _S_ Ed's wife eagerly tore the paper and ribbon off the package. (9) _F_ Discovering a new bathroom scale. (10) _S_ Ed is still missing.

EXERCISE **7.5**

Now correct the fragments you identified in the paragraph above. Use both fragment-fixing techniques we've highlighted for you on pages 95 and 98. Then compare your answers with ours on page 399.

DEPENDENT CLAUSE FRAGMENTS

Any group of words containing a subject and a verb is a clause. There are two kinds of clauses. An **independent clause** is one that makes complete sense. It can stand alone as a sentence; in fact, every sentence MUST contain at least one independent clause. A **dependent clause,** as its name suggests, cannot stand alone as a sentence. It depends on another clause to make complete sense. Dependent clauses (also known as **subordinate clauses**) begin with words or phrases such as these:

Dependent Clause Cues

after	that
although	though
as, as if	unless
as long as	until
as soon as	what, ~~whatever~~
because	when, whenever
before	where, wherever
even if, even though	whether
if	which, whichever
since	while
so that	who, whose

Whenever a clause begins with one of these words or phrases, it is dependent.

A dependent clause must be attached to an independent clause. If it stands alone, it is a sentence fragment.

Here is an independent clause:

I am a hopeless speller.

If we put one of the dependent clause cues in front of it, it can no longer stand alone:

Because I am a hopeless speller.

We can correct this kind of fragment by attaching it to an independent clause:

Because I am a hopeless speller, I have chained my dictionary to my wrist.

EXERCISE **7.6**

Let's start with an easy exercise. Put an "S" before each clause that is independent and therefore a sentence. Put an "F" before each clause that is dependent and therefore a sentence fragment. Highlight the dependent clause cue in each fragment. Then check the answers on page 399.

1. _F_ When we left the party.

2. _F_ If you don't approve.

3. _F_ Although there is another side to the story.

4. _S_ Unless you cheat, I win.

5. _F_ Soon, when you have completed your education.

6. _F_ Even though you thought your effort was enough to win.

7. _F_ All of those who finish before the time is up.

8. _S_ If he were any dumber, he'd have to be watered twice a week.

9. _F_ Repulsive, although my sister seems to be genuinely in love with him.

10. _F_ When you decide to begin, whether the other team is ready or not.

Most sentence fragments are dependent clauses punctuated as sentences. Fortunately, these are the easiest fragments to fix.

> To correct a dependent clause fragment, join it either to the sentence that comes before it or to the one that comes after it—whichever linkage makes the most sense.

Problem: We want to move into our new apartment. As soon as the current tenants leave. It's perfect for our family.

The second "sentence" is incomplete; the dependent clause cue *as soon as* is the clue you need to identify it as a sentence fragment. You could join the fragment to the sentence that follows it, but then you would get "As soon as the current tenants leave, it's perfect for our family," which doesn't make sense. The fragment should be linked to the sentence before it.

Revision: We want to move into our new apartment as soon as the current tenants leave. It's perfect for our family.

If, as in the example above, your revised sentence *ends* with the dependent clause, you do not need to use a comma before it. If, however, your revised sentence *begins* with the dependent clause, put a comma between it and the independent clause that follows.

As soon as the current tenants leave, we want to move into our new apartment. It's perfect for our family. (See Chapter 18, "The Comma," Rule 3, on page 218.)

EXERCISE 7.7

Correct the fragments in Exercise 7.6 by attaching each one to an independent clause that you have made up. Then compare your answers with our suggestions. Be sure to put a comma after a dependent clause that comes at the beginning of a sentence.

Like "missing piece" fragments, dependent clause fragments are harder to identify when they appear in the middle of a paragraph. Check your fragment-finding skills by doing the exercises that follow.

The items in Exercises 7.8 and 7.9 contain one or more dependent clauses masquerading as sentences. They are, in fact, sentence fragments. Highlight the dependent clause(s) in each item.

EXERCISE 7.8

1. Walking is probably the best form of exercise there is, Unless you're in the water. Then, swimming is preferable.

2. The modern world is confusing for all of us. If you can keep your head when all about you are losing theirs, Perhaps you just don't understand the situation.

3. "The world is divided into good and bad people. The good ones sleep better, While the bad ones enjoy their waking hours much more." (Woody Allen)

4. Doing the job right the first time gets the job done, While doing the job wrong again and again gives you job security. This principle explains how my uncle stays employed.

5. You know you have been teaching too long, When capital punishment seems a reasonable response to sentence fragments. Now is the time to think about early retirement.

GO TO WEB
EXERCISE 7.2

WWW.BAREA.NELSON.COM

EXERCISE **7.9**

1. Because bear attacks are so well publicized in the media, Most people do not know that their chances of being killed by a bear are far lower than their chances of being killed by lightning. Bears seldom bother humans, Unless the humans are foolish enough to take food into their tents, approach a bear cub, or get close to a grizzly.

2. While getting lost in a country inhabited by cannibals would be a terrifying experience for most people, I know that my long career as a standup comic will keep me safe from harm. All cannibals know that comics taste funny.

3. The names of many Canadian landmarks have been changed over the years. Until the residents of Lethbridge, for example, petitioned for a change to a more dignified name, The Oldman River used to be called the Belly River.

4. After hearing the same song about 30 times in a week and liking it less each time, I finally took action. I reset all the buttons on my car radio. So

Sentences

that I could avoid any station that plays the top 10, I now listen only to talk radio and the CBC.

5. Superglue is a remarkable product. It can bond almost anything to almost anything else. Nevertheless, all parents of toddlers know there is another substance. Even stronger than Superglue. The glue that outperforms all others is mashed banana, Especially after it has dried in an infant's hair.

GO TO WEB
EXERCISE 7.3

WWW.BAREA.NELSON.COM

EXERCISE **7.10**

Correct the sentence fragments you highlighted in Exercises 7.8 and 7.9 above. Make each fragment into a complete sentence by attaching it to the independent clause that precedes or follows it, whichever makes better sense. Remember to punctuate correctly: if a dependent clause comes at the beginning of your sentence, put a comma after it. Check your answers after each exercise.

EXERCISE **7.11**

In the following paragraph, you'll find a mixture of "missing piece" fragments and dependent clause fragments. Revise the six fragments any way you choose: either by adding the missing piece(s), or by joining fragments to appropriate independent clauses. Check your punctuation carefully.

Because the chances of winning are so small, Lotteries have been called a tax on people with poor math skills. Buying a lottery ticket will gain you about as much as betting that the next U.S. president will come from Moose Jaw, Or that the parrot in the pet store speaks Inuktitut. While winning a lottery is not impossible, It is so unlikely that you'd do better to use your money to light a nice warm fire. Although the winners are highly publicized, No one hears about the huge numbers of losers, Whose money has gone to pay the winners.

In order for the lottery corporation to make its enormous profits, Millions of dollars must be lost whenever a lucky winner is declared.

GO TO WEB
EXERCISE 7.4

WWW.BAREA.NELSON.COM

EXERCISE **7.12**

Sentences

Find and fix the 10 fragment errors in this selection.

A French teacher explaining to her class that in French, unlike English, nouns are either masculine or feminine. An example, "house." In French, "la maison" is feminine. On the other hand, "pencil" is "le crayon" in French, and is masculine. When one of the students asked which gender the French word for "computer" would be. The teacher challenged the class to decide for themselves and give reasons for their choices.

The men in the class decided that "computer" should be feminine. Because no one but their creator understands their internal logic. Also, the language they use to communicate with each other being incomprehensible to anyone else. In addition, computers store even the smallest mistakes in their long-term memory. For later retrieval. Finally, claimed the men, computers had to be feminine because as soon as you commit to one, you find yourself spending half your paycheque buying accessories for it.

Then, the women. They said that "computer" must be masculine. Because, in order to get them to do anything, you have to turn them on. Second, while they have stored a great deal of data. They still can't think for themselves. Third, designed to solve problems, but most of the time they *are* the problem. Finally, according to the women, computers must be masculine because as soon as you commit to one, you realize that if you had waited a little longer you could have gotten a much better model.

8

Solving Run-On Sentence Problems

Some sentences lack essential elements and thus are fragments. Other sentences contain two or more independent clauses that are incorrectly linked together. A sentence with inadequate punctuation between clauses is a **run-on.** Run-ons tend to occur when you write in a hurry, without taking time to organize your thoughts first. If you think about what you want to say and punctuate carefully, you should have few problems with run-ons.

There are two kinds of run-on sentence to watch out for: comma splices and fused sentences.

COMMA SPLICES

As its name suggests, the **comma splice** occurs when two complete sentences (independent clauses) are joined (or spliced) by a comma. Consider these examples:

Yogurt may be good for you, poutine is not.
This film is boring, it has no plot.

FUSED SENTENCES

A **fused sentence** occurs when two complete sentences are joined together with no punctuation between them. For example:

Yogurt may be good for you poutine is not.
This film is boring it has no plot.

There are four ways you can fix comma splices or fused sentences.

1. Make the independent clauses into separate sentences.

Yogurt may be good for you. Poutine is not.
This film is boring. It has no plot.

This solution works well if you do not use it too often. Writing that consists of nothing but single-clause sentences lacks smoothness and sounds immature.

2. Separate the independent clauses with a comma and one of these words: *and, but, or, nor, for, so, yet.*[1]

FANBOYS

Yogurt may be good for you, but poutine is not.
This film is boring, for it has no plot.

---

[1] These words are called coordinating conjunctions. See Appendix A, page 372, for an explanation and illustration of the different kinds of conjunctions and how to use them.

3. Make one clause dependent on the other by adding one of the dependent clause cues listed on page 100.

Yogurt may be good for you although poutine is not.
This film is boring because it has no plot. (*Or:* Because it has no plot, this film is boring.)

4. Use a semicolon, either by itself or with a transitional expression, to separate the independent clauses.[2]

Yogurt may be good for you; poutine is not.
This film is boring; for one thing, it has no plot.

Note: All four solutions to comma splices and fused sentences require you to use a word or punctuation mark strong enough to come between two independent clauses. A comma by itself is too weak, and so is a dash.

The sentences in the following exercises will give you practice in fixing comma splices and fused sentences. Correct the sentences where necessary, and then check your answers, beginning on page 401. Since there are several ways to fix each sentence, your answers may differ from our suggestions. If you're confused about when to use a semicolon and when to use a period, be sure to read pages 227–28 before going on.

EXERCISE **8.1**

1. A fine mess this is, And I'll never forgive you for getting me into this situation.

2. Let's take the shortcut, because we need to get there as quickly as possible.

3. No one in the department supports her; she's arrogant and lazy.

4. I want to play the banjo, ~~unfortunately~~ but I have no musical talent.

---

[2] If you are not sure when or why to use a semicolon, see Chapter 19, pages 227–35.

Sentences

5. "We do not tear your clothing with machinery, we do it carefully by hand." (Sign in a dry cleaner's)

6. I'd rather be lucky than good, on the other hand, I'd rather be good than unlucky.

7. I am busy right now, you'll have to wait.

8. "I don't want to achieve immortality through my work; I want to achieve it through not dying." (Woody Allen)

9. There are many factors to consider when you are looking for a new car; the most important is price.

10. Many good films are made in Canada. I just wish I could tell which ones they were before buying a ticket.

EXERCISE **8.2**

1. I hate computers, *because* they're always making mistakes.

2. Our company wants to hire a telepath, the right person for the job will know where to apply.

3. Stop me if you've heard this one; there was this cab driver on her first day at work.

4. Coffee is Ruth's weakness, *as* she goes to Starbucks at least once a day.

5. Jason offered to take me to a movie, *so* I'll probably be going out tonight.

6. Time is the best teacher, unfortunately it kills all its students.

7. Price and reliability are what I look for in a new car; performance is a long way down the list.

8. I'd love to teach you to play solitaire, *but* I have an assignment to finish first.

9. The English language makes no sense, *because* people recite at a play and play at a recital.

10. We have not inherited the Earth from our ancestors, we are borrowing it from our children.

GO TO WEB
EXERCISE 8.1

WWW.BAREA.NELSON.COM

✳ EXERCISE **8.3**

Some of the items in the following exercise contain more than two independent clauses, so they are a bit more challenging to revise.

1. In Canada, winter is more than a season it's a bad joke.

2. The largest dog in the world is the Irish wolfhound, the strongest dog in the world is the Newfoundland, the stupidest dog in the world is my mutt, he's also the best loved.

3. Twice a week, my wife and I go to a nice restaurant for some good food, a little wine, and pleasant conversation, she goes Tuesdays, and I go Fridays.

4. Jessica backed her car out of the driveway, she forgot to check her rearview mirror, as a result, she produced a significant alteration to the front end of a passing Honda.

5. We understand his feelings of rejection, he discovered that his family had moved to another city while he was out getting a pizza.

6. Fast food is generally less nutritious than home-cooked meals, this is not true of my mother's cooking, hers rates below cardboard in nutritional value as well as taste.

7. The biggest drawbacks to keeping tropical fish are that you get soaked whenever you pet them, and they take a long time to grow big enough to eat.

8. There are two students in this class named Xan, one is from China, the other is from Russia, the latter's name is a nickname, a short form of Alexandra.

9. The first sign of adulthood is the discovery that the volume knob also turns to the left, this realization does not happen overnight for some people, the process takes years.

10. Evaluating Frank's progress is difficult when you realize that he has submitted none of the assignments, written none of the tests, and attended less than a third of the classes, you can see why I despair.

✳ EXERCISE **8.4**

In the paragraph that follows, correct the 10 run-on errors any way you choose. This would be a good time to review the four solutions to run-ons highlighted on pages 107–108. Your goal is to produce a paragraph in which the sentences are both correct and effective. Then compare your revision to our suggestions on pages 402–403.

Last year, an exchange student from the south of France came to live with us her name was Simone, she came to Canada to practise her English and learn something about our culture. Simone was amazed by ice hockey, she had never seen the game before and thought it was very exciting. In her first months here, Simone was surprised by what she perceived as Canadians' devotion to everything American, from television shows to sports events, to music, to fast food, she confessed that she couldn't see much that was uniquely Canadian she was disappointed by our lack of a distinct culture, after she made a week's trip to Chicago, she began to understand some of the differences between the two countries, the relative cleanliness of Canada's cities, our support of multiculturalism, and our respect for law and order impressed her, the vast size of our country, with its huge expanses of untouched wilderness, intimidated her a little. Although she was homesick, especially in the first few weeks, Simone enjoyed her year in Canada when she was packing to return to Provence, she was already planning her next visit, she wants to go camping on Prince Edward Island.

WWW.BAREA.NELSON.COM

✳ EXERCISE **8.5**

The following exercise contains all four kinds of sentence structure error you have studied so far: "missing piece" fragments, dependent clause fragments, comma splices, and fused sentences. Work through the sentences slowly and carefully, and then compare your revisions with our suggestions on page 403.

1. "In answer to your letter, I have given birth to a boy weighing five kilos, I hope this is satisfactory." (From a letter applying for government assistance)

2. "That isn't food that's what food eats." (A meat eater's view of a vegetarian menu)

3. A cup of coffee in the middle of the afternoon. It helps to keep me alert, the caffeine chases away my after-lunch slump.

4. CRNC is the home of the million-dollar guarantee, you give us a million dollars, we guarantee to play any song you want.

5. It's far too hot, no one feels like working. Not even people who claim to like summer temperatures.

6. A fine wine during a special meal being my only vice, otherwise I'm perfect.

7. Eat sensibly, exercise regularly, die anyway.

8. People who do not turn off their cellphones in movie theatres are inconsiderate, they should be ejected without a refund.

9. When a football or hockey game is on TV. My husband becomes deaf, he doesn't hear a word I say.

10. Our dog loves children. Especially when they are eating French fries or hot dogs. In her excitement, she has sometimes frightened a child, she has never bitten anyone.

EXERCISE **8.6**

As a final test of your ability to identify and correct run-on sentence errors, supply appropriate sentence breaks to make this garble into a grammatically correct paragraph. You may need to add or delete a few words to make some of the sentences complete and clear. (There are 10 run-ons.)

If you can identify the difference between a Barolo wine from Italy and a Bordeaux wine from France, or between a Czech pilsner and Belgian blond ale, then you are a connoisseur—a person who makes critical judgments based on taste, in addition to wine and beer, many other foods are the subject of critical analysis by connoisseurs, olives and olive oils, tea, coffee, and maple syrup are analyzed and rated by knowledgeable experts all over the world, even salt comes in a wealth of textures, tastes, and origins that today's chefs appreciate for the special qualities they can impart to food, for example, if you are making an East Indian dish, then you want black salt, also known as Sanchal, if you are creating a Hawaiian dish, then Alaea salt with its reddish tinge is what you need, Celtic salt, which is harvested with wooden rakes from the coastal areas of Brittany in France, is recommended for grilled meats and fresh vegetables, the salt that is considered the finest of all table salts is called Fleur de Sel it consists of "young" salt crystals that form naturally on the surface of the salt ponds along the Mediterranean coast of France, hand-harvested during specific weather conditions by traditional *paludiers* (salt farmers), this rare salt is the pinnacle of the condiment world, as for me, the best I can do on a good day is tell the difference between a cup of fresh-brewed Hawaiian Kona coffee and a cup of instant Nescafé.

GORGEOUS IN THE MOONLIGHT, HER DANGLING MODIFIERS BETRAYED HER.

9 Solving Modifier Problems

After being underwater for 150 years, Dr. Philbrick found the ship in excellent condition.

Both students were expelled because of cheating *by the college registrar*.

For sale: A set of first-year medical textbooks by a needy student *in almost perfect condition*.

How could Dr. Philbrick stay underwater for 150 years? Was the college registrar cheating? Were the medical textbooks written by the needy student, and is this student in almost perfect condition? As you can see, the meaning in these sentences is not clear. The confusion comes from the placement of the modifier in each sentence.

A **modifier** is a word or word group that adds information about another word in a sentence. In the examples above, the italicized words are modifiers.

Used correctly, modifiers describe, explain, or limit another word, making its meaning more precise. Used carelessly, modifiers cause confusion or, even worse, amusement. Few experiences are more embarrassing than being laughed at when you didn't mean to be funny.

You need to be able to recognize and solve two kinds of modifier problems: **misplaced modifiers** and **dangling modifiers**.

MISPLACED MODIFIERS

Modifiers must be as close as possible to the words they apply to. Readers usually assume that a modifier modifies whatever it's next to. It's important to remember this because, as the following examples show, changing the position of a modifier can change the meaning of your sentence.

Only I love you. (No one else loves you.)

I only love you. (I have no other feelings for you.)

I love only you. (You are the only one I love.)

> To make sure a modifier is in the right place, ask yourself "What does it apply to?" and put it beside that word.

When a modifier is not close enough to the word it refers to, it is said to be misplaced.

> • A misplaced modifier can be a single word in the wrong place:

My boss told me that the payroll department needed someone who could use spreadsheets badly .

Is some company really hiring people to do poor work? Or does the company urgently need someone familiar with spreadsheets? The modifier *badly* belongs next to the word it applies to, *needed*:

My boss told me that the payroll department badly needed someone who could use spreadsheets.

Be especially careful with these words: *almost, nearly, just, only, even, hardly, merely, scarcely*. Put them right before the words they modify.

Misplaced: I (nearly) passed every course I took in college.

Correct: I passed (nearly) |every course| I took in college.

Misplaced: The NDP leader was (almost) elected by 50 percent of his riding's voters.

Correct: The NDP leader was elected by (almost) |50 percent| of his riding's voters.

Misplaced: I (only) have eyes for you.

Correct: I have eyes (only) |for you|.

• A misplaced modifier can also be a group of words in the wrong place:

(Playing happily), |the new mother| watched her baby.

The modifier, *playing happily*, is too far away from the word it applies to: *baby*. It seems to modify *mother*, making the sentence ridiculous. We need to revise the sentence.

The new mother watched her baby (playing happily).

Look at this example:

I work for my aunt, who owns a variety store (during the summer.)

During the summer applies to *work* and should be closer to it:

(During the summer,) I work for my aunt, who owns a variety store.

Notice that a modifier does not need to go right next to what it modifies. It should, however, be as close as possible to it.

Occasionally, as in the examples above, the modifier is obviously out of place. The writer's intention is often clear, and the sentence is easy to correct. Sometimes, however, modifiers are misplaced in such a way that the meaning is not clear, as in this example:

My boss told me (on Friday) I was being let go.

Did the boss speak to the employee on Friday? Or did she tell the employee that Friday would be his last day? To avoid confusion, we must move the modifier and, depending on the meaning we want, write

(On Friday), my boss told me I was being let go.

Or

My boss told me I was being let go (on Friday).

Rewrite the following sentences, placing the modifiers correctly. Check your answers to each set before going on. Answers begin on page 403.

EXERCISE **9.1**

1. I almost watched the Leafs lose every night.

2. We were run over by practically every car that passed.

3. This recipe can be made by anyone who has mastered basic cooking skills in about an hour.

4. Alice discovered a magic mushroom walking through Wonderland.

5. She just ate one bite and found herself growing larger.

6. The rabid dog was captured before anyone was bitten by the Canine Control officer.

7. The online classified page lists the names of people who want to buy used cars for less than a dollar.

8. We were only told at the end of the test that it was worth 10 percent of our grade.

9. In the ruins of Minoan Crete, there are wall paintings of boys jumping over bulls with no clothes on.

10. Proud of his new tattoo—a python around his neck—Wayne's father told him to grow a long beard before he even thought of applying for a job.

EXERCISE **9.2**

1. George has almost insulted everyone he's gone out with.

2. After my performance review, the company nearly offered me a raise of $50 a week.

3. Employees who are late frequently are dismissed without notice.

4. I will just ask you once more if you were present when your picture was taken.

5. Each year, 500,000 Canadian men nearly have vasectomies.

6. Unless they are poodles or terriers, most pet owners don't bother having their dogs professionally groomed.

7. I hate parties where food is served to guests who have no place to sit on tiny paper plates.

8. Our instructor reminded us on Monday we would have a test.

9. Badly bruised, Catalina turned the avocados into great guacamole.

10. A rare 1991 Saab convertible is being offered for sale by an elderly lady with only 50,000 km and a recent tune-up.

GO TO WEB
EXERCISE 9.1

WWW.BAREA.NELSON.COM

DANGLING MODIFIERS

A **dangling modifier** occurs when there is no *specific word* or *idea* in the sentence to which the modifier can sensibly refer. With no appropriate word to refer to, the modifier seems to apply to whatever it's next to, often with ridiculous results:

After a good night's sleep , my teachers were impressed by my alertness.

(This sentence seems to say that the teachers had a good night's sleep.)

While paying for our purchases , a security guard watched closely.

(The security guard paid for our purchases?)

Dangling modifiers are harder to fix than misplaced ones. You can't simply move danglers to another spot in the sentence. There are two ways to correct them. One way requires that you remember the following guideline.

> When a modifier comes at the beginning of the sentence, it usually modifies the subject of the sentence.

This means that you can avoid dangling modifiers by choosing the subjects of your sentences carefully. The subject must be an appropriate one for the modifier to apply to. With the guideline in mind, we can correct both examples simply by changing the subjects.

After a good night's sleep , I impressed my teachers with my alertness.

While paying for our purchases , we were closely watched by a security guard.

Another way to correct a dangling modifier is to change it into a dependent clause.

> After I had a good night's sleep, I impressed my teachers with my alertness. While we paid for our purchases, a security guard watched us closely.

Sometimes a dangling modifier comes at the end of a sentence.

A bear blocked our path, (skiing through the park).

Can you correct this sentence? Try it; then look at the suggestions we've given at the bottom of the page.

SUMMARY

1. Ask "What does the modifier refer to?"
2. Be sure there is a word or word group in the sentence for the modifier to apply to.
3. Put the modifier as close as possible to the word or word group it refers to.

The sentences in Exercises 9.3 and 9.4 contain dangling modifiers. Correct them by changing the subject to one the modifier can apply to or by changing the dangler into a dependent clause. Then compare your answers with our suggestions on pages 404–405.

EXERCISE **9.3**

1. As a college English teacher, dangling modifiers are annoying.

2. When writing, a dictionary is your best friend.

3. Lifting the lid carefully and quietly, the cookie jar was empty.

4. The surface must be sanded smooth before applying the varnish.

5. Attempting to hot-wire a '99 Jeep Cherokee, the police were called and made the arrest.

Here are two suggested corrections:

1. Add a subject: (Skiing through the park), we came across a bear blocking our path.
2. Change the dangler to a dependent clause: A bear blocked our path when we were skiing through the park.

6. As an advocate of healthy eating, fast-food restaurants are purveyors of poison, in my opinion.

7. Driving recklessly, the police stopped Tara at a roadblock.

8. Arriving at the meeting room 20 minutes late, everyone had left.

9. In cold weather, the engine should be thoroughly warmed up before attempting to drive.

10. Travelling abroad, much can be learned from the sights you see and the people you meet.

EXERCISE **9.4**

1. After changing the tire, the jack should be released.

2. The next question is whether to order beer or soft drinks, having decided on pizza.

3. After waiting for you for an hour, the evening was ruined.

4. Jogging through Stanley Park, a cluster of totem poles came into view.

5. After four days on the trail, a hot shower and a cold drink were necessities rather than luxuries.

6. Having set the microwave on "Automatic," the turkey was cooked to perfection.

7. Having completed the beginning, the ending is the second most-important part of an essay.

8. Convicted of aggravated assault, the judge sentenced her to two years in the penitentiary.

9. After scoring the goal in overtime, a huge victory parade wound through the city.

10. After living with the same roommate for two years, my parents suggested that I try living alone.

Correct the misplaced and dangling modifiers in Exercises 9.5 and 9.6 in any way you choose. The answers on pages 405 and 405–406 are only suggestions.

EXERCISE **9.5**

1. Looking for style, economy, and performance, a Honda Fit or a Toyota Yaris might be worth a look.

2. Everyone stared as she rode into the ring on a white horse in a sequin-spangled bikini.

3. Looking out the window on a lovely fall day, a squirrel was raiding the bird feeder.

4. With a broken wing and unable to fly, Ruth took the seagull to the Humane Society.

5. Slow-cooked in red wine for two hours, my guests were amazed by how tender the beef was.

6. Gnawing his stolen steak and growling, Henry could not coax his dog to come out from under the table.

7. Made of delicate crystal, my clumsy friends cannot be trusted with my wine glasses.

8. Used to drinking from jam jars, my crystal glasses would be wasted on them, anyway.

9. Because they do not shed hair, our neighbours bought a Cornish Rex cat.

10. Having skipped class for most of the term and not having bothered to buy the textbook, a pass is probably too much for me to hope for.

EXERCISE **9.6**

1. In our program, the women almost outnumber the men by a two-to-one ratio.

2. While sleeping, the blankets became tangled and ended up on the floor.

3. The sign on the door says that students are only admitted to the pub.

4. Having ruled out the other items on the menu, the fully loaded pizza was our choice.

5. Swimming in the bay is not a good idea if polluted.

6. Please summarize what you have read with your textbook closed.

7. Having been to Monte Carlo and visited its magnificent casino, Las Vegas seems trashy and cheap by comparison.

8. Our team's best player was rescued from being thrown out of college in his third term by his girlfriend.

9. I can recommend any of the restaurants almost in this town because I have nearly eaten in all of them.

10. A 53-year-old truck driver, who has lived in Canada since he was a baby, has been deported to England, where he was born after being convicted on drug charges.

GO TO WEB
EXERCISE 9.2

WWW.BAREA.NELSON.COM

EXERCISE **9.7**

Now it's time to test your mastery of modifiers. Carefully read each item in the following exercise before you revise it. Some sentences may contain more than one error.

1. My wedding dress fits as well nearly as it did the day we were married.

2. After three years at Red Deer College, a full-time job with benefits sounded almost too good to be true.

3. Crumbling slowly over the years, the townspeople no longer drive cars or even walk over the ancient bridge.

4. Entering the club just after the show had started, the band's volume level practically knocked us over.

5. Arriving at our table, our appetizers were already waiting for us.

6. While executing a triple Salchow, my costume malfunctioned, and I fell nearly on the ice.

7. Marinated for three days, then slow-roasted in the oven, our guests are sure to love my mother's pot roast.

8. Now almost 40 years old, this photo of me, taken when I was 19, is more than two decades old!

9. Everyone almost says I don't look a day older than I did when I was in college.

10. Of course, anyone who doesn't flatter me outrageously doesn't get invited for free meals in my restaurant or to go for a spin in my Porsche.

The Parallelism Principle 10

Brevity, clarity, and force: these are three characteristics of good writing style. **Parallelism** will reinforce these characteristics in everything you write.

When your sentence contains a series of two or more items, they must be grammatically parallel. That is, they must be written in the same grammatical form. Consider this example:

College requires us *to manage our time, to work independently,* and *critical thinking.*

The three items in this series are not parallel. Two are infinitive phrases (*to manage, to work*), but the third ends in *-ing* and is a noun phrase. To correct the sentence, you must put all of the items in the same grammatical form. You have two choices. You can write

College requires us *to manage* our time, *to work* independently, and *to think* critically. (all infinitive phrases)

Or you can write

College requires *time management, independent work,* and *critical thinking.* (all noun phrases)

Now look at an example with two nonparallel elements:

Most people seek happiness in *long-term relationships* and *work that provides them with satisfaction.*

Again, you could correct this sentence in two ways. You could write "Most people seek happiness *in relationships that are long-term* and *in work that provides them with satisfaction,*" but that solution produces a long and clumsy sentence. The shorter version works better: "Most people seek happiness in *long-term relationships* and *satisfying work.*" This version is concise, clear, and forceful.

Correct faulty parallelism by writing all items in a series in the same grammatical form; that is, all words, or all phrases, or all clauses.

One way to tell whether the items in a series are parallel is to write them out in list form, one below the other. That way, you can see at a glance if all of the elements are in the same grammatical form.

Not Parallel	Parallel
My supervisor is *demanding, short-tempered,* and *an obnoxious person.*	My supervisor is *demanding, short-tempered,* and *obnoxious.*
(This list has two adjectives and a noun phrase.)	(This list has three adjectives.)
I support myself by *delivering pizza, poker,* and *shooting pool.*	I support myself by *delivering pizza, playing poker,* and *shooting pool.*
(This list has two phrases and one single word as objects of the preposition *by.*)	(This list has three phrases as objects of the preposition *by.*)

Not Parallel

Jules wants a job that *will interest him,*
will challenge him,
and *pays well.*

(This series of clauses contains
two future tense verbs and one
present tense verb.)

Parallel

Jules wants a job that *will interest him,*
challenge him,
and *pay him well.*

(All three subordinate clauses
contain future tense verbs.)

As you can see, achieving parallelism is partly a matter of developing an ear for the sound of a correct list. A parallel sentence has a smooth, unbroken rhythm. Practice and the exercises in this chapter will help. Once you have mastered parallelism in your sentences, you will be ready to develop ideas in parallel sequence—in thesis statements, for example—and thus to write clear, well-organized prose. Far from being a frill, parallelism is a fundamental characteristic of good writing.

Correct the sentences where necessary in the following two exercises. As you work through these sentences, try to spot parallelism errors from the change in rhythm that the faulty element produces. Then revise the sentence to bring the faulty element into line with the other element(s) in the series. Check your answers to each set of 10 before going on. Answers for this chapter begin on page 406.

EXERCISE **10.1**

1. My new keyboard is ergonomic, functional, and ~~it looks~~ attractive.

2. The three main kinds of speech are demonstrative, informative, ~~and the~~ *and*
~~kind intended to~~ persuad~~e the audience about something.~~ *sive*

3. Wielding his knife ~~swiftly and with~~ skill, the chef turned a tomato into a *w/ speed and skillfully*
centrepiece that looked just like a rose.

4. I am overworked and ~~not paid enough~~. *under paid*

5. You need to develop skill and strategy and ~~be~~ agile *ity* to be a competitive
skateboarder.

6. On our trip to Finland, we went sailing, explored [ing], and hiked [ing].

7. My doctor advised me to take two aspirins and ~~that I~~ call her in the morning.

8. After winning a hard-fought election campaign, our party leader spoke forcefully and with confidence [-tly].

9. To make your court appearance as painless as possible, prepare your case ~~thoroughly~~ and maintaining a pleasant, positive attitude.

10. We are looking for a car that is reliable, safe, _and cheap/affordable_ ~~and won't cost too much money to buy and maintain.~~

GO TO WEB
EXERCISE 10.1

WWW.BAREA.NELSON.COM

EXERCISE 10.2

1. We're seeking a roommate who is responsible, flexible, ~~has~~ enthusias~~m~~ [-tic], and is reliable.

2. I'm considering a Smart car because they're cheap to run, easy to park, _and fun to drive_ ~~and driving one is fun.~~

3. Tonight's program has all the ingredients of a successful reality show: ambition, greed~~y characters~~, jealous ~~people~~, violence, and sex.

4. The Internet provides us with possibilities ~~for~~ research ③ ~~that are~~ unlimited, ② convenient shopping access, and endless ① ~~ways to waste~~ [wasters] time.

5. Olympic athletes in the modern era can be classified as able bodied, physically challenged, and ~~the ones who are~~ enhanced chemically.

6. Travel teaches us to be tolerant, patient, resourceful~~ness~~, and independ-[-ont] ~~ence.~~

7. Digital cameras are now the standard because they are well made, ~~don't~~ _affordable_ ~~cost very much,~~ and ~~are~~ almost foolproof.

8. The cafeteria now offers a number of healthful menu items, including veggie burgers, homemade soups, and French fries that are low in cholesterol.

9. Why is it that so many movie stars, pop singers, hosts of talk shows, and other performers on television behave badly in public?

10. We are offering this once-in-a-lifetime opportunity for the discriminating buyer to purchase a unique home that is superbly constructed, thought-fully designed, with beautiful landscaping, and a competitive price.

GO TO WEB
EXERCISE 10.2

WWW.BAREA.NELSON.COM

EXERCISE **10.3**

Make the following lists parallel. In each case, there's more than one way to do it because you can make your items parallel with any item in the list. Therefore, your answers may differ from ours. Here's an example:

Incorrect:	prepare reports . . . analysis
Correct:	prepare reports . . . analyze
Also correct:	report preparation . . . analysis

1. Incorrect: mechanically   by using your hands

   Correct:

2. Incorrect: security   valuable   safety

   Correct:

3. Incorrect: achieve her goals   finding true happiness

   Correct:

4. Incorrect: sense of humour   wealthy   intelligent

   Correct:

5. Incorrect: daily exercise   wholesome food   getting a checkup
                                                        regularly

   Correct:

6. Incorrect: nursing   being an engineer

    Correct:

7. Incorrect: speed   comfortable   good manoeuvrability

    Correct:

8. Incorrect: look for bargains   quality should be chosen   value comes first

    Correct:

9. Incorrect: a good cigar   drinking a glass of brandy   catching up on friends' news

    Correct:

10. Incorrect: tanned golden-brown   skimpy bathing suit   big boyfriend

    Correct:

EXERCISE **10.4**

Create a sentence for each of the parallel lists you developed in Exercise 10.3. Example:

Andrea's data analysis was superb, but her report preparation was pitiful.

EXERCISE **10.5**

Many errors in parallelism occur in the bulleted points that are commonly featured in reports and presentations. Working with a partner, create a parallel list out of the bulleted points in each of the following sets. Your answers may vary from our suggestions, depending on which item in each list that you choose as the model for the other items to parallel.

1. In order to improve office morale, our committee recommends that we

    take the following steps:

- Install nameplates on all office doors
- ~~Computers in all offices should be upgraded~~ *upgrade all office compters*
- ~~New furniture to~~ replace damaged ~~items~~ *furniture*

- Institute weekly office meetings
- Flexible hours where practical

2. The consultants' report identifies five changes that must be made to return our team to profitability:

- Improved ~~food at~~ stadium concession stands *food*
- Lower ~~prices for~~ general admission *prices*
- Advertising budget ~~should be~~ increased by 20 percent
- High-profile players ~~should be~~ acquired
- Update team logo and uniforms

3. After a careful study of your son's time management practices, we conclude that the following recommendations, if adopted at once, could salvage his college career:

- Be in bed by 10:00 p.m. on weekdays
- All classes and labs ~~must be~~ attended
- 50 percent less spending on entertainment
- Assignments submitted on time
- Restricted hours for Internet surfing and computer gaming
- ~~His~~ current crowd of friends ~~should be~~ replaced

4. Before we choose your hotel for our convention, we would like to confirm that the following facilities will be available for our delegates' use:

- A conference room ~~for~~ 150 people
- ~~We would like to book a~~ nearby 18-hole golf course
- Full exercise facilities, including pool
- ~~Our~~ dining ~~room must be~~ separate *room from* ~~from~~ restaurants used by other guests
- Wireless Internet access in each room

5. The successful applicant for this position will have these qualifications:

- Able to work independently
- College diploma in Business Administration, Hotel and Restaurant Administration, or related program

- Experience in the travel/tourism industry
- High-level computer skills ~~are required~~
- ~~Must be~~ fluent in ~~at least one of~~ French, German, Spanish, or Italian

EXERCISE **10.6**

Correct the faulty parallelism in the following paragraphs. This exercise contains 10 errors.

There can no longer be any question about the fact that our planet is getting warmer. The melting glaciers, the winters ~~that are getting~~ shorter, record-breaking temperatures, and expanding deserts all point to a rapid warming trend. Many of us shrug our shoulders and leave solutions to this complex problem in the hands of governments, business leaders, ~~those who work in the field of~~ science, and activists. We think, "How can one person ~~do anything to~~ make a difference?" ~~We forget that~~ if we all acted together, we could bring ~~about a~~ significant change for the better.

Buying more fuel-efficient cars, using our automobiles less, and ~~even~~ doing without them ~~altogether~~ would be a start, and imagine the impact if a million city dwellers ~~decided to~~ switch to public transit! We can turn our thermostats down in the winter and up in the summer—~~even~~ a couple of degrees would means a huge energy saving—and changing to energy-efficient light bulbs. Would it be such a hardship to wear an extra sweater in the winter, turning air conditioning off in the summer when we're out, or ~~switching~~ off the lights when we leave a room? Individual actions ~~like these,~~ if undertaken by enough of us, will ~~not only~~ save energy and reduce pollution, and ~~but~~ also will demonstrate to business and governments that we're serious, and motivating ~~them~~ to do more.

On a larger scale, we need to put more resources into research that will enable us to exploit wind power, ~~capture~~ solar energy, and tidal forces ~~must be~~ harnessed. We must insist on intelligently designed, energy-efficient buildings.

Every project, whether large or small, will require the support and encouragement of individuals who buy thoughtfully, consume wisely, and strategically voting. All of us—individuals, corporations, and governments—need to dedicate ourselves to reducing, reusing, and recycling. Our comfort, our children's health, and the lives of our grandchildren depend on it.

GO TO WEB
EXERCISE 10.3

WWW.BAREA.NELSON.COM

EXERCISE **10.7**

As a test of your ability to correct faulty parallelism, revise the following sentences.

1. The apostrophe is used for two purposes: contraction and in possessive constructions.

2. Most first-year students want to meet new friends, financial survival, and passing their courses—not necessarily in that order.

3. The tournament's favoured team turned out to be unprepared, paid too much, and not enthusiastic.

4. Never in our company's history have we offered better prices, quality that is higher, or merchandise that is more attractive.

5. The most successful athletes this year seem to be Albertans, those from Quebec, people from Newfoundland, and British Columbia residents.

6. Winter teaches us patience, to be self-reliant, and respect for nature—all characteristics that define Canadians.

7. We are planning to tour England for its history, Germany for its scenery, food in France, and Italy for its lifestyle.

8. Our new home has windows by Pella, appliances by General Electric, Ikea furniture, Panasonic electronics, and a mortgage by RBC.

9. The incoming town council must address three issues: high property taxes, development that is uncontrolled, and streets that are unsafe.

10. My love of canoeing is a year-round passion: in spring, the rivers run high and fast; summer, for evenings that are long and calm; the gorgeous woods and uncrowded lakes in autumn; and in winter, there is the excitement and anticipation of planning the next year's excursions.

Refining by Combining | 11

SENTENCE COMBINING

To reinforce what you've learned so far about sentence structure, try your hand at sentence combining. Even though you've eliminated fragments, run-ons, modifier problems, and parallelism problems, you may still find that your sentences don't flow smoothly. Although technically correct, they may be choppy or repetitive. You may also be bored with conveying your ideas in the same old way. If you are not bored, you can be pretty sure your reader is. A paper made up of nothing but short, one-clause sentences is enough to put even the most conscientious reader to sleep. Sentence combining accomplishes three things: it reinforces your understanding of sentence structure; it helps you to refine and polish your writing; and it results in a style that will keep your reader alert and interested in what you have to say.

Sentence combining is a technique that enables you to avoid a monotonous style while at the same time producing correct sentences.

Let's look at two short, technically correct sentences that could be combined:

My boss is demanding.
She expects results.

There are several ways of combining statements like these into a single sentence.

FANBOYS

1. You can connect them with an appropriate linking word, such as *and, but, or, nor, for, so,* and *yet.*

My boss is demanding, *and* she expects results.

Dependent

2. You can change one of the sentences into a subordinate clause.

My boss, *who is demanding,* expects results. (Or: *Because my boss is demanding,* she expects results.)

3. You can change one of the sentences into a modifying phrase.

Being demanding, my boss expects results. (Or: My boss, *a demanding supervisor,* expects results.)

4. Sometimes you can reduce one of your sentences to a single-word modifier.

My *demanding* boss expects results.

In sentence combining, you are free to move parts of the sentence around, change words, add or delete words, or make whatever other changes you think necessary. Anything goes, as long as you don't drastically alter the meaning of the base sentences. Remember that your aim in combining sentences is to create effective sentences—not long ones. Clarity is essential, and brevity has force. Consider the following example:

• Correct but choppy sentences conveying an idea:

Water is vital to life.
It is an important Canadian resource.
It must be protected.

- Correct and smooth sentences conveying the same idea:

H_2O

Water, which is vital to life, is an important Canadian resource that must be protected.

An important Canadian resource, water is vital to life and must be protected.

Water is an important Canadian resource that must be protected because it is vital to life.

The skills that you learn by combining sentences develop your understanding of the connections between ideas. They are useful not only in writing and speaking, but also in reading, listening, and problem solving.

In the following exercises, try your answers aloud before you write them. It would be a good idea to read the comma rules in Chapter 18 before you tackle these exercises.

EXERCISE **11.1**

Combine the following sentences, using the cues in parentheses as your guide to linking the ideas together. Answers begin on page 408.

1. This is the car.
   I bought this car with my lottery jackpot. (that)

   With my lottery jackpot, I bought this
   car.

2. Never worry about your heart, ~~for it~~
   ~~Your heart~~ will last as long as you live. (for)

   _____

   _____

3. The preacher talked for over an hour.
   He didn't seem to take a single breath the whole time. (who)

   The preacher, who talked for over an hour
   didn't seem to take a single breath the whole time.

4. This punch bowl contains alcohol, *while*
   ~~T~~hat punch bowl contains only fruit juice and ginger ale. (while)

   _____

   _____

5. The bank has added new service charges, *that*
   I think the service charges are unjustified. (that)

   _____

   _____

6. Canadian football can be a violent game, *even though*
   Canadians love football. (even though)

   _____

   _____

7. I don't like Fords, *nor do I like*
   ~~I don't like~~ Chevrolets. (nor)

   _____

   _____

8. Office morale improve~~d~~ *s*, *when*
   s ~~S~~he changed jobs. (when)

   _____

   _____

9. "Reality" television shows are, in fact, scripted, ~~and that~~
   m ~~M~~any people are not aware ~~of this fact~~. (that)
   ~~that~~ "Reality" shows are scripted

   _____

   _____

10. Ancient scientists looked to the stars for guidance. (while)
    Modern scientists look forward to travelling to the stars. (and)
    Amanda looks for stars in dance clubs.

    While modern scientists look forward

GO TO WEB
EXERCISE 11.1

WWW.BAREA.NELSON.COM

EXERCISE **11.2**

Make each set of independent clauses into a longer, more interesting sentence. Try to use all four sentence-combining techniques as you work through this exercise.

Hint: Read through each set of statements before you begin to combine them. Try several variations aloud or in your head before writing down your preferred solution. There are many ways to combine these short statements to make smooth, effective sentences. Our answers on pages 408–409 are only suggestions.

1. Keep practising your singing.
   Don't give up your day job.

2. English muffins were not invented in England.
   French fries were not invented in France.

Sentences

3. I have a new computer.
   It is a laptop.
   I am going to use it while sitting by the pool.

   _____

   _____

   _____

4. The gates are down.
   The lights are flashing.
   The train isn't coming.

   _____

   _____

   _____

5. Some people enjoy hockey.
   Other people prefer soccer.
   Soccer is the world's most popular spectator sport.

   _____

   _____

   _____

6. You are a polite person.
   You are considerate of the feelings of others.
   You should be more assertive.

   _____

   _____

   _____

Sentences

7. I want to leave class now.
   I want to go home.
   I want to lie down.
   My brain is full.

   _____

   _____

   _____

8. British Columbia is where I was born.
   I was born in Sidney.
   I have not lived there since I was 10.

   _____

   _____

   _____

9. This car has many of the features that I want.
   It is the right price.
   It is the wrong colour.

   _____

   _____

   _____

10. This restaurant is expensive.
    The food is good.
    The service is excellent.
    I don't mind paying the price.

    _____

    _____

    _____

EXERCISE **11.3**

This set of exercises is more challenging. In some questions, you may need to combine the statements into two or even three sentences. Again, be sure to read through all of the statements in each question to identify related ideas before you begin revising. Turn to page 409 to compare your sentences with our suggested revisions.

1. Most of my friends hate cooking.
   I love to cook.
   I create special dishes whenever I can.
   I am going to college.
   I am taking a chef program.
   The program will enable me to do what I love as a career.

2. I have almost no ambition.
   I never move quickly except to avoid work.
   I believe that all deadlines are unreasonable.
   I believe that it is always possible that no one will notice that I am late.
   I believe that it is always possible that no one will notice that my work is unfinished.
   I begin a task when I get around to it.
   I never put off until tomorrow what I can avoid altogether.

3. China is a country with a huge population.
   There are more than a billion people in China.
   It is not easy to be an individual in China.
   You may think of yourself as "one in a million."
   There are a thousand other people just like you!

4. Lawyers are professionals.
   Doctors are professionals.
   Businesspeople are professionals.
   These professionals make up less than 10 percent of Canada's work force.
   These professionals occupy almost three-quarters of the seats in the House of Commons.

5. Blue-collar workers make up nearly 50 percent of the population.
   They hold less than 10 percent of the positions in Parliament.
   Women are also underrepresented in Canada's government.
   First Nations people are also underrepresented in Canada's government.
   Minorities are also underrepresented in Canada's government.

This underrepresentation calls into question Canada's commitment to democracy.

Now that you have completed Unit 2, you are ready to begin revising whatever you write. Read your work aloud. How your sentences sound is important. Test your writing against the seven characteristics of successful sentences.

SUMMARY

1. **Meaning:** Have you said what you meant?
2. **Correctness:** Have you avoided fragments, run-ons, misplaced and dangling modifiers, and unparallel constructions?
3. **Clarity:** Is your sentence clear? Can it be understood on the first reading?
4. **Coherence:** Do the parts of your sentence fit together logically and smoothly?
5. **Emphasis:** Are the most important ideas either at the end or at the beginning of the sentence?
6. **Conciseness:** Is the sentence direct and to the point? Have you cut out all redundant or repetitious words?
7. **Rhythm:** Does the sentence flow smoothly? Are there any interruptions in the development of the key idea(s)? Do the interruptions help to emphasize important points, or do they distract the reader?

If your sentences pass the seven tests of successful sentence style, you may be confident that they are both technically correct and pleasing to the ear. No reader could ask for more.

EXERCISE **11.4**

To practise what you have learned in this unit, write a short paper on a topic of your choice or on one your instructor assigns. When you have completed a first or, preferably, a second draft, read it over carefully. While your spell checker may have corrected some of your errors, remember that no program can flag your use of a correctly spelled wrong word: for example, *accept* instead of *except*, *their* when you mean *they're*, or *than* when the meaning requires *then*. Check your sentence structure by reading your work aloud from the last sentence back to the first. Look for fragments, run-ons, and errors in modifiers and parallelism. Here are some topics you may wish to consider for your paper.

1. Write a letter to a company whose product you use and tell the company why you like it. Even if you are satisfied with the product, you may have a suggestion for improvement. If so, let the company know. Most successful companies welcome positive suggestions.

2. Write a letter of support for a colleague whose probationary period is coming to an end, outlining your reasons for thinking this person is a good employee who should be retained.

3. Write a memorandum to the appropriate administrator of your school requesting exemption from a course you are currently taking. Provide substantial reasons for your request.

4. Write to a club or association requesting information about membership and an application form. Briefly outline why you wish to join this organization.

5. Write to one of your former instructors or employers requesting permission to use that person's name as a reference in your current job search. Explain the nature of the position you are applying for and outline what you have been doing since this instructor/employer last supervised you.

UNIT 2 RAPID REVIEW

As a final test of your ability to use correct sentence structure, read the following passage carefully. It contains a total of 15 errors, including one or more sentence fragments, run-ons, misplaced and dangling modifiers, and unparallel constructions. *Tip:* Read each paragraph through before you begin revising. For errors you miss, the "Answer Key" on page 410 will direct you to the chapter you should review.

[1]Whenever we do something so stupid that we think no one could be as foolish as we are, [2]It is comforting to know that there are people who are even more foolish. [3]The Stupid Awards were created to celebrate those who have committed outstandingly brainless or clumsy acts, *Such as* [4]Forgetting why we came into a room, ~~or~~ tripping over our own feet, or/a cup of coffee ~~spilled~~ *spilling* on our host's white wool carpet. *These are* [5]Merely ~~are~~ minor embarrassments when compared to some of the truly awesome actions of past Stupid Award winners.

[6]For example, the gunman ~~who~~ aimed his .38-calibre handgun at a victim during a holdup in California. *and* [7]When the gun didn't go off, he shook the pistol, peered down the barrel and pulled the trigger ~~again,~~ it worked. [8]Then ~~there was~~ the would-be thief in Arkansas ~~who~~ threw a cinder block at a liquor store window. [9]Made of Plexiglas, the heavy block bounced back off the window and knocked him unconscious. [10]~~Protected by a~~ *Caught on* security camera, the stunned thief was picked up by police before he regained consciousness.

[11]Another thief gave a store clerk a $20 bill and asked for change, ~~and~~ When the clerk opened the cash register, the thief pulled out a gun and demanded all the money. [12]Afraid for his life, the clerk handed over everything in the till, which was [13]~~A~~ a total of less than $15.

[14]The best of the Stupid Awards, in my opinion, took place in Zimbabwe, where a bus driver was hired to transfer 20 mentally ill patients from one asylum to another. [15]Stopping at a bar for a well-earned drink on the way, the ~~bus was empty when the~~ the empty bus. driver returned to ~~it~~ [16]Not wanting to admit his incompetence, he paused at a nearby bus stop and a free ride was offered to everyone. [17]The driver then delivered the passengers to the hospital. [18]Told the staff that the patients were highly delusional, and driving off home as fast as he could go. [19]The deception wasn't discovered for three days.

UNIT 3

Grammar

Grammar

UNIT 3 QUICK QUIZ

The following quiz will show you which chapters of Unit 3 you need to pay special attention to. The paragraph below contains 15 errors in grammar: verb forms, subject–verb agreement, verb tense consistency, pronoun form, pronoun–antecedent agreement, and pronoun consistency.

When you have made your corrections, turn to page 410 and compare your revisions with ours. For each error you miss, the "Answer Key" directs you to the chapter you need to work on.

[1]Every generation have one or two defining moments which are so significant that everyone remembers precisely where they were when the event occurred. [2]Most of the events that have became part of our consciousness are tragic, but there's exceptions. [3]Nobody that was alive when the Allied victory that ended World War II was declared are likely to forget the mingled joy and relief of that occasion. [4]Every Canadian hockey fan, even if they were not watching the game at the time, remember The Goal: Paul Henderson's winner in the 1972 series against the Soviet Union. [5]Neither of these glorious moments are going to fade from the memories of those who experienced them. [6]Memorable tragic moments, however, are more common than joyful ones, and somehow they seemed more important to us as we look back. [7]My contemporaries and me all remember exactly where we were when President John F. Kennedy was shot, while them who were born after 1980 will never

forget the destruction of the World Trade Center in New York City in 2001. [8]No one that saw the televised images of the twin towers as they collapsed and crumbled are ever likely to forget the horror of those moments.

Grammar

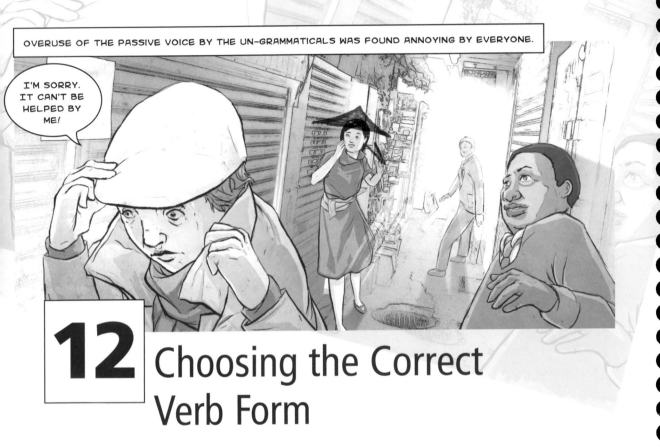

OVERUSE OF THE PASSIVE VOICE BY THE UN-GRAMMATICALS WAS FOUND ANNOYING BY EVERYONE.

I'M SORRY. IT CAN'T BE HELPED BY ME!

12 Choosing the Correct Verb Form

Errors in grammar are like flies in soup. Most of the time, they don't affect meaning any more than flies affect flavour, but they are distracting and irritating. You must eliminate grammar errors from your writing if you want your readers to pay attention to what you say rather than to how you say it.

The **verb** is the most complex and essential part of a sentence. In fact, a verb is to a sentence what an engine is to a car: the source of power and a frequent cause of trouble.

This chapter looks at two verb problems that occur in many people's writing: incorrect use of irregular verbs and difficulties with the passive voice.

THE PRINCIPAL PARTS OF VERBS

All verb formations are based on a verb's **principal parts**. Technically, the principal parts are not the **tenses** (time indicators) of the verb; they are the elements that are used to construct the various tenses.

> Every verb has four forms, called its *principal parts*.
> 1. The **infinitive** form: the form used with *to*
> 2. The **simple past** (also called the **past tense**)
> 3. The **present participle** (the *-ing*) form
> 4. The **past participle**: used with *has* or *have*

Here are some examples:

Infinitive	Simple Past	Present Participle	Past Participle
A. (to) call	called	calling	(has) called
(to) dance	danced	dancing	(has) danced
(to) work	worked	working	(has) worked
B. (to) do	did	doing	(has) done
(to) eat	ate	eating	(has) eaten
(to) say	said	saying	(has) said

If you study the list above, you will notice an important feature of principal parts. In the first group of three verbs (A), the simple past and the past participle are identical: they are both formed by adding *-ed* (or simply *-d* if the verb ends in *-e*, as *dance* does). When both the simple past and the past participle of a verb are formed with *-ed*, the verb is called a **regular verb**. Fortunately, most of the many thousands of English verbs are regular.

The verbs in the second group (B) are called **irregular verbs** because the simple past and past participle are not formed by adding *-ed*. With *do* and *eat*, the simple past and the past participle are different words: *did/done, ate/eaten*. The simple past and past participle of *say* are the same, *said*, but they are not formed with the regular *-ed* ending.

Unfortunately, although there are only a few hundred irregular verbs in English, they are some of the most common verbs in the language; for example, *begin, come, do, go, see,* and *write* are all irregular. Their simple past tenses and past participles are formed in unpredictable ways.

If you are not sure of the principal parts of a verb, check your dictionary. If the verb is irregular, you will find the principal parts listed after the entry

Grammar

for the base form. For instance, if you look up *sing* in your dictionary, you will find *sang* (simple past), *sung* (past participle), and *singing* (present participle). If no principal parts are listed after the verb you are checking, it is regular and forms its simple past and past participle by adding *-ed*.

The verbs we have listed below are used so frequently that you should take the time to learn their principal parts. We have not included the present participle (the *-ing* form) because it rarely causes difficulty. The good news is that only some of the verbs on this list will cause you trouble.

Here's how to identify your problem verbs. Cover the middle and right-hand columns of the list with a piece of paper. Now say the past tense and past participle of *be* and then move the paper down one line to check your responses. If you were right, do the same for *bear* and then move on to the next verb. When you come to a verb whose past tense or past participle you aren't sure of or misidentify, highlight that verb across all three columns. In this way, when you have gone through the list once, you'll have a quick and easy reference to the correct forms of verbs that you need to watch out for.

THE PRINCIPAL PARTS OF
IRREGULAR VERBS

Infinitive (Use with *to* and with helping/auxiliary verbs)	Simple Past	Past Participle (Use with *has*, *have*, *had*)
be (am, is)	was/were	been
bear	bore	borne
beat	beat	beaten
become	became	become
begin	began	begun
bend	bent	bent
bind	bound	bound
bite	bit	bitten
bleed	bled	bled
blow	blew	blown
break	broke	broken
bring	brought (*not* brang)	brought (*not* brung)
broadcast	broadcast	broadcast
build	built	built

Infinitive (Use with *to* and with helping/auxiliary verbs)	Simple Past	Past Participle (Use with *has, have, had*)
burst	burst	burst
buy	bought	bought
catch	caught	caught
choose	chose	chosen
cling	clung	clung
come	came	come
cost	cost	cost
cut	cut	cut
deal	dealt	dealt
dig	dug	dug
dive	dived/dove	dived
do	did (*not* done)	done
draw	drew	drawn
dream	dreamed/dreamt	dreamed/dreamt
drink	drank (*not* drunk)	drunk
drive	drove	driven
eat	ate	eaten
fall	fell	fallen
feed	fed	fed
feel	felt	felt
fight	fought	fought
find	found	found
flee	fled	fled
fling	flung	flung
fly	flew	flown
forbid	forbade	forbidden
forget	forgot	forgotten/forgot
forgive	forgave	forgiven
freeze	froze	frozen
get	got	got/gotten
give	gave	given
go	went	gone (*not* went)
grow	grew	grown
have	had	had
hear	heard	heard
hide	hid	hidden
hit	hit	hit
hold	held	held

Grammar

Infinitive	Simple Past	Past Participle
(Use with *to* and with helping/auxiliary verbs)		(Use with *has, have, had*)
hurt	hurt	hurt
keep	kept	kept
know	knew	known
lay (to put or place)	laid	laid
lead	led	led
leave	left	left
lie (to recline)	lay	lain (*not* layed)
light	lit/lighted	lit/lighted
lose	lost	lost
make	made	made
mean	meant	meant
meet	met	met
mistake	mistook	mistaken
pay	paid	paid
raise	raised	raised
ride	rode	ridden
ring	rang	rung
rise	rose	risen
run	ran	run
say	said	said
see	saw (*not* seen)	seen
seek	sought	sought
sell	sold	sold
set	set	set
shake	shook	shaken (*not* shook)
shine	shone	shone
shoot	shot	shot
show	showed	shown
shrink	shrank	shrunk
sing	sang	sung
sink	sank	sunk
sit	sat	sat
sleep	slept	slept
slide	slid	slid
speak	spoke	spoken
speed	sped	sped
spend	spent	spent
spin	spun	spun

Infinitive (Use with *to* and with helping/auxiliary verbs)	Simple Past	Past Participle (Use with *has, have, had*)
stand	stood	stood
sting	stung	stung
strive	strove	striven
steal	stole	stolen
stick	stuck	stuck
strike (hit)	struck	struck
strike (affect)	struck	stricken
swear	swore	sworn
swim	swam	swum
swing	swung (*not* swang)	swung
take	took	taken
teach	taught	taught
tear	tore	torn
tell	told	told
think	thought	thought
throw	threw	thrown
understand	understood	understood
wear	wore	worn
weave	wove	woven
win	won	won
wind	wound	wound
withdraw	withdrew	withdrawn
write	wrote	written

Grammar

The sentences in the exercises below require both the simple past and the past participle of the verb shown at the left. Write the required form in each blank. Do not add or remove helping verbs. Be sure to check your answers after each set. Answers for this chapter begin on page 411.

EXERCISE **12.1**

1. ride   Having _rode_ a cow once, I wouldn't mind if I never _rode_ one

     again.

2. tear   Albert ~~tore~~ *tore* his sheet into strips, tied the strips he had *tore* into a long cord, and escaped through the window.

3. lie   The cat *lay* defiantly right where the dog had *lain* all morning.

4. shake   After I had ~~shook~~ *shaken* the money out of the envelope, I *shook* the envelope again to be sure I had it all.

5. grow   Britney *grew* the plant in a pot on her balcony, where she had *grown* similar plants successfully in the past.

6. know   We *knew* at the time that we should have *known* better than to believe it was a geranium.

7. lay   Rajiv cautiously *laid* his passport on the officer's desk where other tourists had *laid* theirs.

8. lend   I *lent* Maria the $50 she asked for, even though she hasn't paid back the money I've already *lent* her.

9. take   They *took* sweaters with them to the concert, but when it snowed, they wished they had *taken* parkas.

10. go   We *went* where no human being had ever *gone* before.

GO TO WEB
EXERCISE 12.1

WWW.BAREA.NELSON.COM

EXERCISE **12.2**

Correct the 25 verb errors in the following sentences.

1. The final scene in the play shakened the audience so badly that they have went to a bar to argue over the ending.

2. After laying around all day watching TV, Emma had no time to write her essay, so I loaned her mine.

Grammar

3. "Strike three!" called the umpire as I swang the bat, but I run around the bases anyway.

4. While some of us have swam in the fountain of knowledge, and others have drank from it, Grover just gargles.

5. Lisa should have knowed better than to challenge me at Trivial Pursuit because I have never been beat.

6. I don't mind so much that James has stole my girlfriend and drove off in my car, but he should not have took my coffee mug.

7. All the team's players shined during the game, except for one defence-man who got into a fight and was throwed out in the first period.

8. Near the end of term we were struck to think that if we had went to class and had did the homework, we would have past the course.

9. Television is nature's way of telling us we should have went out and did something enjoyable this evening.

10. The lake had froze solid, so after we had ate supper, we brung our skates out and spended a couple of hours skating.

GO TO WEB
EXERCISE 12.2

WWW.BAREA.NELSON.COM

CHOOSING BETWEEN ACTIVE AND PASSIVE VOICE

Verbs have another quality besides tense (or time). Verbs also have what is called **voice**, which means the quality of being either active or passive. In sentences with **active voice** verbs, the "doer" of the action is the grammatical subject of the sentence.

Active voice: <u>Helmets</u> <u>protect</u> cyclists.
My <u>dog</u> <u>ate</u> my homework.
<u>Someone</u> <u>will show</u> a movie in class.

In sentences with **passive voice** verbs, the grammatical subject of the sentence is the "receiver" of the action (that is, the subject is "passively" acted upon), and the "doer" becomes an object of the preposition *by* or is absent from the sentence entirely, as in the third example below.

Passive voice: <u>Cyclists</u> <u>are protected</u> by helmets.
My <u>homework</u> <u>was eaten</u> by my dog.
A <u>movie</u> <u>will be shown</u> in class.

Notice that active and passive verbs can be in any tense. Present, past, and future tense verbs are used in both sets of examples above.

Passive voice verbs are formed by using a form of *be* + a past participle. To use the passive voice correctly, you must know the past participle form of irregular verbs. For instance, in the third example above, the correct passive construction is *will be shown*, not *will be showed*. In the examples below, note the different tenses and pay special attention to the passive voice verb forms.

	Active	Passive
present	The clerk *signs* the invoice.	The invoice *is signed* by the clerk.
past	The clerk *signed* the invoice.	The invoice *was signed* by the clerk.
future	The clerk *will sign* the invoice.	The invoice *will be signed* by the clerk.
present progressive	The clerk *is signing* the invoice.	The invoice *is being signed* by the clerk.
past progressive	The clerk *was signing* the invoice.	The invoice *was being signed* by the clerk.

EXERCISE **12.3**

Underline the verbs in the sentences with two lines. Then identify them as either active (A) or passive (P). The first one is done for you. The answers to the exercises in this part of the chapter begin on page 412.

1. __A__ Do not <u>number</u> your pages.

2. __P__ Your meal is being prepared by an apprentice chef.

3. __P__ Each year, Mount Washington is visited by thousands of tourists.

4. __A__ "Some weasel took the cork out of my lunch!" (W.C. Fields)

5. __P__ Your essay has not been properly formatted.

6. __A__ This computer is connected to the Internet.

7. __P__ *The English Patient* was written by Canadian author Michael Ondaatje.

8. __A__ Hollywood made Ondaatje's novel into a successful movie.

9. __P__ Mandarin is the language spoken by most of China's 1.3 billion people.

10. __A__ "Children should neither be seen nor heard—ever again." (W.C. Fields)

EXERCISE **12.4**

Now rewrite the sentences in Exercise 12.3, changing active voice verbs to passive and passive voice verbs to active. We've done the first sentence for you as an example.

1. Your pages should not be numbered by you.

2. The apprentice chef is preparing your meal.

3. Each year thousands of tourists visit Mount Washington

4. The cork was taken out of my lunch by some weasel

5. You need to properly format your essay

6. The internet is connected to this computer

7. The Canadian author Micheal Ondaatie wrote the English Pat.

8. Ondaaties novel was made into a <u>successful movie</u>.

9. Most Chinas 1.3 billion ppl speak mandarin.

10. One should never see nor hear children ever again

Exchange papers with a partner, check each other's sentences, and decide whether active or passive voice is preferable in each case.

GO TO WEB
EXERCISE 12.3

WWW.BAREA.NELSON.COM

Active voice verbs are more direct and emphatic than passive verbs. Good writers use the active voice unless there is a specific reason to use the passive. There are three situations in which the passive voice is preferable.

1. The person or agent that performed the action is not known.

This workstation is not ergonomically designed.
The telephone was left off the hook.
The name of our street has been changed from Primate Road to Primrose Lane.

2. You want to place the emphasis on the person, place, or object that was affected by an action rather than on the subject performing the action.

The computer lab was broken into by a group of angry students.

This sentence focuses the reader's attention on the computer lab rather than on the students. If we reconstruct the sentence in the active voice, we produce a quite different effect.

A group of angry students broke into the computer lab.

3. You are writing a technical or scientific report or a legal document.

Passive verbs are the appropriate choice when the focus is on the facts, methods, or procedures involved in an experiment, situation, or event rather than on the person(s) who discovered or performed them. Passive verbs establish an impersonal tone that is appropriate to these kinds of writing. Contrast the emphasis and tone of these sentence pairs:

Passive: The heat <u>was increased</u> to 150°C and <u>was maintained</u> at that temperature.

Active: My lab partner and I <u>increased</u> the heat to 150°C and <u>maintained</u> it at that temperature.

Passive: Our annual report <u>was approved</u> by the board on February 15.

Active: The board <u>approved</u> our annual report on February 15.

In general, because active verbs are more concise and forceful than passive verbs, they add focus and strength to your writing. When you find a passive verb in your writing, think about *who* is doing *what* to *whom*. Ask yourself why the *who* is not the subject of your sentence. If there is a good reason, then use the passive voice. Otherwise, change the verb.

Grammar

EXERCISE **12.5**

Rewrite the sentences below, changing the verbs from passive to active voice. You may need to add a word or word group to identify the doer of the action expressed by the verb.

1. The astronauts were contacted by Mission Control. *contacted the astronauts*
2. The tank was topped up in preparation for the long trip. *We ... the tank*
3. A new recipe is being tried by my sister. *tried a new recipe*
4. After a slow start, three runs were scored in the fourth inning. *the home team scored*
5. A cover of their hit song will be played by a new band. *will cover their hit song*
6. My screen saver, which is a picture of a peaceful scene in Tuscany, was downloaded by my brother. *downloaded my screensaver which was*
7. In English, the sound "ough" can be pronounced eight different ways. *in english*
8. Something must be done about the unreasonable popularity of SUVs. *We ... do something*
9. "Shoes are required to eat in the dining room." (Sign in a hotel restaurant) *Shoes must be worn*
10. This piece of music is thought to have been written by Mozart.

EXERCISE 12.6

Rewrite the sentences below, changing the verbs from passive to active voice. Then compare your revision to the original and, keeping the three reasons for choosing the passive voice in mind (page 160), decide which version is more effective.

1. The white part of the fingernail is called the "lunula." *is the white part of the fingernail*

2. A parade was organized to mark the team's arrival home after the Olympics.

3. A memo will be sent by the Payroll Department to explain why our cheques were late.

4. The person who is responsible cannot be determined by the police.

5. The story was covered by one of the paper's senior journalists.

6. *I ate* More food than necessary ~~was eaten by me~~ when I came off my diet.

7. *Bonnie broke* The remote ~~was broken~~ in a fit of anger ~~by Bonnie~~ when she couldn't watch her favourite show.

8. *The neighbors dog barked @* The letter carrier ~~was barked at by the neighbour's dog~~ until she was too terrified to deliver our mail.

9. *Connects* The two lines ~~that connect~~ your upper lip to the bottom of your nose are ~~known as~~ the "philtrum."

10. *shakespeare created* The word "assassination" ~~was created by Shakespeare.~~

GO TO WEB
EXERCISE 12.4

WWW.BAREA.NELSON.COM

Rewrite the following passage, changing passive voice verbs to active where appropriate. Ten changes are required.

[1]It is thought by many Canadians that our politicians have little wit and no humour. [2]However, there are many examples of instances when clever things have been said by our political leaders. [3]A story about Bob Rae is told by John Robert Colombo. [4]When Rae was premier of Ontario, he was criticized by some of his opponents as being from a privileged background, even though he was the leader of a socialist party. [5]He was called a "silver spoon socialist" by Joe Clark. [6]After all, he was the son of a diplomat, a Rhodes Scholar, a graduate of Oxford University, and a law degree was held by him. [7]His reply to these criticisms was reported in the *Toronto Star*. [8]"That's not true," he said. [9]"That [remark] is resented by me. [10]It is resented by my nanny. [11]It is resented by my chauffeur."

IN THIS VICTIM'S SENTENCES, THE SUBJECTS AND VERBS DOESN'T AGREE.

YOU HAVE THE RIGHT TO REMAIN SILENT...

13 Mastering Subject–Verb Agreement

SINGULAR AND PLURAL

One of the most common writing errors is lack of agreement between subject and verb. Both must be singular, or both must be plural. If one is singular and the other plural, you have an agreement problem. You have another kind of agreement problem if your subject and verb are not both in the same "person" (see Chapter 17).

Let's clarify some terms. First, it's important to distinguish between **singular** and **plural**.

- "Singular" means one person or thing.
- "Plural" means more than one person or thing.

Second, it's important to know what we mean when we refer to the concept of person:

- "First person" is the person(s) speaking or writing: *I, me*; *we, us*
- "Second person" is the person(s) being addressed: *you*
- "Third person" is the person(s) being spoken or written about: *he, she, it; they, them*

Here's an example of the singular and plural forms of a regular verb in the present tense.

	Singular	**Plural**
First person	I win	we win
Second person	you win	you win
Third person	she wins (*or* he, it, the horse wins)	they win (*or* the horses win)

The form that most often causes trouble is the third person because the verb endings do not match the subject endings. Third-person singular present tense verbs end in *-s*, but their singular subjects do not. Third-person plural verbs never end in *-s*, while their subjects normally do. Look at these examples.

A fire burns.
The car skids.
Our neighbour cares for the children.

The three singular verbs, all of which end in *-s* (*burns, skids, cares*), agree with their singular subjects (*fire, car, neighbour*), none of which ends in *-s*. When the subjects become plural, the verbs change form, too.

Four fires burn.
The cars skid.
Our neighbours care for the children.

Now all of the subjects end in *-s*, and none of the verbs do.
To ensure **subject–verb agreement**, follow this basic rule:

Subjects and verbs must both be either singular or plural.

This rule causes difficulty only when the writer doesn't know which word in the sentence is the subject and so makes the verb agree with the wrong word.

Grammar

As long as you decode the sentence correctly (see Chapter 6), you'll have no problem making every subject agree with its verb.

If you have not already done so, now is the time to memorize this next rule:

The subject of a sentence is NEVER in a prepositional phrase.

Here's an example of how errors occur.

Only one of the 2,000 ticket buyers are going to win.

What is the subject of this sentence? It's not *buyers*, but *one*. The verb must agree with *one*, which is clearly singular. The verb *are* does not agree with *one*, so the sentence is incorrect. It should read

Only <u>one</u> ~~of the 2,000 ticket buyers~~ <u>is going</u> to win.

Pay special attention to words that end in *-one, -thing,* or *-body.* They cause problems for nearly every writer.

Words ending in *-one, -thing,* or *-body* are always singular.

When used as subjects, these pronouns require singular verbs.

anyone	anything	anybody
everyone	everything	everybody
no one	nothing	nobody
someone	something	somebody

The last part of the pronoun subject is the tip-off here: every*one*, any*thing*, no*body*. If you focus on this last part, you'll remember to use a singular verb with these subjects. Usually, these words cause trouble only when modifiers crop up between them and their verbs. For example, you would never write "Everyone are here." The trouble starts when you insert a group of words in between the subject and the verb. You might, if you weren't careful, write this: "Everyone involved in implementing the company's new policies and procedures are here." The meaning is plural: several people are present. But the subject (*everyone*) is singular, so the verb must be *is.*

More subject–verb agreement errors are caused by violations of this rule than any other. Be sure you understand it. Memorize it, and then test your understanding by doing the following exercise before you go any further.

EXERCISE **13.1**

Circle the correct verb for each of the following sentences. Answers for this chapter begin on page 413.

1. Somebody with a taste for Smarties (has/~~have~~) found my hidden stash of candy.
2. I wonder why it is that everyone in my photos (has/~~have~~) red eyes.
3. Nothing (~~succeed~~/succeeds) like success.
4. Everybody on the team (~~show~~/shows) great respect for the coach.
5. No one carrying a pager, a cellphone, or a recording device (is/~~are~~) permitted into the theatre.
6. Something about the way he moves (~~make~~/makes) me uncomfortable.
7. I hope nobody in our classes ever (~~overhear~~/overhears) us gossiping in the faculty lounge.
8. The police are looking for anyone who (was/~~were~~) in the vicinity when the crime took place.
9. Anybody with any sense of civic pride (~~dispose~~/disposes) of empty cans and coffee cups in the appropriate recycling box.
10. After Labour Day, almost no one ever (~~visit~~/visits) the provincial park campsites.

The next two exercises will give you practice in pairing singular subjects with singular verbs and plural subjects with plural verbs.

EXERCISE **13.2**

Change the subject and verb in each sentence from plural to singular. Underline the subject once and the verb twice. Then check your answers.

1. Girls just want to have fun. [The] [s]
2. Articles on the Internet do not always contain reliable information. [An] [es]
3. Have the lucky winners collected the lottery money? [s]
4. Students often prefer to attend college away from home. [A]
5. College students often complain that they didn't learn anything in high school. [The] [s] [he/she]

EXERCISE **13.3**

Rewrite each sentence, changing the subject as indicated and revising the verb accordingly. Then check your answers. For example:

Computer <u>games</u> <u>are</u> my favourite pastime.
My favourite <u>pastime</u> <u>is</u> computer games.

1. Trees are a primary source of Earth's oxygen.

   A primary source _____

2. British Columbia wines regularly win international awards.

   British Columbia wine _____

3. Good managers consult with their subordinates before making decisions.

   A good manager _____

4. They insist on doing whatever they please.

   She _____

5. He does his best work when he is unsupervised.

   We _____

GO TO WEB
EXERCISE 13.1

WWW.BAREA.NELSON.COM

So far, so good. You can find the subject, even when it's hiding on the far side of the verb or buried under a load of prepositional phrases. You can match up singular subjects with singular verbs and plural subjects with plural verbs. Now let's take a look at a few of the complications that make subject–verb agreement such a disagreeable problem.

FIVE SPECIAL CASES

Some subjects are tricky. They look singular but are actually plural, or they look plural when they're really singular. There are five kinds of these slippery subjects, all of them common and all of them likely to trip up the unwary writer.

> 1. Multiple subjects joined by *or; either . . . or; neither . . . nor;* or *not . . . but.*

Most multiple subjects we've dealt with so far have been joined by *and* and have required plural verbs, so agreement hasn't been a problem. But watch out when the two or more elements of a compound subject are joined by *or; either . . . or; neither . . . nor;* or *not . . . but.* In these cases, the verb agrees in number with the nearest subject. That is, if the subject closest to the verb is singular, the verb will be singular; if the subject closest to the verb is plural, the verb must be plural, too.

Neither the <u>federal government</u> nor the <u>provinces</u> effectively <u>control</u> environmental pollution.

Neither the <u>provinces</u> nor the <u>federal government</u> effectively <u>controls</u> environmental pollution.

EXERCISE **13.4**

Circle the correct verb.

1. Either "Dr." or "Ms." (is/~~are~~) fine with me.
2. Not the dog but the cats (sleep/~~sleeps~~) on our bed.
3. A sad song, onions, or happiness (is/~~are~~) likely to make her cry.
4. Either your friend or you (~~is~~/are) paying for the damage.
5. Not lower taxes but friendly people (~~is~~/are) what I miss most about Alberta.
6. The salesman said that neither the manufacturer nor the suppliers (~~suggests~~/suggest) loading a T-shirt into the printer.
7. According to a recent survey, not financial worries but disagreement over children (~~cause~~/causes) the most strain on a marriage.
8. Not the politicians nor the issues but voter apathy (~~seem~~/seems) to be the main concern of the analysts.
9. Neither voter apathy nor the analysts (~~interests~~/~~interest~~) me.
10. Not the callers but the talk-show host (sounds/~~sound~~) completely ignorant of the facts.

2. Subjects that look multiple but really aren't.

Don't be fooled by phrases beginning with words such as *with, like, as well as, together with, in addition to,* and *including.* These prepositional phrases are NOT part of the subject of the sentence. Since they do not affect the verb, you can mentally cross them out.

My math professor, ~~as well as my counsellor,~~ has advised me to change my major.

Two people were involved in the advising; nevertheless, the subject (math professor) is singular, so the verb must be singular (has advised).

All of my courses, ~~including English,~~ seem easier this term.

If you mentally cross out the phrase "including English," you can easily see that the verb (seem) must be plural to agree with the plural subject (courses).

EXERCISE **13.5**

Circle the correct verb.

1. One hotdog with all the trimmings (has/~~have~~) more calories than you would believe.
2. Margaret Atwood, like many contemporary Canadian authors, (~~write~~/writes) novels with political themes.
3. This play, like everything else the author has written, (is/~~are~~) guaranteed to put you to sleep in the first act.
4. Full employment, like lower taxes, (has/~~have~~) become an impossible dream.
5. Even on sale, this computer package, including monitor, disk drive, printer, and software, (is/~~are~~) too expensive for us.
6. My brother, as well as my parents, (~~want~~/wants) me to move out.
7. The food he serves, along with the musical entertainment he provides, (is/~~are~~) barely worth the free admission.
8. Anger, together with denial and despair, (is/~~are~~) almost inevitable during the grieving process.
9. The waiter, like the busboys and the wine steward, (is/~~are~~) hoping that we will tip generously.
10. Television, with its reality shows, game shows, dramas, and sitcoms, (~~remain~~/remains) the most popular form of mass entertainment.

3. *Each (of), either (of), neither (of).*

Used as subjects, these words take singular verbs. (Remember, the subject is never located in a prepositional phrase.)

<u>Either</u> <u>is</u> suitable for the job.

<u>Each</u> of us <u>dreams</u> of scoring the winning goal.

<u>Neither</u> of these stores <u>is</u> open after six o'clock.

EXERCISE **13.6**

Circle the correct verb.

1. Neither of the celebrity parents (~~deserves~~/deserve) custody of their children.
2. Neither of the union's proposals (is/~~are~~) acceptable to management.
3. Each of the contestants in the karaoke competition (thinks/~~think~~) stardom is just around the corner.
4. I understand that neither of you (is/~~are~~) interested in online dating.
5. If either of the teams (scores/~~score~~) more than four goals, I win the money in the pool.
6. It's unbelievable that each of these actors (has/~~have~~) won several awards.
7. It's clear that neither of us (is/~~are~~) ready to be tested on this material.
8. My mother was delighted to announce that each of my cousins (has/~~have~~) won a scholarship to the college that rejected my application.
9. Either of those two professors (is/~~are~~) fun to watch in a lecture hall full of first-year students.
10. If neither of these software programs (works/~~work~~) with our computer system, we'll have to find another supplier.

4. Collective nouns.

A collective noun is a word naming a group. Some examples are *band, gang, orchestra, company, class, committee, team, crowd, public, family, audience, group,* and *majority.* When you are referring to the group acting as a unit, use a singular verb. When you are referring to the members of the group acting individually, use a plural verb.

> The <u>team</u> <u>is</u> sure to win tomorrow's game. (Here *team* refers to the group acting as a whole.)

> The <u>team</u> <u>are</u> getting into their uniforms now. (The separate members of the team are acting individually.)

EXERCISE **13.7**

Circle the correct verb.

1. The nuclear family (is/~~are~~) the fundamental unit of society.
2. The class (~~is~~/are) making Valentine cards for their parents.
3. My department (~~pride~~/prides) itself on a high degree of efficiency.
4. The budget committee (~~fight~~/fights) among themselves continually.
5. (~~Has~~/Have) the jury reached a verdict?
6. Having waited for almost an hour, the crowd (was/~~were~~) growing restless.
7. Our office (~~give~~/gives) a farewell party whenever anyone leaves.
8. The majority of immigrants (~~find~~/finds) Canada a tolerant country.
9. The entire gang, without exception, (is/~~are~~) getting together this weekend.
10. The audience (~~wait~~/waits) impatiently, eager for the concert to begin.

---

5. Units of money, time, mass, length, and distance.

These expressions require singular verbs.

<u>Twelve dollars</u> <u>is</u> too much to pay for a hamburger.

<u>Two hours</u> <u>seems</u> like four in our sociology class.

<u>Eighty kilograms</u> <u>is</u> the mass of an average man.

<u>Ten kilometres</u> <u>is</u> too far to walk.

EXERCISE **13.8**

Circle the correct verb.

1. Six metres (is/~~are~~) the minimum amount of cloth you need to make a sari.
2. Two hours of watching martial arts films (seems/~~seem~~) like seven hours to me.
3. Twenty kilograms of food for a four-day hike (is/~~are~~) far too much to expect us to carry.
4. Twenty dollars an hour for flipping burgers (sounds/~~sound~~) like a good deal to me.
5. Thirty kilometres on good roads (doesn't/~~don't~~) seem very far unless you're cycling against the wind.
6. Forty years in the desert (is/~~are~~) a very long time between baths.
7. Twenty centimetres of snow in four hours (was/~~were~~) enough to paralyze the city.
8. Seven hours of classes without a break (makes/~~make~~) for a very long day.
9. Thirty years of working at the same job, doing the same tasks, (~~seem~~/seems) like sixty.
10. Twelve kilos of turkey, stuffed, together with roasted potatoes and mashed turnip, (takes/~~take~~) about seven hours to cook.

In Exercises 13.9 and 13.10, correct the errors in subject–verb agreement. Check your answers to each exercise before going on.

EXERCISE **13.9**

1. A group of unbiased students and faculty ~~have~~ *has* been asked to study the problem.
2. Anybody who really want*s* to succeed will do so.
3. Over the past 20 years, the number of couples living together has more than doubled.
4. The lack of these four nutrients ~~are~~ *is* thought to contribute to depression.
5. You'll find that not only ragweed but also cat hairs make*s* you sneeze.

6. If there ~~is~~ *are* no bubbles, then you have patched your tire successfully.

7. Neither the twins nor their mother ~~were~~ *was* willing to enter the water.

8. The lack of things to write about ~~cause~~ *causes* the headaches.

9. Nicole, together with her agent, her stylist, two bodyguards, and three Chihuahuas, ~~were~~ *was* seen boarding a private jet.

10. The amount of money generated by rock bands on tour ~~are~~ *is* astonishing.

GO TO WEB
EXERCISE 13.2

WWW.BAREA.NELSON.COM

EXERCISE **13.10**

There are 10 errors in this paragraph. Can you find and correct them?

There's *are* many good reasons for staying fit. The diminished strength, flexibility, and endurance that results from lack of exercise are compelling factors, but everyone who joins the many health clubs in this city ~~have~~ *has* individual reasons as well. The people I talked with says appearance or weight loss ~~are~~ *is* their main motivation for working out. No one among the 200 patrons of a local health club ~~were~~ *was* there for the social life, according to my poll. Either weightlifting or daily aerobic workouts ~~was~~ *were* what they wanted from the club, and the intensity of the workouts ~~were~~ *was* clear evidence that they were serious. The manager of the club, along with all the members of the staff, ~~were~~ *was* careful to point out that supervised exercise is essential for best results, but neither she nor her staff ~~was~~ *were* in favour of fad diets or sweat programs.

Correct the following passage, which contains 10 errors in subject–verb agreement.

The rewards of obtaining a good summer or part-time job goes well beyond the money you earn from your labour. Contacts that may be valuable in the future and experience in the working world is an important part of school-time employment. Even if the jobs you get while attending school has nothing to do with your future ambitions, they offers many benefits. For example, when scanning your résumé, an employer always like to see that you know what working for other people require: arriving at the work site on time, getting along with co-workers, following directions. Neither instinct nor instruction take the place of experience in teaching these basic facts of working life. These long-term considerations, in addition to the money that is the immediate reward, is what make part-time work so valuable. Everyone who have gone to school and worked part-time or during vacations are able to confirm these observations.

Complete the sentences below using present tense verbs. After you complete each set, check the answers on page 415 to see whether the verbs should be singular or plural.

1. Neither my boss nor the receptionist

2. Everybody with two or more pets

3. Not the lead singer but the musicians

4. A flock of birds

5. Every one of his employees

6. Fifty dollars

7. The whole family, including two aunts and six cousins,

Grammar

8. The actors, as well as the director,

9. Either a Big Mac or a Whopper

10. No one among the hundreds present

GO TO WEB
EXERCISE 13.3

WWW.BAREA.NELSON.COM

SUMMARY

- Subjects and verbs must agree: both must be singular, or both must be plural.
- The subject of a sentence is never in a prepositional phrase.
- Pronouns ending in *-one, -thing*, or *-body* are singular and require singular verbs.
- Subjects joined by *and* are always plural.
- When subjects are joined by *or; either . . . or; neither . . . nor;* or *not . . . but*, the verb agrees with the subject that is closest to it.
- When looking for the subject in a sentence, ignore phrases beginning with *as well as, including, in addition to, like, together with*, etc. They are prepositional phrases.
- When *each, either,* and *neither* are used as subjects, they require singular verbs.
- Collective nouns are usually singular.
- Units of money, time, mass, length, and distance are always singular.

As a final check of your mastery of subject–verb agreement, correct the following sentences. We suggest that you review the information in the Summary box on the preceding page before you tackle this exercise.

1. According to our survey, not charm nor looks, but success are what make a man attractive.

2. It seems that everyone, even the most die-hard indoor enthusiasts, eat outdoors on Canada Day; it's the oven's day off.

3. There's two things I cannot understand: numbers and arithmetic.

4. Appearing live on prime-time television tonight is the captain of the Montreal Canadiens and the goalie of the Calgary Flames.

5. Because you defaulted on your loan payments, neither the bank nor your other creditors is willing to lend you more money.

6. We put up an awning over the deck because, in the fall, a flock of Canada geese fly over our house almost every morning.

7. Alice Munro, along with Carol Shields and Margaret Atwood, have won international acclaim for novels and short stories.

8. Each of the experts we consulted agree that your condition can be improved by fresh air, reduced stress, good food, and lots of sun; of course, they're travel experts, not medical experts.

9. Either the students or the teacher who was supposed to be supervising them are going to have to pay for the damage.

10. Did you know that the original NHL team in Toronto were called the Arenas?

14 Keeping Your Tenses Consistent

Verbs are time markers. Changes in tense express changes in time: past, present, or future.

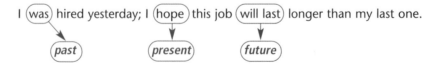

I (was) hired yesterday; I (hope) this job (will last) longer than my last one.

  (past)   (present)   (future)

Sometimes, as in the sentence above, it is necessary to use several different tenses in a single sentence to get the meaning across. But most of the time, whether you're writing a sentence or a paragraph, you use one tense throughout. Normally, you choose either the past or the present tense, depending on the nature of your topic. (Few paragraphs are written completely in the future tense.) Here is the rule to follow:

> Don't change tense unless the meaning of the sentence requires it.

Readers like and expect consistency. If you begin a sentence with "I argued, protested, and even appealed to his masculine pride," the reader will tune in to the past tense verbs and expect any other verbs in the sentence to be in the past tense, too. So, if you finish the sentence with ". . . but he looks at me with those big brown eyes and gets me to pay for dinner," your readers will be jolted abruptly out of one time frame into another. This sort of jolting is uncomfortable, and readers don't like it.

Shifting tenses is like shifting gears: it should be done smoothly and when necessary—never abruptly, out of carelessness, or on a whim. Avoid causing verbal whiplash; keep your tenses consistent.

Consider these two examples, both of which mix tenses inappropriately.

Problem: I*'m standing* right behind Sula when she suddenly *screamed.*
Solution 1:   I *was standing* right behind Sula when she suddenly *screamed.*
Solution 2:   I*'m standing* right behind Sula when she suddenly *screams.*

Problem: Tony *delayed* until the last possible minute and then *begins* to write his paper. When he *gets* halfway through, he *decided* to change his topic.
Solution 1:   Tony *delayed* until the last possible minute and then *began* to write his paper. When he *got* halfway through, he *decided* to change his topic.
Solution 2:   Tony *delays* until the last possible minute and then *begins* to write his paper. When he *gets* halfway through, he *decides* to change his topic.

Now look at this example, which expresses a more complex idea.

Problem: I *handed* my paper in just before the deadline. The next day, however, when I *see* the professor, she *says* that it was late, so I *will lose* marks.

This sentence is a hopeless muddle. It begins with the past tense, shifts to the present for no reason, and ends with the future.

Solution: I *handed* my paper in just before the deadline. The next day, however, when I *saw* the professor, she *said* that it was late, so I *will lose* marks.

Here the past tense is used consistently until the last clause, where the shift to future tense is appropriate to the meaning.

In the following exercises, most—but not all—of the sentences contain unnecessary tense shifts. Use the first verb in each sentence as your time marker and
change the tense(s) of the other verb(s) to agree with it. Answers for exercises
in this chapter begin on page 415.

EXERCISE 14.1

1. I met Dana and ~~tell~~ [told] her what happened after she left.

2. After supper, even though he was tired from his long day at work, Rico
   ~~plays~~ [played] with the twins.

3. I enjoy my work, but I ~~was~~ [am] not going to let it take over my life.

4. "The abdominal cavity contains the bowels, of which there ~~were~~ [are] five: a, e,
   i, o, and u." (Student answer on a science test)

5. There ~~will be~~ [is] a parade on Canada Day and the mayor is the grand marshal.

6. The goalie must not move from his stand until the penalty kicker ~~makes~~
   contact ~~with~~ the ball.

7. When the server went down, no one in the office ~~is~~ [was] able to work.

8. The umpire ~~stands~~ [stood] there, unable to believe what he was seeing.

9. She ~~goes~~ [went] to the fridge, ~~gets~~ [got] a cold can of pop, and proceeded to drink it
   without offering me anything.

10. "I keep liquor on hand just in case I ~~saw~~ [see] a snake, which I also ~~kept~~ [keep] on
    hand." (W. C. Fields)

EXERCISE 14.2

1. First, he backcombed his hair into spikes, and then he ~~coats~~ [coated] it with glue.

2. The lights dimmed and the crowd held its breath; Ricky ~~keeps~~ [kept] them
   waiting for another minute or so before he ~~explodes~~ [exploded] onto the stage.

3. The couple next door ~~had~~ [has] a boa constrictor that keeps getting loose and
   terrorizing the neighbourhood.

4. Typewriters were a vital piece of technology in the first two-thirds of the
   20th century, but the advent of the personal computer ~~makes~~ [made] them obsolete within a decade.

5. Just as time ran [runs] out, Emil launches [d] a three-point attempt from mid-court, but it misses the basket and the Chiefs lost [s] their final home game.

6. The Peter Principle states that every employee will rise to his or her level of incompetence.

7. I will have a first draft of my essay done by Thursday so the tutor could [can] examine it for structural errors.

8. You will live a happy and healthy life until your forties, when you meet [will] a beautiful dark-haired woman who makes [will] you miserable, breaks [s] your heart, ruined [leave] your health, and left [leave] you for another man.

9. I used to smoke, drink, and eat poutine whenever I could until I have [had] a case of indigestion that I think [thought was] is a heart attack and scared myself into eating a healthier diet.

10. The opposing coach was quoted in the paper as saying that Shack is [was] too dumb to spell "goal," but after scoring the winning goal that night, Shack skates [d] up to the coach and snarls [ed], "Goal. G-O-A-L!"

EXERCISE **14.3**

Correct the 15 faulty time shifts in the following paragraph. Use the italicized verb as your time marker. Then check your answers.

My most embarrassing moment *occurred* just last month when I meet an old friend whom I have not seen in years. We greet each other and begin to chat, and I tell her that I have been reading her daughter's columns in the newspaper. I congratulate her on her daughter's talent. I tell her that she must be very proud to see her offspring's name in print. My friend looks puzzled for a minute, then she laughs and tells me that the writer I am praising so highly isn't her daughter. My friend had divorced long ago; her former husband remarries, and the columnist is her ex-husband's new wife.

GO TO WEB
EXERCISE 14.1

WWW.BAREA.NELSON.COM

EXERCISE **14.4**

Correct the 15 faulty time shifts in the following paragraph. Use the italicized verb as your time marker.

Stephen Leacock *was* a great Canadian humorist who is also a respected professor of economics at McGill. Not long after he receives his doctorate in political economy from the University of Chicago, he travels by boat to Europe and proudly registers himself on the passenger list as Dr. Stephen Leacock. During the Atlantic crossing, a waitress in the ship's dining room will fall and injure her leg. Leacock is in his cabin when the steward knocks and asks for Dr. Leacock. When Leacock identifies himself, the steward requests that he examine the waitress's leg. Leacock delightedly agrees to do what he can, but as he tells audiences at his talks for years afterward, he is beaten to the scene of the injury by another "doctor," this one a doctor of divinity!

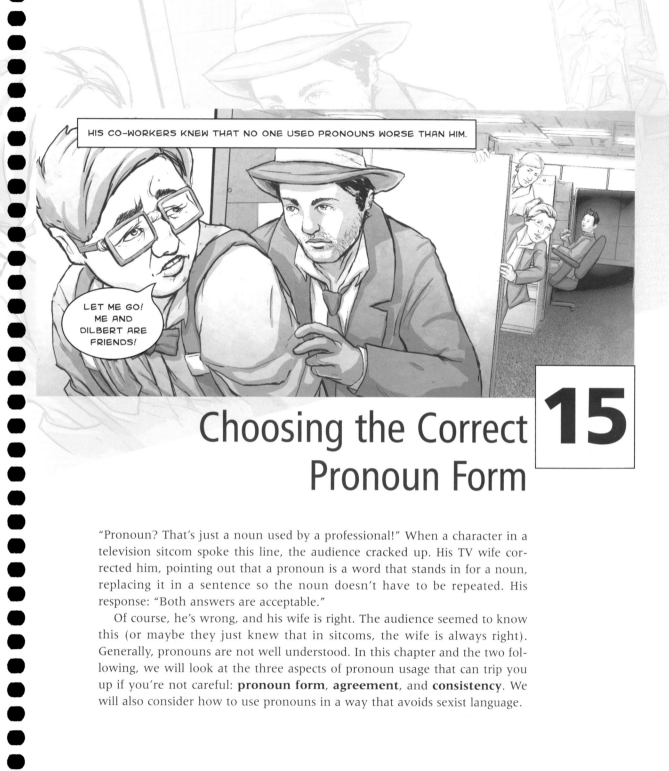

Choosing the Correct Pronoun Form

15

"Pronoun? That's just a noun used by a professional!" When a character in a television sitcom spoke this line, the audience cracked up. His TV wife corrected him, pointing out that a pronoun is a word that stands in for a noun, replacing it in a sentence so the noun doesn't have to be repeated. His response: "Both answers are acceptable."

Of course, he's wrong, and his wife is right. The audience seemed to know this (or maybe they just knew that in sitcoms, the wife is always right). Generally, pronouns are not well understood. In this chapter and the two following, we will look at the three aspects of pronoun usage that can trip you up if you're not careful: **pronoun form**, **agreement**, and **consistency**. We will also consider how to use pronouns in a way that avoids sexist language.

There are <u>three kinds</u> of pronouns that are likely to cause difficulty for writers:

Personal pronouns	I, we, she, they, etc.
Relative pronouns	who, which, that, etc.
Indefinite pronouns	any, somebody, none, each, etc.

(See Appendix A, pages 368–70, for complete lists of these pronouns.)

Your first challenge is to be sure that you are using correct pronoun forms. Look at these examples of incorrect pronoun usage:

~~Her~~ *She* and ~~me~~ *I* offered to pick up a video.

Between you and ~~I~~ *me*, Paul's mother does his homework.

How do you know which form of a pronoun to use? The answer depends on the pronoun's place and function in your sentence.

SUBJECT AND OBJECT PRONOUNS

There are two forms of personal pronouns. One is used for subjects, and one is used for objects. Pronoun errors occur when you confuse the two. In Chapter 6, you learned to identify the subject of a sentence. Keep that information in mind as you learn the following basic rule.

> When the subject of a sentence is (or is referred to by) a pronoun, that pronoun must be in **subject form**; otherwise, use the **object form**.

Subject Pronouns

Singular	Plural
I	we
you	you
he, she, it, one	they

She and *I* <u>decided</u> to rent a video.
(The pronouns are the subject of the sentence.)

The lucky <u>winners</u> of the free tickets to the World Wrestling Championships <u>are</u> *they*.
(The pronoun refers to the subject of the sentence, *winners*.)

The only <u>person</u> who got an A in the course <u>was</u> *she*.
(The pronoun refers to the subject of the sentence, *person*.)

We serious <u>bikers</u> <u>prefer</u> Harleys to Hondas.
(The pronoun refers to the subject of the sentence, *bikers*.)

Object Pronouns

Singular	*Plural*
me	us
you	you
him, her, it, one	them

Between you and *me*, Paul's <u>mother</u> <u>does</u> his homework.
(*Me* is not the subject of the sentence; it is one of the objects of the preposition *between*.)

<u>Sasha</u> <u>saw</u> *him* and *me* having coffee at Tim Hortons.
(*Him* and *me* are not the subject of the verb *saw*; *Sasha* is, so the pronouns must be in the object form.)

The <u>police</u> <u>are</u> always suspicious of *us* bikers.
(*Us* does not refer to the subject of the sentence, *police*; it refers to *bikers*, the object of the preposition *of*.)

Be especially careful with pronouns that occur in multiple subjects or after prepositions. If you remember the following two rules, you'll be able to eliminate most potential errors in pronoun form.

1. All pronouns in a multiple subject are *always* in subject form.
2. Pronouns that follow a preposition are *always* in object form.

She and *I* <u>have</u> season's tickets.
(The pronouns are used as a multiple subject.)

We are very happy for *you* and *her*.
(The pronouns follow the preposition *for*.)

When you're dealing with a pair of pronouns and can't decide which form to use, try this test. Mentally cross out one pronoun at a time, then read aloud the sentence you've created. Applying this technique to the first example above, you get "*She* has tickets" and "*I* have tickets." Both sound right and are correct. In the second sentence, if you try the pronouns separately, you get "We are happy for *you*" and "We are very happy for *her*." Again, you know by the sound that these are the correct forms. (You would never say "*Her* had

Grammar

tickets," or "*Me* had tickets," or "We are very happy for *she*.") If you deal with paired pronouns one at a time, you are unlikely to choose the wrong form.

Note, too, that when a pair of pronouns includes "I" or "me," that pronoun comes last. For example, we write "between *you* and *me*" (not "between *me* and *you*"); we write "*she* and *I*" (not "*I* and *she*"). There is no grammatical reason for this rule. It's based on courtesy. Good manners require that you speak of others first and yourself last.

EXERCISE **15.1**

Choose the correct pronouns from the words given in parentheses. Answers for exercises in this chapter begin on page 416.

1. Computers and (I/ ~~me~~) are incompatible.
2. The photographer and (I/~~me~~) agree that you look better out of focus.
3. With (us/~~we~~) away skiing, the dogs will relax at the Pooch Parlour Spa.
4. (He/~~Him~~) and (I/~~me~~) disagree about practically everything.
5. Neither they nor (~~us~~/we) deserve to be treated this way.
6. The agreement between your company and (us/~~we~~) will not be renewed.
7. It would be better for (them/~~they~~) to come here rather than for (us/~~we~~) to go there.
8. (~~Me and Britney~~/~~Britney and me~~/~~I and Britney~~/Britney and I) wrote, shot, and edited the film over the weekend.
9. If I have to choose between you and (~~he~~/him), it is (~~he~~/him) who will get the job.
10. Mainlanders might have more respect for (us/~~we~~) Newfoundlanders if (~~us~~/we) got to know each other better.

EXERCISE **15.2**

The following exercise contains 10 errors in pronoun form. Can you find and correct them?

1. ~~Her~~ and her family are strict vegetarians; they don't eat honey, use leather products, or even wear wool.

2. From time to time, my boyfriend and ~~me~~ have gone skinny dipping in moonlight.

3. Him and ~~me~~ agree, however, that no sane person would go bungee jumping in the dark, with or without clothes.

4. Amanda returned the videos before ~~me and~~ my boyfriend and I had a chance to see them.

5. It is not up to you or ~~I~~ me to discipline your brother's children; that responsibility belongs to ~~he~~ him and his partner.

6. Ted seems to be quite comfortable living with his mother; do you think ~~him and~~ he and Terry will ever get married?

7. The contract was not signed by the deadline, so ~~me and~~ Alex and I will have to negotiate it all over again.

8. Just as Kate and ~~me~~ I approached it, the geyser erupted, and we got soaked.

GO TO WEB
EXERCISE 15.1

WWW.BAREA.NELSON.COM

USING PRONOUNS IN CONTRAST CONSTRUCTIONS

Choosing the correct pronoun form is more than a matter of wanting not to appear ignorant or careless. Sometimes the form determines the meaning of your sentence. Consider these two sentences:

Jill treats her dog better than *I*.
Jill treats her dog better than *me*.

There's a world of difference between the meaning of the subject form—"Jill treats her dog better than *I* [do]"—and the object form—"Jill treats her dog better than [she treats] *me*."

When using a pronoun after *than, as well as,* or *as,* decide whether you mean to contrast the pronoun with the subject of the sentence. If you do, use the subject form of the pronoun. If not, use the object form.

Minnie would rather listen to Nelly Furtado than I.
(*I* is contrasted with *Minnie.*)

Minnie would rather listen to Nelly Furtado than me.
(*Me* is contrasted with *Nelly Furtado.*)

Here's a quick way to check that you've used the correct pronoun form. If you've used a subject form, mentally insert a verb after it. If you've used an object form, mentally insert a preposition before it. If your imagined sentences make sense, you have chosen correctly. For example,

Minnie would rather listen to Nelly Furtado than I [would].
Minnie would rather listen to Nelly Furtado than [to] me.

Some writers prefer to leave the additional verb or preposition in place, a practice that eliminates any possibility of confusion.

EXERCISE **15.3**

Correct the errors in the following sentences.

1. Nobody likes old movies more than ~~me~~. [I]
2. Andrea is more afraid of being alone than ~~him~~. [he]
3. At last, I have met someone who enjoys barbecued eel as much as ~~me~~! [I]
4. While they have more talent than ~~us~~, our team is in better condition. [we]
5. You seem to have even more trouble with English than ~~me~~. [I]
6. No one in the world eats more doughnuts per capita than ~~us~~ Canadians. [we]
7. Everyone wanted to watch the game except Max and ~~I~~. [Me]
8. Gary drafts and revises on the computer more than ~~me~~. [I]
9. He doesn't write as well as ~~me~~, but he does write faster. [I]
10. Not many rock groups have sold as many albums as ~~them~~. [they]

GO TO WEB
EXERCISE 15.2

WWW.BAREA.NELSON.COM

EXERCISE **15.4**

Correct the faulty pronoun forms in the following sentences.

1. Lynne and ~~me~~ [*I*] are splitting up; ~~her~~ [*she*] and her pet iguana are moving out tomorrow.

2. Once my brother and ~~me~~ [*I*] had experienced our first prairie winter, we decided to move on to Victoria.

3. The landlord has written you and ~~I~~ [*me*] requesting an appointment to inspect the apartment.

4. Sandrine would much rather drink coffee than ~~me; her~~ [*I*] [*she*], of all my friends, spends the most time in Tim Hortons.

5. Saving 10 percent of our monthly income has been a priority for my husband and ~~I~~ [*me*] ever since we were married.

6. ~~Her~~ [*She*] and her sister have travelled with us to the Caribbean many times, and every time they take twice as much luggage as ~~us~~ [*we*].

7. Between you and ~~I~~ [*me*], the real reason he got fired was that ~~him~~ [*he*] and his supervisor were dating the same woman.

8. After the exam, ~~him~~ [*he*] and ~~me~~ [*I*] were convinced we had failed, but when we got the results, it turned out that ~~us~~ [*we*] "failures" got two of the highest marks.

9. Our supervisor says she respects Gavin and ~~I~~ [*me*] equally, but she gives him more responsibility and a higher salary than ~~I~~ [*me*].

10. Americans are more demonstrative than ~~us~~ [*we*] Canadians; while ~~us~~ [*we*] and ~~them~~ [*they*] have much in common, history and culture have given us different national personalities.

Grammar

16 Mastering Pronoun–Antecedent Agreement

I am writing in response to your ad for a waiter and bartender, male or female. Being both, I am applying for the position.

Pronoun confusion can take several forms, and some of the resulting sentences can be unintentionally hilarious. In this chapter, we'll look at how to use pronouns consistently throughout a sentence or paragraph to avoid confusing (and embarrassing) mistakes.

PRONOUN—ANTECEDENT AGREEMENT

The name of this pronoun problem may sound difficult, but the idea is simple. Pronouns are words that substitute for or refer to a person, place, or thing mentioned elsewhere in your sentence or paragraph. The word(s) that a pronoun substitutes for or refers to is called the **antecedent**.

Hannibal had his own way of doing things. (*His* refers to *Hannibal.*)

Chantal respects her boss. (*Her* refers to *Chantal.*)

The computer is processing as fast as it can. (*It* substitutes for *the computer.*)

Usually, as in these three examples, the antecedent comes before the pronoun[1] that refers to it. Here is the rule to remember.

> A pronoun must agree with its antecedent in
> * number (singular or plural)
> * person (first, second, or third)
> * gender (masculine, feminine, or neuter)

Most of the time, you follow this rule without even realizing that you know it. For example, you would never write

Hannibal had *your* own way of doing things.

Chantal respects *its* boss.

The computer is processing as fast as *she* can.

You know these sentences are incorrect even if you may not know precisely why they are wrong.

There are three kinds of pronoun–antecedent agreement that you need to learn. Unlike the examples above, they are not obvious, and you need to know them so you can watch out for them. The rules you need to learn involve **indefinite pronouns ending in *-one, -body,* or *-thing*; vague references;** and **relative pronouns**.

---

[1] Strictly speaking, possessive words such as *my, his, her, our,* and *their* are pronominal adjectives rather than pronouns. We are dealing with them in this chapter, however, because they follow the same agreement rule that governs pronouns.

PRONOUNS ENDING IN *-ONE*, *-BODY*, *-THING*

The most common pronoun–antecedent agreement problem involves **indefinite pronouns**:

anyone	anybody	anything
everyone	everybody	everything
no one	nobody	nothing
someone	somebody	something
each (one)		

In Chapter 13, you learned that when these words are used as subjects, they are singular and require singular verbs. So it makes sense that the pronouns that stand for or refer to them must also be singular.

Antecedents ending in *-one*, *-body*, and *-thing* are singular. They must be referred to by singular pronouns: *he, she, it; his, her, its.*

Everyone deserves a break from *her* children now and then.

Everything has *its* place and should be in it.

Everybody is expected to do *his* share of the work.

No one had the courage to express *his* true feelings.

But take another look at the last two sentences. Until about 30 years ago, the pronouns *he, him,* and *his* were used with singular antecedents to refer to both men and women. Most modern readers are sensitive to gender bias in writing and think that it is not appropriate to use the masculine pronoun to refer to both genders. As a writer, you should be aware of this sensitivity. If you want to appeal to the broadest possible audience, you should avoid what readers may consider to be sexist language.

In informal usage, it has become acceptable to use plural pronouns with *-one*, *-body*, and *-thing* antecedents. Although they are grammatically singular, they are often plural in meaning, and in conversation we tend to say

Everybody is expected to do *their* share of the work.

No one had the courage to express *their* true feelings.

This usage is acceptable in speech, but it is not acceptable in academic or professional writing.

Writers sometimes make errors in pronoun–antecedent agreement because they are trying to write without indicating whether the person referred to is male or female. "Everybody is expected to do *their* share of the work" is incorrect, as we have seen; however, it does avoid making "everybody" male. The writer could replace the plural *their* with the singular and nonsexist *his or her*— "Everybody is expected to do *his or her* share of the work"—but *his or her* sounds clumsy if it is used frequently.

There are two better ways to solve the problem.

1. Revise the sentence to leave out the pronoun.

Everybody is expected to share the work.

No one had the courage to speak honestly.

Such creative avoidance of gender-specific language or incorrect constructions can be an interesting intellectual challenge. The results sometimes sound a little artificial, however. The second solution is easier to accomplish.

2. Revise the sentence to make both the antecedent and the pronoun plural.

We are all expected to do *our* share of the work.

The *teachers* did not have the courage to express *their* true feelings.

Here are a couple of examples for you to study:

Problem: Everybody has been given his assignment.
Revision 1:   Everybody has been given an assignment.
Revision 2:   All of the students have been given their assignments.

Problem: No one wants his copy edited.
Revision 1:   No one wants copy editing.
Revision 2:   Most writers object to having their copy edited.

If you are writing on a word processor, you can use the grammar checker to ensure agreement between indefinite pronouns and their antecedents. This is one error that grammar checkers tend to catch. The revisions offered by the checker might not be elegant, but they *are* correct. This step takes less time than you might think and is well worth it, especially if your instructor has asked for a formal paper or report.

EXERCISE **16.1**

Identify the most appropriate word(s) from the choices given in parentheses. You may have to modify some sentences to avoid sexist or clumsy language. Check your answers carefully before continuing. Answers for this chapter begin on page 417.

1. It seemed that everybody in the mall was talking on (~~his or her, their~~, a) cellphone.
2. Anything found in the locker room will be returned to (its/~~their~~) owner, if possible.
3. A bandleader is someone who is not afraid to face (his or her/their/the) music.
4. According to the reviews, not one of the movies at the mall is worth (its/~~their~~/the) admission price.
5. Everyone is expected to pay (~~his or her/their~~/a) share of the expenses.
6. Would someone kindly lend (~~his/her/their~~/a) copy of the text to Mel?
7. Is there anybody here who can bring (her/~~their~~) own car?
8. Our hockey team is superstitious, so everyone has agreed not to wash (~~our~~/his/~~their~~) sweater until after the playoffs.
9. A bore is someone who persists in (his/~~their~~) own opinion even after we have enlightened (him/~~them~~) with ours.
10. Anyone who wants an A for (~~his/their~~/this) essay should see me after class and give me (~~his/their~~/a) cheque.

EXERCISE **16.2**

Correct the errors in the following sentences, being careful to avoid awkward repetition and sexist language. Because there is more than one way to correct these errors, your answers may differ from our suggestions.

1. Everyone is a product of their environment as well as heredity.

2. Nobody who is as smart as you needs to have help with their homework.

3. Each car in all categories will be judged on their bodywork, engine, and interior.

4. Everybody who really tried should be satisfied with their performance.

5. Every movie-, theatre-, and concert-goer knows how annoying it is to have their evening's enjoyment spoiled by a ringing cellphone.

6. Put the sign at the curb so anyone looking for our yard sale won't have to waste their time driving around the neighbourhood.

7. Everyone who pays their membership fee in advance will receive a free session with a personal trainer.

8. A true geek is somebody who has trouble deciding between buying flowers for ~~their~~ *his* girlfriend and upgrading ~~their~~ *his* RAM.

9. The accident could not have been avoided, and fortunately no one was hurt, so no one should have to say they are sorry.

10. Ultimate is a game in which everyone who participates enjoys themselves, whether their team finishes first or last.

GO TO WEB
EXERCISE 16.1

WWW.BAREA.NELSON.COM

VAGUE REFERENCES

Avoiding the second potential difficulty with pronoun–antecedent agreement requires common sense and the ability to put yourself in your reader's place. If you look at your writing from your reader's point of view, it is unlikely that you will break the following rule.

> Every pronoun must have a clearly identifiable antecedent.

The mistake that occurs when you fail to follow this rule is called **vague reference**.

Luc pointed to his brother and said that he had saved his life.

Who saved whom? Here's another:

> Danielle wrote a song about her sister when she was five years old.

Is the song about a five-year-old sister, or was Danielle a musically talented child?

In sentences like these, you can only guess the meaning because you don't know who is being referred to by the pronouns. The antecedents are not clear. You can make such sentences less confusing either by using proper names (Luc, Danielle) more frequently or by changing the sentences around. These solutions aren't difficult; they just take a little time and some imagination. Try them on our examples.

Another type of vague reference occurs when there is no antecedent for the pronoun to refer to.

> Jeff loves off-road rallies and would like to try *it* himself. (Try what?)

> Snowboarding is Anna's favourite sport, and she's hoping to get *one* for her birthday. (One what?)

> My roommate smokes constantly, *which* I hate. (There is no noun or pronoun for *which* to refer to.)

> My sister's work schedule overlaps with her husband's. *This* creates childcare problems. (There is no noun or pronoun for *this* to refer to.)

How would you revise these sentences? Try it, then see our suggestions below.

Suggestions: Jeff loves off-road rallies and would like to try *the sport* himself.

Snowboarding is Anna's favourite sport, and she's hoping to get *a board* for her birthday.

My roommate is constantly smoking, *which* I hate.

My sister's work schedule overlaps with her husband's. *This* conflict creates child-care problems.

Make sure that every pronoun has a clear antecedent and that every pronoun agrees with its antecedent. Both must be singular, or both must be plural. Once you have mastered this principle, you'll have no trouble with pronoun–antecedent agreement.

EXERCISE **16.3**

Correct the following sentences where necessary. There are several ways to fix these sentences. In some cases, the antecedent is missing, and you need to supply one. In other cases, the antecedent is so vague that the meaning of the sentence can be interpreted in more than one way; you need to rewrite these sentences to make the meaning clear.

1. Our college strictly enforces the "no smoking" policy, so you can't even ~~have one~~ *smoke* outside on campus.

2. Fishing is fun even when I don't catch ~~one~~ *a fish*.

3. Every time David looked at the dog, *dog* he barked.

4. In a rage, Max hurled his cellphone at the computer and broke ~~it~~ *his cell phone.*

5. When the baby has finished drinking, ~~it~~ *the bottle* should be rinsed in cool water.

6. If the baby does not thrive on fresh milk, ~~it~~ *The milk* should be boiled.

7. When I learned that reading for at least an hour a day reduces the threat of Alzheimer's, I went to the library and took out three *books* to read over the weekend.

8. The forest is spectacular at this time of year, especially those *trees* with red and gold leaves.

9. My boyfriend and I took a sailing course last summer, and now we're saving every dollar we can so that eventually we'll be able to afford to buy *a boat.* ~~one.~~

10. Her son scored the winning goal three minutes into overtime, ~~which~~ Nell *missed the goal* ~~missed~~ because she was arguing with another parent.

GO TO WEB
EXERCISE 16.2

WWW.BAREA.NELSON.COM

fane   Phone

RELATIVE PRONOUNS

The third potential difficulty with pronoun–antecedent agreement is how to use relative pronouns—*who*, *which*, and *that*—correctly. Relative pronouns must refer to someone or something already mentioned in the sentence. Here is the guideline to follow.

> Use *who* and *whom* to refer to people.
> Use *that* and *which* to refer to everything else.

The chef *who* prepared this meal deserves a medal.

The servers *who* presented it deserve to be fired.

The appetizer *that* I ordered was buried under wilted parsley.

My soup, *which* was cold, arrived at the same time as my main course.

My father's meal, *which* was delicious, demonstrated the talent *that* the chef is famous for.

Whether you need *who* or *whom*[2] depends on the pronoun's place and function in your sentence. Apply the basic pronoun rule:

> If the pronoun is, or refers to, the subject of the sentence, use *who*. Otherwise, use *whom*. Or you can revise the sentence to eliminate the pronoun.

It was Sheila *who* drew the winning ticket for a week's holiday in Moose Factory. (The pronoun refers to the subject of the sentence, *Sheila*.)

The trip's promoters were willing to settle for *whom* they could get. (The pronoun does not refer to the subject, *promoters*; it is the object of the preposition *for*.)

A better solution is to solve the problem by rewriting the sentence so that you don't need either *who* or *whom*.

Sheila drew the winning ticket for a week's holiday in Moose Factory.

The trip's promoters were willing to settle for anyone they could get.

---

[2] The distinction between *who* and *whom* has all but disappeared in spoken English and is becoming rarer in written English. Ask your instructor for guidance.

That is required more often than *which*. You should use *which* only in a clause that is separated from the rest of the sentence by commas. (See comma Rule 4, page 219.)

The moose *that* I met looked hostile.
The moose, *which* was standing right in front of my car, looked hostile.

EXERCISE **16.4**

Correct the pronoun errors in the following sentences. Remember: use *who* to refer to people; use *that* or *which* to refer to everything else.

1. A grouch is a person that knows himself and isn't happy about it. [who]

2. The salesclerk, that sold me my DVD player didn't know what he was talking about. [who]

3. Everyone, that was at the party had a good time, although a few had more punch than was good for them. [who]

4. The open-office concept sounds good to anyone, that has worked in a stuffy little cubicle all day. [who]

5. The open-office concept, that many corporations have experimented with over the years, contributes to cooperative problem solving among workers that feel part of a community. [who]

6. Is this the dog which attacked the mail carrier that carries a squirt gun? [that] [who]

7. Thanks to the computer, I regularly order supplies from companies which are located in cities all across the country. [that]

8. The tests which we wrote today were designed to discourage anyone that didn't have the knowledge, preparation, and stamina to endure them. [that] [who]

9. Sales staff that want to earn promotion must have good people skills as well as a thorough knowledge of the products which they are selling. [who] [that]

10. WestJet, who offers discount fares across the country, encourages its employees to communicate in a friendly fashion with all customers that board its planes. [which] [who]

GO TO WEB
EXERCISE 16.3

WWW.BAREA.NELSON.COM

EXERCISE **16.5**

Revise the following paragraph, which contains 15 errors representing the three different kinds of pronoun–antecedent agreement errors. If you change a subject from singular to plural, don't forget to change the verb to agree. Some of your answers may differ from our suggestions and still be correct.

Everyone ~~that~~ *who* has been to Newfoundland knows that an outport is a small fishing community along the coast of that vast island province. Ladle Cove, for example, is a tiny outport with fewer than 200 residents ~~who~~ live there all year. Despite its small population, Ladle Cove is a village ~~which~~ *that* enjoyed a nation-wide moment of fame when a man ~~that~~ *who* lives there met the Queen. Fred had left Ladle Cove, as just about every man does when ~~they~~ *he* need to find work, and ~~gone~~ *went* to St. John's. Fred wanted to work, but he had few marketable skills to help him get ~~one~~ *a job*. Fortunately, he had relatives in St. John's ~~that~~ *who* helped him find a place to stay and eventually found him a job at Purity Foods, a company famous for ~~their~~ baked goods—and for Newfoundland's favourite treat, Jam Jam cookies.

During Queen Elizabeth's visit to St. John's, the officials ~~that~~ *who* organized her tour decided it would be a good idea for her to visit a local industry ~~which~~ *that* had a national reputation. Purity Foods was the logical choice. While touring the plant, the Queen stopped to talk to a few of the men and women ~~that~~ *who* were on the production line. Near the end of the tour, ~~that~~ *which* was being filmed by the national media, the Queen stopped by one of the workers ~~that were~~ *who was* making the famous Jam Jams: Fred. As the television lights glared and each reporter held ~~their~~ *a* pencil poised over their notebook, the Queen leaned toward Fred and asked, "And what are we making here?" With a courteous bow in Her Majesty's direction, Fred replied, "Ten-fifty an hour, Ma'am. Ten-fifty an hour."

SUMMARY

- Every pronoun must agree with its antecedent (a word or word group mentioned, usually earlier, in the sentence or paragraph). Both must be singular, or both must be plural.
- Antecedents ending in *-one*, *-body*, and *-thing* are singular and must be referred to by singular pronouns: *he, she, it; his, her, its.*
- A pronoun must clearly refer to a specific antecedent.
- Use *who/whom* to refer to people; use *that* and *which* to refer to animals, objects, and ideas.

EXERCISE **16.6**

Correct the 15 errors in the following paragraph. Part of the challenge in this Mastery Test is to make the paragraph not only grammatically correct but also free of sexist language. Before you try the test, we suggest that you review the rules for pronoun–antecedent agreement in the "Summary" box above.

Anyone that drives in Canada knows that, in the springtime, they take his or her lives in their hands when they go too fast along our roads. A driver that ventures out after the spring thaw will encounter moon-crater-sized potholes which will loosen every joint in their car. Our roads are a challenge to any car owner, no matter how new or powerful theirs may be. Maybe no one in their right mind will agree with me, but I think potholes are a government plot to reduce greenhouse gas emissions.

Road engineers, which are paid by the government, design faults into the roads, knowing that the frost will attack these flaws and create enormous potholes. The potholes deter a driver from using their car, forcing them to consider mass transit, cycling, or walking in order to protect the huge investment which they have in their automobile. I believe that this subtle plan is our government's way of trying to meet their international commitments to reduce carbon dioxide emissions.

17 Maintaining Person Agreement

So far, we have focused on using pronouns correctly and clearly within a sentence. Now let's turn to the problem of **person agreement**, which means using pronouns consistently throughout a sentence, a paragraph, or an essay. There are three categories of person that we use when we write or speak:

	Singular	Plural
First person	I; me	we; us
Second person	you	you
Third person	she, he, it, one; her, him *and all pronouns ending in* -one, -body, -thing	they; them

Here is the rule for person agreement.

Do not mix "persons" unless meaning requires it.

In other words, be consistent. If you begin a sentence (or a paragraph, or an essay) using a second-person pronoun, you should use the second person all the way through. Look at this sentence:

If *you* wish to succeed, *one* must work hard.

This is the most common error—mixing second-person *you* with third-person *one.* Sometimes mixed pronouns can confuse or mislead the reader, as in this sentence:

Everyone must shower when you go into the pool.

Most of the time, however, lack of agreement among pronouns is just poor style, as this example illustrates:

One can live happily in Vancouver if *you* have a sturdy umbrella.

We can correct this error by using the second person throughout:

(1) *You* can live happily in Vancouver if *you* have a sturdy umbrella.

We can also correct it by using the third person throughout:

(2) *One* can live happily in Vancouver if *one* has a sturdy umbrella.

or

(3) *One* can live happily in Vancouver if *he or she* has a sturdy umbrella.

These last three sentences raise two points of style that you should consider.

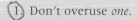 1. Don't overuse *one.*

All three revised sentences are grammatically correct, but they make different impressions on the reader, and impressions are an important part of communication.

- The first sentence, in the second person, sounds the most informal—like something you would say. It's a bit casual for general writing purposes.
- The second sentence, which uses *one* twice, sounds the most formal—even a little pretentious.
- The third sentence falls between the other two in formality. It is the one you'd be most likely to use in writing for school or business.

Although it is grammatically correct and nonsexist, this third sentence raises another problem. Frequent use of *he or she* in a continuous prose passage, whether that passage is as short as a paragraph or as long as a paper, is guaranteed to irritate your reader.

2. Don't overuse *he or she*.

He or she is inclusive, but it is a wordy construction. If used too frequently, the reader cannot help shifting focus from what you're saying to how you're saying it. The best writing is transparent—that is, it doesn't call attention to itself. If your reader becomes distracted by your style, your meaning is lost. Consider this sentence:

> A student can easily pass this course if he or she applies himself or herself to his or her studies.

Readers deserve better. A paper—or even a single paragraph—filled with this clumsy construction will annoy the most patient reader. There are two better solutions to this problem, and they are already familiar to you because they are the same as those for making pronouns ending in *-one*, *-body*, or *-thing* agree with their antecedents.

- You can change the whole sentence to the plural.

> Students can easily pass this course if they apply themselves to their studies.

- You can rewrite the sentence without using pronouns.

> A student can easily pass this course by applying good study habits.

EXERCISE **17.1**

Select the most appropriate word(s) from the choices given in parentheses. Answers for exercises in this chapter begin on page 419.

1. One should not annoy the instructor if (~~you want~~/one wants) to pass the course.

2. If you are looking for cheap shoes, (~~one~~/you) can get a pair at the bowling alley for only two dollars.

3. Any man will be irresistible if (he/~~she/one~~) uses the new L'Homme cologne.

4. (~~One~~/You) should never challenge Professor Snapes because he becomes nasty and sarcastic, and you don't want that to happen.

5. Too late, we realized the test would have been easy if (~~one/you~~/we) had done (~~their/your~~/our) homework during the term.

6. When we came out of the bush, (~~one/you~~/we) discovered that our guide had taken our Jeep and left (~~one/you~~/us) stranded.

7. Even worse, he had also taken our lunch, so (~~one/you~~/we) (~~was~~/were) both stranded and starving.

8. After wasting a few minutes' energy cursing and swearing, we started trekking back to the highway, where (~~one/you~~/we) were lucky enough to get a lift into town.

9. The driver who had given us a ride kindly dropped (~~one/you~~/us) off in the centre of town, right in front of the local pub, where (~~one's~~/our/~~your~~) guide had parked the Jeep and was inside enjoying our lunch and a few beers with his buddies.

10. This story has a happy ending—for (~~him/one~~/us). After (~~one~~/we) had settled our account, that guide was in no shape to take city slickers hiking in the bush for a very long time.

EXERCISE **17.2**

Correct the errors in pronoun consistency in the following sentences.

1. A speed limit is the speed you go as soon as ~~one~~ see**s** a police car. *(you)*

2. People who don't learn from history are doomed to find ~~yourself~~ back in Grade 9 for a second try. *(them)*

3. If we think we can't learn these rules, then ~~you~~'re not really trying to grasp them. *(we)*

4. If you are convicted on that charge, a fine is the least of ~~one's~~ worries. *(your)*

5. After we had driven almost four hours, it became difficult to keep ~~your~~ eyes open. *(our)*

6. One cannot lead any farther than ~~you have~~ already gone. *(one has)*

7. The penalties for plagiarism are severe, but most of us don't think about the consequences of ~~y~~our actions until ~~you~~ *we* 've been caught.

8. "Middle age is that time of life when you've met so many people that everyone ~~one~~ *you* meets reminds ~~one~~ *you* of somebody else." (Ogden Nash)

9. "Never try to impress a woman, because if one does, she'll expect you to keep up that standard for the rest of ~~their~~ *your* life." (W.C. Fields)

10. Many people are happy to ride with ~~one~~ *you* in the limo, but what you want is someone who will take the bus with us when the limo breaks down.

GO TO WEB
EXERCISE 17.1

WWW.BAREA.NELSON.COM

EXERCISE **17.3**

Correct the following sentences where necessary. For those sentences containing language that might be considered sexist, try correcting them twice: first, to ensure person agreement; second, to avoid gender bias. Turn to page 420 to compare your answers with our suggestions.

1. It has taken Canadians far too long to acknowledge the seriousness of your environmental problems.

2. No one tests the depth of a river with both of their feet. (Ashanti proverb)

3. If you can't cope with the pressure, one must expect to be replaced by someone who can.

4. If any of you are planning to attend the class party next Friday, their tickets are now available in the Student Association office.

5. Some people are like Slinkies: they have no useful purpose, but you can't help but smile when one sees them tumble down the stairs.

6. When they feel frustrated or angry, it can sometimes be difficult for a teenager to control his temper.

7. "Good health" is nothing more than the slowest rate at which he or she can die.

8. In the '60s, some people took LSD to make the world seem weird; now the world *is* weird, and you take Prozac to make it seem normal.

9. When taking multiple-choice tests, don't stop and think about questions you aren't sure of. Finish the test and then to back to the questions that stumped one.

10. When you're gardening, the best way to make sure one is removing a weed and not a valuable plant is to grasp it firmly at the base of the stem and pull. If it comes out easily, it is a valuable plant.

EXERCISE **17.4**

Rewrite the following paragraphs, changing the 25 third-person pronouns to second-person pronouns and correcting any verb errors that result from your revisions.

How can one fight the common cold? If one had the energy to research the subject, he or she would find books, videos, and thousands of articles in newspapers and magazines advising one how to cope with a cold. A cold cannot be prevented or cured since it is not known what organism actually causes it. However, one's research will not be wasted: one will find no shortage of folk remedies and "personally guaranteed" cures, most of which do nothing more than make one feel better while he or she waits for the cold to go away. Advertisements for pharmaceutical companies promise their pills, syrups, lozenges, and capsules will relieve one's symptoms, but no one claims to offer a cure.

There is something strangely comforting in this fact. Since the only thing one can do for a cold is wait for it to go away, one need not waste time visiting a doctor or seeking a miraculous remedy. One might as well relax, spend a day or two indulging himself or herself snuggled up in bed, and enjoy whatever restorative one finds most to his or her liking. One might discover, for example, that chicken soup is his or her treatment of choice. Or one might prefer hot tea with brown sugar and lemon.

Whatever one's preferred treatment, one should indulge and enjoy oneself! This is one of the few times in one's life when he or she can pamper himself or herself not just without guilt but also in the knowledge that self-indulgence is good for one.

EXERCISE **17.5**

Rewrite the paragraph in Exercise 17.4 by changing the pronouns from third-person singular to third-person plural throughout. Your first two sentences will read "How can people fight the common cold? If they had the energy to research the subject, they would find. . . ."

EXERCISE **17.6**

Find and correct the inconsistencies in pronoun person in the following paragraph. Revise the paragraph twice: (1) once in the second person and (2) once in the third person. Then compare your two revisions. Which version do you prefer? Why?

If one is a sports fan, you are already familiar with the astronomical salaries major players make. We fans sometimes lose sight of the fact that our favourite players live in the real world, and their salaries are sometimes out of touch with real life, at least as most people live it. You may be aware, for example, that all-time-favourite basketball player Michael Jordan made nearly $200,000 per day in the last year of his contract. If we compare Jordan's salary with the incomes of other famous people, however, one finds some interesting numbers. For instance, you learn that, in his last year in professional basketball, Jordan earned 200 percent more than the total income of all the presidents of the United States, from George Washington to George W. Bush, *combined*. If we do a little more research, we also discover that, if Jordan were to save and invest all of his income for 250 years, he would accumulate less money than Bill Gates has now.

GO TO WEB
EXERCISE 17.2

WWW.BAREA.NELSON.COM

EXERCISE **17.7**

Find and correct the inconsistencies in pronoun person in the following.

1. I enjoy living in a home without air conditioning because you can leave the windows open in the summer and enjoy the sounds of nature.

2. A sure way to lose all of one's friends is to eat all the popcorn yourself.

3. People always seem to want what they don't have, and have what one doesn't really need.

4. When we walked into the room after our performance, the applause was enough to make you blush.

5. When you are dyeing your hair, be sure to start at the roots and work one's way to the ends.

6. "Most men commit great crimes only because of his scruples about petty ones." (Cardinal de Retz)

7. Any member of the team who played during the championship game must line up in the foyer to get your photo taken by the newspaper.

8. Each participant will get an egg, some straws, a section of newspaper, and a roll of tape; your task is to make a vehicle for the egg that will allow it to drop unbroken from a height of two metres.

9. The emotional turmoil that results from breast cancer can affect a woman's physical health as well as their psychological well-being.

10. I can hardly believe this unit is almost finished. Sometimes one gets so tired of grammar that you want to give up.

UNIT 3 RAPID REVIEW

The passage below contains a total of 15 errors in verb form, subject–verb agreement, pronoun form, pronoun–antecedent agreement, and tense and pronoun consistency. When you've made your corrections, turn to page 422 and compare your answers with ours. For each error you miss, the "Answer Key" directs you to the chapter you need to review.

[1]A professor at our college ~~begun~~ *began* the last week of term by giving a demonstration to her Business Administration students. [2]For 15 weeks, she had spoken about the need for balance in life, but she felt that she had not yet gotten her message across. [3]She suspected that most of the students that sat before her ~~was~~ *were* still primarily focused on money and career advancement. [4]"People in business," she began, "sometimes have a hard time remembering ~~one's~~ *their* true priorities." [5]She placed a large glass jar on the desk and ~~fills~~ *filled* it with golf balls and asked the students if the jar was full. [6]~~Each~~ *All* of the students nodded their heads. [7]She then ~~pours~~ *poured* pebbles into the jar, which filled up the spaces around the golf balls. [8]"Is it full now?" she asked. [9]~~Everyone~~ *All the students* laughed and said that they thought it was full. [10]Then sand was poured into the jar by the professor, filling ~~it~~ *the jar* to the brim. [11]Everyone ~~that~~ *who* was watching agreed that the jar was now full. [12]Then the professor poured two cups of coffee into the jar. [13]She brought the demonstration to a close with this explanation. [14]"The golf balls represents the important things in your life: health, family, and rela-

tionships. [15]The pebbles are the less important things such as jobs, hobbies,

cars, and houses. [16]And the sand ~~is~~ *are* the small, unimportant stuff. [17]If I had

filled the jar with sand, there wouldn't have been room for anything else.

[18]The same thing is true in life: if you fill your life with small stuff, ~~we'll~~ *you'll* have

no room for the important things. [19]Take care of the important things first;

there is always room for the small stuff."

[20]One student asked what the coffee represents. [21]"No matter how full your

life may seem," the professor replied with a smile, "there's always room for a

cup of coffee with a friend!"

UNIT 4

Punctuation

Punctuation

UNIT 4 QUICK QUIZ

This Quick Quiz will let you see at a glance which chapters of Unit 4 you need to concentrate on. In the paragraph below, 15 punctuation marks are missing. Go through the paragraph carefully and supply the missing punctuation. (Note: Each pair of quotation marks counts as one punctuation mark.) When you've finished your corrections, turn to page 423 and compare your answers with ours. For each error you miss, the Answer Key that follows the corrected version directs you to the chapter you need to work on.

[1]As a woman was leaving a convenience store a man grabbed her purse and ran. [2]Help she cried. [3]The store clerk thinking quickly called 911, the police arrived in minutes. [4]The woman was able to give a clear description of the thief, a small man with bleached blond hair wearing a green leather jacket baggy denims and old canvas running shoes. [5]Within minutes the police captured a man answering this description. [6]Could there be any doubt. [7]He was asked to stand in front of the woman for a positive identification. [8]Yes, officer said the young man, that's her. [9]That's the lady I stole the purse from.

SHE HAD LEFT OUT THE COMMAS THAT ARE NEEDED TO SEPARATE WORDS PHRASES OR CLAUSES IN A LIST.

SMALL THINGS LIKE DIAMONDS, COMPUTER CHIPS, AND COMMAS CAN, IN SOME CASES, BE IMPORTANT.

The Comma 18

Many writers-in-training tend to sprinkle punctuation over their pages like pepper. Do not use punctuation to spice up or decorate your writing. Punctuation marks are functional: they indicate to the reader how the various parts of a sentence relate to one another. By changing the punctuation, you can change the meaning of a sentence. Here are two examples to prove the point.

1. An instructor wrote the following sentence on the board and asked the class to punctuate it appropriately: "woman without her man is nothing."

The men wrote, "Woman, without her man, is nothing."
The women wrote, "Woman! Without her, man is nothing."

2. Now it's your turn. Punctuate this sentence: "I think there is only one person to blame myself."

If you wrote, "I think there is only one person to blame, myself" the reader will understand that you believe only one person—who may or may not be known to you—is to blame.

If you wrote, "I think there is only one person to blame: myself" the reader will understand that you are personally accepting responsibility for the blame.

The comma is the most frequently used—and misused—punctuation mark in English. Perhaps nothing is as sure a sign of a competent writer as the correct use of commas. This chapter presents four comma rules that cover most situations in which commas are required. If you apply these four rules faithfully, your reader will never be confused by missing or misplaced commas in your writing. And if, as occasionally happens, the sentence you are writing is not covered by one of our four rules, remember the first commandment of comma usage: WHEN IN DOUBT, LEAVE IT OUT.

FOUR COMMA RULES

RULE 1

Use commas to separate three or more items in a series. The items may be expressed as words, phrases, or clauses.

Words	The required subjects in this program are math, physics, and English.
Phrases	"Punctuation marks are the traffic signals of prose: they tell us to slow down, notice this, take a detour, and stop." (Lynne Truss)
Clauses	The wedding was delayed an hour because the groom was hung over, the best man had forgotten the ring, and the bride was in tears.

The comma before the *and* at the end of the list is optional, but we advise you to use it. Occasionally, misunderstandings occur if it is left out.

EXERCISE **18.1**

Insert commas where necessary in the following sentences, and then check your answers on page 423.

1. Does anyone remember Scary, Baby, Ginger, Posh, and Sporty?
2. A panda is a bearlike, marsupial that eats shoots, and leaves.

3. In the typical Hollywood B Western, the villain rides into town ,and eats ,shoots ,and leaves.

4. Macdonald ,Laurier ,Borden, and Pearson were four dissimilar men, who had one thing in common.

5. Arnold is an all-round athlete; he enjoys skiing ,cycling ,swimming, and showering.

6. Nicole has strong ambition a cool head ,good health ,and an inquiring mind; everyone hates her.

7. Chicken Kiev, pork tenderloin ,with prune stuffing rack of lamb with rosemary ,and garlic ,and baked tofu au gratin were our choices for the banquet menu.

8. A good education ,long-range planning, and pure luck led him to wealth ,acclaim ,and happiness.

9. Much of the world sees Canada as a land where French is spoken, ice ,and snow are year-round hazards ,and violent hockey is a favourite pastime.

10. In fluent English ,and Italian, our tour guide described the construction of Notre Dame Cathedral, explained the causes of the French Revolution ,and listed the ingredients in bouillabaisse.

The second comma rule is already familiar to you. You encountered it in Chapter 8, "Solving Run-On Sentence Problems."

RULE 2

Put a comma between independent clauses when they are joined by

for	but	so
and	or	
nor	yet	

(You can remember these words easily if you notice that their first letters spell "fanboys.")

I hope I do well in the interview, for I really want this job.

I like Feist, but I prefer Norah Jones.

"We shape our tools, and our tools shape us." (Marshall McLuhan)

I knew I was going to be late, so I went back to sleep.

Be sure that the sentence you are punctuating contains two independent clauses rather than one clause with a single subject and a multiple verb.

We loved the book but hated the movie.
(We is the subject, and there are two verbs, *loved* and *hated*. Do not put a comma between two or more verbs that share a single subject.)

We both loved the book, but Kim hated the movie.
(This sentence contains two independent clauses — *We loved* and *Kim hated* — joined by *but*. The comma is required here.)

EXERCISE **18.2**

Insert commas where they are needed in the following sentences. Check your answers when you're done.

1. Pierre and I are good friends, yet we often disagree.
2. I wonder why the sun lightens our hair, but darkens our skin.
3. Noah had the last two of every creature on his ark, yet he didn't swat those mosquitoes.
4. Money can't buy happiness, but it makes misery easier to live with.
5. *Con* is the opposite of *pro*, so Congress must be the opposite of progress.
6. Canada and the United States have a complex relationship that is characterized by ignorance, on one side and apprehension on the other.
7. Flying may be the safest form of transportation, but why is the place where planes land called a "terminal"?
8. Pack an extra jacket or sweater, for evenings in September can be cold.
9. The phone hasn't worked for days, and the television has been broken for a month, but I haven't missed either of them.
10. Please pay close attention for the instructions are a little complicated, and failure to follow the process precisely can result in disaster.

RULE 3

Put a comma after an introductory word, phrase, or dependent clause that comes before an independent clause.

Rob, you aren't paying attention.

Exhausted and cranky from staying up all night, I staggered into class.

No matter how hard I try, I will never forget you.

If that's their idea of a large pizza, we'd better order two.

Until she got her promotion, she was quite friendly.

EXERCISE **18.3**

Insert commas where they are needed in the following sentences. Check your answers when you have finished all 10.

1. First, we need to understand what an independent clause is.
2. In the end we will be judged by how much happiness we have given others.
3. "Unless I get my husband's money pretty soon, I will be forced to live an immortal life." (From an application for government assistance)
4. According to company policy, you may not personally collect Air Mile points accumulated on business-related travel.
5. If you live by the calendar, your days are numbered.
6. According to my stomach, lunch time came and went about an hour ago.
7. In most newspaper and magazine advertisements, the time shown on a watch is 10:10.
8. Even if a mixed metaphor sings, it should be stifled.
9. As her 40th birthday approached, Stella met the challenge by trading in her minivan for a sports car and one boyfriend for another who is 20 years her junior.
10. When the first robin heralds the return of spring, I begin to dream of lazy summer days beside the pool, with a cool drink in my hand and a ball game on the radio.

RULE 4
Use commas to set off any word, phrase, or dependent clause that is NOT ESSENTIAL to the main idea of the sentence.

Following this rule can make the difference between your readers' understanding and misunderstanding of what you write. For example, the following two sentences are identical, except for a pair of commas. But notice what a difference those two tiny marks make to meaning:

The children who were dressed in Halloween costumes had ice cream.
(Only the children wearing costumes ate ice cream.)

The children, who were dressed in Halloween costumes, had ice cream.
(All of the children wore costumes and had ice cream.)

To test whether a word, phrase, or clause is essential to the meaning of your sentence, mentally put parentheses around it. If the sentence still makes complete sense (i.e., the main idea is unchanged; the sentence just delivers less information), the material in parentheses is *not essential* and should be set off from the rest of the sentence by a comma or commas.

Nonessential information can appear at the beginning of a sentence,[1] in the middle, or at the end of a sentence. Study the following examples.

Alice Munro (one of Canada's best-known novelists) spends the summer in Clinton and the winter in Comox.

Most readers would be puzzled the first time they read this sentence because all of the information is presented without punctuation, so the reader assumes it is all equally important. In fact, the material in broken parentheses is extra information, a supplementary detail. It can be deleted without changing the sentence's meaning, and so it should be separated from the rest of the sentence by commas:

Alice Munro, one of Canada's best-known novelists, spends the summer in Clinton and the winter in Comox.

Here's another example to consider:

The Queen (who has twice as many birthdays as anyone else) officially celebrates her birthday on May 24.

Again, the sentence is hard to read. You can't count on your readers to go back and re-read every sentence they don't understand at first glance. As a writer, your responsibility is to give readers the clues they need as to what is crucial information and what isn't. In the example above, the information in broken parentheses is not essential to the meaning of the sentence, so it should be set off by commas:

The Queen, who has twice as many birthdays as anyone else, officially celebrates her birthday on May 24.

---

[1] Rule 3 covers nonessential information at the beginning of a sentence.

In this next sentence, the nonessential information comes at the end.

Writing a good letter of application isn't difficult (if you're careful).

The phrase "if you're careful" is not essential to the main idea, so it should be separated from the rest of the sentence by a comma:

Writing a good letter of application isn't difficult, if you're careful.

And finally, consider this sentence:

Writing a letter of application (that is clear, complete, and concise) is a challenge.

If you take out "that is clear, complete, and concise," you change the meaning of the sentence. Not all letters of application are a challenge to write. Writing vague and wordy letters is easy; anyone can do it. The words "that is clear, complete, and concise" are essential to the meaning of the sentence, and so they are not set off by commas.

Writing a letter of application that is clear, complete, and concise is a challenge.

Insert commas where they are missing in the following sentences. Check your answers on pages 424–425.

1. Commas like capitals are clues to meaning.
2. Our hope of course is that the thieves will be caught and punished.
3. Our adventure began in Barcelona which is the site of a famous unfinished cathedral designed by Gaudi.
4. Gaudi who was killed by a bus in his 50s began the cathedral as an atonement for the sins of mankind.
5. An opportunist is someone who goes ahead and does what the rest of us wish we had the courage to do.
6. A compliment like a good perfume should be pleasing but not overpowering.
7. Trevor's job requires largely but not exclusively that he be available 24 hours a day to clean up any of senior management's mistakes.
8. Anyone who arrives during the early weeks of August will have to get acclimatized to the overwhelming heat and humidity before trying to do anything productive.

Punctuation

9. One of our most experienced salespeople suggested to our surprise that we concentrate on making a better product, instead of spending millions to persuade people to buy our current line.

10. The new office manager, now in her second month at the job has made many changes to our procedures not all of them welcome.

The rest of the exercises in this chapter require you to apply all four comma rules. Before you begin, write the four rules on a sheet of paper and keep the sheet in front of you as you work through the exercises. Refer to the four rules frequently as you punctuate the sentences that follow. After you've finished each exercise, check your answers and make sure you understand any mistakes you make.

EXERCISE **18.5**

1. All power corrupts, but we need electricity.
2. In January, the birds compete with the chipmunks over control of our backyard feeder.
3. No words in the English language, rhyme with month, orange, silver, and purple.
4. My scanner, which is less than a year old, cannot reproduce a 20 dollar bill.
5. "Our Superstore is unrivalled in size, unmatched in variety, and unparalleled inconvenience." (Sign posted at a "big box" store opening)
6. The train would not get us to Saskatoon, until after 8:00 p.m. so we decided to take the bus.
7. Unless the union intervenes, tomorrow will be her last day on the job.
8. Early diagnosis often the key to successful treatment, is responsible for his recovery.
9. Yield to temptation, for it may not pass your way again.
10. Cleverly disguised as a fountain pen, the camera recorded the entire conversation.

EXERCISE **18.6**

In this exercise, after you have punctuated each sentence, identify the rule(s) you applied. For example:

On Tuesday I go to the dentist.

On Tuesday, I go to the dentist. **(Rule 3)**

1. There is something wrong with this proposal, but I haven't yet figured out what it is.
2. George Washington, the first president of the United States was an officer in the British army before the American Revolution.
3. While I respect your opinion, and your right to express it, I disagree with everything you say.
4. "Politics is the art of looking for trouble, finding it, misdiagnosing it, and then misapplying the wrong remedies." (Groucho Marx)
5. Did you know that pound for pound, the amoeba is the most vicious animal on earth?
6. This department cannot support your proposal, nor can we recommend that any other department provide funding.
7. The word *allegro*, thought by some to be a type of leg fertilizer, is actually a musical notation meaning "lively" or "quick."
8. Further to your letter of last week, our personnel director will be pleased to meet with you on Thursday, but she can spare only 10 minutes for the meeting.
9. The best feature of this book a compact, concise, and clever guide to grammar is its convenient spiral binding.
10. Charlottetown Quebec, and Kingston were the sites of the conferences that eventually led to Confederation the birth of our nation in 1867.

GO TO WEB
EXERCISE 18.1

WWW.BAREA.NELSON.COM

EXERCISE **18.7**

Insert the 15 commas that are missing in the following paragraph.

John Robert Colombo tells this story about Conrad Black the discredited media tycoon and his wife columnist Barbara Amiel. Long before Black was disgraced tried and convicted for defrauding investors the couple was invited for dinner by Cardinal Carter the Roman Catholic Archbishop of Toronto. Unfortunately they were late in arriving and Cardinal Carter expressed his displeasure. He told them that when he dined with Pope John Paul II the pope never kept him waiting. Black who was well known for his haughty demeanour refusal to accept blame and quick wit replied instantly. "Your Eminence that is because he does not have a wife."

GO TO WEB
EXERCISE 18.2

WWW.BAREA.NELSON.COM

EXERCISE **18.8**

Insert the 20 commas that are missing in the following paragraph.

As long as you are prepared and confident you'll find that an employment interview need not be a terrifying experience. Some people believe it or not actually enjoy employment interviews and attend them with enthusiasm. Most of us however are intimidated by the prospect of being interrogated by an interviewer or even worse a team of interviewers. To prepare for an interview the first thing you should do is to find out as much as you can about the company. Among the things you need to know are the title of the job you are applying for approximately how much it pays the name of the person or persons who will conduct the interview the address of the company how long it will take you to get there and the location of the washrooms. Employment consultants usually recommend that you make an advance visit to the office of the firm to which you've applied in order to confirm how long it takes to get there and where the interview room is. While on your scouting mission you can learn valuable information about the company's working conditions employee attitudes and even dress code. On the day of the interview be sure to show up 10 or 15 minutes in advance of your scheduled appointment. When the interviewer greets you you should do three things: memorize his or her name identify yourself and extend your hand. Your handshake should be brief and firm not limply passive or bone-crushingly aggressive. Practise! Now all you have to do is relax and enjoy the interview.

WWW.BAREA.NELSON.COM

SUMMARY

THE FOUR COMMA RULES

1. Use commas to separate items in a series of three or more. The items may be expressed as words, phrases, or clauses.
2. Put a comma between independent clauses when they are joined by *for, and, nor, but, or, yet,* or *so*.
3. Put a comma after an introductory word, phrase, or dependent clause that comes before an independent clause.
4. Use commas to set off a word, phrase, or dependent clause that is NOT ESSENTIAL to the main idea of the sentence.

EXERCISE **18.9**

Insert commas where they are needed in the following sentences.

1. To me a night at the opera means watching a play I don't like which is sung in a language I don't understand and wearing a suit that doesn't fit.

2. Starting a small business while full of risks has become a realistic option for many young people as an alternative to trying to find a job when they have no experience.

3. Nowadays we can watch television in our cars on our phones and through our computers.

Punctuation

4. When the nurse calls your name identify yourself right away because nurses have better things to do than wait around for you.

5. Naturally she knows a better way to do it and she's only too willing to tell the rest of us what it is.

6. The best way to get a child to wear something she loathes aside from resorting to bribery or threats is to pretend you loathe it even more than she does.

7. Remember computers can't think for themselves so in at least one respect they're just like every other worker in this office.

8. Just think if Shakespeare had used a computer he might have accidentally erased *King Lear* thus bringing joy to the hearts of the thousands of high-school students forced to study it each year.

9. According to cowboy philosopher Will Rogers if there was ever a time to save money it's now: "When you give a dog a bone he doesn't go out and make the first payment on a bigger bone; he buries the one he's got."

10. Finally emphasizing principally but not exclusively the political social geographic architectural and historical aspects of warfare in Europe the Middle East and Asia trace the impact of gunpowder from its invention to the present day. You have 20 minutes. (*Tip*: This monster requires 10 commas.)

THE UN-GRAMMATICALS WERE BECOMING DESPERATE, THEY HAD NO IDEA WHERE OR WHEN TO USE A SEMICOLON.

The Semicolon | 19

The semicolon and the colon are often confused and used as if they were interchangeable. They have distinct purposes, however, and their correct use can dramatically improve a reader's understanding of your writing. The semicolon has three functions.

1. A semicolon can replace a period; in other words, it can appear between two independent clauses.

You should use a semicolon when the two clauses (sentences) you are joining are closely connected in meaning, or when there is a cause-and-effect relationship between them.

I'm too tired; I can't stay awake any longer.

Montreal is not the city's original name; it was once called Ville Marie.

A period could have been used instead of a semicolon in either of these sentences, but the close connection between the clauses makes a semicolon more effective in communicating the writer's meaning.

2. Certain transitional words or phrases can be put between independent clauses to show a cause-and-effect relationship or the continuation of an idea.

Words or phrases used in this way are usually preceded by a semicolon and followed by a comma:

; also,	; furthermore,	; nevertheless,
; as a result,	; however,	; on the other hand,
; besides,	; in addition,	; otherwise,
; consequently,	; in fact,	; then,
; finally,	; instead,	; therefore,
; for example,	; moreover,	; thus,

The forecast called for sun; instead, we got snow.

My monitor went blank; nevertheless, I kept on typing.

"I'm not offended by dumb blonde jokes because I know I'm not dumb; besides, I also know I'm not blonde." (Dolly Parton)

In other words, *a semicolon* + *a transitional word/phrase* + *a comma* = a link strong enough to come between two related independent clauses.

Note, however, that, when transitional words and phrases are used as nonessential expressions rather than as connecting words, they are separated from the rest of the sentence by commas (Chapter 18, Rule 4, page 219).

I just can't seem to master particle physics, however hard I try.

The emissions test, moreover, will ensure that your car is running well.

3. To make a COMPLEX LIST easier to read and understand, put semicolons between the items instead of commas.

A complex list is one in which at least one component part already contains commas. Here are two examples:

I grew up in a series of small towns: Cumberland, British Columbia; Red Deer, Alberta; and Timmins, Ontario.

When we opened the refrigerator, we found a limp, brown head of lettuce; two small containers of yogurt, whose "best before" dates had long since passed; and a hard, dried-up piece of cheddar cheese.

EXERCISE **19.1**

Put a check mark (✓) before the sentences that are correctly punctuated. Answers for exercises in this chapter begin on page 426.

1. __✓__ Your paper was due last week; I cannot accept it now.

2. __✗__ I need to replace my computer because it continually freezes.

3. _____ It's a beautiful day, perfect for a long walk.

4. __✓__ We reached the campsite in time to meet the others; in fact, we arrived a little ahead of time.

5. _____ I do not approve of political jokes, because I've seen too many of them get elected.

6. __✓__ Six of the First Nations bands joined together in a loose confederacy; they were called *Iroquois*.

7. _____ The lawn, a little ragged after all the rain, needs to be cut, the hedge, shrubs, and ivy need to be trimmed, the roses need to be pruned, and, most important, the gardener needs to be paid.

8. _____ The label on the bag of potato chips proclaimed, "You could be a winner! No purchase is necessary, details are inside."

9. __✓__ I think animal testing is wrong; the animals get terribly nervous and give the wrong answers.

10. _____ Here are the twins, looking adorable, their parents, who look in need of a good night's sleep, their baby-sitter, who appears to be on the verge of a nervous breakdown, and the family's four pet Schnauzers.

EXERCISE **19.2**

Correct the faulty punctuation in Exercise 19.1.

EXERCISE **19.3**

Put a check mark before the following sentences that are correctly punctuated.

1. _____ If life deals you a handful of lemons; make lemonade.

2. _____ Sadly, the swimming pool was closed; however, the hot tub was working just fine.

3. _✓_ The price of coffee is outrageous, yet that doesn't prevent me from having my morning cup or three.

4. _____ Our vacation in Europe was a huge success; except for Euro-Disney, which was a major disappointment.

5. _✓_ Krystal is always late; however, she is worth waiting for.

6. _____ She made herself feel better by shopping for new shoes; a guaranteed strategy for chasing the blues.

7. _____ Cookie pieces have no calories; because all the calories leak out when the cookie is broken.

8. _____ Some people are skilled in many fields; Kumari, for example, is both a good plumber and a great cook.

9. _____ The weather is terrible, as it has been all month; I have a head cold that is making me miserable; the power has been out for several hours; so I can't cook; and, to top it all off, my in-laws are arriving for dinner in about an hour.

10. _✓_ Keep this book on your desk; that way, you can easily refer to it when you need to check how or where to use semicolons.

EXERCISE **19.4**

Correct the faulty punctuation in Exercise 19.3.

EXERCISE **19.5**

Correct the following sentences by changing commas to semicolons where necessary.

1. I can't afford a Porsche, therefore, I drive a Focus.

2. Sometimes I stare at the blank page in front of me for hours, waiting for inspiration, it's very discouraging.

3. On my shopping list are carrots and onions for the stew, rhubarb and strawberries for the pie, Parmesan cheese, which Paula likes to grate over the salad, and espresso coffee to have after the meal.

4. I'm reading a fascinating book on levitation, I just can't seem to put it down.

5. The fact is I already have a boyfriend, however, don't let that stop you from worshipping me from afar.

6. Please turn off your cellphone, you will be asked to leave the room if it rings during class.

7. Newfoundland and Labrador is Canada's newest province, actually, it was known as Newfoundland until 2004, when the full name was officially recognized.

8. I love Michael Moore's films, however, I recognize that he presents a one-sided view of political issues.

9. When it comes to office politics, it's best to avoid being distracted by unproductive or irrelevant conflicts, I find that reading the comic strip *Dilbert* is a great help.

10. "For the physics section of your exam, explain the nature of matter, include in your answer an evaluation of the impact of the development of mathematics on the study of science." (From "The *Final* Exam")

GO TO WEB
EXERCISE 19.1

WWW.BAREA.NELSON.COM

EXERCISE **19.6**

Insert commas and semicolons where necessary in the following sentences. Then check your answers carefully.

1. Turn left when you come to the fork in the road otherwise you will end up at the nuclear waste-disposal site and come out all aglow.

2. Watch your pennies the government will take care of your dollars.

Punctuation

3. As gasoline prices continue to rise hybrid cars make more and more sense the problem is their high initial purchase price.

4. If you can afford one however it will pay for itself in gas savings over the life of the vehicle in fact my calculations indicate that a hybrid will save me money after only three years.

5. The Lord's Prayer is 66 words long the Gettysburg address is 286 words the Declaration of Independence is 1,322 words but U.S. government regulations on the sale of cabbage total 26,911 words.

6. When I am tired I listen to classic rock 'n' roll because it energizes me however when I am working at home nothing stimulates my creativity like Mozart.

7. I am nobody and nobody is perfect therefore I must be perfect.

8. "From the moment I picked up your book until I put it down I was convulsed with laughter someday I intend to read it." (Groucho Marx)

9. Buying a house involves enormous responsibilities not to mention enormous debt consequently I plan to live with my parents until I find a wealthy woman with her own home.

10. I'm sure you understand that I would like nothing better than for you to pass this course however there may be a small fee involved.

EXERCISE **19.7**

Correct the faulty punctuation in these sentences.

1. I saw Elvis, he sat right between the Sasquatch and me on the UFO.

2. There are only 190 shopping days left until my next birthday that's barely enough time to plan the enormous party and select an appropriate gift.

3. My new office chair was supposed to have been custom-fitted however when I sat down I quickly discovered that it had been custom-fitted for someone else.

4. When we skied silently through the north woods we saw the tracks of a lynx that was stalking a snowshoe rabbit we heard the cracking, groaning,

and sighing of the river as ice solidified on its surface and we felt the minus 40-degree-temperatures nipping at our noses and fingers.

5. One movie reviewer loved this movie another hated it and a third thought it was so-so however audiences flocked to it and made the producers very rich. Apparently, critics do not have as much influence as they like to think.

6. My pager beeped just as I was answering my cellphone. The pager message was my computer reminding me not to forget my girlfriend's birthday the phone call was from my answering service, telling me I had a message from my mother.

7. We're unhappy about our instructor's evaluation process, in fact we believe it is irrational arbitrary and unfair.

8. One of the products of the computer age was supposed to be increased leisure, however most of us are working longer hours and even taking our work into our cars homes and gardens.

9. I read a lot of books consequently I rarely watch television which is why I assumed my friends were talking about the evening news when they mentioned a "reality show."

10. Every year at tax time, I am faced with the same problem: assembling my bills and receipts, figuring out my gas consumption, trying to recall which expenses were business-related and which were personal, finding my T-4s, T-5s, and other T-forms, and organizing this mess so my accountant can attempt to keep me out of jail for another year.

EXERCISE **19.8**

All of the punctuation marks that appear in the following paragraph are correct; however, 15 punctuation marks are missing. Correct the paragraph by inserting commas and semicolons where they are needed.

A friend of mine had not been feeling very well for some time so he finally went to the doctor for a complete physical examination. After many tests and two more visits he was told to come back once more he was also asked to bring

Punctuation

his wife. When they arrived at the doctor's office the doctor asked the wife to wait outside while he examined her husband. After several minutes the husband emerged from the office and told his wife to go in the doctor wanted to see her alone. The doctor asked the wife to sit down, and then he told her that her husband was seriously ill. While she listened attentively, the doctor outlined what she must do to save her husband. The doctor revealed that stress was the cause of the husband's illness stress must be eliminated from his life. He must stop working immediately and stay at home. She would have to make sure he sat quietly in a comfortable chair while she brought him whatever he wanted. Even driving would be too stressful she would have to take him wherever he wanted to go. She would have to cook his favourite meals screen his telephone calls bring him snacks while he watched TV keep the children away from him, and cater to his every wish. The wife listened to these instructions with concern she left the office deep in thought. On the way home the husband finally asked her, "What did the doctor say, dear?"

She replied, "My dear, I'm so sorry unfortunately nothing can be done."

WWW.BAREA.NELSON.COM

EXERCISE **19.9**

Have you mastered the semicolon? Try this exercise and find out. Insert semicolons and commas as required, and change commas to semicolons and semicolons to commas where necessary in the following sentences.

1. Don't try to be irreplaceable, if you can't be replaced you can't be promoted.

2. Clothes it is said make the man, this must be true because naked people have little or no influence in society.

3. If it weren't for our pitching we would be in last place, our hitting is pathetic, our fielding is laughable; and our base-stealing is nonexistent.

4. The class began on time, however; it quickly became obvious to everyone that no one had done the assigned reading.

5. For some reason my parents are not as enthusiastic as I am about my plan to live at home until I have saved enough money for the apartment of my dreams, in fact they seem downright hostile.

6. A college diploma is a piece of paper that says this phase of your education is complete, now it's time to go out into the world and start paying for it.

7. The great thing about having dogs as pets is that; no matter what kind of day you've had, no matter how badly the world has treated you, when you come home you are greeted as if you were lord of the universe.

8. On my last trip to the French Riviera my Porsche broke down in the middle of Nice; I lost money in the casino at Monaco; and the fashion models who promised to meet me in Antibes never showed up, in short, the vacation was a complete disaster.

9. While making a long story short; saving the best to last; and talking a blue streak; Dennis bored us to tears with his cliché-filled tale of woe.

10. This department runs collaboratively; thanks to a manager who frequently consults before making decisions, staff who take responsibility for the company's success and seek to further the company's goals, and a front office based in Montreal that provides us with both freedom and support.

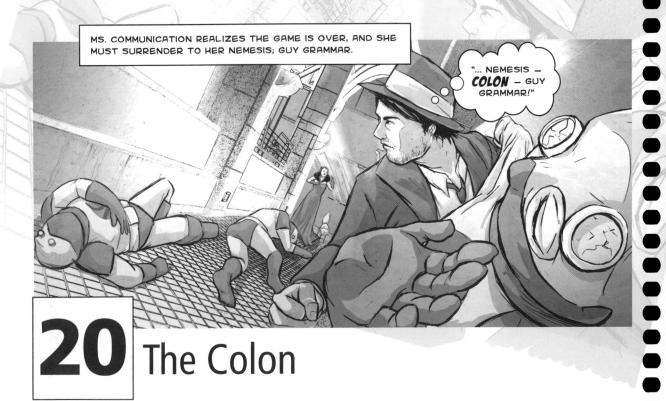

MS. COMMUNICATION REALIZES THE GAME IS OVER, AND SHE MUST SURRENDER TO HER NEMESIS; GUY GRAMMAR.

"... NEMESIS — *COLON* — GUY GRAMMAR!"

20 The Colon

The *colon* functions as an introducer. When a statement is followed by a list, one or more examples, or a quotation, the colon alerts the reader that some sort of explanatory detail is coming up.

When I travel, I am never without three things: sturdy shoes, a money belt, and my journal.

There is only one enemy we cannot defeat: time.

We have two choices: to study or to fail.

Early in his career, Robert Fulford did not think very highly of intellectual life in Canada: "My generation of Canadians grew up believing that, if we were very good or very smart, or both, we would someday *graduate* from Canada."

The statement that precedes the colon must be a complete sentence (independent clause).

A colon should never come immediately after *is* or *are.* Here's an example of what *not* to write.

The only things I am violently allergic to are: cats, ragweed, and country music.

This is incorrect because the statement before the colon is not a complete sentence.

Use a colon between an independent clause and a LIST or one or more EXAMPLES that define, explain, or illustrate the independent clause.

The information after the colon often answers the question "What?" or "Who?"

I am violently allergic to three things: (What?) cats, ragweed, and country music.

Business and industry face a new challenge: (What?) offshore outsourcing.

The president has found the ideal candidate for the position: (Who?) her brother.

Use a colon after a complete sentence introducing a quotation.

Maude Barlow of the Council of Canadians encouraged young people to vote: "If you want to know who is going to change this country, go home and look in the mirror."

Finally, use a colon to separate the title of a book, film, or television show from a subtitle.

Word Play: What Happens When People Talk

Ace Ventura: Pet Detective

Trading Spouses: Meet Your New Mommy

Punctuation

If you remember this summary, you'll have no more trouble with colons: the colon follows an independent clause and introduces an example, a list, or a quotation that amplifies the meaning of that clause.

EXERCISE 20.1

Put a check mark (✓) next to those sentences that are correctly punctuated. Answers for the exercises in this chapter begin on page 429.

1. _____ Two of the most common causes of failure are poor time management and inadequate preparation.

2. _____ We cannot write the report until we are given: accurate data.

3. _____ Our weekly grocery shopping always includes: pizza, pretzels, and pastries.

4. _____ The instructor's first words were not encouraging: "Half of you are going to fail this course."

5. _____ The essential characteristics of a good manager are: decisive leadership, clear communication, and meaningful consultation.

6. _____ There are three kinds of people: those who can count and those who can't.

7. _____ A shin is: a device for finding furniture in the dark.

8. _____ We are looking for a computer firm that can supply several important components; reliable hardware, adaptable software, and timely support.

9. _____ Let me give you an example, Joey Smallwood.

10. _____ In an effort to encourage me, my parents gave me a book for my birthday: *The Dog Ate My Résumé, Survival Tips for Life After College*.

EXERCISE 20.2

Correct the faulty sentences in Exercise 20.1.

GO TO WEB
EXERCISE 20.1

WWW.BAREA.NELSON.COM

EXERCISE **20.3**

Correct the faulty punctuation in the following sentences, and then check your answers. If you've made any mistakes, review the explanation and examples, and be sure you understand why your answers were incorrect.

1. The only ways to get rich quickly are: to win the lottery or marry money.

2. According to Samantha, men are like Kleenex, soft, strong, and disposable.

3. The pioneers made their own: candles, soap, butter, and beer.

4. The supplies cabinet is low on pencils, highlighters, scratch pads, and staples.

5. We expect to do well in two venues: the pool and the track.

6. My roommate, who loves horror movies persuaded me to go with her to see *Nosferatu, the Vampire* and *Evil Dead 2; Dead by Dawn*.

7. There are two sides to every divorce, yours and the idiot's.

8. My parents think I am: lazy, selfish, ignorant, and inconsiderate, but what do they know?

9. Your paper lacks three essential features, a title page, a Works Cited list, and some original content in between.

10. Every time I walk into a singles bar, I can hear my mother's warning "Don't pick that up! You don't know where it's been."

GO TO WEB
EXERCISE 20.2

WWW.BAREA.NELSON.COM

Punctuation

EXERCISE **20.4**

The following paragraph will test all you have learned in the last three chapters. Insert commas, semicolons, and colons where appropriate in this passage. There are 15 errors.

Imagine if you can Oscar's surprise on being told that he had won a big prize in the lottery, one million dollars. At first he didn't believe it it was simply too good to be true. Once the reality had sunk in however he began to make plans for his fortune. As he thought about how to spend the money he kept one goal in mind "I want to help others as well as myself." He talked to the counsellors at the college who advised him that setting up a scholarship would be a good use of his funds. Every year five thousand dollars would go to three students who were doing well in school but who couldn't afford to continue their education without assistance. It was a perfect way for Oscar to share his good fortune with others. Of course he also bought himself the car of his dreams a sleek silver Porsche.

EXERCISE **20.5**

Now test your ability to use colons correctly. Revise the punctuation in the following sentences where necessary.

1. For each and every action there is: an equal and opposite criticism.

2. Several features of rural life appeal to me, such as: clean air, closeness to nature, and low housing costs.

3. You are probably a Canadian if: you know what a Robertson screwdriver is, you have Canadian Tire money in your kitchen drawer, and you know what a toque is used for.

4. You can tell that Oswald is cautious and conservative from the way he dresses, he wears both a belt and suspenders.

5. If you are an avid gardener, an enthusiastic bird-watcher, and enjoy quiet evenings with a good book, you are exactly my kind of man: please contact me at the address provided.

6. The characteristics of a good player are: patience, quick reflexes, and a knowledge of all sorts of trivia.

7. It's time to go to the showers: your outing on the pitching mound is over.

8. Everybody wants to be more successful than the next guy: therefore, be sure to stand next to someone who isn't doing very well.

9. I just received my new Canadian passport and now I know exactly what Will Kommen meant when he said: "If you look like your passport photo, you're too ill to travel."

10. I have a very old-fashioned cellphone: some people even call it "quaint" because it has only two functions: it makes and receives calls.

Punctuation

AS SHAKESPEARE SAID, LOVE CONQUERS ALL.

QUOTE LOVE CONQUERS ALL, UNQUOTE!

21 Quotation Marks

USING QUOTATION MARKS CORRECTLY

A quotation is one or more words originally spoken or written by another person that you want to include in your paper. Quotations can enhance meaning and add interest to your writing—as long as they are used sparingly, like spice. If you insert quotations into every other sentence, your own ideas will be buried under the weight of other people's words. Your reader wants to hear what YOU think about your topic. Use the words of others to support your ideas, not as substitutes for them.

When you quote, you need to provide a signal to your reader that these words are borrowed, not your own. **Quotation marks** (" ") are used to set off dialogue, short passages of quoted material, and some titles. Long passages of quoted material are handled differently, as we'll see later.

Quotation marks come in pairs. There must be a set to show where the quotation or title begins and a set to show where it ends. The words in between must be *exactly* what you heard or read. (If you wish to omit or change a word or words and can do so without changing the meaning of your source, you may do so, but again you must signal your reader that you have altered the quotation. To find out how, see the Student Resources page on this book's website at **www.barea.nelson.com**, go to "Other Information," and click on "Format and Documentation.") The only other thing you need to know about quotations is how to introduce and punctuate them.

PUNCTUATING DIALOGUE

When you quote direct speech, start with a double quotation mark (") and use normal sentence punctuation. If you include the speaker's name in your sentence, set it off with commas. Put a comma or an end punctuation mark—whichever is appropriate—inside the final set of quotation marks.

> "Yes, officer," said the young man, "that's her. That's the lady I stole the purse from."

Be careful to put quotation marks only around a speaker's exact words. Do not use quotation marks with indirect speech (a paraphrase of someone's words).

> The young man confessed that the woman the officer pointed to was the woman from whom he had stolen the purse.

PUNCTUATING AND FORMATTING QUOTATIONS

Inserting quotations from print and electronic sources into your own writing smoothly and seamlessly is not easy. It takes practice. Quotations cannot simply be dropped (splash!) into your paragraphs. Every quotation MUST be introduced, usually in a phrase or clause that identifies the source.

When you quote a *short passage* (three lines of print or less), you should work it into your own sentence using appropriate punctuation.

1. Normally, you use a short phrase and a comma to mark off a quotation of one or more sentences. Put your quotation marks at the beginning

Punctuation

and end of the passage you are quoting, including the end punctuation mark.

> According to Margaret Atwood, "If you like men, you can like Americans. Cautiously. Selectively. Beginning with the feet. One at a time."

> "As you grow old," wrote Richard Needham, "you lose your interest in sex, your friends drift away, your children ignore you. There are other advantages, of course, but these would seem to me the outstanding ones."

> "My idea of long-range planning is lunch," confesses Frank Ogden, one of Canada's foremost futurists.

2. If your own introductory words form a complete sentence, use a colon to introduce the quotation.

> Frank Ogden, one of Canada's foremost futurists, confesses that he has little respect for traditional business-planning cycles: "My idea of long-range planning is lunch."

3. If the passage you are quoting is a couple of words, a phrase, or anything less than a complete sentence, do not use any punctuation to introduce it.

> Woody Allen's one regret in life is that he is "not someone else."

> Neil Bissoondath argues that racism is based on "willful ignorance and an acceptance of—and comfort with—stereotype."

4. A quotation *within* a quotation is punctuated by single quotation marks.

> According to John Robert Colombo, "the most widely quoted Canadian aphorism of all time is Marshall McLuhan's 'The medium is the message.' "

EXERCISE **21.1**

In the following sentences, place quotation marks where they are needed and insert any necessary punctuation before and after each quotation. Answers for this chapter begin on page 430.

1. There are not many quotations that everyone who speaks English knows, but Shakespeare's "To be or not to be, that is the question" must be one of the most familiar.

2. On the subject of exercise, Fred Allen remarked that he liked long walks, especially when they were taken by people who annoyed him.

3. "It is good to obey the rules when you are young," wrote Mark Twain, "so that you'll have the strength to break them when you're old."

4. A dedicated non-athlete, Twain also observed "I take my exercise acting as pallbearer at the funerals of those who exercised regularly."

5. Will and Ian Ferguson describe Canadian cuisine in simple terms: "If you let a Canadian anywhere near a piece of food [he or she is] sure to fling it into a deep fryer. Or cover it with sugar. Or fling it into a deep fryer and *then* cover it with sugar."

EXERCISE **21.2**

For each of the topics below, read the quotation and write, in your own words, two or three sentences about the subject. Then revise your sentences to incorporate the quotation smoothly and effectively. You should end up with a short paragraph. Here's an example:

Topic: College
Quotation: "A place where pebbles are polished and diamonds are dimmed."
Source: Robert G. Ingersoll

Original sentences:

My college experience has been positive, probably because I am taking courses that interest me and are directly related to the career I want. Some of my friends, however, are struggling, even though they did much better than I in high school. If I can keep up this success, then I will feel that I made a wise investment of money and time.

Revision:

My college experience has been positive, probably because I am taking courses that interest me and are directly related to the career I want. Some of my friends, however, are struggling, even though they did much better than I did in high school. I like to think that Robert G. Ingersoll got it right when he defined college as "a place where pebbles are polished and diamonds are dimmed." If I can graduate as a smoothly polished pebble, then I will feel that I made a wise investment of both money and time.

1. **Topic:**   Canadian culture
   Quotation: "Canada has never been a melting pot; more like a tossed salad."
   Source: Arnold Edinborough

2. **Topic:**   Winter
   Quotation: "In Canada, we have nine months of winter and three months of road repair."
   Source: Peter Hanson

3. **Topic:**   Lies
   Quotation: "A lie gets halfway around the world before the truth has a chance to get its pants on."
   Source: Sir Winston Churchill

4. **Topic:**   Equality of the sexes
   Quotation: "Whatever women do they must do twice as well as men to be thought half as good. Luckily, this is not difficult."
   Source: Charlotte Whitton (former mayor of Ottawa)

5. **Topic:**   Work/leisure
   Quotation: "No man on his deathbed ever said, 'I wish I'd spent more time at the office.'"
   Source: The originator of this modern proverb is unknown.

All of the lines of a *long quotation* (more than three lines of print) should be indented 10 spaces (2 cm) from the left margin. Do not use quotation marks around a long quotation that is set off from the text.

A block indentation indicates to the reader that the words set off in this way are not yours but some other writer's. Here is an example:

> In "An Immigrant's Split Personality," Sun-Kyung Yi describes the painful dilemma faced by the children of immigrants, who often feel torn between two worlds. She cites her own case as an example. Neither Korean nor Canadian, she
>
> > remain[s] slightly distant from both cultures, fully accepted by neither. The hyphenated Canadian personifies the ideal

of multiculturalism, but unless the host culture and the immigrant cultures can find ways to merge their distinct identities, sharing the best of both, this cultural schizo-phrenia will continue. (345)

College writing normally requires that you indicate the source of any material you quote. The easiest way to do this is to give the author's name (if it's not already included in your paragraph), the name of the article and/or publication from which the quotation was taken, and the page reference in parentheses at the end of the quotation. That's what the "345" at the end of the quotation above refers to: if you turn to that page in this book, you will find the paragraph from which the quotation was taken.

The following examples illustrate the two basic ways to incorporate a quotation—short or long—into your own writing and credit your source. The first example identifies the author in the sentence introducing the quotation; the second does not.

Second marriages, according to Dr. Samuel Johnson, are "the triumph of hope over experience" (402).

In the 18th century, a lifelong bachelor observed that second marriages were "the triumph of hope over experience" (Johnson 402).

These source identifications are called *parenthetical citations* and refer to entries in what is called a "Works Cited" or "References" list, depending on the style of documentation required by your instructor. For further information on format and documentation, see our website at **www.barea.nelson.com**.

Some instructors prefer footnotes or endnotes to parenthetical citations. Find out what format your instructor requires and follow it. Some institutions are very particular about documentation, so you would be wise to ask your instructor which style to use.

As a general rule, if you are writing a paper for a humanities course and need more details than we provide on this text's website, we suggest you consult the *MLA Handbook for Writers of Research Papers*, 7th ed. (New York: MLA, 2009), or access the MLA website at **www.mla.org**. These MLA sources provide information on citing all types of sources, including material obtained from Internet sites.

For papers in the social sciences, the standard reference is the *Publication Manual of the American Psychological Association*, 5th ed. (Washington, DC: APA, 2001). Check **www.apastyle.org** for specific details on using APA style, including instruction on citing online information.

The information and exercises that follow are based on the MLA format.

Punctuation

PUNCTUATING AND FORMATTING TITLES

Titles of books and other entire works should be *italicized*.

Titles of parts of books and other works should be put in quotation marks.

The title of anything that is published or produced as a separate entity (e.g., books, magazines, newspapers, pamphlets, plays, movies, TV shows, albums) should be italicized. The title of anything that has been published or produced as part of a separate entity (e.g., articles, essays, stories, poems, a single episode of a TV series, songs) should be placed in quotation marks. As you can see from the following examples, this rule is very simple, and it applies to all types of source references, including print and electronic.

Book:	*The Bare Essentials, Form A*
Chapter in a book:	"Quotation Marks"
Magazine:	*Maclean's*
Article in magazine:	"Man the Barricades: Film Tax Credits Are Taking Fire"
Newspaper:	*Calgary Herald*
Article in newspaper:	"Judge Tosses Out Fine for 'Wardrobe Malfunction'"
TV program:	*The Nature of Things*
TV episode:	"The Hobbit Enigma"
Music CD:	*Hard Candy*
Song on CD:	"The Confessions Tour"
Website sponsor:	*National Film Board of Canada*
Website page:	"The Facebook Challenge"

Why the difference? The way you format and punctuate a title tells your reader what sort of document you are quoting from or referring to: it may be a complete work that the reader can find listed by title, author, or subject in a library, or it may be an excerpt that the reader can find only by looking up the name of the work in which it was published.

EXERCISE **21.3**

Insert the necessary punctuation (quotation marks or italics) in the following sentences. Check your answers before continuing.

1. While *Casablanca* is on most lists of the best movies of all time, and *Citizen Kane* is on all of them, *The Spy Who Shagged Me* is on none.

2. Mel Gibson's *The Passion of the Christ* caused as much controversy and discussion as Michael Moore's *Sicko*, but among very different audiences.

3. Canada's national anthem, "O Canada," was written by Calixa Lavallée.

4. In her best-selling book, *Eats, Shoots & Leaves*, Lynne Truss devotes a chapter entitled "Airs and Graces" to colons and semicolons.

5. In his book *Open Secrets*, John Robert Colombo warns "Do not confuse citizenship with nationality. One does not have to be a Canadian to be Canadian."

6. Today's headline in the *Newark Times* made me smile: "New Jersey Judge to Rule on Nude Beach."

7. Pierre Elliott Trudeau made many memorable statements during his years in Parliament, but he is probably best known for two: "Just watch me!" and "Fuddle-duddle."

8. In an article entitled "Family: You Can't Live With It and You Can't Live Without It" Dana writes, "My mother is the world's top travel agent for guilt trips."

9. The latest issue of *Consumer Universe* features an article about shopping on board a cruise ship. The article is called "Veni, Vidi, Visa," which can roughly be translated as "I Came, I Saw, I Shopped."

10. Dawn Hanna begins her essay "Hooked on Trek" by confessing that she is a *Star Trek* junkie: "My heart beats just a little faster when I hear William Shatner intone 'Space . . . the final frontier.' . . . "

Punctuation

EXERCISE **21.4**

This exercise is designed to test your understanding of how to punctuate short quotations and titles in your writing. When and where do you use quotation marks? Italics? Which punctuation marks precede and follow a quotation?

1. The CBC's Hockey Night in Canada competed head to head with a rerun of CTV's Corner Gas and Global's airing of the movie Alexander.

2. In the chapter entitled Weasel Words, in his book The Joy of Writing, Pierre Berton describes an encounter between the great novelist Margaret Laurence and her physician.

3. In what he thought was a relaxing bedside manner, the doctor said to Laurence, A writer, eh? When I retire I intend to become a writer myself.

4. Laurence, the author of such classics as The Stone Angel, The Diviners, and A Jest of God, replied Yes, and when I retire, I intend to become a brain surgeon.

5. Have you heard the song Promiscuous from Nellie Furtado's album Loose? She also has a video of that tune and Maneater from the same album.

6. The original soundtrack for the movie Brokeback Mountain was by Gustavo Santaolalla and featured songs like Snow and Riding Horses. Willie Nelson's He Was a Friend of Mine and Linda Ronstadt's It's So Easy were also heard in the movie.

7. The most frequently played songs on my iPod are the Rascalz' hit single Movie Star from their album Reloaded and Buck 65's great song Pants on Fire from his CD Man Overboard.

8. The classic French dish cassoulet, takes three days to prepare unless you follow the quick and easy directions in Anna and Michael Olson's book

Cook At Home, where you'll find their shortcut to great cassoulet in the chapter called Casual Bistro.

9. Vincent van Gogh's great painting Starry Night was the inspiration for Don McLean's famous song Vincent, also known as Starry Starry Night, which ends with the line, I could have told you, Vincent, this world was never meant for one as beautiful as you.

10. Mae West cultivated the persona of a happily sinful woman in movies like Belle of the Nineties, in which she observed A man in the house is worth two on the street, and Klondike Annie, in which she said When I have a choice between two evils, I always pick the one I never tried before.

Punctuation

22 Question Marks, Exclamation Marks, and Punctuation Review

THE QUESTION MARK

Everyone knows that a **question mark** follows an interrogative, or asking, sentence, but we all sometimes forget to include it. Let this chapter serve as a reminder not to forget!

Put a question mark at the end of every interrogative sentence.

The question mark gives your readers an important clue to the meaning of your sentence. "There's more?" (interrogative) means something quite different from

"There's more!" (exclamatory), and both are different from "There's more." (declarative). When you speak, your tone of voice conveys the meaning you intend; when you write, your punctuation tells your reader what you mean.

The only time you don't end a question with a question mark is when the question is part of a statement.

Question	Statement
Are you going?	I asked whether you were going.
Do you know them?	I wonder if you know them.
Is there enough evidence to convict him?	The jury deliberated whether there was enough evidence to convict him.

EXERCISE **22.1**

Write the correct end punctuation for the following sentences, and then check your answers on pages 430–431.

1. If we succeed, who will know ?
2. I wonder who won the game last night .
3. Does the name Pavlov ring any bells ?
4. Wouldn't it be great if, whenever we messed up our lives, we could simply press "Ctrl Alt Delete" and start all over?
5. Who could have predicted that a game like Trivial Pursuit would enrich so many lives, especially the lives of those who developed it ?
6. I am curious about what the new chief financial officer plans to do about our chronic deficit .
7. Please have a look at these exams and tell me if you agree that some of the students may have been cheating .
8. Our manager queried the vice president about the likelihood of completing this project on time or on budget .
9. If we continue to make a profit, I question whether the new owners would close us down or move our operation offshore .
10. I do not understand why the Americans don't adopt a health care system like ours instead of leaving millions of people with no coverage for medical problems or emergencies .

GO TO WEB
EXERCISE 22.1

WWW.BAREA.NELSON.COM

Punctuation

THE EXCLAMATION MARK

Consider the difference in tone between these two sentences:

There's a man behind you.
There's a man behind you!

In the first sentence, information is being supplied, perhaps about the line of people waiting their turn at a grocery store checkout counter. The second sentence might be a shouted warning about a mugger.

> Use an **exclamation mark** as end punctuation only in sentences requiring extreme emphasis or dramatic effect.

Note that the exclamation mark will have "punch" or dramatic effect only if you use it sparingly. If you use an exclamation mark after every other sentence, how will your readers know when you really mean to indicate excitement? Overuse of exclamation marks is a technique used by comic book writers to try to heighten the impact of their characters' words. Ironically, the effect is to neutralize the impact. You will seldom find exclamation marks in academic or business writing.

Practically any sentence could have an exclamation mark after it, but remember that the punctuation changes the meaning of the sentence. Read the following sentences with and without an exclamation mark, and picture the situation that would call for each reading.

They've moved   Don't touch that button
The file was empty   Listen to that noise

EXERCISE 22.2

Add the appropriate punctuation in the following sentences. Then compare your answers with our suggestions on page 431. (Answers may vary, depending on the tone and impact the writer wants to convey.)

1. Row faster! It's gaining on us!
2. Never introduce a quotation with a semicolon.
3. Don't even think about it!
4. Just imagine! She actually got a job!
5. Turn the heat up. I'm freezing!

6. She's here at last! Let the celebrations begin!
7. Try it. You'll like it !
8. The fans were on their feet, screaming "Skate!"
9. "Lights, camera, action!"
10. Go for it! You'll never know unless you try.

EXERCISE **22.3**

Supply appropriate punctuation for the 15 sentences in the following paragraph.

[1]I used to wonder why my great-grandfather never talked about his youth, even when we youngsters pestered him with questions [2]Then, to my surprise, I discovered that he was ashamed of his past as a circus clown [3]How could anyone be embarrassed about such a fascinating career [4]It has been my life-long ambition to become a comedian like Matthew Perry or Jim Carrey, so what more prestigious pedigree could I claim [5]Grandpapa, however, didn't see his past from my perspective [6]Because his father was a lawyer and his two brothers were doctors, he always felt his choice of career was second-rate [7]"How could a circus buffoon hold his head up around such serious professionals " he asked [8]I tried to tell Grandpapa that he was a kind of doctor, too [9]After all, don't people say that laughter is the best form of medicine [10]Researchers have conducted studies to confirm this truth [11]I question whether there is any higher calling than helping people laugh [12]Laughter not only breaks down social barriers, it also releases powerful brain chemicals called *endorphins* [13]Endorphins create such an overwhelming feeling of relaxation and well-being that they can actually ease pain [14]Comedy functions as such effective natural medicine that you could say clowns and comedians serve as naturopathic doctors [15]Is there, then, any more noble way to spend one's career than clowning around

Punctuation

PUNCTUATION REVIEW

The exercises that follow will test your knowledge of all the punctuation marks you have studied in Unit 4. All of the sentences below contain errors: punctuation is either missing or misused. Work through the sentences slowly and carefully. Check your answers to each set before continuing. If you make a mistake, go back to the chapter that deals with the punctuation mark you missed, and review the explanation and examples. If you're still confused, log on to **www.barea.nelson.com** and ask the authors to help you solve your problem.

EXERCISE 22.4

1. Did you know that in English, the word "karate" means empty hands?

2. If your goal is to be a millionaire before you are 35, you will have to: make work the focus of your life and be uncommonly lucky.

3. The question of whether evolution is fact or myth doesn't worry most of the people in my biology class; they're more concerned about whether there's a dance on Friday night

4. Do you think Sara has any idea how lucky she is that her supervisor didn't find out she took the day off to go to the casino?

5. The cure is readily at hand; drink plenty of liquids, take an aspirin with each meal, get lots of rest, and take three grams of Vitamin C daily

6. When her grandfather told her how large computers used to be, the wide-eyed child exclaimed, "Gosh! How big was the mouse?"

7. I think it was Mark Twain who once said, "Clothes make the man; naked people have little or no influence in society."

8. This is the first entry in my new book, Words of Wisdom: If at first you don't succeed, skydiving is not the sport for you.

9. Your résumé is the second piece of writing that an employer will see; the first is the cover letter, which is one of the most important documents you will write in your career.

10. Today's passenger jets are so fast, and the airlines so efficient that when you land in Amsterdam, it takes them only a couple of days to locate your luggage and fly it in from Brazil !

WWW.BAREA.NELSON.COM

EXERCISE **22.5**

Correct the 20 misused or missing punctuation marks in this passage.

All too often it seems that the Canadian national pastime is complaining about the weather! Our summers are criticized because they're too hot while our springs are too wet our autumns too cool and our winters too long. If the climate is so bad here why does anyone live north of the U.S. border. Perhaps the answer is not that Canadians don't like living in Canada but that they love to complain.

Two of the most popular sports teams in Canada were at one time those with the worst records; the Argonauts and the Maple Leafs. Could their popularity have been due to the ample opportunity and scope they gave to their fans for complaint. Not only do we moan about the records of such teams when they lose but when they win we dwell with glee on the possibilities of disaster for next year.

The same syndrome can be seen in our attitude toward Canadian heroes, it has often been said that we are a nation without heroes but I suspect that we have plenty of candidates: it's just that we enjoy complaining so much we try to find fault wherever we can, and prefer to focus on failure rather than success. One cannot help but wonder how Canadians fare in heaven where everything is perfect? I suspect they must be desperately unhappy?

EXERCISE **22.6**

Insert the 25 punctuation marks that are missing or misused in the following paragraph.

When most of us think of Chinese food we think of the dozen or so dishes offered on Chinese restaurant menus in towns and villages across Canada. In China however the cuisine like the nation itself is remarkably diverse. Each province in China has a unique cuisine! Some of these regional specialties are available in Canada particularly in communities where enough immigrants have settled to create a demand for regional dishes. In addition to Cantonese cooking which is what most of us think of as "Chinese food" we can now choose among Szechwan Hunan Beijing Guangdong and Shanghai cuisine. Szechwan and Hunan are provinces famous for spicy food it is highly seasoned with locally grown hot peppers. Be careful when tasting this food. The most famous dish from Beijing is Peking duck but Beijing is also home to many other delicious dishes including Mongolian hot pot and Beggar's Chicken. Each region of China not only boasts its own culinary specialties but also influences the cuisine of its neighbours. The result is a gourmet's dream a delectable patchwork of diverse and delicious foods. Given its astonishing variety, how can we define Chinese food. To attempt such a definition is like trying to describe the Chinese people themselves infinitely variable often surprising and always interesting. Whoever said Variety is the spice of life might well have been describing Chinese cuisine.

EXERCISE **22.7**

Insert the punctuation marks that are missing in the following. You will need to use at least one colon, semicolon, and question mark, in addition to quotation marks, numerous commas, and italics.

1. When a national contest invited Canadians to come up with an alternative to the expression as American as apple pie the winning entry was as Canadian as possible under the circumstances.

2. Mike Weir and Stephen Ames are two golfers who are making the world take notice of Canadian golf and we should be proud of them.

3. When W. C. Fields was asked if he had ever had trouble sleeping this was his reply A good cure for insomnia is: to get plenty of sleep.

4. In 1850 Henry David Thoreau spent a week in Canada but was not much impressed by his experience I fear that I have not got much to say about Canada, not having seen much, what I got by going to Canada was a cold.

5. Babe Ruth who started his professional career in Baltimore played for Boston became famous as a New York Yankee and hit his first home run as a pro in Toronto.

6. In a quick-witted response to a question about violence on television, Dick Cavett once said There's so much comedy on TV nowadays. Does that cause comedy in the streets.

7. As far as Albert is concerned a livable city must have three important things an NHL hockey team a CFL football team and a Swiss Chalet with delivery service.

8. What is the Canadian equivalent to Patrick Henry's famous pronouncement during the American War of Independence Give me liberty or give me death

9. Since I've had a regular job I've been trying to save up for a rainy day, so far I can handle a light mist.

10. After much consideration my uncle decided to stop subscribing to The Globe and Mail instead he decided to order three new papers the National Post The Vancouver Sun and The St. John's Telegram.

UNIT 4 RAPID REVIEW

Supply the 15 punctuation marks that are missing in the following paragraph. (Note: Each pair of quotation marks counts as one punctuation mark.)

[1]At a meeting of the college faculty, an angel suddenly appears and tells the head of the philosophy department, I will grant you whichever of three blessings you choose: wisdom, beauty, or 10 million dollars. [2]Immediately, the professor chooses wisdom. [3]Lightning flashes and a tremendous clap of thunder reverberates throughout the room. [4]The professor appears to be transformed, but he just sits there staring down at the table. [5]One of his colleagues whispers, Say something. [6]The professor says, I should have taken the money.

(Adapted from a passage in Thomas Cathcart and Daniel Klein, *Plato and a Platypus Walk into a Bar . . . Understanding Philosophy through Jokes*. New York: Abrams Image, 2007: 79.)

UNIT 5

Paragraphs and Essays

Paragraphs and Essays

23 Finding Something to Write About

Every writer knows that content is important. Not so many seem to know that form is just as important. In fact, you can't really separate the two: *what you say is how you say it*. Writing a paper (or an essay, or a report, or a letter, or anything else) is like doing a chemistry experiment or baking a cake: you need the right amount of the right ingredients put together in the right proportions and in the right order. There are five steps to follow.

1. Choose a satisfactory subject.
2. Discover your thesis and main points.
3. Write a thesis statement and/or an outline.
4. Write the paragraphs.
5. Revise the paper.

If you follow these steps faithfully, in order, we guarantee that you will write clear, organized papers.

Note that, when you get to step 3, you have a choice. You can choose to plan your paper with a thesis statement, or with an outline, or with both. The thesis statement approach works well for short papers—about 500 words or less. An outline is necessary for longer papers. Ideally, you should learn to use both methods of organizing your writing. In fact, your teacher may require that you do so.

Steps 1, 2, and 3 make up the planning stage of the writing process. Be warned: done properly, these three steps will take you at least as long as steps 4 and 5, which involve the actual writing. The longer you spend on planning, the less time you'll spend on drafting and revising, and the better your paper will be.

CHOOSE A SATISFACTORY SUBJECT

Unless you are assigned a specific subject by a teacher or supervisor, choosing your subject can be the most difficult part of writing a paper. Apply the following guidelines carefully, because no amount of instruction can help you to write a good paper on something you don't know anything about or on something that is inappropriate for your audience or purpose. Your subject should satisfy the **4-S test**.

A satisfactory subject is SIGNIFICANT, SINGLE, SPECIFIC, and SUPPORTABLE.

1. Your subject should be **significant**. Write about something that your reader needs or might want to know. Consider your audience and choose a subject that they will find significant. This doesn't mean that you can't ever be humorous, but, unless you're another Stephen Leacock, an essay on "How I Deposit Money in My Bank" will probably be of little significance to your readers. The subject you choose must be worthy of the time and attention you expect your readers to give to your paper.

2. Your subject should be **single**. Don't try to cover too much in your paper. A thorough discussion of one topic is more satisfying to a reader than a skimpy, superficial treatment of several topics. A subject such as "The challenge of government funding cutbacks to colleges and universities" includes too much to deal with in one paper. Limit yourself to a single topic, such as "How private sector donations are helping our college meet the challenge of funding cutbacks."

Paragraphs and Essays

3. Your subject should be **specific**. This requirement is closely tied to the "single" requirement. Given a choice between a general topic and a specific one, you should choose the latter. In a short paper, you can't hope to say anything new or significant about a large topic: "Employment opportunities in Canada," for example. But you could write an interesting, detailed discussion on a more specific topic, such as "Employment opportunities in Nova Scotia's hospitality industry."

   You can narrow a broad subject by applying one or more **limiting factors** to it. Try thinking of your subject in terms of a specific *kind*, or *time*, or *place*, or *number*, or *person* associated with it. To come up with the hospitality topic, for example, we limited the subject of employment opportunities in Canada in terms of both place and kind.

4. Your subject must be **supportable**. You must know something about the subject (preferably, more than your reader does), or you must be able to find out about it. Your discussion of your subject will be clear and convincing only if you can include examples, facts, quotations, descriptions, anecdotes, and other details. Supporting evidence can be taken from your own experience or from the experience of other people. In other words, your topic may require you to do some research.[1]

EXERCISE **23.1**

Imagine that you have been asked to write a 500-word paper and given this list of subjects to choose from. Test each subject against the 4-S guidelines and identify what's wrong with it. Answers for exercises in this chapter begin on page 433.

1. Cellphone plans
2. The five senses
3. Recharging your iPod
4. The dangers of obesity and anorexia
5. How to insert a European-back earring
6. Characteristics of Baby Boomers, Generation X, and the Millennials
7. The Olympics in 2020

---

[1] Many colleges and most universities require students to write formal research papers in their first year. The five steps to essay writing that we outline in this unit apply to research papers as well as to informal and in-class essays. In addition, a research paper requires that you find and use information from sources in your essay, and that you format and document your paper according to specific guidelines. Go to **www.barea.nelson.com** to find out how to produce a paper in MLA or APA style—the two styles most frequently required in courses at the undergraduate level.

8. Problems our children will face as parents
9. How to parasail or bungee-jump safely
10. Astrophysics

Apply the 4-S guidelines to the following subjects. Some are possibilities for short papers but fail to satisfy one or more of the guidelines. Others are hopeless. Revise the "possible" subjects to make them significant, single, specific, and supportable.

1. Bottled water
2. Some people are very attractive.
3. The proper way to load the dishwasher
4. The Russian economy
5. Plug-in electric cars
6. How to mix paint
7. Predicting the future
8. Canadian war heroes
9. Global positioning systems
10. Internet piracy

List three subjects that you might choose to write about. Make sure each subject is *significant*, *single*, *specific*, and *supportable*.

GO TO WEB
EXERCISE 23.1

WWW.BAREA.NELSON.COM

Paragraphs and Essays

DISCOVER YOUR THESIS AND MAIN POINTS

Once you've chosen a suitable subject for your paper, you need to decide what you want to say about it. There are many possible ways of thinking and writing about any subject. In a short paper, you can deal effectively with only a few aspects of your topic. How do you decide what approach to take?

The approach to your subject that you choose is your **thesis**: a thesis is an *idea about a limited subject*. It is an opinion or point of view that needs to be explained or proved. A thesis is not a statement of fact. Compare the examples that follow.

Fact	Thesis
Most people experience some anxiety when they begin a first job.	The stress I experienced in my first job was caused by my employer, my co-workers, and—surprisingly—myself. (Needs to be explained.)
For several years, Canada ranked first on the UN's list of the world's best countries to live in.	Canadians don't know how lucky they are. (Needs to be explained.)
Some universities do not require students to demonstrate writing competence before graduation.	All universities should require students to demonstrate writing competence before graduation. (Needs to be proved.)

A thesis can be discovered in several ways. Brainstorming, freewriting, listing, and clustering are strategies that many college students are familiar with from high school. You should continue to use any technique you've learned that produces results. Some students, however, need a more structured approach to discovering what it is they can and want to say about a subject.

If none of the informal approaches you've experimented with work for you, you can try questioning—asking lead-in questions about your subject. A lead-in question is one that guides you into your subject by pointing to an angle or viewpoint—a thesis—that you can explore in your paper. The answers to your lead-in question become the main points your paper will explain.

Six Questions to Ask about Your Subject

1. How can my subject be defined or explained? What are its significant features or characteristics? Examples: "Generation Y," "HDTV," "The Canadian personality"
2. How is my subject made or done? How does it work? Examples: "How to choose the right college," "Hybrid electric cars," "How to set up a home network"
3. What are the main kinds, components, or functions of my subject? Examples: "Internet addicts," "The perfect workout," "What does a floor director do?"

4. What are the main similarities and/or differences between my subject and _____? Examples: "Toyota and Honda hybrid systems," "A fan's view of professional vs. amateur hockey," "Differences between college and university"
5. What are the causes or effects of my subject? Examples: "Why parents and teenagers disagree," "The causes of ADD," "Some effects of high fuel prices"
6. What are the advantages or disadvantages of my subject? What are the reasons for or against it? Examples: "Our city's new recycling program," "Fast food," "Toll roads"

These questions suggest some common ways of looking at or thinking about a subject. Some questions will yield better results than others, and most subjects will produce answers to more than one of the questions. Choose as your subject the question that produces the answers you can or want to say most about.

Here's an example of how the process works. Let's assume you've been asked to write a paper on the topic "A satisfying career."[2] Apply each question to your subject and make notes of the answers.

1. "What is a satisfying career?" What are its significant features or characteristics?
   This question produces useful answers. Answers might include a career that is interesting, highly paid, and respected, and that provides opportunities for advancement.

2. "How is a satisfying career made or chosen?"
   This question would also work. Some answers might include self-analysis, career counselling, experience (perhaps through part-time or volunteer work), research, or taking aptitude tests.

3. "What are the main parts or components of a satisfying career?"
   We could use this question, too. The components of a satisfying career might include challenging work, good pay, compatible co-workers, and respect in the community.

---

[2] If your instructor has assigned the topic of your essay, don't grumble—be grateful. The way your instructor words the assignment may contain information that will help you decide what approach to take. Assignment instructions usually contain "direction words," which are reliable clues to the kind of paper your instructor is looking for. For example, *Define* points you to question 1; *Describe* means you should apply questions 1 and 2; *Discuss* and *Explain* tell you to apply questions 3, 4, 5, and possibly 6; and *Evaluate* points you to question 6.

Paragraphs and Essays

4. "How is a satisfying career different from something else?"
   This question has limited possibilities. We could develop a contrast between a satisfying career and an unsatisfying one, but there isn't much new to say. The main points are obvious and could be explained more easily in response to question 1 than to question 4.

5. "Does a satisfying career have causes or effects?"
   It has both.

   What causes a satisfying career?
   Preparation, planning, self-analysis.

   What are the effects of a satisfying career?
   Confidence, stability, recognition, happiness.

6. "What are the advantages or disadvantages of a satisfying career?"
   Unless you can think of some unusual advantages (i.e., ones that are not covered by the answers to question 3), this question doesn't produce answers that are worth spending our own or our readers' time on. We've already discovered the advantages in answering question 3, and there aren't many disadvantages to a satisfying career!

Asking these six questions about your subject will help you decide what approach would be best for your paper. The "best" approach is the one that is most original and most convincing: the main points your paper discusses should not only seem fresh to your readers but should also sound reasonable to an educated audience.

The questioning strategy we've outlined above will

- help you define your thesis by identifying the point of view you can best explain or defend and
- put you on the path to drafting your paper by providing some solid main points to work with.

Don't rush this process. The more time you spend exploring your subject in the planning stage, the easier the actual drafting of the paper will be.

Below you will find eight sample subjects, together with main points that were discovered by applying the questions on pages 266–67. Study these examples carefully. Figure out the logic that leads from subject to question to main points in each case. When you're finished, you should have a good understanding of how the questioning process can work for you.

Subject	Selected Question	Main Points
A good teacher	1. What are the characteristics of a good teacher?	• knowledge of subject • ability to communicate • respect for students

Subject	Selected Question	Main Points
The hybrid automobile	1. What are the features of a hybrid car?	• gas engine for high speeds • electric engine for low speeds • momentum from gas engine and brakes to recharge batteries
A successful party	2. How do you give a successful party?	• invite the right mix of people • plan the entertainment • prepare the food in advance • provide a relaxed, friendly atmosphere
Internet users	3. What are the main categories of Internet users?	• dabblers • regulars • addicts
Quitting smoking	3. What are the main ways to quit smoking?	• cold turkey • taper off gradually • medical/chemical support (pills, gum, patch)
Refugees in Canada	5. What are the main causes of refugees coming to Canada?	• persecution in homeland • war in homeland • poverty in homeland
Nursing as a career	6. What are the main advantages of a career in nursing?	• opportunities to help people • opportunities for travel • career security
PDAs	6. What are the main disadvantages of using a PDA?	• prevents escape from work • creates a disturbance in theatres, restaurants, etc. • can put drivers at risk • replaces social interaction

Paragraphs and Essays

As a general rule, you should try to identify between *two* (the absolute minimum) and *five* main ideas to support your subject. If you have only one main idea, your subject is suitable for a paragraph or two, not for an essay. If you have discovered more than five main ideas that require discussion, you have too much material for a short paper. Either select the most important aspects of the subject, or take another look at it to see how you can focus it more specifically.

EXERCISE **23.4**

In this exercise, select a question from the highlighted list on pages 266–67 and generate good main points for each subject.

Subject	Selected Question	Main Points
1. My chosen career	•	•
		•
		•
2. Owning a car vs. using public transit	•	•
		•
		•
3. My family's (or my ancestor's) immigration to Canada	•	•
		•
		•
4. Leaving home	•	•
		•
		•
5. Reality television	•	•
		•
		•

Subject	Selected Question	Main Points
6. Dressing for success	•	• • •
7. Time management	•	• • •
8. Blogs	•	• • •
9. Tattoos	•	• • •
10. Achieving a balanced life	•	• • •

EXERCISE **23.5**

For each of the three subjects you chose in Exercise 23.3, list two to five main points. To discover suitable main points, apply to your subject the six questions highlighted on pages 266–67, one at a time, until you find the question that fits best. The answers to that question are your main points.

Paragraphs and Essays

GO TO WEB
EXERCISE 23.2

WWW.BAREA.NELSON.COM

TESTING YOUR MAIN POINTS

Now take a close look at the main points you've chosen for each subject in Exercise 23.5. It may be necessary to revise some of them before going any further. Are some points too trivial to bother with? Do any of the points overlap in meaning? Are there any points that are not directly related to the subject?

Main points must be SIGNIFICANT, DISTINCT, and RELEVANT.

To be satisfactory, the main points you have chosen to write about must all be **significant**: they must require a paragraph or more of explanation. If you have any trivial ideas mixed in with the important ones, now is the time to discard them.

Each of the main points you've chosen must also be **distinct**. That is, each must be different from all the others. There must be no overlap in meaning. Check to be sure you haven't given two different labels to what is really one aspect of the subject.

Finally, each main point must be **relevant**; it must be clearly **related** to the subject. It must be an aspect of the subject you are writing about, not some other subject. For example, if you're writing about the advantages of a subject, cross out any disadvantages that may have appeared on your list.

EXERCISE **23.6**

Each of the following subjects is followed by some possible main points. Circle the unsatisfactory point(s) in each group.

1. Popular Canadian sports teams
   - Edmonton Oilers
   - Winnipeg Blue Bombers
   - Montreal Canadiens
   - Oromocto Blues
   - Hamilton Tiger Cats

2. The advantages of getting into shape
- improved muscle tone
- weight loss
- improved appearance
- improved stamina
- better looks

3. Problems faced by new immigrants in Canada
- finding suitable work
- learning a new language
- finding a suitable place to live
- shovelling snow
- adjusting to the climate

4. The main kinds of daytime television
- talk shows
- quiz shows
- soap operas
- *Oprah*
- game shows

5. Characteristics of sharks
- tiny brains
- cartilaginous skeleton
- must move to breathe and float
- sharp, triangular teeth
- great white shark

6. Advantages of digitized online books
- available on a single, multi-function device
- links to information available
- eyestrain from video screens
- online dictionary and reference works available
- downloadable and erasable

7. Alternative energy sources
- wind
- tides
- geothermal
- solar
- coal

8. Lower taxes stimulate the economy
- Businesses have more money to hire workers.
- Individuals have more money to buy goods and services.
- Low-tax economic environment attracts foreign investment.
- Government has less money to spend on social services.

Paragraphs and Essays

GO TO WEB
EXERCISE 23.3

WWW.BAREA.NELSON.COM

EXERCISE **23.7**

Study the main points you chose in Exercise 23.5 on page 271. Cross out any that are not *significant*, *distinct*, or *relevant* to the subject. If necessary, add new main points so that you end up with at least three main points for each subject.

ORGANIZING YOUR MAIN POINTS

Now that you've decided on three or four main points to discuss, you need to decide on the order in which to present them in your paper. Choose the order that is most appropriate for your subject and audience.

There are four basic ways to arrange main points in an essay: CHRONOLOGICAL, CLIMACTIC, LOGICALLY LINKED, and RANDOM order.

1. **Chronological order** means in order of time sequence, from first to last. Here's an example:

Subject	Main Points
The development of a relationship	• attraction • meeting • discovery • intimacy

2. **Climactic order** means presenting your strongest or most important point last. Generally, you would discuss your second-strongest point first and the others in between, like this:

Subject	Main Points
Reasons for the federal government to legislate lower carbon emissions	• Airborne pollutants endanger the health of individual Canadians.

Main Points (continued)

- Damage to trees hurts the economy.
- Our emissions affect the U.S. as well as Canada.
- Global warming caused by carbon emissions threatens our very existence.

3. **Logically linked order** means that the main points are connected in such a way that one point must be explained before the next can be understood. Consider this example:

Subject	Main Points
Main causes of gang involvement	• lack of opportunity for work • lack of recreational facilities • boredom • need for an accepting peer group

The logical link here is this: because of unemployment, recreational facilities are needed, and because of both unemployment and inadequate recreational facilities, boredom becomes a problem. Bored by having nothing to do and nowhere to go, young people need an accepting peer group to bolster their self-esteem. The first three points must be explained before the reader can fully understand the fourth.

4. **Random order** means the points can be satisfactorily explained in any order. A random arrangement of points is acceptable only if the main points are *equally significant* and *not chronologically or causally linked*, as in this example:

Subject	Main Points
Reasons to cycle to school	• fitness • economy • enjoyment

These three points are equally important; they can be effectively explained in any order.

Paragraphs and Essays

EXERCISE **23.8**

Below, we have identified eight subjects, together with several main points that could be used to develop them. For each subject, number the points so that they are arranged in the suggested order.

Subject	Order	Main Points
1. How to prepare for a job interview	chronological	_____ Visit the company's website.
		_____ Dress appropriately.
		_____ Prepare answers to standard interview questions.
		_____ Ask a friend to role-play the interview with you.
2. Differences between spoken and written language	climactic	_____ Speech is transitory; writing is permanent.
		_____ Speech is spontaneous; writing isn't.
		_____ Speech can't be revised; writing can.
3. How to write a research paper	chronological	_____ Read and take notes on selected research sources.
		_____ Draft the paper.
		_____ Compile a working bibliography of research sources.
		_____ Define the subject.
		_____ Type and proofread final draft.
		_____ Insert source citations and reference list.
		_____ Revise the paper.
4. How colleges benefit society	logical	_____ They provide students with a higher level of education.

Subject	Order	Main Points
		_____ They contribute to increased national productivity.
		_____ They provide students with job skills.
5. Effects of malnutrition	logical	_____ Malnutrition affects the productivity and prosperity of nations as a whole.
		_____ Malnutrition impedes the mental and physical development of children.
		_____ Undernourished children become sickly adults unable to participate fully in their society.
6. Why pornography should be banned	chronological	_____ It degrades those who make it.
		_____ It brutalizes society as a whole.
		_____ It desensitizes those who view it.
7. Reasons for student poverty	climactic	_____ lack of parental assistance
		_____ lack of government loan assistance
		_____ inability to manage money effectively
		_____ inability to find part-time work
8. Why Canadian professionals emigrate to the United States	climactic	_____ higher salaries
		_____ more jobs to choose from
		_____ warmer climate
		_____ better working conditions

Paragraphs and Essays

EXERCISE **23.9**

Using your list of subjects and main points from Exercise 23.7, arrange the main points for each subject in the most appropriate order. (*Note:* Keep your answer sheet. You will need it in some of the exercises that follow in the next chapter.)

In this chapter, you've learned how to choose a satisfactory subject; how to discover a thesis; and how to find, test, and arrange main points that support your thesis. Now it's time to think about how to plan your paper. Which will work best for you: the thesis statement method? Or the outline method? We think the former generally works best for short papers and the latter for long papers, but this distinction isn't hard and fast. Your wisest choice is to learn both. You will often get the best results if you use them together.

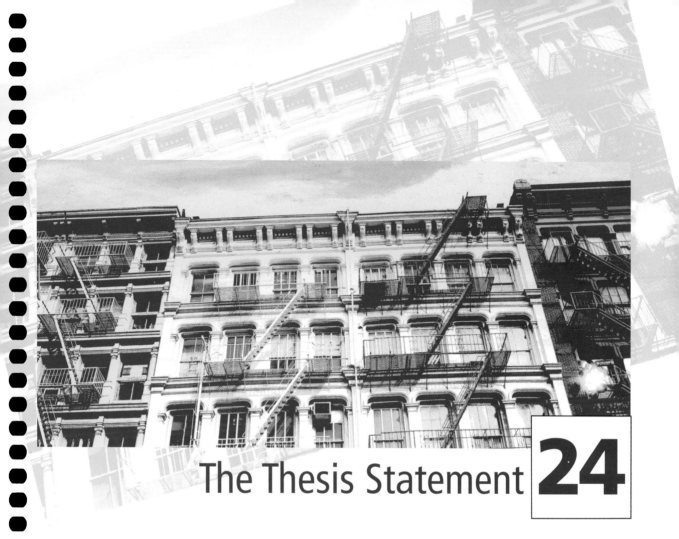

The Thesis Statement 24

In Chapter 23, you chose a topic and selected some aspects of it to discuss. Your next task is to outline your paper. There are several different methods to choose from, ranging from a sentence or two (a thesis statement) to a formal outline. For short papers, we recommend that you use the method presented in this chapter. For longer papers, or if your teacher requires a more detailed outline, you will find instructions in Chapter 25, "The Outline."

The key to a well-organized paper is a **thesis statement**—a statement near the beginning of your paper that announces its subject and scope. The thesis statement helps both you and your readers because it previews the plan of your paper. It tells your readers exactly what they are going to read about.

In fiction, telling readers in advance what they are going to find would never do. But for practical, everyday kinds of writing, advance notice works well. Term papers, technical reports, research papers, office memoranda, and business letters are no place for suspense or surprises. In these kinds of writing, you're more likely to get and keep your readers' attention if you indicate the subject and scope of your paper at the outset. A thesis statement acts like a table of contents. It's a kind of map of the territory covered in your paper: it keeps your reader (and you) on the right track.

> A thesis statement clearly and concisely indicates the SUBJECT of your paper, the MAIN POINTS you will discuss, and the ORDER in which you will discuss them.[1]

To write a thesis statement, you join your **subject** to your **main points,** which you have arranged in an appropriate order. To join the two parts of a thesis statement, you use a **link**. Your link can be a word or a phrase such as *are, include, consist of, because,* or *since,* or it can be a colon.[2] Here is a simple formula for constructing a thesis statement. (S stands for your subject.)

> *subject*   *link*   *main points*
>
> S   consists of   1, 2, 3 . . . n.

Here's an example:

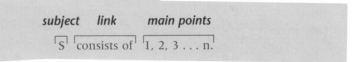

subject   *link* *main points 1, 2, and 3*

Three characteristics of a good professional letter (are) conciseness, clarity, and courtesy.

EXERCISE **24.1**

In each of the following thesis statements, underline the subject with a wavy line, circle the link, and underline the main points with a straight line. Answers for this chapter begin on page 435.

1. Three essential components of a strong and lasting relationship are good

   communication, sexual compatibility, and mutual respect.

---

[1] Not all thesis statements retain the preview portion (i.e., the main points in order of discussion) in the final draft. Nevertheless, we recommend that you begin the drafting process with a full thesis statement. You can always omit the preview of main points in your final copy if it seems redundant.

[2] Remember that a colon can be used only after an independent clause. See Chapter 20 if you need a review.

2. Don Cherry simultaneously amuses and provokes viewers with his opinions about hockey violence, his taste in clothing, and his perspective on international hockey.

3. If I were you, I would avoid eating in the cafeteria because the food is expensive, tasteless, and unhealthy.

4. The responsibilities of a modern union include protecting jobs, increasing wages, improving working conditions, and enhancing pensions and benefits.

5. If we are to compete internationally, our company needs a strong board of directors, creative executives, and dynamic middle managers.

6. The original Volkswagen Beetle, the Citroen CV, and the Morris Minor are three cars that will be remembered for their endearing oddness.

7. Fad diets are not the quick and easy fixes to weight problems that they may seem to be; in fact, they are often costly, ineffective, and even dangerous.

8. Taking the time and trouble to buy locally grown foods is better not only for you, but also for the local economy and the environment.

9. Do you lack basic skills, study skills, or motivation? If so, you are at high risk of failing your first year of college.

10. What makes a great movie? Not top stars or a huge budget. Great movies—those that are destined to be viewed generations from now—are based on a fortuitous combination of memorable stories, unforgettable characters, and brilliant direction.

When you combine your subject with your main points to form a thesis statement, there is an important rule to remember.

Main points must be stated in **grammatically parallel form (parallelism)**.

This rule means that, if main point 1 is a word, then main points 2 and 3 and so on must be words too. If main point 1 is a phrase, then the rest must be

Paragraphs and Essays

phrases. If your first main point is a dependent clause, then the rest must be dependent clauses. Study the model thesis statements you analyzed in Exercise 24.1. In every example, the main points are in grammatically parallel form. For each of those thesis statements, decide whether words, phrases, or dependent clauses were used. If you think your understanding of parallelism is a bit wobbly, review Chapter 10 and do Web Exercise 24.1 before continuing.

WWW.BAREA.NELSON.COM

EXERCISE **24.2**

Put a check mark (✓) before the sentences that are grammatically parallel. When you have completed the exercise, check your answers on page 436.

1. _____ A good counsellor must have knowledge, insight, patience, and compassion.

2. _____ Good writing involves applying the principles of organization, sentence structure, spelling, and you have to punctuate correctly.

3. _____ Our company requires employees to be knowledgeable, totally honest, disciplined, and we have to be able to rely on them.

4. _____ Hobbies are important because they provide us with recreational activities, stimulation, and they are relaxing.

5. _____ Some of the negative effects of caffeine are nervousness, you have difficulty sleeping, and heart palpitations.

EXERCISE **24.3**

Now revise the incorrect sentences in Exercise 24.2.

WWW.BAREA.NELSON.COM

EXERCISE **24.4**

Revise the following draft thesis statements. Be sure that the main points of each statement are significant, distinct, relevant, and grammatically parallel. Some sentences contain more than one kind of error. Make corrections as needed; then compare your revisions with our suggested answers.

1. The four kinds of essay writing are description, narrative, expository, and argumentation.

2. To survive, this corporation needs improved products, increase its sales, and a reduction in the work force.

3. Increasingly, scientists are finding links between the weather and diseases such as colds, cancer, arthritic ailments, and aging.

4. The most prolific producers of pretentious language are politicians, teachers, those who write advertising copy, educators, and sports writers.

5. There are three categories of students whom teachers find difficult: those who skip class, sleeping in class, and those who disrupt class.

EXERCISE **24.5**

With a partner, for each of the following subjects, assess the main points we've provided to see if they are suitable for inclusion in a short essay. Then, using the points that pass the test, write a grammatically parallel thesis statement. Underline the subject with a wavy line, circle the link, and underline the main points with straight lines. We've done part of the first question for you as an example. (*Tip*: Read each question all the way through before you decide which main points can be kept and which should be discarded.)

1. Subject: Watching television is a valuable way to spend time.

Choose main points that support the subject:

- learn things? Yes, you can learn many things watching TV.

- relax and laugh? Yes, TV provides good entertainment.

- wastes time? No, TV may do that, but this point doesn't support the thesis.

Paragraphs and Essays

- provides topics for discussion? Yes, talking about shows we've watched brings us together with friends and family.
- violent video games? No (why?) _____

A. Thesis statement: <u>Watching television is a valuable way to spend time</u> (because) <u>it teaches us many things</u>, <u>it provides relaxation</u>, and <u>it supplies us with topics to discuss with others</u>.

Now rewrite the thesis statement using a colon as a link.

B. There are three reasons _____

_____

_____

_____

2. A 30-hour work week would increase our company's productivity.
- Employees will be less tired, more focused, and more productive.
- It would allow employees to get part-time jobs.
- Increased family time and leisure time make an employee more satisfied.
- Work hours will not be in sync with those of suppliers and clients.
- Reduction in work hours will be compensated for by reduction in absenteeism and sick leave.

A. Thesis statement: Three reasons why our company should reduce the work week to 30 hours are _____

_____

_____

_____

Rewrite the thesis statement using *because* as a link.

B. _____

_____

_____

_____

3. Immigration is a good policy for Canada.

- immigrants offer new skills

- immigrants may find it difficult to adjust to life in Canada

- immigrants may bring investment dollars

- immigrants must often learn a new language

- immigrants enrich Canadian culture

A. **Thesis statement:** Immigration is a good policy for Canada because _____

_____

_____

_____

Rewrite the thesis statement using a colon as the link.

B. _____

_____

_____

_____

4. Most of us look forward to vacations, but the kind of vacation we enjoy depends on the kind of people we are.

- beach resorts
- gambling trips (e.g., Las Vegas, Orillia, Atlantic City)
- Cancun, Mexico
- adventure vacations
- Buckingham Palace
- too much sun

Paragraphs and Essays

- mountain climbing
- touring cultural attractions

A. **Thesis statement:** Different people like different kinds of vacation; for

example, <u>some people like to relax at a beach resort</u>, _____

_____

_____

Rewrite the thesis statement using *are* as a link.

B. _____

_____

_____

_____

In the following question, you need first to create a subject statement. Next, decide which points are usable (significant, distinct, and relevant). After deleting any unsatisfactory points, write two different thesis statements, making sure that both are grammatically parallel.

5. A satisfying career
   - interesting
   - well paid
   - respected
   - provides opportunities for advancement
   - makes employee feel needed and appreciated

A. **Thesis statement:** _____

_____

_____

_____

B. Thesis statement: _____

_____

_____

_____

EXERCISE **24.6**

Exchange with another student team the thesis statements you created for Exercise 24.5. Check each thesis statement for completeness and grammatical parallelism. Then decide which team's thesis statement for each subject you prefer, and why. Be prepared to defend your choice by referring to the four highlighted guidelines found on pages 272–81.

EXERCISE **24.7**

For each of the topics below, provide main points and write a thesis statement.

1. Starting a new job

    •

    •

    •

Thesis statement: _____

_____

_____

_____

2. What I've learned from my family since I became an adult

    •

    •

    •

Thesis statement: _____

_____

_____

_____

Paragraphs and Essays

3. What success means to me

-
-
-

Thesis statement: _____

_____

_____

_____

4. What makes us laugh

-
-
-

Thesis statement: _____

_____

_____

_____

5. How to save money

-
-
-

Thesis statement: _____

_____

_____

_____

GO TO WEB
EXERCISE 24.3

WWW.BAREA.NELSON.COM

EXERCISE **24.8**

Find the subjects and main points you produced for Exercise 23.9 in Chapter 23. Combine each subject with its main points to make a thesis statement. Be sure the main points are expressed in parallel form.

We said at the beginning of this chapter that a thesis statement outlines your paper for you. Before we turn to the actual writing of the paper, you should have a general idea of what the finished product will look like.

In a short paper, each main point can be explained in a single paragraph. The main points of your subject become the **topics** of the paragraphs, as shown below in the model format for a paper with three main points.[3] Once you've mastered this simple structure, you can modify, expand, and develop it to suit papers of any length or kind.

Please note that the model format on the next page is a basic guideline for anyone who is learning to write English prose. Not all essays are—or should be—five paragraphs long. As you will see in Unit 6, unified, coherent essays can be shorter or longer, depending on the subject and purpose. As you gain writing experience, you will learn how to adapt the basic format to suit your needs. A competent and confident writer always adapts form to content, never the other way around. But learners must start somewhere, and the five-paragraph format is an excellent structure with which to begin.

Notice the proportions of the paragraphs in the model format. This format is for a paper whose main points are approximately equal in significance, so the body paragraphs are approximately equal in length. (In a paper in which your last main point is more important than the other points, however, the paragraph that explains it will probably be longer than the other paragraphs.)

Notice, too, that the introductory and concluding paragraphs are shorter than the ones that explain the main points. Your introduction should not ramble on, and your conclusion should not trail off. Get to your main points as quickly as you can, and end with a bang, not a whimper.

Paragraphs and Essays

---

[3] Chapter 26 will show you how to develop your paragraphs fully and convincingly.

Title
_____

Paragraph 1:
Contains your
introduction
and thesis
statement
{
_____
_____
_____

S consists of 1, 2, and 3.

Paragraph 2:
Explains your
first main point
{
Topic sentence introducing main point 1.
_____
_____
_____
_____
_____
_____ .

Paragraph 3:
Explains your
second main
point
{
Topic sentence introducing main point 2.
_____
_____
_____
_____
_____
_____ .

Paragraph 4:
Explains your
third main point
{
Topic sentence introducing main point 3.
_____
_____
_____
_____
_____
_____ .

Paragraph 5:
States your
conclusion
{
_____
_____
_____
_____ .

EXERCISE **24.9**

An example of a paper based on the model format above is Brian Green's "Career Consciousness" on pages 336–37. Read it through; then go back and underline the thesis statement and the topic sentences.

The Outline 25

For longer compositions—business and technical reports, research papers, and the like—an outline is often necessary. A good outline maps out your paper from beginning to end. It shows you what you have to say about each of your main points before you begin drafting. Outlining spares you the agony of discovering too late that you have too much information about one point and little or nothing to say about another.

Once you've chosen a satisfactory subject and main points to discuss, the next step is to expand this material into an organized plan for your finished paper. To do this, you may need to do some more thinking or reading to gather additional information and supporting details. (For ideas about what kinds of information you might use, see "Developing Your Paragraphs" in Chapter 26.) After you've assembled all the information you think you'll need, prepare the outline.

There are as many different kinds of outlines as there are writers. The kind of outline you prepare for a paper will vary depending on your approach to the topic, the amount of time before the due date, and your instructor's preference (or requirement). Here are a few of the strategies you can choose from:

- People who like to begin the writing process with brainstorming, freewriting, or another inductive technique often choose to postpone outlining until after they see what their creative juices produce on paper.
- Some writers prefer to start with a "scratch" outline, which consists of one- or two-word points that act as a bare-bones guide.
- Others like an informal outline that sketches out the parts of the paper in more detail, showing major headings and supporting points.
- Some writers do best with a full, formal outline with numbered points and subheadings.

Whatever approach is appropriate for you, your topic, and your instructor, the time you spend outlining is invested, not wasted. The more time you spend at this stage of the process, the less time you'll need to devote to drafting.

SCRATCH OUTLINE

As we've seen in Chapters 23 and 24, after choosing a subject to write about, your next steps are to come up with main points and to arrange them in an order that will make sense to your reader. A thesis and main points are the beginnings of a scratch outline. Write these down, leaving enough space to jot down a few of the things you might say as you expand on each of the main points. Now you have a bare-bones outline to guide you as you draft the body of your paper. Here's an example:

Thesis: A satisfying career—interesting, rewarding, productive
- Interesting
  - enjoyable
  - like hobbies
  - Max Ward
- Rewarding
  - financial rewards
  - emotional rewards
- Productive
  - need to contribute
  - unproductive jobs

This is the skeleton of a paper. Put some meat on the bones, add an introduction and a conclusion, and you'll have a good first draft.

INFORMAL OUTLINE

An informal outline carries the scratch outline a step further, adding notes and ideas that will form the content of each paragraph. If whole sentences occur to you, write them down, but generally the informal outline is in point form.

Introduction
> What is a career?
> Thesis: "A satisfying career should be interesting, rewarding, and productive"
> - Interesting
>   1. Look forward to going to work
>   2. Leisure activities are stimulating, why not your career?
>   Examples: artists, Max Ward
>   3. Important not to spend rest of your life doing something you hate
> - Rewarding
>   1. Know yourself: What do you need?
>   Are you ambitious? Do you need status, high salary?
>   Low stress?
>   2. Success is what it means to you
>   Examples: technician, news director . . . which one is "successful"?
> - Productive
>   1. Human nature to want to contribute, to make a difference
>   2. Some jobs are easy, but meaningless
>   Examples: factory job, night shift

Conclusion
> Need to understand yourself is key
> Don't be swayed by opinions of others
> Keep working at it. Strive to improve for your own sake, not your employer's.

FORMAL OUTLINE

A formal outline is more detailed than the scratch or informal outline. It may be drafted in point form, but the finished outline usually consists of complete sentences.

Paragraphs and Essays

First, write down your main points in the order you've decided is best for your presentation. Leave at least a half-page between points. Using Roman numerals (I, II, III, and so on), number your main points. Now, under each main point, indent and list the examples, facts, quotations, or other supporting information you're going to use to explain it. Again, leave lots of space. Check to make sure these items are arranged in an order that will be clear to your reader.[1] Label your supporting points *A, B, C,* and so on.

If some of these supporting points need to be explained or developed, indent again and list the second level of supporting points, numbering them *1, 2, 3,* and so on. Third-level supporting details, if there are any, should be indented under the points to which they relate and labelled *a, b, c,* and so on. Add the introduction and the conclusion, and you're done. Your outline might look something like this.

Introduction
    Attention-getter
    Thesis statement/statement of subject

I. First main point
   A. Item that develops first main point
   B. Item that develops first main point
        1. Supporting material that develops item B
        2. Supporting material that develops item B

II. Second main point
   A. Item that develops second main point
   B. Item that develops second main point
   C. Item that develops second main point

III. Third main point
   A. Item that develops third main point
        1. Supporting material that develops item A
           a. Detail
           b. Detail
        2. Supporting material that develops item A
   B. Item that develops third main point

Conclusion
    Summary
    Memorable statement

---

[1] The four kinds of order explained in Chapter 23 apply to the arrangement of ideas within a paragraph as well as to the arrangement of main points in a paper.

Questions about how to arrange your information under each main point and how much time to spend on a particular point should be considered carefully at the outline stage. If, for example, you find you have six subheadings under main point I and only one under main point II, you need to do some rethinking to balance your paper. Main points should be supported by approximately equal amounts of information.

Preparing a satisfactory outline takes time. Be prepared to spend time adding, deleting, and rearranging your ideas and supporting details until you're completely satisfied with the arrangement and proportions of your outline.

If you have access to a word-processing program with an outline feature, try it out. These programs can be very helpful to an inexperienced writer with little knowledge of how to organize a writing assignment.

After you have written and revised your outline, you are ready to draft your paper. Make the main points into paragraph divisions, develop the supporting points, and add an introduction and a conclusion. Chapter 26 explains how.

To show you the relationship between an outline and the final product, we've re-created the outline that was used to write "Career Consciousness," which you will find on pages 336–37.

Introduction

    Attention-getter: Choosing your life's vocation is not a decision to be taken lightly.

    Thesis statement: A satisfying career is one that is stimulating, rewarding, and productive.

I. A satisfying career is stimulating.
   A. When you get up in the morning, you look forward to your day.
       1. While not the image most people have of work, it is achievable.
       2. Most people can enjoy work just as they enjoy leisure activities.
   B. Many successful people have turned their interests into careers.
       1. Career professionals in the arts get paid for what they love to do.
          a. write, compose, paint, sculpt, etc.
          b. act, dance, sing, etc.
       2. Max Ward turned his love of flying into the development of one of Canada's first charter airlines.
   C. If you deny yourself the chance to do what you love, you will spend most of your life wishing you were doing something else.

II. A satisfying career is rewarding, both financially and emotionally.
    A. To choose the right career, you must know yourself.
        1. Do you seek power and status?
        2. Or would you prefer a lower-profile position with less stress?
    B. Success is a state of mind.
        1. Contrast the careers of a small-town TV tech and a big-city news director.
            a. TV tech loves his job, family, community, and volunteer activities.
            b. News director thrives on deadlines, big-city life, money, and the recognition her job provides.
        2. Both feel they are successful in their careers.

III. A satisfying career is productive.
    A. People need meaningful work.
        1. People need to feel they make a difference.
        2. Friendly co-workers, a pleasant routine, and money do not make up for lack of appreciation.
    B. Many people go unnoticed in their working lives.
        1. Some boast about reading paperbacks on the job.
        2. Some sleep through the night shift and fish or golf during the day.
    C. Knowing that you are doing something worthwhile is essential to your sense of well-being.

Conclusion
    Summary: It's not easy to find a career that provides stimulating, enjoyable, and meaningful work.
    A. You need to understand yourself.
    B. Make career decisions consistent with your values and goals.
    C. Once you have found a satisfying career, keep working at it.
        1. Seek challenges and opportunities that stimulate you.
        2. Enjoy the rewards of doing your job well.
        3. Strive for improvement for your own sake, not your employer's.
    Memorable statement: Your career will occupy three-quarters of your life, so make the most of it!

Once you've mapped out your plan in an outline, the task of writing the essay is much easier. You can see at a glance where you're going and how to get there.

EXERCISE **25.1**

Turn to "Career Consciousness" on pages 336–37. Work with a partner to find the paragraphs and sentences that correspond to the various headings and subheadings in the outline on page 294. Use a coloured pen to label the paragraphs and sentences with the symbols that indicate where they fit into the outline: Attention-getter, Thesis statement, I, A, 1, 2, and so on.

EXERCISE **25.2**

1. With a partner, choose one of the essays in Unit 6 that interests you. Read the essay carefully, and create for it
   - a scratch outline
   - an informal outline
   - a formal outline.

2. Exchange your work with another team that selected the same reading, and compare outlines. Are there significant differences between the two teams' outlines? If so, which set of outlines best captures the essence of the essay?

EXERCISE **25.3**

Turn to the subjects and main points you developed for Exercise 23.9 in Chapter 23 and create scratch, informal, and formal outlines for a paper on one of those subjects.

26 Paragraphs

With your thesis statement and outline in front of you, you are ready to turn your main points into paragraphs. Does that sound like a magician's trick? It isn't. All you need to know is what a paragraph looks like and how to put one together.

A paragraph looks like this:

<u>A sentence that introduces the **topic** (or main idea) of the paragraph goes here.</u>

Three or more sentences that specifically support or explain the topic go in here.

<u>A sentence that concludes your explanation of the topic goes here.</u>

Sometimes you can explain a main point satisfactorily in a single paragraph. If the main point is complicated and requires lots of support, you will need two or more paragraphs. Nevertheless, whether it is explaining a main point or a supporting point, every paragraph must contain two things: a **topic sentence** (usually the first sentence in the paragraph) and several sentences that develop the topic.

A sentence clearly stating your main idea is a good way to start a paragraph. The sentences that follow should support or expand on the topic. The key to making the paragraph *unified* (an important quality of paragraphs) is to make sure that each of your supporting sentences relates directly to the main idea introduced in the topic sentence.

EXERCISE **26.1**

Turn to page 346 and read Brian Green's "The Case against Quickspeak." Study the fourth, fifth, and sixth paragraphs, and find in each the three basic components of a paragraph: the topic sentence, the supporting sentences, and the conclusion. Then compare your answer with ours. Answers for exercises in this chapter begin on page 438.

DEVELOPING YOUR PARAGRAPHS

How do you put a paragraph together? First, write your topic sentence, telling your reader what topic (main point or key idea) you're going to discuss in the paragraph. Next, develop your topic. An adequately developed paragraph gives enough supporting information to make the topic completely clear to the reader. An average paragraph runs between 75 and 200 words (except for introductions and conclusions, which are shorter), so you will need lots of supporting information for each point.

Unless you are writing from a detailed outline and have all the supporting ideas you need listed in front of you, you need to do some more thinking at this point. Put yourself in your reader's place. What does your reader need to know in order to understand your point clearly? If you ask yourself the six questions listed below, you'll be able to decide what **kind(s) of development** to use to support a particular topic sentence. The kind of development you choose is up to you. Let your topic and your reader be your guides.

Paragraphs and Essays

1. Is a **definition** necessary?

If you're using a term that may be unfamiliar to your reader, you should define it. Use your own words in the definition. The reader needs to know what *you* mean by the term—and, besides, quoting from the dictionary is a boring way to develop a paragraph. In the following paragraph, Al Gore defines a Chinese expression that is a key term in his article.

> Clichés are, by definition, over used. But here is a rare exception—a certifiable cliché that warrants more exposure, because it carries meaning deeply relevant to the biggest challenge our civilization has ever confronted. The Chinese expression for "crisis" consists of two characters: 危機. The first is a symbol for "danger"; the second is a symbol for "opportunity." (355)[1]

You should include a definition, too, if you're using a familiar term in a specific or unusual way. In the following paragraph, Nina Kovac offers two specific definitions of "quality food."

> The term "high-quality food" means different things to different people. For some, it means food that is produced organically—without the use of fertilizer, pesticides, or other chemical additives—and is not genetically modified. For other less demanding consumers, "high quality" means food that is free of added sugar, fat, or chemical enhancers. Whatever their definition of "quality food," the important point is that people should think about what they eat and choose their foods based on nutrition and taste rather than on popularity and convenience. (350)

EXERCISE **26.2**

Write a paragraph in which you define one of the following terms:

a geek	a good (or bad) movie/TV show	success/failure
friendship	creativity	leadership
racism	a bully	a good (or bad) relationship

---

[1] The page numbers in parentheses at the end of some of the examples in this chapter indicate page numbers in Unit 6, "Readings," where you will find the paragraphs in context. For source information on examples by writers other than the authors of this text, refer to the "Credits" page at the back of the book.

2. Would examples help to clarify the point?

Listing a number of examples is probably the most common method of developing a topic. Readers become confused, even suspicious, when they read unsupported generalizations or statements of opinion. One of the most effective ways of communicating your idea is by providing clear, relevant examples. In the following paragraph, excerpted from a reading in Unit 6, Sun-Kyung Yi uses examples to explain why her job with a Korean company proved to be a "painful and frustrating experience."

> When the president of the company boasted that he "operated a little Korea," he meant it literally. A Canadianized Korean was not tolerated. I looked like a Korean; therefore, I had to talk, act, and think like one, too. Being accepted meant a total surrender to ancient codes of behaviour rooted in Confucian thought, while leaving the "Canadian" part of me out in the parking lot with my '86 Buick. In the first few days at work, I was bombarded with inquiries about my marital status. When I told them I was single, they spent the following days trying to match me up with available bachelors in the company and the community. I was expected to accept my inferior position as a woman and had to behave accordingly. It was not a place to practise my feminist views, or be an individual without being condemned. Little Korea is a place for men (who filled all the senior positions) and women don't dare to speak up or disagree with their male counterparts. The president (all employees bow to him and call him Mr. President) asked me to act more like a lady and smile. I was openly scorned by a senior employee because I spoke more fluent English than Korean. The cook in the kitchen shook her head in disbelief upon discovering that my cooking skills were limited to boiling a package of instant noodles. "You want a good husband, learn to cook," she advised me. (344–45)

Sometimes one example developed in detail is enough to communicate your point to the reader. In the following paragraph, Al Gore describes what global warming is doing to Earth's oceans.

> More than 70 percent of the planet's surface is covered by ocean, and a series of new, comprehensive studies show that the amount of CO_2 being absorbed into the oceans is about one-third of what we have put into the environment with the burning of fossil fuels. As a result, the oceans of the world are becoming more acid, and the total amount of carbonic acid— even though it is a relatively weak acid—is beginning to change the mix of carbonate and bicarbonate ions in the oceans. This interferes with the ability of corals to form their calcium-carbonate skeletons, which constitute

Paragraphs and Essays

the base of many food chains in the oceans. Even more ominously, the amounts of carbonic acid we are continuing to sink into the oceans will, if we don't change the current reckless pattern, make it more difficult for many ocean creatures, large and tiny, to make shells, because the shells would instantly dissolve in the newly acid ocean water, the way chalk (also calcium carbonate) dissolves in vinegar. Continuing on our current path will return the oceans to a chemical pH balance that last existed 300 million years ago—when the Earth was a very different planet from the one that gave birth to and nurtured the human species. (356–57)

GO TO WEB
EXERCISE 26.1

WWW.BAREA.NELSON.COM

EXERCISE **26.3**

Write a six- to ten-sentence paragraph based on one of the topic sentences below, using examples to develop it.

Fast food is the new tobacco.
Most Americans do not understand why their country is so unpopular abroad.
Internet dating sites are beneficial (*or* harmful).
The teenage years are the hardest.
Sports are fascinating (*or* boring) entertainment.

3. Is a **series of steps** or **stages** involved?

Sometimes the most effective way to develop the main idea of your paragraph is by explaining how to do it—that is, by relating the process or series of steps involved. Make sure you break down the process into its component parts and explain the steps logically and precisely. The following paragraph explains the process of writing an effective e-mail message. As you read it, number the steps the author identifies as the parts of the process. Has he left anything out?

E-mail is no different from any other business correspondence: it must be clear and concise. Achieving clarity and conciseness is not difficult, but it does require planning. Begin with an introduction that briefly explains the purpose of your message. Next, outline how you are going to develop that message. Use numbered or bulleted points to guide the reader from your position statement through your reasoning to your conclusion.

Reinforce your message with a conclusion that states any follow-up actions you require and that confirms the time, place, and responsibilities of those who are contributing to the project. Next, re-read your message as if you were seeing it for the first time. Revise to be sure that you have included all the necessary details: dates, reference numbers, times and places of meetings, and whatever other information is needed to get the right people together in the right places, on the right days, at the right times, with the right information in their briefcases. Use a spell-checker, but don't count on it to catch all your errors and typos. Remember: A clear message, clearly delivered, is the essence of effective communication. (Green 347)

EXERCISE **26.4**

Write a paragraph developed as a series of steps telling your reader how to make or do something you are good at. (Choose a significant topic, not a trivial one.)

---

4. Would **specific details** be useful?

Providing your reader with concrete, specific, descriptive details can be an effective way of developing your main point. In the following paragraph, highlight the specific details that Nina Kovac uses to develop her topic, the benefits of shared family meals.

> Not surprisingly, the research also finds that adolescents who regularly eat with their families consume more fruit and vegetables, more calcium, less fat, and significantly fewer soft drinks. A healthier diet can account for some of the superior physical, mental, and emotional health of children in families who eat together, but not all. The very act of sitting down together without the distractions of video games, television, and computers encourages family members to communicate and share experiences. The shared meal need not be supper; in some shift-working households, a family breakfast may be more appropriate. While a thoughtfully prepared three-course feast might be the ideal, a quicker, easy-to-fix dish such as pasta or a stir-fry can also provide a tasty and nutritious main course for a sit-down family supper. And the research studies demonstrated that the benefits to children increase in direct proportion to the number of family meals they participate in each week. (352–53)

In some paragraphs, numerical facts or statistics can be used to support your point effectively. Ever since Benjamin Disraeli's immortal condemnation of the media's "lies, damned lies, and statistics," however, critical readers tend to be suspicious of statistics, so be very sure that your facts are correct and that your statistics are current.

> Canadians are great travellers. We not only travel around our own country, exploring every nook and cranny from Beaver Creek in the Yukon Territory to Bay Bulls in Newfoundland, but we also can be found touring around every other country on Earth. Statistics Canada reports that we take more than 175 million overnight trips a year within our own borders. Abroad, we favour our next-door neighbour by a wide margin above other destinations, averaging around 16 million overnight trips a year to the United States. Mexico is our second favourite destination, with over 841,000 visits, followed by the United Kingdom (778,000) and France (645,000). Of the Caribbean Islands, Cuba is our favourite winter escape, ranking fifth overall, with about 278,000 visits a year by Canadians. China ranks ninth in popularity with 250,000 visits, but Hong Kong, now part of China, attracts an additional 150,000 Canadian visitors, making their combined total just behind the Dominican Republic and ahead of Germany and Italy, while the top 15 are rounded out by more European nations: the Netherlands, Spain, Switzerland, Ireland, and Austria. We can make a rough estimate from these figures that, on average, a Canadian travels within Canada five times a year and takes a trip abroad twice in three years.

EXERCISE **26.5**

Write an eight- to ten-sentence paragraph describing one of the following topics. Include details that involve several of the physical senses: sight, hearing, touch, smell, and taste. Be sure to begin with a clearly identifiable topic sentence.

Your favourite summer/winter sport
The best video game/movie ever
Your favourite club/bar/coffee shop
A great/terrible concert
A locker room after a game
Your favourite family meal

---

5. Would a **comparison** or **contrast** help to clarify your point?

A **comparison** points out similarities between objects, people, or ideas; it shows how two different things are alike. A **contrast** points out dissimilarities between things; it shows how two objects, people, or ideas are different. In the paragraph below, Sun-Kyung Yi contrasts the two sides of her "split personality."

> When I was younger, toying with the idea of entertaining two separate identities was a real treat, like a secret game for which no one knew the rules but me. I was known as Angela to the outside world, and as Sun-Kyung at home. I ate bologna sandwiches in the school lunch room and rice and kimchee for dinner. I chatted about teen idols and giggled with my girlfriends during my classes, and ambitiously practised piano and studied in the evenings, planning to become a doctor when I grew up. I waved hellos and goodbyes to my teachers, but bowed to my parents' friends visiting our home. I could also look straight in the eyes of my teachers and friends and talk frankly with them instead of staring at my feet with my mouth shut when Koreans talked to me. Going outside the home meant I was able to relax from the constraints of my cultural conditioning, until I walked back in the door and had to return to being an obedient and submissive daughter. (343–44)

In the following paragraph, the writer develops his topic—how lack of planning can kill a city—by comparing the anatomy of a city to that of the human body.

> A poorly planned city dies from the centre out. When an unplanned urban area is growing rapidly, businesses and residential developments spring up wherever it is advantageous for them to locate. In time, they become plaque deposits on the very arteries that they chose to build on, gradually narrowing and choking the city's passages. New routes cannot be constructed without major surgery, nor can the old ones be widened because of the poorly planned developments that line them. Without sufficient flow along its arteries, an organism begins to experience high pressure . . . whether from traffic or blood. As the pressure builds, those who live and work in the city core seek to relocate to more convenient, less stressful surroundings, and the centre begins to die. Keeping arteries open and healthy requires advance planning and constant vigilance. In the human organism, a healthy diet and physical exercise will keep the blood flowing; in the urban organism, mass transit and well-planned traffic corridors will do the trick.

EXERCISE **26.6**

Write a paragraph comparing or contrasting two cities (or countries, co-workers, generations, musicians, jokes, clothing brands, vacation destinations). Begin your paragraph with a clearly identifiable topic sentence.

6. Would a **quotation** or **paraphrase** be appropriate?

Occasionally, you will find that someone else—an expert in a particular field, a well-known author, or a respected public figure—has said what you want to say better or more convincingly than you could ever hope to say it. In these cases, quotations—as long as they are kept short and not used too frequently—are useful in developing your topic. In the following paragraph, Al Gore quotes Winston Churchill's memorable remarks in his appeal to the British Parliament to take action against Nazi Germany.

> Nearly 70 years ago, when a horrible and unprecedented storm . . . was gathering in Europe, British prime minister Neville Chamberlain found it inconvenient to see the truth about the nature of the evil threat posed by the Nazis. In criticizing his government's blinding lack of awareness, Winston Churchill said, "So they go on in strange paradox, decided only to be undecided, resolved to be irresolute, adamant for drift, solid for fluidity, all-powerful to be impotent." After the appeasement at Munich, Churchill said, "This is only the first sip, the first foretaste, of a bitter cup which will be proffered to us year by year—unless by supreme recovery of moral health and martial vigor we rise again and take our stand for freedom." Then he warned prophetically that "the era of procrastination, of half measures, of soothing and baffling expedients, of delays, is coming to a close. In its place, we are entering a period of consequences." (357–58)

A paraphrase is a summary in your own words of someone else's idea. Be sure to identify the source of the idea you are paraphrasing, as we have done in the following example, a paraphrase of paragraph 3 from "Food for Thought" (pages 350–51).

Original

> The term "high-quality food" means different things to different people. For some, it means food that is produced organically—without the use of fertilizer, pesticides, or other chemical additives—and is not genetically modified. For other, less-demanding consumers, "high quality" means food that is free of added sugar, fat, or chemical enhancers. In either case, the important point is that people should think about what they eat and choose their foods based on nutrition and taste rather than on popularity, packaging, and convenience. Educating consumers to know how to select quality food is one of the Slow Food movement's main objectives.

Paraphrase

In an essay entitled "Food for Thought," Nina Kovac explains that the meaning of the term "high-quality food" varies depending on whom you talk to. Strict interpreters use it to refer to organic products grown without chemicals from natural, not genetically modified, seeds. At the other end of the scale, more relaxed consumers use the phrase to refer to foods that are processed without added fat, sugar, or chemicals. One of the goals of the Slow Food movement is to teach consumers how to choose foods based on their nutritional value and taste, rather than on clever advertising or widespread availability.

College writing normally requires that you indicate the source of any material you quote. The easiest way to do this is to give the reference in parentheses at the end of your quotation. If the author's name is already mentioned in your introduction to the quotation, you need give only the page number(s) on which you found the quotation. If the author's name is not given in your introduction to the quotation, you need to include it along with the page number(s).

If your quotation is short and included in your sentence, you use the same citation format, but you insert the parenthetical reference—author's name (if not already mentioned) and page number—before the end punctuation. For example:

According to Brian Green, "A career can be defined as the employment you prepare for during the first quarter of your life, engage in during the best years of your life, and reap the rewards from when you are least able to enjoy them" (336).

One writer takes a fairly cynical view of the typical career cycle: "A career can be defined as the employment you prepare for during the first quarter of your life, engage in during the best years of your life, and reap the rewards from when you are least able to enjoy them" (Green 336).

At the end of your paper, include a Works Cited or References list: a list in alphabetical order by authors' surnames of all of the books, articles, and other publications from which you have quoted in your paper. For an example of a Works Cited list in the Modern Language Association (MLA) format, go to page 342 ("The Slender Trap"), and for an example of an American Psychological Association (APA) References list, go to page 354 ("Food for Thought"). Be sure to follow the documentation style required by your instructor! For further information about both the MLA and the APA documentation styles, go to the Student Resources page of this book's website at

Paragraphs and Essays

www.barea.nelson.com; click on "More Information" and then on "Formatting and Documentation."

When you plan the paragraphs of your essay, remember that you will often need to use more than one method of development to explain each point. The six methods outlined above can be used in any combination. Choose whichever kinds of development will best help your reader understand what he or she needs to know about your topic.

EXERCISE **26.7**

Working with a partner, identify the kinds of development used in the following paragraphs from essays in Unit 6. (More than one kind of development may be present in each.) Then turn to page 439 to check your answers.

1. "The Case against Quickspeak," paragraph 5
2. "Food for Thought," paragraph 2
3. "Food for Thought" paragraph 4
4. "The Slender Trap," paragraph 4
5. "Career Consciousness," paragraph 3
6. "The Case against Quickspeak," paragraph 4
7. "The Moment of Truth," paragraph 4
8. "The Slender Trap," paragraph 3
9. "An Immigrant's Split Personality," paragraph 4
10. "An Immigrant's Split Personality," paragraph 10

EXERCISE **26.8**

Choose one of the following topics (or make up one of your own) and write a paragraph of approximately six to ten sentences using one or more of the methods of paragraph development we have discussed in this chapter. At the end of your paragraph, name the development method(s) you've used.

1. You can't trust everything you find on the Net.
2. Life is like a game of _____.
3. Failing at college requires careful planning.
4. Radio will never die.
5. How to "get away from it all."
6. _____ is a profession with a future.
7. Yesterday's music is (not) better than today's.
8. How to assess a potential partner.
9. Canadians don't appreciate how lucky they are.
10. A lucky escape.

WRITING INTRODUCTIONS AND CONCLUSIONS

Two paragraphs in your paper are not developed in the way we've just outlined: the introduction and the conclusion. All too often, these paragraphs are dull or clumsy and detract from a paper's effectiveness. But they needn't. Here's how to write good ones.

The introduction is worth special attention because that's where your reader either sits up and takes notice of your paper or sighs and pitches it into the wastebasket. Occasionally, for a short paper, you can begin simply with your thesis statement or statement of subject. More usually, though, an **attention-getter** comes before the thesis statement. An attention-getter is a sentence or two designed to get the reader interested in what you have to say.

There are several kinds of attention-getter to choose from.

1. A question (see "Food for Thought," page 350)
2. A little-known or striking fact (see "An Immigrant's Split Personality," page 343; "The Slender Trap," page 339)
3. A statement of opinion you intend to challenge (see "The Moment of Truth," page 355)
4. An interesting incident or anecdote related to your subject (see "The Case against Quickspeak," page 346)
5. A definition (see "Career Consciousness," page 336)

Add your thesis statement to the attention-getter to complete the introduction.

The closing paragraph, too, usually has two parts: a **summary** of the main points of your paper (phrased differently, please—not a word-for-word repetition of your thesis statement or your topic sentences) and a **memorable statement**. Your memorable statement may take several forms.

1. Refer to the content of your opening paragraph (see "Career Consciousness," page 337).
2. Include a relevant or thought-provoking quotation, statement (see "The Moment of Truth," page 360), or question (see "Food for Thought," page 353).
3. Emphasize the value or significance of your subject (see "The Case against Quickspeak," page 347).
4. Make a suggestion for change (see "An Immigrant's Split Personality," page 345).
5. Offer a solution, make a prediction, or invite the reader to get involved (see "The Slender Trap," page 342).

Paragraphs and Essays

EXERCISE **26.9**

Using as many of the different kinds as you can, write an attention-getter and a memorable statement for each of the following topics.

1. Taxes on gasoline should (not) be raised to reduce fuel consumption.
2. Video game content should (not) be censored.
3. Honesty is (not) always the best policy.
4. College professors should (not) be required to take courses in how to teach.
5. Travel is the best form of education.
6. What you wear tells who you are.
7. It's not easy being a man (woman).
8. Canada's new preferred immigrant categories will (not) benefit the country over time.
9. The notion of employer-supported lifelong learning (i.e., continual retraining throughout my career) is (not) appealing to me.
10. We can learn much from our grandparents/children.

KEEPING YOUR READER WITH YOU

As you write your paragraphs, keep in mind that you want to make it as easy as possible for your reader to follow you through your paper. Clear **transitions** and an appropriate **tone** can make the difference between a paper that confuses or annoys readers and one that enlightens and pleases them.

TRANSITIONS

Transitions are those words or phrases that show the relationship between one point and the next, helping a paragraph or a paper to read smoothly. Like turn signals on a car, they tell the person following you where you're going. Here are some common transitions you can use to keep your reader on track.

1. *To show a time relationship:* first, second, third, next, before, during, after, now, then, finally, last
2. *To add an idea or example:* in addition, also, another, furthermore, similarly, for example, for instance
3. *To show contrast:* although, but, however, instead, nevertheless, on the other hand, in contrast, on the contrary
4. *To show a cause–effect relationship:* as a result, consequently, because, since, therefore, thus

Here is a paragraph that has adequate development but no transitions:

> There are several good reasons why you should not smoke. Smoking is harmful to your lungs and heart. It is annoying and dangerous to those around you who do not smoke. Smoking is an unattractive and dirty habit. It is difficult to quit. Most worthwhile things in life are hard to achieve.

Not very easy to read, is it? Readers are jerked from point to point until, battered and bruised, they reach the end. This kind of writing is unfair to readers. It makes them do too much of the work. The ideas may all be there, but the readers have to figure out for themselves how they fit together. After a couple of paragraphs like this one, even a patient reader can become annoyed.

Now read the same paragraph with the transitions added:

> There are several good reasons why you should not smoke. *Among them, three stand out as the most persuasive. First*, smoking is harmful to your lungs and heart. *Second*, it is *both* annoying and dangerous to those around you who do not smoke. *In addition to these compelling facts*, smoking is an unattractive and dirty habit. *Furthermore, once you begin*, it is difficult to quit; *but then*, most worthwhile things in life are hard to achieve.

In the revised paragraph, readers are gently guided from one point to the next. By the time they reach the conclusion, they know not only what ideas the writer had in mind but also how they fit together. Transitions make the reader's job easier and more rewarding.

TONE

One final point. As you write the paragraphs of your paper, be conscious of your **tone.** Your audience, purpose, and subject will all influence the tone you choose, which must be appropriate to all three. The words you use, the examples, quotations, and other supporting materials you choose to help explain your main points—all of these contribute to your tone.

When you are trying to explain something to someone, particularly if it's something you feel strongly about, you may be tempted to be highly emotional in your discussion. If you allow yourself to get emotional, chances are you won't be convincing. What will be communicated is the strength of your feelings, not the depth of your understanding or the validity of your opinion. To be clear and credible, you need to restrain your enthusiasm or anger and present your points in a calm, reasonable way.

Paragraphs and Essays

Here are a few suggestions to help you find and maintain the right tone.

- Be tactful. Avoid phrases such as "Any idiot can see," "No sane person could believe," and "It is obvious that. . . . " What is obvious to you isn't necessarily obvious to someone who has a limited understanding of your subject or who disagrees with your opinion.

- Don't talk down to your readers as though they were children or hopelessly ignorant. Don't use sarcasm, profanity, or slang.

- Don't apologize for your interpretation of your subject. Have confidence in yourself. You've thought long and hard about your subject, you've found good supporting material to help explain it, and you believe in its significance. Present your subject in a positive manner. If you hang back, using phrases such as "I may be wrong, but . . . " or "I tend to feel that . . . ", your reader won't be inclined to give your points the consideration they deserve. If you present your ideas with confidence and courtesy, your paper will be clear and convincing.

The following paragraph is an example of inappropriate tone. The writer is enthusiastic about the topic, but the tone is arrogant, bossy, and tactless. Few readers would be persuaded.

It is time that governments at all levels did something completely out of character: take action. We need laws requiring the addition of 10 percent ethanol to gasoline. Ethanol burns cleaner than gas and also boosts octane, so it's completely obvious that the oil companies don't have to put so many poison additives in the gas to make our already too powerful cars go even faster. For another thing, anybody who has done any reading knows that ethanol is made out of corn, which is grown on farms and is a renewable resource. Growing it will make farmers happy, and drivers should also be cheerful because it can be produced for less than the outrageous prices we pay for straight gasoline. Adding 10 percent of the cheaper fuel should bring pump prices down, although I'm sure the oil companies will find a way to gouge the consumer. Obviously, the government is going to have to pass laws forcing the oil companies to add ethanol because there's no way they're going to do what is good for the environment and the economy at the expense of lining their own pockets. However, relying on government to do the right thing is just as precarious a proposition; I wouldn't hold my breath.

Now read the following paragraph, which argues the same point but in a courteous, tactful way.

Legislation requiring the addition of ethanol to gasoline is both sensible and overdue. The addition of 10 percent ethanol to the gasoline that is sold at the pump is sensible for two reasons. First, it makes the fuel that is burned in our cars and trucks cleaner. Ethanol burns hotter than gasoline and burns up more of the pollutants, rather than sending them out of the tailpipe. Because it provides a higher octane fuel, ethanol also eliminates the need for some of the very nasty additives currently used to boost octane. Second, ethanol is a renewable source of energy that will provide jobs in rural Canada because it is made from corn. At current oil prices, ethanol is cheaper than gasoline, so its addition to our fuel will help to reduce costs for consumers. Why should governments have to legislate such a sensible course of action? The petroleum industry, from exploration to retail, is not about to voluntarily dilute its product, and, more importantly, its profits, by any amount, let alone 10 percent!

EXERCISE **26.10**

The following paragraph is a draft written for a general reader. The writer's purpose is to persuade her audience that city dwellers should be more aware of the labour that lies behind every packaged product we eat. Revise the paragraph to make it appropriate to its audience and purpose by deleting or rewording any lapses in tone. Then compare your answer with ours on page 439.

I'm from the city, so I may not know much about the subject, but it seems to me that we urban-dwellers have lost touch with the food we eat. By this I mean, obviously, that we no longer appreciate the farmers and farm workers who supply the food that we enjoy every day. Anyone with half a brain should realize that most of the food we buy is prepackaged in Styrofoam, wrapped in plastic, or precooked and frozen by huge corporations whose goal is to make humongous profits by selling us the packaging, not the contents. Do any urban consumers understand that their ketchup is made from farm-grown tomatoes? Do any advertising-driven supermarket shoppers really think about the fact that those over-packaged frozen pork chops, so irresistible with their sprig of parsley, were once a pig, raised by a farmer? Not only are we ignorant, but also

Paragraphs and Essays

we couldn't care less about the journey our food makes from farm to fridge. My guess is that if you asked most city kids where their food comes from, they'd say, "the food factory."

EXERCISE **26.11**

Do either A or B.

A. Using one of the thesis statements you prepared in Chapter 24, Exercise 24.7, write a paper of approximately 400 words.
B. Using one of the outlines you prepared in Chapter 25, Exercise 25.3, write a paper of approximately 500 words.

Revising Your Paper 27

No one can write in a single draft an essay that is perfectly organized and developed, let alone one that is free of errors. The purpose of the first draft is to get down on paper something you can work with until it meets your reader's needs and expectations. Planning and drafting should take about half the time you devote to writing a paper. The rest should be devoted to revision.

Revision is the process of refining your message until

- it says what you want it to say
- your reader(s) will understand it and
- your reader(s) will receive it favourably

These three goals are the essentials of good communication. You can achieve them only if you keep your readers in mind as you revise. Because a first draft reflects the contents of the writer's mind, it often seems all right to the writer. But in order to transfer an idea as clearly as possible from the mind of the writer to the mind of the reader, revision is necessary. The idea needs to be honed and refined until it is as clear to your reader as it is to you. By revising from your reader's point of view, you can avoid misunderstandings before they happen.

WHAT IS REVISION?

Revision means "re-seeing." It does *not* mean re-copying. The aim of revision is to improve your writing's organization, accuracy, and style. Revising is a three-stage process. Each step requires that you read through your entire essay, painful though this may be. The goal of your first reading is to ensure that you've organized and developed your ideas in a way that communicates with your reader. In your second reading, you focus on structure. Your third reading concentrates on correctness. Here are the steps to follow in revising a paper.

1. Improve the whole paper by revising its content and organization.
2. Refine paragraph and sentence structure, and correct any errors in grammar.
3. Edit and proofread to catch errors in word choice, spelling, and punctuation.

Inexperienced writers often skip the first two stages and concentrate on the third, thinking they will save time. This is a mistake. In fact, they waste time—both theirs and their readers'—because the result is writing that doesn't communicate clearly and won't make a positive impression.

The best way to begin revising is to do nothing to the early version of your paper for several days. Let as much time as possible pass between completing your first draft and re-reading it. Ten minutes, or even half a day, is not enough. The danger in re-reading too soon is that you're likely to "read" what you *think* you've written—what exists in your head, not on the page.

If you haven't allowed enough time for this cooling-off period, don't despair. There are two other things you can do to help you get some distance from your draft. If your first draft is handwritten, type it out. Reading your essay in a different form helps you to "re-see" its content. Alternatively, read your paper aloud and listen to it from the point of view of your reader. Hear how your explanation unfolds, and mark every place your reader may find something unclear, irrelevant, inadequately developed, or out of order.

STEP 1:
REVISE CONTENT AND ORGANIZATION

As you read your paper aloud, keep in mind the three possible kinds of changes you can make at this stage:

1. You can **rearrange** information. This is the kind of revision that is most often needed but least often done. Consider the order in which you've arranged your paragraphs. From your reader's point of view, is this the most effective order in which to present your ideas? If you are not already using a word-processing program, now is the time to begin. With a good word processor, moving blocks of text around is as easy as dealing a deck of cards.
2. You can **add** information. Adding new main ideas or more development is often necessary to make your message interesting and convincing as well as clear. It's a good idea to ask a friend to read your draft and identify what needs to be expanded or clarified. (Be sure to return the favour. You can learn a great deal by critiquing other people's writing.)
3. You can **delete** information. Now is the time to cut out anything that is repetitious, insignificant, or irrelevant to your subject and reader.

Use the checklist that follows to guide you as you review your paper's form and content.

Content and Organization Checklist

ACCURACY
Is everything you have said accurate?
- Is your information consistent with your own experience and observations or with what you have discovered through research?
- Are all your facts and evidence up to date?

COMPLETENESS
Have you included enough main ideas and development to explain your subject and convince your reader? (Remember that "enough" means from the reader's point of view, not the writer's.)
- If your paper is based on research, have you provided an appropriate source citation for every quotation and/or paraphrase?
- Have you attached a Works Cited or References list, if one is required?

Paragraphs and Essays

SUBJECT

Is your subject

- significant? Does it avoid the trivial or the obvious?
- single? Does it avoid double or combined subjects?
- specific? Is it focused and precise?
- supportable? Have you provided enough evidence to make your meaning clear?

MAIN POINTS

Are your main points

- significant? Have you deleted any unimportant ones?
- distinct? Are they all different from one another, or is there an overlap in content?
- relevant? Do all points relate directly to your subject?
- arranged in the most appropriate order? Again, "appropriate" means from the reader's perspective. Choose chronological, climactic, logical, or random order, depending on which is most likely to help the reader make sense of your information.

INTRODUCTION

Does your introduction

- catch attention and make the reader want to read on?
- contain a clearly identifiable thesis statement?
- identify the main points that your paper will explain?

CONCLUSION

Does your conclusion

- contain a summary or reinforcement of your main points, rephrased to avoid word-for-word repetition?
- contain a statement that effectively clinches your argument and leaves the reader with something to think about?

TONE

Is your tone consistent, reasonable, courteous, and confident throughout your essay?

When you have carefully considered these questions, it's time to move on to the second stage of the revision process.

Read through the following draft outline for an essay on how to write effective e-mails in a business environment. Working with a partner, delete any unnecessary supporting points and arrange the remaining ones in chronological order. Write a thesis statement to complete your working outline for the essay. Then compare your results with our suggestion on page 440.

E-Mail Excellence

Attention-getter: As the recipient of approximately 1,000 business-related e-mail messages every month, I am something of an expert on what is effective and what is not in e-mail correspondence.

Thesis statement: _____

                              _____

                              _____

                              _____

Main points:

I. Subject line

    A. always include one

    B. make sure it states clearly what the message is about

    C. never use vague subject lines such as "hello," or "message," or "are you there?"

    D. never leave the subject line blank

II. Attachments

    A. use sparingly

    B. may carry viruses

    C. take time to transfer and to open

    D. attach text-only files unless a graphic is absolutely necessary

    E. use only if necessary

III. Message

    A. Content

        1. be concise and to the point

        2. tell the reader what action is needed, by whom, and when

        3. don't be a novelist or a "Chatty Cathy"

        4. use plain English, not "cyberspeak"

        5. use an appropriate level of language in your message as well as in your salutation and signature

    B. Format

        1. use bullets to identify points you want to emphasize

        2. leave white space between points

        3. avoid sending your message in uppercase letters (shouting)

        4. avoid smilies and other "cute" computer shorthand symbols

Summary: If you follow my recommendations on these three points whenever you write an e-mail, you will make the recipient of your message very happy.

Memorable statement: Especially if you're writing to me.

STEP 2:
REVISE PARAGRAPHS AND SENTENCES

Here, too, you should allow time—at least a couple of days—between your first revision and your second. Enough time must elapse to allow you to approach your paper as if you were seeing it for the first time. Once again, read your draft aloud, and use this list of questions to help you improve it.

Paragraph and Sentence Checklist

PARAGRAPHS

Does each paragraph

- begin with a clear, identifiable topic sentence?
- develop one—and only one—main idea?
- present one or more kinds of development appropriate to the main idea?
- contain clear and effective transitions to signal the relationship between sentences? Between paragraphs?

SENTENCES

Sentence Structure

1. Is each sentence clear and complete?
   - Are there any fragments or run-ons?
   - Are there any misplaced or dangling modifiers?
   - Are all lists (whether words, phrases, or clauses) expressed in parallel form?
2. Are your sentences varied in length? Could some be combined to improve the clarity and impact of your message?

Grammar

1. Have you used verbs correctly?
   - Are all verbs in the correct form?
   - Do all verbs agree with their subjects?
   - Are all verbs in the correct tense?
   - Are there any confusing shifts in verb tense within a paragraph?
2. Have you used pronouns correctly?
   - Are all pronouns in the correct form?
   - Do all pronouns agree with their antecedents?
   - Have any vague pronoun references been eliminated?

When you're sure you've answered these questions satisfactorily, go to the third and last stage of the revision process.

EXERCISE **27.2**

Here is the draft of the essay on e-mail. Revise it to correct errors in paragraph structure, sentence structure, and grammar. Don't worry about word usage, spelling, or punctuation at this stage. Then compare your answer with our suggestion on pages 440–41.

1   As the recipient of approximately 1,000 business-related e-mail messages

every month, I am something of an expert on what is effective in e-mail correspondence and what is not. The three areas that need attention in most e-mail messages are the subject line, the content, the format of the message and the use of attachments.

2   Some people leave the subject line blank, this is a mistake. I want to know what the message is about before I open it so I can decide if it needs my immediate attention. Or can wait until later. A message with no subject line or with a line that didn't tell me nothing about the content of the e-mail get sent to the bottom of my "to-do" list. There are lots of readers like me busy people who receive tons of e-mail, much of it unsolicited advertising that clutter up their inboxes. For this reason the subject line should always clearly state the subject of the message and should never be vague or cute like "hello" or "message" or "are you there?"

3   As for the message itself, it's function should be to tell the reader what action one wants, you need to be clear about this and be as brief as possible. What is it that you want the recipient to do. Who else needs to be involved. By when does the action need to take place. Communicate your message in plain English, not in "cyberspeak." Not everyone knows Net lingo, and even some who are famliar with it find it irritating not charming. Use an appropriate level of language (general-level Standard English will always be appropriate) to convey you're message. Use the same level of language in you're salutation and closing or "signature." One should definitely not sign off a message to your client or your boss with "love and kisses." Format you're message so that the recipient

will be able to read it quickly and understanding it easily. Use bullets to identify points you want to emphasize, separate the bullets with white space so they can be read at a glance and reviewed individually if necessary. There are some important points of e-mail etiquette that you should observe. Don't type your message in uppercase letters, that's considered "shouting." Do avoid "smilies" and other "cute" computer shorthand symbols. Some of you're readers won't understand them, others will have seen them so often they will be turned off.

4   Attachments should be included only if they are really necessary, for one thing, attachments can carry virruses so some people won't open them. Another disadvantage is that they take time to send download and open. Unless I am sure that an attachment is both urgent and vitally important—the agenda of tomorrow's meeting, for example—I don't bother to open it, for all I know, it might contain not only a virus but also footage of the sender's toddler doing her latest photogenic trick. As a general rule attach only what you must and attach text-only files. Try to include everything you need to say in the message itself and use attachments only as a last resort. Think of them as equivalent to footnotes, supplementary to the message not an essential part of it.

5   If you follow my recommendations on these three points whenever you write an e-mail, you will make the recipient of your message very happy. Especially if you're writing to me.

Paragraphs and Essays

STEP 3:
EDIT AND PROOFREAD

By now you're probably so tired of refining your paper that you may be tempted to skip **editing**—correcting errors in word choice, spelling, punctuation, and formatting—and **proofreading**—correcting errors in typing or writing that appear in the final draft. But these final tasks are essential if you want your paper to make a positive impression.

Misspellings, faulty punctuation, and messiness don't always create misunderstandings, but they do cause the reader to form a lower opinion of you and your work. Careful editing and proofreading are necessary if you want your writing to be favourably received.

Most word-processing programs include a grammar checker and a spell checker. It is worthwhile running your writing through these programs at the editing stage. The newer programs have some useful features. For example, they will question (but not correct) your use of apostrophes, they will sometimes catch errors in subject–verb agreement, and they will catch obvious misspellings and typos.

But don't make the mistake of assuming these programs will do all of your editing for you. Many errors slip past a computer's database, no matter how comprehensive the salesperson told you it is. Only you or a knowledgeable and patient friend can find and correct all errors.

If spelling is a particular problem for you, you should first run your paper through a spell checker. After that, you're on your own. Read your paper backward, word by word, from the end to the beginning. Reading backward forces you to look at each word by itself and helps you to spot those that look suspicious. Whenever you're in doubt about the spelling of a word, look it up! If you find this task too tedious to bear, ask a good speller to read through your paper for you and identify any errors. (Then take this person out for dinner. If you get an A, add a show.)

Here are the questions to ask yourself when you are editing.

Editing Checklist
WORDS

Usage
Have you used words to convey meaning rather than to impress?
- Have you eliminated any slang, pretentious language, or offensive language?
- Have you cut out any unnecessary words?
- Have you corrected any "abusages"?

Spelling

Are all words spelled correctly?

- Have you double-checked any homonyms?
- Have you used capital letters where they are needed?
- Have you used apostrophes correctly for possessives and omitted them from plurals?

PUNCTUATION

Within Sentences

- Have you eliminated any unnecessary commas and included commas where needed? (Refer to the four comma rules in Chapter 18 as you consider this question.)
- Have you used colons and semicolons where appropriate?
- Are all quotations appropriately marked?

Beginnings and Endings

- Does each sentence begin with a capital letter?
- Do all questions—and only questions—end with a question mark?
- Are all quotation marks correctly placed?

FORMATTING AND DOCUMENTATION (If required)

- Does your paper satisfy all details of the format specified by your instructor?
- Have you provided a citation for the source of every quotation and paraphrase?
- Have you attached a properly formatted Works Cited or References list?

EXERCISE **27.3**

Now scan or key into your word processor the revised draft of the essay you produced for Exercise 27.2.[1] This is your last chance to make this essay error-free. There are two parts to this exercise.

1. Using the "Editing Checklist" above, revise errors in word usage, spelling, and punctuation. Save your file as "Draft 3" and print it.

2. Follow the "Tips for Effective Proofreading" below to find and correct any errors or typos you may have missed. Save your file under a new name ("Draft 4" or "Final Draft") and print it.

Finally, compare your results with our suggestions on pages 441–42. Don't make any corrections to your work; just see how close you came to finding and correcting all errors.

Paragraphs and Essays

---

[1] If you do not have access to a word processor, complete this exercise using a different colour of pen for each draft. In order to learn your strengths and weaknesses, you must be able to identify the changes you made at each stage of the revision process.

TIPS FOR EFFECTIVE PROOFREADING

By the time you have finished editing, you will have gone over your paper so many times you may have practically memorized it. When you are very familiar with a piece of writing, it's hard to spot the small mistakes that may have crept in as you produced your final copy. Here are some tips to help you find those tiny, elusive errors.

1. Read through your essay line by line, using a ruler to guide you.
2. If you've been keeping a list of your most frequent errors in this course, scan your essay for the mistakes you are most likely to make.
3. Use the "Quick Revision Guide" on the inside front cover of this book to make a final check of all aspects of your paper.
4. Use the list of correction marks on the inside back cover to check for errors your instructor has identified in your writing.

Your "last" draft may need further revision after your proofreading review. If so, take the time to rewrite the paper so that the version you hand in is clean and easy to read. If a word processor is available to you, use it. Computers make editing and proofreading almost painless, since errors are so easy to correct.

At long last, you're ready to submit your paper. If you've followed the three steps to revision conscientiously, you can hand it in with confidence that it says what you want it to say, both about your subject and about you. One last word of advice:

DON'T FORGET TO KEEP A COPY FOR YOUR FILES!

GO TO WEB
EXERCISE 27.1

WWW.BAREA.NELSON.COM

EXERCISE **27.4**

Revise the passage on the following page in three stages: first, apply all of the questions in the Step 2 "Paragraph and Sentence Checklist" on page 321, and then apply all of the questions in the Step 3 "Editing Checklist" on pages 324–25. Finally, review "Tips for Effective Proofreading" above. Then compare your final draft with ours on pages 442–43.

Do you find it a struggle to pay the bills every month. When living beyond your means, even a small shortfall at the end of each month can quickly add up to a humongous debt. To beat this problem you can basically choose to spend less or earning more. At first, the former may seem the more difficulty choice, cutting back on what you spend may mean giving up some of the things you "need" such as eating out, movies, or the latest fashions. Doing without such expensive pleasures, however, often produce significant savings, you may even save enough to balance the monthly books.

Earning more money than what you now bring in and continuing to spend at your present pace may seem like a more attractive way to go, but is it realistic. There is the challenge of finding another job that pays better. Or adding part-time work to the job you already have, either way your going to loose even more of your already scarce study and leisure time. There is the fact that most people continue to spend at the same rate, regardless of how much money we make so its likely that, even with additional income, you'll still be in the hole at the end of the month. The best solution to the end-of-month budget blues is likely a combination of cutting costs where practical and adding to income where possible.

EXERCISE **27.5**

Turn to the draft paper you wrote for Exercise 26.11 in Chapter 26. Revise the paper by applying to it the three steps of the revision process.

28 | Using Research Resources Responsibly

PARAPHRASE OR PLAGIARISM?

In our culture, using someone else's words or ideas in your own writing without acknowledging their source is considered to be **plagiarism**, and it is a punishable offence. At its most serious, plagiarism is an attempt to deceive the reader into thinking you wrote the material. In the academic world, even when plagiarism is unintentional, it can lead to consequences ranging from a grade of zero on a paper, a failing grade in the course, or even expulsion from the college or university. In the business world and in the media, a writer who plagiarizes can expect to be fired.

Many students think that it is all right to use information they've found if they change the wording of the material they want to "borrow." This is not so. *Any information or ideas that cannot be considered common knowledge must be acknowledged or credited. Even if you put someone else's original idea into your own words, you must tell your reader the source of the information.* Any material that is taken word for word from another writer must be put in quotation marks and its source given. (See "Crediting Your Sources," below.)

PARAPHRASING VS. PLAGIARISM

Paraphrasing is including another writer's idea in your essay, but expressing it in your own words. The ability to paraphrase well is an immensely useful skill, but it is not easy to learn. You will need much experience before you can produce effective paraphrases. One of the reasons you are assigned research papers in college or university is to give you practice in paraphrasing. Here are the guidelines to follow:

1. A paraphrase must be a clear and accurate rewording of the author's idea.
2. A paraphrase must express the author's idea in your own words and sentences.
3. The source of your paraphrase must be included, using the documentation format that has been specified by your instructor or chosen by you.

To see the differences between paraphrase and plagiarism, study the paragraphs that follow. We have taken as our example a paragraph from "Career Consciousness," which you will find on page 337.

Original

It is not easy to find a career that provides stimulating, enjoyable, and meaningful work. Understanding yourself—your interests, needs, values, and goals—is an essential first step. Making long-term decisions consistent with your values and goals is the difficult second step. Too many people spend their lives in careers that make them miserable because they allow themselves to be governed by parents, friends, or simple inertia. Finally, once you have launched your career, never rest. Actively seek challenges and opportunities that stimulate you. Relish the rewards of meeting those challenges, being productive, and doing your job well. Continually strive to improve, not for the sake of your employer, but for your own sake. Your career will occupy three-quarters of your life, so make the most of it!

Unacceptable paraphrase

In "Career Consciousness," Brian Green points out that it is not easy to find a career that is stimulating, enjoyable, and meaningful. The first step is to understand yourself, your interests, needs, values, and goals. The second step is making long-term decisions consistent with your values and goals. Too often, people devote their lives to careers that make them unhappy because they permit themselves to be influenced by family, friends, or plain laziness. Once you have decided on a career, look for challenges and opportunities that are stimulating, and keep striving to improve, not for the sake of the employer, but for your own sake. Make the most of your career because it will occupy three-quarters of your life.

Neither a quotation nor a true paraphrase, this paragraph is an example of plagiarism.

Its phrasing is too close to that of the original. Even though the paragraph acknowledges the source of the ideas, it presents those ideas in the same order, and often in the same words as the original. And when the words are not identical, the sentence structure is. For example, compare these two sentences and note the correspondence between the two sets of italicized words:

Original

Too many people *spend* their lives in careers that make them *miserable* because they *allow* themselves to be *governed* by *parents*, friends, or *simple inertia*.

and

Unacceptable paraphrase

Too often, people *devote* their lives to careers that make them *unhappy* because they *permit* themselves to be influenced by *family*, friends, or *plain laziness*.

The second sentence is an example of what happens when an inexperienced writer tries to create a paraphrase by relying on a thesaurus to "translate" the original. The identical sentence structure is a dead giveaway—not only of what the writer was trying to do, but also of how he or she was trying to do it.

Better paraphrase

Two factors are essential to long-term career satisfaction. In "Career Consciousness," Brian Green says that the first is to know yourself and make a career choice that is consistent with your personal values and goals, rather than allow the decision to be made for you by others. The second, according to Green, is to continue to look for opportunities once you have begun your career. By continually seeking ways to improve your performance and meet new challenges, you will not only please your employer, but you will also make your job stimulating and satisfying.

USING ONLINE SOURCES

When using Internet sources for research, remember that the Internet is largely unregulated. Even seasoned researchers are sometimes fooled into thinking that a particular posting is factual when it is only someone's—and not necessarily an expert's—opinion. One of your responsibilities as a student researcher is to evaluate the sources of information you use to ensure that they are authoritative and creditable. Many websites try to give the appearance of being official and objective when in fact they have a distinct point of view that they are trying to promote. Unfortunately, there is no standard test or measure you can apply to distinguish between fact and propaganda.

One of the most popular sites for research material is Wikipedia, which is a gold mine of information. However, researchers must be aware that the entries in Wikipedia are written by subscribers. Can this information be trusted? Since entries are closely monitored by professional scholars and expert amateurs, as well as by Wikipedia employees, in many cases it can. But there is no guarantee that a Wikipedia entry is accurate, up to date, or unbiased. If you cannot rely on Wikipedia without question, imagine how careful you must be in using information from blogs and discussion forums!

Always check the trustworthiness of an Internet source. One way to confirm the accuracy of information you want to use is by consulting several different sources to see if they agree. If you are unsure about a source, check with your instructor to confirm whether information from that source is reliable for the research project you are doing.

CREDITING YOUR SOURCES: MLA AND APA DOCUMENTATION

When you use material that you have found in your reading, you must tell the reader where that material came from. This process is called *documentation*, and it consists of two parts: parenthetical citations, which you insert into the text of your paper immediately after the quotations or paraphrases that you've used to support a main point, and a list at the end of the paper of all of the sources you refer to in your paper.

There are two reasons why you must use source citations: first, they protect you from the charge of plagiarism, and, second, they enable your readers to locate your sources if they want to read more about your subject. Unfortunately, you cannot just name the author and title of the work(s) you have borrowed from. The standard style for papers in the humanities (English, history, art, philosophy, etc.) differs from the standard style required for papers in the social sciences (economics, psychology, sociology, political science, etc.). Your instructors may have specific requirements for acknowledging sources; if so, follow them to the letter. And don't be surprised if different teachers have different requirements.

Paragraphs and Essays

As a student researcher, you need to be familiar with at least two documentation systems: MLA and APA. The initials stand for the organizations (Modern Language Association and American Psychological Association) that developed these formats for writers who want to submit papers for publication by these organizations in their respective journals.

In MLA and APA styles, in-text citations (basic information about sources) are given in parentheses immediately following the quoted or referenced material in the main body of your paper. Normally, in-text citations provide the author's last name and the page number in the document where the material was found. At the end of the essay, a Works Cited (MLA) or References (APA) page gives detailed information about each source, including the author's name, title of the work, publisher, place of publication, and year of publication—not always in that order. The format you use depends on where you found the information: on the Internet, in a book, journal, magazine, interview, and so on. In Unit 6, you will find an essay in MLA format (page 339) and one in APA format (page 349). For specific instructions on how to credit various kinds of sources in both MLA and APA styles, go to the Student Resources page on this book's website at **www.nelson.barea.com**; click on "More Information" and then on "Format and Documentation."

EXERCISE **28.1**

Below we have provided three paragraphs (taken from readings in Unit 6), each of which is followed by a paragraph that is intended to be a paraphrase of the original. Compare each paraphrase to the original and determine if it is an acceptable paraphrase or if it is plagiarism. Check your answers with ours on page 443 and then revise the plagiarized paragraphs to make them true paraphrases.

1. From "An Immigrant's Split Personality," pages 343–44:

Original:

When I was younger, toying with the idea of entertaining two separate identities was a real treat, like a secret game for which no one knew the rules but me. I was known as Angela to the outside world, and as Sun-Kyung at home. I ate bologna sandwiches in the school lunch room and rice and kimchee for dinner. I chatted about teen idols and giggled with my girlfriends during my classes, and ambitiously practised piano and studied in the evenings, planning to become a doctor when I grew up. I waved hellos and goodbyes to my teachers, but bowed to my parents' friends visiting our home. I could also look straight into the eyes of my teachers and friends and talk frankly with them instead of staring at my feet with my mouth shut when Koreans talked to me. Going outside the home meant I was able to relax from the constraints of my cultural conditioning, until I walked back in the door and had to return to being an obedient and submissive daughter.

Paraphrase?

First-generation immigrants sometimes adopt two personalities: one outside the home and a different one inside. In her essay "An Immigrant's Split Personality," Sun-Kyung Yi says that she thought of her two identities as a secret game for which no one knew the rules but her. She was Angela in the outside world and Sun-Kyung at home. She ate bologna sandwiches, gossiped about teen idols with girlfriends, and waved hello and goodbye when outside her home. But in her home, she ate rice and kimchee, practised the piano and studied in the evenings, and bowed to her parents' friends. She could look directly at her teachers and friends and talk openly with them, but when she was with Koreans, she stared at her feet with her mouth closed. Outside, she was free of cultural constraints, but at home she was expected to behave like an obedient and submissive daughter.

2. From "The Case against Quickspeak," page 347:

Original:

People who write in quickspeak ignore the reason that rules for correct writing evolved in the first place. Writing that communicates accurately depends upon precise thinking. A message with a statement of purpose, logically arranged points, and a confirming summary is the work of a writer whose message has been thought through and can be trusted. In contrast, quickspeak, which can be bashed out in no time, reflects no planning, little coherent thought, and no sense of order or priority. The message, the reader, and ultimately, the worker all suffer as a result.

Paraphrase?

In "The Case against Quickspeak," a criticism of thoughtless writing in e-mails, Brian Green points out that writers who plan each message to include a topic sentence, carefully organized points, and a summation gain the trust of the reader; their messages are clear and credible. Those who write sloppily, with little thought or preparation, risk being misunderstood and often leave the reader confused and suspicious.

Paragraphs and Essays

3. From "The Slender Trap," page 342:

Original:

If the media do not begin to provide young women with a positive and healthy image of femininity, we will see no lessening in the numbers of anorexia victims. If our cultural ideal of female beauty does not change to reflect a range of healthy body types, the pressures to realize idealized and unhealthy physical standards will continue, and young women's feelings of helplessness and inadequacy will persist. In order for anorexia to become less prominent among young women, healthier associations must replace the existing connections among beauty, success, and thinness. Young women must realize that self-inflicted starvation is not a means to empowerment, but a process of self-destruction.

Paraphrase?

In summing up her essay on *anorexia nervosa*, "The Slender Trap," Trina Piscitelli blames the media for not providing young women with a positive and healthy image of femininity; our culture for its unrealistic standards of beauty; and societal pressures that equate beauty, success, and thinness. Young women, Rys concludes, must realize that starving themselves does not empower them, but leads to their own destruction.

Readings

Readings

CAREER CONSCIOUSNESS
Brian Green

1   A career can be defined as the employment you prepare for during the first quarter of your life, engage in during the best years of your life, and reap the rewards from when you are least able to enjoy them. Behind the cynicism of this observation lies an important truth: choosing a life's vocation is not a decision to be taken lightly. To justify the time and effort you will invest in your career, it should be stimulating, rewarding, and productive. The better you know yourself, the more likely you are to choose a career you can live with happily.

2   What would a stimulating career be like? Picture yourself getting up in the morning and looking forward to your day with eager anticipation. This may not be the popular image of most jobs, but it is one that can be achieved. Most people participate in leisure activities that they find interesting, even energizing. There's no rule that says you can't be as enthusiastic about your work as you are about your play. Many successful people have turned their interests into careers, thus getting paid for what they like to do. Many career professionals in the arts, for example, make their living by doing what they feel they were born to do: write, act, paint, dance, play or compose music, sing, design, or sculpt. Max Ward loved to fly, and from that passion grew his career as a bush pilot, and, later, his founding of one of Canada's first charter airlines. Of course it is not always possible to turn a passion into a career, but to deny what excites you, to relegate it to after-hours activities without trying to incorporate it into your working life, means you will spend most of your life wishing you were doing something else.

3   If your career is stimulating, then chances are good that it can also be rewarding. A good career offers two kinds of rewards: financial and emotional. Rewarding work doesn't just happen; it's something you need to plan for. The first and most important step is to know yourself. Only if you know who you are and what makes you happy can you consciously seek out career experiences that will bring you satisfaction and steer clear of those that will annoy or stress you. Are you genuinely ambitious, or is power something you seek because you think it is expected of you? The pursuit of status and a high salary brings some people pure pleasure. Many people, however, find leadership positions excruciatingly stressful. Career enjoyment depends to some extent on whether or not you are successful, and success is a state of mind. Consider two graduates from the same college program. One is a technician in a small-town television station who loves his work, takes pride in keeping the station on the air, and delights in raising his family in a community where he is involved in volunteer activities ranging from sports to fire-fighting. The other is a news director at one of Canada's major television networks; her work is highly

NFL

stressful, full of risks, and continually scrutinized by viewers, competitors, and her supervisors. She thrives on the adrenaline rush of nightly production, and loves the big-city life, the financial rewards of her position, and the national recognition she receives. Which graduate is "successful"? Certainly, both feel their careers are rewarding, according to their individual definitions of the term.

4   A job at which you do not feel useful cannot be either rewarding or stimulating for very long. It is human nature to want to contribute, to feel that your efforts make a difference. Camaraderie with co-workers, a pleasant daily routine, and even a good salary cannot compensate in the long run for a sense that your work is meaningless or unappreciated. Sadly, some people spend their entire working lives at jobs in which their contribution is so insignificant that their absence would scarcely be noticed. Everyone knows people who boast about reading magazines or surfing the Net on the job, and others who sleep through their night shift so they can spend their days fishing or golfing. Is this the way you want to spend 45 years of your life? All the junk literature and the rounds of golf don't add up to much without a sense that you are doing something worthwhile. It may take a few years, but when it comes, the realization that your work lacks meaning is soul-destroying.

5   It is not easy to find a career that provides stimulating, enjoyable, and meaningful work. Understanding yourself—your interests, needs, values, and goals—is an essential first step. Making long-term decisions consistent with your values and goals is the difficult second step. Too many people spend their lives in careers that make them miserable because they allow themselves to be governed by parents, friends, or simple inertia. Finally, once you have launched your career, never rest. Actively seek challenges and opportunities that stimulate you. Relish the rewards of meeting those challenges, being productive, and doing your job well. Continually strive to improve, not for the sake of your employer, but for your own sake. Your career will occupy three-quarters of your life, so make the most of it!

QUESTIONS FOR DISCUSSION

1. What kind of attention-getter does the writer use to open his essay?
2. In paragraph 5, identify the two main parts of the author's conclusion: the summary of the essay's main points and the memorable statement. What kind of memorable statement has he used? Is it appropriate for this essay? Why?
3. In what order has Green arranged his points: chronological, logically linked, climactic, or random? Can you rearrange the points without diminishing the effectiveness of the piece?
4. What kinds of development has the author used to develop paragraph 2? Paragraph 3? Paragraph 4?

Readings

5. How do the topic sentences of paragraphs 2, 3, 4, and 5 contribute to the coherence of this essay? Identify three or four transitional words or phrases the author has used within his paragraphs to make them read smoothly.

SUGGESTIONS FOR WRITING

1. How would you define a satisfying career?
2. Who is the most satisfied worker you know? What makes him or her happy with the job? How can you tell that this person is highly contented with his/her employment?
3. Who is the most dissatisfied worker you know? What makes him or her unhappy with the job? How does this person compensate for the lack of interest in his/her job?
4. If you had enough money invested so that you could live comfortably without paid employment, would you be happy? Why or why not?

THE SLENDER TRAP

Trina Piscitelli

The following is a short documented essay prepared in the Modern Language Association (MLA) style. The annotations point out some features of MLA format and documentation. If your instructor requires a separate title page, ask for guidelines.

1.25 cm

2.5 cm

Writer's last name and page number on every page → Piscitelli 1

Trina Piscitelli

2.5 cm Professor C. Carpenter

CS 200-03

15 February 2007

The Slender Trap

> Starvation is not a pleasant way to expire. In advanced stages of famine, as the body begins to consume itself, the victim suffers muscle pain, heart disturbances, loss of hair, dizziness, shortness of breath, extreme sensitivity to cold, physical and mental exhaustion. The skin becomes discoloured. In the absence of key nutrients, a severe chemical imbalance develops in the brain, inducing convulsions and hallucinations. (Krakauer 198)

Every day, millions die of hunger. The symptoms of starvation are so horrific that it seems unthinkable anyone would choose this way of death. How is it possible that in the Western world, one in 200 young women from upper- and middle-class families practises starvation as a method of weight control? How do young women become so obsessed with being thin that they develop *anorexia nervosa*? To cause such a fearsome and potentially fatal condition, the influencing factors must be powerful indeed. And they are powerful: the psychological pressures of adolescence, the inescapable expectations of family and peers, and the potent influence of the media.

A tendency to perfectionism, lack of identity, and feelings of helplessness are three aspects of a young woman's psychology that can contribute to the develop-

Author's name, instructor's name, course name and section number, and date

Title centred, not underlined

Block quote indented

Author and page reference of source

Each paragraph indented 1.25 cm

Thesis statement

Readings

Piscitelli 2

ment of *anorexia nervosa*. Young women who exhibit perfectionism are particu-

larly susceptible to the disease because they often have unrealistic expectations

about their physical appearance. These expectations can lead to feelings of help-

lessness and powerlessness, and some young women with these feelings see

starving themselves as a means to empowerment. Their diet is often the only thing

they can control, and they control it with a single-mindedness that astonishes and

horrifies their families and friends. As well as the need for control, anorexia in

young women can be caused by a weak or unformed identity. Confused about who

they are, many young women define themselves by how closely they approximate

our society's notion of the ideal woman. Unfortunately, for the past half-century,

Western society's ideal female image has been that of an unrealistically thin young

woman. When women focus on this impossible image as the ideal and strive to

starve their bodies into submission, they suffer emotional and physical damage.

In addition to an unstable psychological state, family and peer pressure can con-

tribute to a fragile young woman's development of *anorexia nervosa*. By empha-

sizing physical appearance, by criticizing physical features, and even by restricting

junk food, family members can push a young woman over the cliff edge that sepa-

rates health from illness. A home environment in which physical attractiveness is

overvalued can be destructive for young women. Surrounded by family members

and friends who seem to be concerned primarily about appearance, a young woman

can begin to feel insecure about how she looks. This uncertainty can produce the

desire—and then the need—to look better. And better means thinner. This flawed

Piscitelli 3

logic underlies the disease in many young women. A family or peer group that over-
values physical appearance is often also critical of physical flaws. Critical comments
about weight and general appearance, even when spoken jokingly, can be instru-
mental in a young woman's desire to be thin. Ironically, food restrictions imposed by
parents can also contribute to anorexia in young women. Restricting the consumption of junk food, for example, has been known to cause bingeing and purging, a
condition associated with anorexia.

While a young woman's developing psyche and the pressures of those close to
her can exert tremendous influence, the root cause of the "thin is beautiful" trap is
a media-inspired body image. Television, fashion magazines, and stereotypical
Hollywood images of popular stars provide young women with an unrealistic
image of the ideal female body. While only 5 percent of North American females
are actually underweight, 32 percent of female television and movie personalities
are unhealthily thin ("What causes . . .?" para 6). The media's unrealistic portrayal
of a woman's ideal body can cause a young woman to develop a sense of inadequacy. To be considered attractive, she feels she must be ultra-thin. Television's
unrealistic portrayal of the way young women should look is reinforced on the
pages of fashion magazines. Magazine ads feature tall, beautiful, *thin* women.
Media images also perpetuate the stereotype that a woman must be thin in order
to be successful. Thanks to television and movies, when we think of a successful
woman, the image that comes to mind is that of a tall, well-dressed, *thin* woman.
This stereotypical image leads impressionable young women to associate success

*Paraphrase
followed by
source
reference*

Piscitelli 4

with body weight and image. When internalized by young women, these artificial

standards can result in the development of *anorexia nervosa.*

If the media do not begin to provide young women with a positive and healthy

image of femininity, we will see no lessening in the numbers of anorexia victims.

If our cultural ideal of female beauty does not change to reflect a range of healthy

body types, the pressures to realize idealized and unhealthy physical standards

will continue, and young women's feelings of helplessness and inadequacy will

persist. In order for anorexia to become less prominent among young women,

healthier associations must replace the existing connections among beauty, suc-

cess, and thinness. Young women must realize that self-inflicted starvation is not a

means to empowerment, but a process of self-destruction.

Works Cited list begins on a new page.

Piscitelli 5

Heading centred, not underlined

Works Cited

First line, flush left; subsequent lines indented 1.25 cm

"What causes eating disorders?" *Section 1: General information.* Anorexia and

    Related Eating Disorders Inc. (ANRED), 2004. Web. 12 June 2004.

Krakauer, Jon. *Into the Wild.* New York: Villard, 1996. Print.

Entries in alphabet-ical order; double-spaced throughout

QUESTIONS FOR DISCUSSION

1. We've identified for you the author's thesis statement and plan of development. Compose a single sentence combining both the thesis statement and the main points Piscitelli uses to develop her thesis.
2. What two supporting points does the author use to develop the main point of paragraph 2? (See the fifth sentence ["as well as . . ."], which serves as a transition between the two supporting ideas.)
3. What kind of development does Piscitelli use in paragraph 3?
4. Study the concluding paragraph carefully. The author's treatment of her summary and memorable statement is unusual and interesting. The second sentence of the conclusion summarizes the three main points that have been developed in the essay, but in an original, unpredictable way. Underline the clauses of this sentence, and write above each clause the number of the main point it reinforces.
5. What audience did Piscitelli have in mind when she wrote this essay? How do you know?

SUGGESTIONS FOR WRITING

1. Do you know something about eating disorders? If you have a friend or family member who suffers from bulimia, gorging, anorexia, or another related disorder, write an essay describing the causes, effects, and symptoms (features) of the problem, or how it developed.
2. Men also suffer from eating disorders. How are their eating disorders different from those of women? Why do you think we seldom read about male anorexia, bulimia, etc.?
3. In April 2008, the French Parliament's National Assembly adopted a bill that would make it illegal for anyone (including fashion magazines, advertisers, and websites) to publicly encourage extreme thinness. What do you think about this approach to combating anorexia?

AN IMMIGRANT'S SPLIT PERSONALITY
Sun-Kyung Yi

1   I am Korean-Canadian. But the hyphen often snaps in two, obliging me to choose to act as either a Korean or a Canadian, depending on where I am and who I'm with.

2   When I was younger, toying with the idea of entertaining two separate identities was a real treat, like a secret game for which no one knew the rules but

Readings

me. I was known as Angela to the outside world, and as Sun-Kyung at home. I ate bologna sandwiches in the school lunch room and rice and kimchee for dinner. I chatted about teen idols and giggled with my girlfriends during my classes, and ambitiously practised piano and studied in the evenings, planning to become a doctor when I grew up. I waved hellos and goodbyes to my teachers, but bowed to my parents' friends visiting our home. I could also look straight into the eyes of my teachers and friends and talk frankly with them instead of staring at my feet with my mouth shut when Koreans talked to me. Going outside the home meant I was able to relax from the constraints of my cultural conditioning, until I walked back in the door and had to return to being an obedient and submissive daughter.

3   The game soon ended when I realized that it had become a way of life, that I couldn't change the rules without disappointing my parents and questioning all the cultural implications and consequences that came with being a hyphenated Canadian.

4   Many have tried to convince me that I am a Canadian, like all other immigrants in the country, but those same people also ask me which country I came from with great curiosity, following with questions about the type of food I ate and the language I spoke. It's difficult to feel a sense of belonging and acceptance when you are regarded as "one of them." "Those Koreans, they work hard. . . . You must be fantastic at math and science." (No.) "Do your parents own a corner store?" (No.)

5   Koreans and Canadians just can't seem to merge into "us" and "we."

6   Some people advised me that I should just take the best of both worlds and disregard the rest. That's ideal, but unrealistic when my old culture demands a complete conformity with very little room to manoeuvre for new and different ideas.

7   After a lifetime of practice, I thought I could change faces and become Korean on demand with grace and perfection. But working with a small Korean company in Toronto proved me wrong. I quickly became estranged from my own people. My parents were ecstatic at the thought of their daughter finally finding her roots and having a working opportunity to speak my native tongue and absorb the culture. For me, it was the most painful and frustrating two and one-half months of my life.

8   When the president of the company boasted that he "operated little Korea," he meant it literally. A Canadianized Korean was not tolerated. I looked like a Korean; therefore, I had to talk, act, and think like one, too. Being accepted meant a total surrender to ancient codes of behaviour rooted in Confucian thought, while leaving the "Canadian" part of me out in the parking lot with my '86 Buick. In the first few days at work, I was bombarded with inquiries about my marital status. When I told them I was single, they spent the following days trying to match me up with available bachelors in the company and the community. I was expected to accept my inferior position as a woman

and had to behave accordingly. It was not a place to practise my feminist views, or be an individual without being condemned. Little Korea is a place for men (who filled all the senior positions) and women don't dare speak up or disagree with their male counterparts. The president (all employees bow to him and call him Mr. President) asked me to act more like a lady and smile. I was openly scorned by a senior employee because I spoke more fluent English than Korean. The cook in the kitchen shook her head in disbelief upon discovering that my cooking skills were limited to boiling a package of instant noodles. "You want a good husband, learn to cook," she advised me.

9   In less than a week I became an outsider because I refused to conform and blindly nod my head in agreement to what my elders (which happened to be everybody else in the company) said. A month later, I was demoted because "members of the workplace and the Korean community" had complained that I just wasn't "Korean enough," and I had "too much power for a single woman." My father suggested that "when in Rome do as the Romans." But that's exactly what I was doing. I am in Canada so I was freely acting like a Canadian, and it cost me my job.

10   My father also said, "It doesn't matter how Canadian you think you are, just look in the mirror and it'll tell you who you *really* are." But what he didn't realize is that an immigrant has to embrace the new culture to enjoy and benefit from what it has to offer. Of course, I will always be Korean by virtue of my appearance and early conditioning, but I am also happily Canadian and want to take full advantage of all that such citizenship confers. But for now I remain slightly distant from both cultures, accepted fully by neither. The hyphenated Canadian personifies the ideal of multiculturalism, but unless the host culture and the immigrant cultures can find ways to merge their distinct identities, sharing the best of both, this cultural schizophrenia will continue.

QUESTIONS FOR DISCUSSION

1. For what audience was this essay originally intended? (*Hint:* Notice the number of one-sentence paragraphs, which are not usually acceptable in academic writing.)
2. In point form, summarize the main characteristics of the Korean and the Canadian parts of the author's personality.
3. What method of paragraph development does the author use in paragraph 8?
4. Identify five examples of parallel structure in paragraph 2. How does the author's use of parallelism serve to reinforce her thesis?
5. Identify the summary of main points and the memorable statement in paragraph 10.
6. Do you agree that "the hyphenated Canadian personifies the ideal of multiculturalism"?

Readings

SUGGESTIONS FOR WRITING

1. Do you sometimes feel that you are two people trapped inside a single body? Write an essay in which you contrast the two sides of your personality.
2. Contrast three or four significant values of your generation with those of your parents' (or grandparents') generation.

THE CASE AGAINST QUICKSPEAK
Brian Green

"Thx fr yr rply. no prob. ill call mtg fr tues @ 9 ok? :-)"

1   If you aren't familiar with e-mail jargon, this message may look like something in military code or from outer space. Those who use e-mail regularly, however, will recognize it as an example of a new form of communication that I call "quickspeak." Many people these days are in such a hurry that they can't take time to spell, punctuate, or write complete sentences in their electronic correspondence. Of course, these folks wouldn't dream of writing messages like this on paper, but there's something about e-mail that makes them think it's acceptable, even fashionable, to ignore everything they ever knew about writing in order to "save time." Call me a dinosaur, an antique from the days of the inkwell and quill pen, but I will not succumb to quickspeak. I will continue to ensure that my e-mail is as structured and correct as any other mail I send. Why? Because I want my message to be clearly understood, I want to send messages that are thoughtful and complete, and I want to present a positive image to my readers.

2   "But you know what I mean!" protests an e-mail correspondent (written as "bt u no wht i meen :-]".) And it's true that, with some effort, I can make out what I think she means, but I'd also understand if she said, "Duh—we gonna eat soon?" while scratching her stomach. Any written message, whether stored in print or electrons, communicates more than the bare meaning of its words. It tells the reader something about the importance of the message, the ability and intelligence of the writer, and the writer's consideration for the reader.

3   Quickspeak tells the reader that the writer doesn't care much about the message or the reader. It also implies that the writer may not be capable of writing correctly. At the very least, quickspeak betrays a writer as sloppy and disorganized. My father used to describe this approach to communication as "slap-dash," and that's as good a term as any. A slap-dash writer is unlikely to make it into the executive suite.

4   Although I am usually able to decipher the gist of quickspeak, I'm seldom sure that I have translated the message accurately. In many cases, this failure stems from the fact that the writer didn't provide complete or accurate information. Take the example that introduces this essay. I know there will be a meeting (about what?) on Tuesday (which week?) at 9:00 (a.m. or p.m.?). Where is this meeting? Who will be present? What documents am I expected to bring? Without the answers to these questions, how can I prepare? Far from saving time, quickspeak actually wastes it. Now I have to respond to the e-mail sender to find out the answers to these questions. At least three messages will be needed where one would have done. If only the writer had recognized this basic rule of writing: to be brief takes time!

5   E-mail is no different from any other business correspondence: it must be clear and concise. Achieving clarity and conciseness is not difficult, but it does require planning. Begin with an introduction that briefly explains the purpose of your message. Next, outline how you are going to develop that message. Use numbered or bulleted points to guide the reader from your position statement through your reasoning to your conclusion. Reinforce your message with a conclusion that states any follow-up actions you require and that confirms the time, place, and responsibilities of those who are contributing to the project. Next, re-read your message as if you were reading it for the first time. Revise to be sure that you have included all the necessary details: dates, reference numbers, times and places of meetings, and whatever other information is needed to get the right people together in the right places, on the right days, at the right times, with the right information in their briefcases. Use a spell-checker, but don't rely on it to catch all your errors and typos. Remember: A clear message, clearly delivered, is the essence of effective communication.

6   People who write in quickspeak ignore the reason that rules for correct writing evolved in the first place. Writing that communicates accurately depends upon precise thinking. A message with a statement of purpose, logically arranged points, and a confirming summary is the work of a writer whose message has been thought through and can be trusted. In contrast, quickspeak, which can be bashed out in no time, reflects no planning, little coherent thought, and no sense of order or priority. The message, the reader, and, ultimately, the writer all suffer as a result.

7   My co-worker who wrote the e-mail message that introduces this argument is "slap-dash" and may be semi-literate. That, at least, is the impression she gives. She has wasted not only my time but also her own. And, by using quickspeak, she hasn't taken advantage of the power of precise, structured language to produce clear, complete messages. Her trendy message communicates more about her than it does about the subject of her e-mail, and what it says is far from flattering.

Readings

QUESTIONS FOR DISCUSSION

1. In your own words, write a one-sentence summary of the thesis and main points of this essay.
2. Is this essay written in informal, general, or formal English? Give examples of vocabulary, sentence structure, and tone to support your answer.
3. What is the main kind of development used by the author in paragraph 5?
4. What is the effect of the questions included in the body of paragraph 4? How do they draw the reader onside?
5. The concluding paragraph does contain a summary of the essay's main points, but they are subtly rather than obviously stated. Find and underline them.

SUGGESTIONS FOR WRITING

1. Is e-mail a time-saver or a time-waster in an office environment? Support your opinion with at least two reasons.
2. Write an essay in which you contrast e-mail with text messaging.

FOOD FOR THOUGHT
by Nina Kovac

The following is a short research paper prepared in the American Psychological Association (APA) style. The annotations point out some features of APA format and documentation.

1.25 cm

Food for Thought

2.5 cm

First two or three words of the title + page number on every page

Food for Thought

Nina Kovac

COM 102-14

Professor B. Green

January 10, 2008

Title, author's name, course name and section number, instructor's name, date; centred on page, double-spaced

Readings

Title centred, not underlined →

Food for Thought

Paragraphs indented 1.25 cm

↔ *2.5 cm*

What relatively simple action can ordinary people take to improve the lives of their families, contribute to the local economy, and even help ease the global food crisis? The answer may be surprisingly simple: sit down to healthy, locally grown family meals. Certainly the 100,000 people who belong to the Slow Food movement think so.

Begun in Italy, the movement has now spread around the world. Each of the 1,000 local chapters, called "convivia," promotes the philosophy that "the food we eat should taste good; it should be produced in a clean way that does not harm the environment, animal welfare, or human health, and its producers should receive fair compensation for their work" (Malatesta, et al., 2007). In reaction to the fast-food culture that has pervaded North America over the last 50 years and is now a global blight of mass-produced meals eaten on the run in factory-like environments, the Slow Food movement promotes choosing high-quality local foods and taking time to enjoy them.

Citation of secondary source

The term "high-quality food" means different things to different people. For some, it means food that is produced organically—without the use of fertilizer, pesticides, or other chemical additives—and is not genetically modified. For other, less-demanding consumers, "high-quality" means food that is free of added sugar, fat, or chemical enhancers. Whatever their definition of quality, the important point is that people should think about what they eat and choose their foods based on nutrition and taste rather than on commercial advertising and convenience.

Paper is double-spaced throughout

Food for Thought 3

Educating consumers to know how to select quality food is one of the Slow Food movement's main objectives.

At a recent Slow Food event in Ontario's Niagara Region, volunteer tasters were asked to sample two chicken dishes, prepared identically, but using chicken from different suppliers. The meat in one dish had been purchased at a super-market; it came from a large poultry factory that grows its birds in dark, crowded sheds and water-chills the meat before packaging it. The chicken in the second dish came from an organic producer who raises free-range birds and air-chills the meat before packaging. Once a chicken is slaughtered, it must be cooled quickly; the most common way to do this is to dunk the meat into a cold-water bath. During this process, the chicken absorbs water, which adds weight that consumers pay for when they buy chicken. Air-cooled chickens are chilled by blasts of cold air. This is a more expensive process because it is less efficient, but it produces denser, tastier meat. With up to 80 percent less bacteria than water-chilled chicken, the meat is longer lasting, too ("Chilled-out chicken," 2000). The tasters unanimously found the air-chilled organic chicken superior in appearance, texture, and flavour to the pale, flabby water-chilled product.

Paraphrase

Electronic source citation (author not known)

Food that is produced locally is superior, both in quality and value. According to the Environmental News Service, the ingredients for a typical North American meal travel between 2,500 and 4,000 km from farm or orchard to our tables (Lazaroff, 2002). Think of all the gasoline that journey requires. Think of all the freshness lost along the way. Think of all the packaging and preservatives neces-

Source citation of the study referred to

Readings

Food for Thought 4

sary for the food to make the trip. And when it finally reaches its destination, produce from faraway growers is often disgusting in texture and taste. Strawberries the size of golf balls and the basketball-sized melons that appear in our supermarkets in February have the texture of snowballs and about as much taste.

We live in a cold climate, and it would be impossible for anyone but a fanatic to stick religiously to a diet of nothing but local foods. We all buy coffee and sugar and oranges and pepper and olive oil, but we can choose to go to local markets for seasonal vegetables and fruit and to a butcher who sells locally produced meat. By doing so, we support our local agricultural economy rather than contributing to the profits of some far-off factory farm that relies on heavy-duty machinery, chemical fertilizers, and toxic pesticides to sustain its single-crop production.

Sitting down for dinner with the family may seem like an outdated notion, something from a '60s sitcom, but we should think again. Research shows that no other factor is as likely to increase the probability of a child's academic success; reduce the likelihood of drug, alcohol, and tobacco use; and decrease the incidence of adolescent obesity and depression. One major study statistically eliminated all significant variables such as socioeconomic status and even the cohesiveness of the family, and concluded that shared family mealtimes is the primary determining factor in children's health and well-being, especially among girls (*Family meals promote healthy eating*, 2004).

Source citation of study referred to

Not surprisingly, the research also finds that adolescents who regularly eat with their families consume more fruit and vegetables, more calcium, less fat, and

Food for Thought 5

significantly fewer soft drinks. A healthier diet can account for some of the supe-

rior physical, mental, and emotional health of children in families who eat

together, but not all. The very act of sitting down together without the distractions

of video games, television, and computers encourages family members to commu-

nicate and share experiences. The shared meal need not be the evening meal; in

some shift-working households, a family breakfast may be more appropriate.

While a thoughtfully prepared three-course feast might be the ideal, a quicker,

easy-to-fix dish such as pasta or a stir-fry can also provide a tasty and nutritious   *← Paraphrase*

main course for a sit-down family meal. And the research studies demonstrated

that the benefits to children increase in direct proportion to the number of family

meals they participate in each week (*Family meals promote healthy eating*, 2004).   *Source citation*

The Slow Food movement is the culmination of a trend that has been quietly

gaining momentum for years. Our awareness of the benefits of organic food and

the introduction of natural products into mainstream stores has grown dramati-   *Quotation integrated into author's sentence*

cally in the last decade. For example, the Whole Foods Market, which bills itself

as "the world's leading natural and organic foods supermarket" has annual sales in

excess of $10 billion at its almost 300 supermarkets (*Selling the highest quality*,   *Source citation*

2008). Other trends underlie the Slow Food philosophy: the mushrooming "green"

movement and our ever-growing interest in health and wellness both reinforce the

Slow Food concept. Who could argue against an organization whose aim is to con-

vince us to eat good, fresh food in a convivial and enjoyable setting?

Readings

Food for Thought 6

Heading centred, not underlined →

References

Entries in alphabetical order

"Chilled-out chickens." (September, 2000). *Research Nebraska*. University of

Nebraska-Lincoln Agricultural Research Division. Retrieved May 8, 2008,

from http://ard.unl.edu/rn/0900/chick.html

First line, flush left; subsequent lines indented 1.25 cm →

Family meals promote healthy eating. (November 9, 2004). University of

Minnesota, Academic Health Center. News release. Retrieved May 6, 2008,

from www.ahc.umn.edu/news/releases/meals110904

Lazaroff, Cat. (November, 2002). *Food travels far to reach your table*.

Double-spaced throughout →

Environmental News Service. Retrieved May 15, 2008, from www.ens-

newswire.com/ens/nov2002/2002-11-21-06.asp

Malatesta, Simona, et al. (2007). *The Slow Food companion* (4th ed., p. 3). Bra,

Italy: Slow Food.

Selling the highest quality natural and organic products available. (2008). Fast

Facts. Whole Foods Market. Retrieved May 6, 2008, from http://media .whole-

foodsmarket.com/pr/wf/fast-facts.aspx

QUESTIONS FOR DISCUSSION

1. Identify the thesis statement for this essay and list the three main points that develop the thesis.
2. The basic essay format that we outline on page 290 is five paragraphs long. It consists of an introduction, a paragraph for each main point, and a conclusion. This essay has nine paragraphs. Map out a scratch outline of the essay, showing how each paragraph fits into the structure.
3. What methods of development does the author use in paragraph 4?
4. Identify the summary of main points and the memorable statement in paragraph 9.

SUGGESTIONS FOR WRITING

1. Describe a typical evening meal in your household. Does it bear any resemblance to the idea of a "family meal" described in the essay? Based on your observations and experience, do you believe the author's contention that shared family meals can make the kind of significant improvements described in paragraph 7? Why?

2. In paragraph 9, the author says that the philosophy and principles of the Slow Food movement are gathering momentum globally. Describe any evidence you have encountered that suggests this may or may not be the case.

THE MOMENT OF TRUTH

Al Gore

1   Clichés are, by definition, over used. But here is a rare exception—a certifiable cliché that warrants more exposure, because it carries meaning deeply relevant to the biggest challenge our civilization has ever confronted. The Chinese expression for "crisis" consists of two characters: 危機. The first is a symbol for "danger"; the second is a symbol for "opportunity."

2   The rapid accumulation of global-warming pollution in the Earth's atmosphere is now confronting human civilization with a crisis like no other we have ever encountered. This climate crisis is, indeed, extremely dangerous, but it also presents unprecedented opportunities. Before we can get to the opportunities, however, it is crucial to define the danger, and to discuss how it is that we in the United States seem to be having such difficulty perceiving that danger.

危

3   The climate crisis may at times appear to be happening slowly, but in fact it is a true planetary emergency. The voluminous evidence suggests strongly that, unless we act boldly and quickly to deal with the causes of global warming, our world will likely experience a string of catastrophes, including deadlier Hurricane Katrinas in both the Atlantic and Pacific.

4   We are melting virtually all of the mountain glaciers in the world—including those in the Rockies, the Sierras, the Andes, and the Alps—and, more ominously, the massive ice field on the roof of the world, on the enormous Tibetan Plateau, which has 100 times more ice than the Alps, and which supplies up to half of the drinking water of 40 percent of the world's people, through seven river systems that all originate there: the Indus, the Ganges, the Brahmaputra, the Salween, the Mekong, the Yangtze and the Yellow.

5   Even more important, we are rapidly melting the vast, but relatively thin, floating ice cap that covers the Arctic Ocean. For the first time, scientists are finding significant numbers of polar bears that have died by drowning, as the distance from the shores of the Arctic to the edge of the ice cap has stretched in places to 60 kilometers or more. At present, the North Polar cap helps to cool the planet by reflecting the vast majority of the sunlight that hits the Arctic during six months of the year. It is like a gigantic mirror larger than the entire United States. But the growing areas of open water left as the ice cap melts are absorbing the vast majority of the energy coming from the Sun, raising temperatures at the top of our planet far more rapidly than anywhere else.

6   We are beginning to melt—and possibly de-stabilize—the enormous, 10,000-foot-thick mound of ice on top of Greenland and the equally enormous mass of ice of West Antarctica, which is propped up precariously against the tops of islands, poised to slip into the sea. Either of these massive, land-based ice sheets would, if it melted or broke up and slid into the ocean, raise the sea level worldwide by more than 20 feet. The largest ice mass of all on the planet—East Antarctica—was long thought to be still growing. Until recently, that is, when a new, in-depth scientific survey showed that it, too, may be beginning to melt.

7   Since the entire climate system of Earth is formed by the planetwide pattern of wind and ocean currents, which redistribute heat from the tropics to the poles, there is growing concern that the relatively stable pattern that has persisted for 11,000 years—since the last ice age and before the first appearance of cities—may now be on the verge of radical and disruptive changes. The Gulf Stream, the monsoon cycle in the Indian Ocean, the El Niño/La Niña cycle in the Eastern Pacific, and the jet streams, among the other circulatory phenomena, are all at risk of being pushed into new and unfamiliar patterns.

8   Global warming, together with the cutting and burning of forests and the destruction of other critical habitats, is causing the loss of living species at a rate comparable to that of the extinction of dinosaurs 65 million years ago. Most scientists theorize that that event, by the way, was caused by a giant asteroid colliding with the Earth. This time it is not an asteroid wreaking havoc; it is us. We are recklessly dumping so much carbon dioxide into the Earth's atmosphere that we have literally changed the relationship between the Earth and the Sun, altering the balance of energy between our planet and the rest of the universe, so the buildup of heat energy that should be re-radiated by the Earth is beginning to wilt, melt, dry out, and parch delicate components of the planet's living systems.

9   More than 70 percent of the planet's surface is covered by ocean, and a series of new, comprehensive studies show that the amount of CO_2 being absorbed into the oceans is about one-third of what we have put into the environment with the burning of fossil fuels. As a result, the oceans of the world are becoming more acid, and the total amount of carbonic acid—even though

it is a relatively weak acid—is beginning to change the mix of carbonate and bicarbonate ions in the oceans. This interferes with the ability of corals to form their calcium-carbonate skeletons, which constitute the base of many food chains in the oceans. Even more ominously, the amounts of carbonic acid we are continuing to sink into the oceans will, if we don't change the current reckless pattern, make it more difficult for many ocean creatures, large and tiny, to make shells, because the shells would instantly dissolve in the newly acid ocean water, the way chalk (also calcium carbonate) dissolves in vinegar. Continuing on our current path will return the oceans to a chemical pH balance that last existed 300 million years ago—when the Earth was a very different planet from the one that gave birth to and nurtured the human species.

10   All of this, incredibly, could be set in motion in the lifetime of the children already living—unless we act boldly and quickly. Even more incredibly, some of the leading scientific experts are now telling us that without dramatic changes we are in grave danger of crossing a point of no return within the next ten years! So the message is unmistakable. This crisis means danger!

11   But in order to move through the danger to seize the opportunity, we have first to recognize that we are in fact facing a crisis. So why is it that our leaders seem not to hear such clarion warnings? Are they resisting the truth because they know that the moment they acknowledge it they will face a moral imperative to act? Is it simply more convenient to ignore the warnings? Perhaps, but inconvenient truths do not go away just because they are not seen. Indeed, when they are not responded to, their significance doesn't diminish; it grows.

12   For example, the Bush administration was warned on August 6, 2001, of an attack by al-Qaeda: "Bin Ladin Determined to Strike in US," said the intelligence community in a message so important that it was the headline of the president's daily briefing that day, five weeks before the attacks of September 11. Didn't he see that clear warning? Why were no questions asked, meetings called, evidence marshaled, clarifications sought?

13   The Bible says, "Where there is no vision, the people perish."

14   Four Augusts later, as Hurricane Katrina was roaring across the unusually warm water of the Gulf of Mexico and growing into a deadly monster that was less than two days away from slamming into New Orleans, the administration received another clear warning: the levees—which had been built to protect the city against smaller, less powerful hurricanes—were in grave danger. But once again an urgent warning was ignored. The videotapes of one session make clear that the president heard the warnings but, again, asked not a single question.

. . .

15   Where there is a blinding lack of situational awareness, the people perish.

16   Nearly 70 years ago, when a horrible and unprecedented storm of another kind was gathering in Europe, British prime minister Neville Chamberlain found

it inconvenient to see the truth about the nature of the evil threat posed by the Nazis. In criticizing his government's blinding lack of awareness, Winston Churchill said, "So they go on in strange paradox, decided only to be undecided, resolved to be irresolute, adamant for drift, solid for fluidity, all-powerful to be impotent." After the appeasement at Munich, Churchill said, "This is only the first sip, the first foretaste, of a bitter cup which will be proffered to us year by year—unless by supreme recovery of moral health and martial vigor we rise again and take our stand for freedom." Then he warned prophetically that "the era of procrastination, of half measures, of soothing and baffling expedients, of delays, is coming to a close. In its place, we are entering a period of consequences."

17   Today, there are dire warnings that the worst catastrophe in the history of human civilization is bearing down on us, gathering strength as it comes. And these warnings have also been met with a blinding lack of awareness, by the Congress as well as by the administration.

18   After the tragedy of Hurricane Katrina, many Americans now believe that we have entered a period of consequences—that Katrina, as horrible as it was, may have been the first sip of a bitter cup which will proffered to us over and over again until we act on the truth we have wished would go away. And they are beginning to demand that the administration open its eyes and look at the truth, no matter how inconvenient it might be for all of us—not least for the special interests that want us to ignore global warming.

19   As Abraham Lincoln said during our time of greatest trial, "We must disenthrall ourselves, and then we shall save our country." America is beginning to awaken. And now we will save our planet.

20   So it is time for the good news: we can solve this crisis, and as we finally do accept the truth of our situation and turn to boldly face down the danger that is stalking us, we will find that it is also bringing us unprecedented opportunity. I'm not referring just to new jobs and new profits, though there will be plenty of both. Today we have all the technologies we need to start the fight against global warming. We can build clean engines. We can harness the sun and wind. We can stop wasting energy. We can use the Earth's plentiful coal resources without heating the planet.

21   The procrastinators and deniers would have us believe that this will be painful and impossibly expensive. But in recent years dozens of companies have cut emissions of heat-trapping gases and saved money. Some of the world's largest companies are moving aggressively to capture the enormous economic opportunities in a clean-energy future.

22   But there's something far more precious than the economic gains that will be made. This crisis is bringing us an opportunity to experience what few generations in history ever have the privilege of knowing: a generational mission; the exhilaration of a compelling moral purpose; a shared and unifying cause; the thrill of being forced by circumstances to put aside the pettiness and conflict that so often stifle the restless human need for transcendence; the opportunity to rise.

23   When we do rise, it will fill our spirits and bind us together. Those who are now suffocating in cynicism and despair will be able to breathe freely. Those who are now suffering from a loss of meaning in their lives will find hope. When we rise, we will experience an epiphany as we discover that this crisis is not really about politics at all. It is a moral and spiritual challenge.

24   What is at stake is the survival of our civilization and the habitability of the Earth. Or as one eminent scientist put it, the pending question is whether an opposable thumb and a neocortex are a viable combination on this planet.

25   The new understanding we will gain—about who we really are—will give us the moral capacity to comprehend the true nature of other, related challenges that are also desperately in need of being defined as moral imperatives with practical solutions: HIV/AIDS and other pandemics that are ravaging large parts of humankind, global poverty, the ongoing redistribution of the world's wealth from the poor to the rich, the ongoing genocide in Darfur, famines in other parts of Africa, chronic civil wars, the destruction of ocean fisheries, families that don't function, communities that don't commune, the erosion of democracy in America, and the re-feudalization of the public forum.

26   Consider once again what happened during the crisis of global Fascism. When England and then America and our allies ultimately did rise to meet the threat, we won two wars simultaneously, in Europe and in the Pacific. And by the end of those terrible wars, the Allies had gained the moral authority and vision to create the Marshall Plan—and persuade the taxpayers to pay for it! They had gained the spiritual capacity and wisdom to rebuild Japan and Europe and launch the renewal of the very nations they had just defeated in the war. In the process, they laid the foundation for 50 years of peace and prosperity. One of their commanders, General Omar Bradley, said at the end of World War II, "It is time we steered by the stars and not by the lights of each passing ship."

27   And now so must we. For this, too, is a critical moment. Ultimately, it is not about any scientific discussion or political dialogue; it is about who we are as human beings. It is about our capacity to transcend our limitations, to rise to this new occasion. To see with our hearts, as well as our heads, the response that is now called for. This is a moral, ethical, and spiritual challenge.

28   Just as we can no longer ignore this challenge, neither should we fear it. Instead, we should welcome it. Both the danger and the opportunity. And then

we will meet it because we must. We have accepted and met other great challenges in the past. We declared our liberty and then won it. We designed a new form of government. We freed the slaves. We gave women the right to vote. We took on Jim Crow and segregation. We cured polio and helped eradicate smallpox, we landed on the moon, we brought down Communism, and we helped end apartheid. We even solved a global environmental crisis—the hole in the stratospheric ozone layer—because Republicans and Democrats, rich nations and poor nations, businessmen and scientists, all came together to shape a solution.

29   And now we face a crisis with unprecedented danger that also presents an opportunity like no other. As we rise to meet this historic challenge, it promises us prosperity, common purpose, and the renewal of our moral authority.

30   We should not wait. We cannot wait. We must not wait.

31   The only thing missing is political will. But in our democracy, political will is a renewable resource.

QUESTIONS FOR DISCUSSION

1. Where does Gore state his THESIS? Which paragraphs deal with dangers? Which deal with opportunities? What is the focus of paragraphs 11 to 19?

2. What kind of development does Gore use for support in paragraph 4? In paragraphs 16 and 19?

3. What is the major point of TRANSITION in the essay? Is it effective? (If there are any Chinese speakers in your class, consult them.)

4. Identify the economic opportunities that Gore argues will result from the political decision to solve the crisis of global warming.

5. Beyond the economic gains that Gore says will come with the resolution of global warming, he maintains that a sense of "generational mission" (paragraph 22) will offer people a variety of rewards. What are they? Do you agree or disagree? Why?

6. What kind of encouragement does Gore offer in paragraph 28? In other words, why does he remain an optimist about a crisis that he sees as threatening life on the planet?

7. What examples of "political will" can you identify in the recent history of Canada and/or the U.S. (from 2008)?

SUGGESTIONS FOR WRITING

1. Do you agree with Gore's position on the crisis of global warming? Do some research and then write an essay that argues either for or against the ideas in "The Moment of Truth."

2. Write an essay contrasting the effectiveness of this essay with that of Gore's film on the same topic, *An Inconvenient Truth*. Which version of his argument do you prefer and why?

Appendixes

APPENDIX A

A Review of the Basics

This appendix contains a brief overview of the basic building-blocks of the English language. At the very least, you should know the kinds and parts of a sentence and the parts of speech before you tackle the complex tasks involved in correcting and refining your writing.

SENTENCES: KINDS AND PARTS

A sentence is a group of words expressing a complete thought. Sentences can be classified in two different ways: by function and by structure.

FUNCTION: FOUR KINDS OF SENTENCES

1. The **declarative** sentence makes a statement or conveys information.

George Clooney starred in *O Brother, Where Art Thou?*, a Coen brothers' film.

He played a character named Ulysses Everett McGill.

2. The **interrogative** sentence asks a question.

Did George Clooney do his own singing in *O Brother, Where Art Thou?*

Was Pete really turned into a frog, or was he turned in to the police?

3. The **imperative** (command) sentence gives an order or a directive.

Stop talking! I'm trying to listen!

The **request** is a modified form of imperative sentence. Its tone is softer:

Let's rent a DVD of *O Brother* and watch it tonight.

4. The **exclamatory** sentence is a strong statement of opinion or warning.

The scene in which Clooney insists on wearing a hair net to bed is hilarious!

Don't answer the phone! This is my favourite part of the movie!

STRUCTURE: BASIC SENTENCE PATTERNS

Every sentence can be classified into one of four patterns, depending on the number and kind of clauses the sentence contains. (In the examples below, subjects are underlined with one line, verbs with two.)

1. A **simple** sentence consists of one independent clause. It has one subject and one verb, either or both of which may be compound (multiple).

a. Matt plays hockey for McGill. (one subject, one verb)

b. Matt and Caro play hockey with their friends on weekends. (compound subject, one verb)

c. Matt and Caro play hockey and drink beer with their friends on weekends. (compound subject, compound verb)

2. A **compound** sentence is made up of two or more independent clauses. The clauses may be joined by a *coordinating conjunction* or by a semicolon. (See Chapters 8 and 19.)

Geoff paid for the flight to Cuba, *and* Kendra paid for their accommodation.

Either or both clauses in a compound sentence may contain a compound subject and/or a compound verb:

Geoff and Kendra flew to Cuba, *but* Matt and Caro stayed home and sulked.

3. A **complex** sentence has one independent clause and one or more dependent clauses introduced by *subordinate conjunctions* (dependent clause cues). (See page 100.)

We <u>flew</u> to Cuba for our vacation *while* my <u>brother</u> <u>stayed</u> home to take care of our dogs.

<u>Geoff</u> and <u>Kendra</u> <u>flew</u> to Cuba, *but* <u>Matt</u> and <u>Caro</u> <u>stayed</u> home *because* <u>they</u> <u>couldn't</u> <u>afford</u> the trip.

4. The **compound-complex** sentence combines the features of sentence patterns 2 and 3 above. That is, it contains two (or more) independent clauses, together with one or more dependent clauses.

<u>Geoff</u> and <u>Kendra</u> <u>flew</u> to Cuba, *but* <u>Matt</u> and <u>Caro</u> <u>stayed</u> home *because* <u>they</u> <u>couldn't</u> <u>afford</u> the trip and *because* <u>someone</u> <u>needed</u> to care for the dogs.

PARTS OF A SENTENCE

Every sentence or independent clause can be divided into two parts: subject and predicate. The subject half contains the **subject** (simple or compound), together with its modifiers. The predicate half contains the **verb** (simple or compound), with its modifiers and any other words or phrases that complete the sentence's meaning. These predicate completers may be **direct objects**, **indirect objects**, or **complements**. (In the examples below, <u>direct objects</u> are indicated by a triple underline; <u>indirect objects</u> by a dotted underline; and <u>complements</u> by a broken underline.)

1. The **subject** of a sentence is a noun/pronoun (or phrase or clause used as a noun).

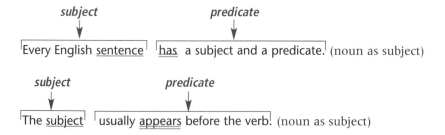

subject   *predicate*

Every English <u>sentence</u> | <u>has</u> a subject and a predicate. (noun as subject)

subject   *predicate*

The <u>subject</u> | usually <u>appears</u> before the verb. (noun as subject)

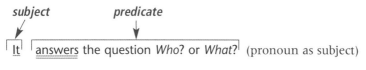

subject   *predicate*

It | answers the question *Who*? or *What*? (pronoun as subject)

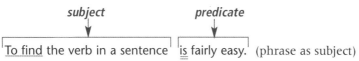

subject   *predicate*

To find the verb in a sentence | is fairly easy. (phrase as subject)

2. The **verb** is the word or phrase that tells the reader what the subject is or does.

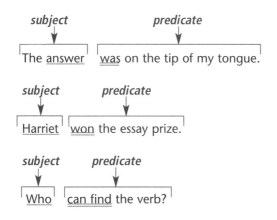

subject   *predicate*

The answer | was on the tip of my tongue.

subject   *predicate*

Harriet | won the essay prize.

subject   *predicate*

Who | can find the verb?

3. The **direct object** is the noun or pronoun that names the receiver of the action of the verb.

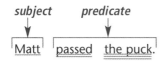

subject   *predicate*

Matt | passed   the puck.

4. The **indirect object** is a noun or pronoun that tells to whom something is (was/will be) done. The indirect object normally comes before the direct object.

subject   *predicate*

Matt | passed Caro the puck.

5. An **object of a preposition** is a noun or pronoun that follows the preposition in a prepositional phrase.

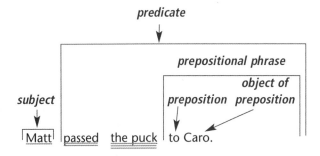

6. A **complement** is a noun, pronoun, or modifier that explains, renames, or describes the subject of a linking verb (e.g., *is, seems, appears, smells, tastes,* etc.).

Caro is the captain of the team. (noun complement)
The goal and the game are ours! (pronoun complement)
The crowd went wild. (adjective complement)

PARTS OF SPEECH

The words that make up sentences can be classified into nine grammatical categories or word classes. The function of a word in a sentence determines what part of speech it is. The word *rock,* for example, can belong to any one of three categories, depending on its context.

We stopped to rest in the shadow of an enormous *rock.* (noun)

The baby will usually stop fussing if you *rock* her. (verb)

I used to listen only to *rock* music, but now I prefer rap. (adjective)

Here's another example, illustrating three functions of the word *since.*

We have not seen Lucy *since* Saturday. (preposition)

We haven't seen Lucy *since* she left. (subordinate conjunction)

We haven't seen Lucy *since.* (adverb)

1. NOUNS

A noun is a word that names a person, place, object, quality, or concept.

A. **Common nouns** are general names for persons, places, and objects: e.g., *artist, politician; city, suburb; train, computer.*
  - **Concrete** nouns name things that can be seen and touched: *telephone, sister, puppy.*
  - **Abstract** nouns name thoughts, emotions, qualities, or values—things that cannot be seen or touched: e.g., *ambition, success, honesty.*
B. **Proper nouns** name specific persons, places, and things and are capitalized: *Queen Elizabeth, Homer Simpson, Bugs Bunny, CN Tower, Calgary, General Motors.*
C. **Collective nouns** name groups of people or things that act as a single unit: *jury, class, committee, herd.*

2. VERBS

A. A verb is a word or phrase that tells what the subject of the clause is or does.

- **Action verbs** tell what the subject does: The <u>driver</u> <u>braked</u> suddenly.
- **Linking** (or **copula**) **verbs** connect the subject to a word or phrase identifying or describing the subject of a sentence: The <u>driver</u> <u>was</u> my older brother. <u>He</u> <u>felt</u> sleepy.

B. All verbs have different forms (called tenses) to indicate past, present, or future time.

Our team <u>played</u> badly last night. (action verb in past tense)

Mario <u>thinks</u> that we <u>will win</u> tonight. (present tense, future tense)

I <u>am</u> not so confident. (linking verb in present tense)

C. **Auxiliary** (or **helping**) **verbs** are used with a main verb to show tense or voice.

The auxiliary verbs are *be, have, do, may, can, ought, must, shall, will,* and their various forms.

By November, <u>we will have spent</u> six months in Canada. (future perfect tense)

D. The way verbs interact with their subjects is shown through a quality called **voice**. Active voice and passive voice verbs give different messages to the reader.

- **Active voice** verbs show the subject doing or acting:

  A <u>woman</u> in a BMW <u>took</u> my parking place.

  The <u>tornado</u> <u>destroyed</u> everything in its path.

- **Passive voice** verbs show the subject being acted upon:

  My parking <u>place</u> <u>was taken</u> by a woman in a BMW.

  Our <u>home</u> <u>was destroyed</u> by the tornado.

  (See Chapter 12, page 160, for instructions on when to use passive voice verbs.)

3. PRONOUNS

Pronouns are words that substitute for nouns. They can act as subjects or objects.

There are seven classes of pronouns:

1. Personal Pronouns

	Singular (Subject/Object)	Plural (Subject/Object)
1st person	I/me	we/us
2nd person	you/you	you/you
3rd person	he, she, it/him, her, it	they/them

We would like *you* to come with *us*, but *they* can fit only four people into the car.

2. Possessive Pronouns

	Singular	*Plural*
1st person	mine	ours
2nd person	yours	yours
3rd person	his, hers, its	theirs

The wonton soup is *yours*; the chicken wings are *hers*; the spareribs are *mine*; and the spring rolls are *ours* to share.

3. Indefinite Pronouns

	Singular	*Plural*
	any, anyone, anybody, anything	some, all, many
	everyone, everybody, everything	some, all, many
	someone, somebody, something	some people, some things
	no one, nobody, nothing, none (sing.)	none (pl.)
	one	several
	each	both
	either, neither	few, several, many

Is *no one* curious about *anything someone* is doing for the good of us *all*?

4. Demonstrative Pronouns

	Singular	*Plural*
	this	these
	that	those

This paper is mine; *these* papers are yours.

That is my magazine; I've read *those*, so you can have them.

5. Relative Pronouns

Singular and Plural
(Subject/Object)

who/whom; whoever/whomever; which/whichever; what/whatever; that; whose

The Order of Canada, *which* was created in 1967, is awarded each year to Canadians *who* have distinguished themselves in the arts and sciences, politics, or community service, and *whose* contributions in *whatever* field are deemed worthy of national honour.

6. Interrogative Pronouns   *Singular and Plural*
                                       (Subject/Object)

                                       who?/whom?
                                       which? what?/which? what?

Jan is the leader on *whom* the team depended. *Who* could take her place?
What can the team do now?

7. Reflexive/Emphatic
Pronouns   *Singular*   *Plural*

1st person   myself   ourselves
2nd person   yourself   yourselves
3rd person   himself, herself, itself   themselves

We had planned to go by *ourselves*, but since Sharon invited *herself* along,
Leo and Jon should have included *themselves* on the outing, too.

4. ADJECTIVES

An adjective is a word that modifies or describes a noun or pronoun.

- Adjectives usually answer one of these questions: "What kind?" "Which?"
  "How many?"

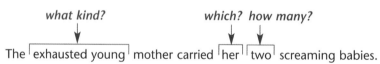

- Pay special attention to the possessive pronoun adjectives: *my, our; your; his,
  her, their.* These words follow the same rules for agreement that govern the
  possessive pronouns listed above. See Chapter 16, pages 191–92.
- Most adjectives have three forms:

Positive (Base) Form: e.g., short, brief, concise

Comparative Form:

- Add *-er* to one-syllable words: e.g., shorter, briefer
- Use *more* + base form for adjectives of two or more syllables: e.g., more
  concise

Superlative Form:

- Add *-est* to one-syllable words: e.g., shortest, briefest
- Use *most* + base form for adjectives of two or more syllables: e.g.,
  most concise

A few adjectives such as *bad* have irregular comparatives (*worse*) and superlatives (*worst*). Your dictionary will list these irregular forms.

5. ADVERBS

> An adverb is a word that modifies or describes a verb, an adjective, or another adverb.

- Adverbs commonly answer the questions "When?" "Where?" "How?"
- Adverbs often—but not always—end in *-ly*.

Rocco *foolishly* challenged the police officer. (adverb modifies verb)

The baby is an *extremely* fussy eater. (adverb modifies adjective)

My elderly father drives *very slowly.* (adverb modifies another adverb; adverb phrase modifies verb)

6. PREPOSITIONS

> A preposition is a word (or words) such as *in, on, among, to, for, according to, instead of* that introduces a prepositional phrase. A prepositional phrase = preposition + object of the preposition (a noun or pronoun).

Prepositional phrases can function as adjectives, adverbs, or nouns.

Celeste is an old friend *of mine* *from Paris.* (prepositional phrases as adjectives modifying noun *friend*)

I'll wait *until seven o'clock.* (prepositional phrase as adverb modifying verb *wait*)

We all hope *for a better world.* (prepositional phrase as noun object of verb *hope*)

7. CONJUNCTIONS

Conjunctions are connecting words used to join two words, two phrases, or two clauses.

- **Coordinating conjunctions** (*and, but, or, for, so, nor, yet*) join grammatically equal elements in a sentence (e.g., the two parts of a compound subject; two independent clauses).

  Moreen *and* Gina are coming, *but* Tessa is not.

- **Subordinating conjunctions** are dependent clause cues: *because, although, when, since,* etc. They link dependent (or subordinate) clauses to independent clauses.

  Tom must go home early *because* he promised to cook dinner.

- **Conjunctive adverbs** are transitional expressions (e.g., *however, therefore, nevertheless, in fact*) usually used after a semicolon to join two independent clauses.

  I would like to go to the club tonight; *however,* I have no money.

- **Correlative conjunctions** are conjunctions used in pairs: e.g., *both . . . and, not only . . . but (also), either . . . or, neither . . . nor*. These constructions are intensifiers. They make the meaning of a statement more emphatic by focusing the reader's attention on each element separately.
  For example,

  Helen is beautiful *and* intelligent. (coordinating conjunction = statement)

  Helen is *both* beautiful *and* intelligent. (correlative conjunctions = emphatic statement)

  Luca invited all his friends to the party *and* gave everyone a gift. (coordinating conjunction = statement)

  Not only did Luca invite all his friends to the party, *but (also)* he gave everyone a gift. (correlative conjunctions = emphatic statement)

8. ARTICLES

An article precedes the noun it modifies. The **definite article**, *the*, may be used with a singular or a plural noun; it denotes a particular person or thing. The **indefinite article,** *a/an,* is generally used with a singular, countable noun, and signals an unspecified one of a number of others. (Use *an* before vowel *sounds,* not just vowels: e.g., *an apple, an honest* person.)

The student sitting next to you is asleep. (a particular student)

A student in the back row is snoring. (one of a number of students)

A number of factors determine the use or non-use of articles. For a summary of rules governing articles, go to "ESL Tips" under "More Information" on the Student Resources page of our website, **www.barea.nelson.com**.

9. EXPLETIVES

Here and *There* are expletives, which are words used at the beginning of a sentence to postpone the subject until after the verb and thus emphasize it.

Here is your mail. (= Your mail is here.)

There are hundreds of copies still available. (= Hundreds of copies are still available.)

See Chapter 6, page 80.

APPENDIX B

List of Grammatical Terms

abstract and **concrete**
See **noun**.

adjective
A word that modifies (describes, restricts, relates to, makes more precise) a noun or pronoun. Adjectives answer the questions **What kind? How many? Which?**—e.g., the *competent* student; *five* home runs; my *last* class.

adverb
A word that modifies a verb, adjective, or other adverb. Adverbs answer the questions **When? How? Where? Why? How much?**—e.g., Nino talks *fast* (*fast* modifies the verb *talks*); he is a *very* fast talker (*very* modifies the adjective *fast*); he talks *really* fast (*really* modifies the adverb *fast*). Adverbs often—but not always—end in *-ly.*

anecdote
A short account of an event or incident, often humorous, that is used to catch the reader's interest and illustrate a point.

antecedent
The word that a pronoun refers to or stands for. Literally, it means "coming before, preceding." The antecedent usually comes before the pronoun that refers to it—e.g., *Karen* believes *she* is possessed. (*Karen* is the antecedent to which the pronoun *she* refers.)

article
A determiner that precedes a noun. *A/an* is the **indefinite article** that signals an unspecified one of others—e.g., *a* stockbroker, *an* accountant, *a* village, *an* animal, *an* opportunity. Use *a/an* with a singular count noun when making a generalization: *A stockbroker's job is stressful.*

The is the **definite article** that signals a particular person, place, or thing that has been singled out from others—e.g., *the* stockbroker who lives next door; *the* accountant who audits our books; *the* village where I was born. *The* is used when the speaker or writer and the audience are thinking about the same specific person(s) or thing(s). *The* is also used when an unspecified noun is mentioned a second time: I bought a box of chocolates, and my roommate ate half of *the* box.

No article is used in general statements with noncount and plural nouns unless the noun is particularized or made specific in some way—e.g., *Tea* contains less caffeine than *coffee*. *Diamonds* are a girl's best friend. (Compare: *The diamond in my ring* weighs 1.25 carats.)

audience The writer's intended reader or readers. Knowledge of your audience's level of understanding, interests, attitude toward the subject, and expectations of you as a writer are critically important to successful communication. Your level of vocabulary, sentence structure, organization of material, the amount of specific detail you include, and tone will all be influenced by the needs of your audience.

chronological order Events or ideas that are organized chronologically are discussed in order of time sequence.

clause A group of words that contains a subject and a verb. If the group of words can stand by itself and makes complete sense, it is called an **independent clause** (or **principal clause** or **main clause**). If the group of words does not make complete sense on its own but depends on another clause for its meaning, it is called a **dependent** or **subordinate clause**. Here's an example: The porch collapsed. This group of words can stand by itself, so it is called an independent clause. Now consider this clause: When Kalim removed the railing with his tractor. This group of words has a subject, *Kalim,* and a verb, *removed,* but it does not make complete sense on its own. It depends for its meaning on *the porch collapsed*; therefore, it is a dependent clause.

climactic order The arrangement of key ideas in order of importance. The most important or strongest idea comes last. Thus, the paper builds to a climax.

colloquialism A word or phrase that we use in casual conversation or in informal writing. Not appropriate in academic or professional writing.

Steve *flunked* his accounting exam.
Did you *get* what the teacher said about job placement?
I can't believe that *guy* is serious about learning.

comma splice The error that results when the writer joins two independent clauses with a comma—e.g., The comma splice is an error, it is a kind of run-on sentence. See Chapter 8.

compound   A compound construction is made up of two or more equal parts. For example:

> Matt and Caro are late. (compound subject)
>
> Matt came late and left early. (compound verb)
>
> Caro is sick and tired. (compound complement)
>
> The team had no time to warm up, but they won the game anyway. (compound sentence)

count noun   A common noun that has a plural form and can be preceded by an indefinite article *(a/an)* or a quantity expression such as *one*, *many*, *several*, *a few of*, *hundreds of*. Examples: car, letter, dollar.

dependent clause cue   A word or phrase that introduces a dependent clause—e.g., when, because, in order that, as soon as. See page 100.

homonyms   Two or more words that are identical in sound (e.g., bear, bare) or spelling (e.g., bank—a place for money; bank—a slope) but different in meaning. See Chapter 2, page 26.

logically linked order   A pattern of organization that depends on a causal connection among the main points. One point must be explained before the next can be understood.

modifier   A word or group of words that adds information about another word (or phrase or clause) in a sentence. See **adjective, adverb, dependent clause cue,** and Chapter 9.

noncount noun   A common noun that cannot be preceded by an indefinite article *(a/an)* or by a quantity expression (e.g., *one*, *several*, *many*, *a couple of*) and that has no plural form. Examples: traffic, mail, money.

noun   A word that names a person, place, thing, or concept and that has the grammatical capability of being possessive. Nouns are most often used as subjects and objects. There are two classes of nouns: concrete and abstract.

Concrete nouns name things we perceive through our senses; we can see, hear, touch, taste, or smell what they stand for. Some concrete nouns are **proper**: they name people, places, or things and are capitalized—e.g., Babe Ruth, Beijing, Canada's Wonderland. Other concrete nouns are **common** (woman, city, car, coffee); still others are **collective** (group, audience, swarm, committee).

Abstract nouns name concepts, ideas, characteristics—things we know or experience through our intellect rather than through our senses—e.g., truth, pride, feminism, self-esteem.

object   The "receiving" part of a sentence. The **direct object** is a noun or noun substitute (pronoun, phrase, or clause) that is the target or receiver of the action expressed by the verb. It answers the question **What?** or **Whom?**—e.g., John threw the *ball.* (John threw *what?*)

> He wondered where the money went. (He wondered *what?*)
> Munira loves Abdul. (Munira loves *whom?*)

The **indirect object** is a noun or pronoun that is the indirect target or receiver of the action expressed by the verb in a sentence. It is *always* placed in front of the direct object. It answers the question **To whom?** or **To what?**

> Doug threw *me* the ball. (Doug threw *to whom?*)
> Lisa forgot to give her *essay* a title. (Give *to what?*)

The **object of a preposition** is a noun or noun substitute (pronoun, phrase, or clause) that follows a preposition—e.g., after the *storm* (*storm* is a noun, object of the preposition *after*); before *signing the lease* (*signing the lease* is a phrase, object of the preposition *before*); he thought about *what he wanted to do* (*what he wanted to do* is a clause, object of the preposition *about*). Notice that what follows a preposition is always its object. That is why the subject of a sentence or clause is never in a prepositional phrase.

parallelism   Consistent grammatical structure. In a sentence, for example, all items in a series would be expressed in the same grammatical form: words, phrases, or clauses. Julius Caesar's famous pronouncement, "I came, I saw, I conquered," is a classic example of parallel structure. The symmetry of parallelism appeals to readers and makes a sentence read smoothly and rhythmically. Lack of parallelism, on the other hand, is jarring: "My favourite sports are water-skiing, swimming, and I particularly love to sail."

paraphrase   To paraphrase is to rephrase another writer's idea in your own words. A good paraphrase reflects both the meaning and the tone of the original; it is usually about the same length as or shorter than the original. Whenever you paraphrase another writer's idea(s), you must acknowledge your source. If you don't you are guilty of plagiarism.

participle   The form of a verb that can be used as an adjective (the *completed* work, the *laughing* children) or as part of a verb phrase (am *working,* have *rented*).

> The **present participle** of a verb ends in *-ing.*
> The **past participle** of a **regular verb** ends in *-d* or in *-ed.*
> For a list of **irregular verbs,** see pages 152–55.

person   A category of pronouns and verbs. **First person** refers to the person who is speaking (I, we). **Second person** refers to the person being spoken to (you). **Third person** is the person or thing being spoken about (he, she, it, they). Regular verb forms remain constant except in the present tense, third-person singular, which ends in *-s:* I run; *you* run; *she* runs.

phrase   A group of meaning-related words that acts as a noun, a verb, an adjective, or an adverb within a sentence. Phrases do not make complete sense on their own because they do not contain both a subject and a verb.

> Please order *legal-size manila file folders.* (phrase acting as a noun)
> I *must have been sleeping* when you called. (verb phrase)
> *Sightseeing in Ottawa,* we photographed the monuments *on Parliament Hill.* (phrases acting as adjectives)
> Portaging a canoe *in this weather* is no fun. (phrase acting as an adverb)

prefix   A meaningful letter or group of letters added to the beginning of a word either (1) to change its meaning or (2) to change its word class.

> 1. *a* + moral = amoral
>   *bi* + sexual = bisexual
>   *contra* + diction = contradiction
>   *dys* + functional = dysfunctional
> 2. *a* + board (noun) = aboard (adverb, preposition)
>   *con* + temporary (adjective) = contemporary (noun, adjective)
>   *dis* + robe (noun) = disrobe (verb)
>   *in* + put (verb) = input (noun)

Some prefixes require a hyphen, as here:
all-Canadian
de-emphasize
mid-morning

preposition   A word that connects a noun, pronoun, or phrase to some other word(s) in a sentence. The noun, pronoun, or phrase is the **object** of the preposition.

> I prepared the minutes *of the meeting*. (*of* relates *meeting* to *minutes*)
> One *of the parents* checks the children every half hour. (*of* relates *parents* to *One*)

prepositional phrase   A group of grammatically related words beginning with a preposition and having the function of a noun, adjective, or adverb. See the list on page 86.

pretentious language   Sometimes called *gobbledygook*, pretentious language is characterized by vague, abstract, multi-syllable words and long, complicated sentences. Intended to impress the reader, pretentious language is noise without meaning; readers find it irritating, even exasperating.

pronoun   A word that functions like a noun in a sentence (e.g., as a subject, or as an object of a verb or a preposition). Pronouns usually substitute for nouns, but sometimes they substitute for other pronouns.

> *He* will promote *anything that* brings in money.
>
> *Everyone* earns *her* own reward.

There are several kinds of pronouns:

> **personal:** *I, we; you; he, she, it, they; me, us; him, her, them*
> **possessive:** *mine, ours; yours; his, her, its, theirs*
> **demonstrative:** *this, these; that, those*
> **relative:** *who, whom, whose; which, that*
> **interrogative:** *who? whose? whom? which? what?*
> **indefinite:** all *-one, -thing, -body* pronouns, such as *everyone, something,* and *anybody; each; neither; either; few; none; several*

Note: Possessive pronouns also have adjective forms: *my, our; your; his, her, their.* Possessive adjectives follow the same rules for agreement that govern pronouns. They must agree with their antecedents in person, number, and gender. E.g.,

> Every young *hockey player* dreams of playing goal for *his* team. (Not *their* team.)

random order   A shopping-list kind of arrangement of main points in a paper. The points could be explained in any order. Random order is appropriate only when all points are equal in significance and are not chronologically or causally connected to one another.

subject In a sentence, the person, thing, or concept that the sentence is about (see Chapter 6). In an essay, the person, thing, or concept that the paper is about (see Chapter 23).

suffix A letter or group of letters that is added to the end of a word (1) to change its meaning, (2) to change its grammatical function, or (3) to change its word class.

1. king + *dom* = kingdom
   few + *er* = fewer
   tooth + *less* = toothless
2. buy (base form) + *s* = buys (third-person singular, present tense)
   eat (base form) + *en* = eaten (past participle)
   instructor + *s* = instructors (plural)
   instructor + *'s* = instructor's (possessive singular)
3. your (adjective) + *s* = yours (pronoun)
   act (verb) + *ive* = active (adjective)
   active (adjective) + *ly* = actively (adverb)
   manage (verb) + *ment* = management (noun)

Some words add two or more prefixes and/or suffixes to the base form. Look at antidisestablishmentarianism, for example. How many prefixes and suffixes can you identify?

tenses The different forms of a verb that indicate past, present, or future time are called **tenses.** The verb ending (e.g., plays, played) and any helping verbs associated with the main verb (*is* playing, *will* play, *has* played, *had* played, *will have* played) indicate the tense of the verb.

There are simple tenses: **present:** *ask, asks*
 past: *asked*
 future: *will ask*

and perfect tenses: **present:** *has (have) asked*
 past: *had asked*
 future: *will (shall) have asked*

The simple and perfect tenses can also be **progressive:** am asking, have been asking, etc.

thesis A thesis is the idea or point about a subject that the writer wants to explain or prove to the reader in an essay. A summary of the writer's thesis is often expressed in a *thesis statement.* See Chapter 24.

tone	Reflects the writer's attitude toward his or her topic and intended audience. For instance, a writer who is looking back with longing to the past might use a nostalgic tone. An angry writer might use an indignant tone or an understated, ironic tone—depending on the subject and purpose of the paper.
topic sentence	A sentence that identifies the point or key idea developed in a paragraph. The topic sentence is usually found at or near the beginning of the paragraph.
transition	A word or phrase that helps readers to follow the writer's thinking from one sentence to the next or from one paragraph to another. See Chapter 26.
verb	A word or phrase that says something about a person, place, or thing and whose form may be changed to indicate tense. Verbs may express action (physical or mental), occurrence, or condition (state of being). See Chapter 6.

> Wesley *hit* an inside curve for a home run. (physical action)
> Laurence *believed* the Blue Jays would win. (mental action)
> Father's Day *falls* on the third Sunday of June. (occurrence)
> Reva eventually *became* interested in English. (condition)

Some verbs are called **linking verbs:** they help to make a statement by linking the subject to a word or phrase that describes it.

> William Hubbard *was* Toronto's first black mayor. (*was* links *William Hubbard* to *mayor*)
> Mohammed *looks* tired. (*looks* links *Mohammed* and *tired*)

In addition to am, is, are, was, were, and been, some common linking verbs are appear, become, feel, grow, look, taste, remain, seem, smell, sound.

Another class of verbs is called **auxiliary** or **helping verbs.** They show the time of a verb as future or past (*will* go, *has* gone) or as a continuing action (*is* reading). They also show the passive voice (*is* completed, *have been* submitted).

voice	Verbs may be **active** or **passive,** depending on whether the subject of the verb is *acting* (active voice) or *being acted upon* (passive voice).

> In 2008, the government *introduced* a new set of tax reforms. (active)

> A new set of tax reforms *was introduced* in 2008. (passive)

APPENDIX C
Answers to Exercises

Answers for Unit 1 Quick Quiz (page 2)

Note: Triple asterisks (***) indicate that a word or words have been deleted and not replaced. Each set of triple asterisks counts as one error.

[1]Yesterday I was in the city to do some shopping and enjoy an evening of fine **dining**. [2]It was my girlfriend's birthday, so I intended to **buy two** tickets to a play and then **take her** for dinner at an expensive restaurant. [3]First, I went to a **stationery** store to find a card, and when I came out, **there** was a **police officer**, writing a parking ticket. [4]Suddenly I got what I thought was a great *** idea. [5]I approached the **officer** and asked that he **accept** my apology and not write the ticket. [6]He ignored me and continued to write. [7]Determined to get a **response** from him, I called him a miserable swine. [8]He glared at me and began to write another ticket because the car had worn tires. [9]It was **then** that I insulted his ancestors and his **ancestors'** ancestors. [10]He finished the second ticket and began filling out a third, then a **fourth**. [11]Even though he pretended not to hear me, I knew my abuse was **annoying** him since he kept writing **tickets**. [12]I didn't care because I had no idea **whose** car it was. [13]I always come into the city by public transit, but I think **it's** important to have a little fun every day.

Answer Key

If you missed the error(s) in sentence. . .	See Chapter. . .
1 *dinning*	2 Hazardous Homonyms
2 *Birthday*	4 Capital Letters
score	1 Slang
a pair	1 Slang
go for broke	1 Slang
3 *stationary*	2 Hazardous Homonyms
their	2 Hazardous Homonyms
the heat	1 Slang
4 *utterly brilliant, out-of-this world*	1 Wordiness
5 *Officer*	4 Capital Letters
except	2 Hazardous Homonyms
7 *get a rise out of*	1 Clichés
9 *at this point in time*	1 Wordiness
ancestors	3 The Apostrophe
10 *2nd*	5 Numbers
forth	2 Hazardous Homonyms
11 *getting under his skin*	1 Clichés
ticket's	3 The Apostrophe

12 *who's*   2 Hazardous Homonyms

13 *it's*   3 The Apostrophe

Answers for Chapter 1: Choosing the Right Words (pages 4 to 25)

Exercise 1.1

1. *humor.* You must use the root *humor* when adding an ending: e.g., *humorous.*
2. The word is spelled *harassment.* The stress is on the second syllable: har-<u>ass</u>-ment.
3. The word is spelled *tattoo* and can be used both as a noun and as a verb.
4. People in Saskatchewan are more likely to experience a *tornado*; a *tsunami* is a gigantic sea wave and a *typhoon* is a tropical storm.
5. *program, centre, skilful, traveller, judgment,* which are the preferred Canadian spellings.

Exercise 1.2

1. bases   4. ratios   8. phenomena
2. criteria   5. nuclei (*or* nucleuses)   9. mothers-in-law
3. data   6. appendixes (*or* appendices) 10. syllabuses
   (the *singular* is datum) 7. formulas (*or* formulae)   (*or* syllabi)

Exercise 1.3

1. delayed   5. repayment   8. easier
2. journeys   6. loneliness   9. laziness
3. player   7. policies   10. necessarily
4. destroying

The root words in 1 to 5 end in a **vowel** plus *y*; these words do not change spelling when you add an ending. The root words in 6 to 10 end in a **consonant** plus *y*; change *y* to *i* when you add an ending to such words.

Exercise 1.4

1. cof-fee   5. pro-cess   9. dic-tion-ary (*not*
2. arrange-ment   6. moni-tor   dic-tion-ar-y. *Use*
3. pre-cise   7. grad-ually   *a hyphen to divide*
4. night (*words of*   8. poli-tics   *a word only if three*
   one syllable cannot be divided)   *or more letters will*
                                              begin the next line)
                                          10. *pre-nup-tial*

Exercise 1.6

Informal paragraph: The vocabulary is casual and includes contractions and colloquialisms (e.g., "paying through the nose," "a lot of," "the best bets"). Written in the second person, the paragraph addresses the reader informally as "you." Most of the sentences are short and simple; two are exclamatory—common in speech, but not in formal writing.

General paragraph: Sentences here are longer and more complex than in the informal paragraph, but still easily understood. The vocabulary is less casual and more abstract (e.g., contrast the informal expression "We will have to change everything" with the general-level "We will have to transform our entire oil-based infrastructure"; and the informal "That's a big job!" with the general "That's an enormous undertaking!").

Written in the first person, the paragraph is still friendly in tone, but less conversational than the previous paragraph.

Formal paragraph: The vocabulary is more abstract than concrete; there are no contractions or colloquialisms. Complex sentences are relatively long; the parallel structure of phrases and clauses contributes to the formality of the passage, as does the third-person point of view. The tone is serious. The reader cannot imagine anyone speaking this paragraph; clearly, it was written for educated readers.

Exercise 1.7
1. formal
2. informal
3. general

Exercise 1.8 (suggested answers)
1. I do not think there is any basis for believing in UFOs.
2. Getting up at 5 a.m. and repeating the same routine daily for three weeks wore me out.
3. Our competitor's products, although inferior to ours, are selling better than ours.
4. My essay is as good as Jill's and deserves an equivalent mark, but the professor hates me.
5. Nothing suggests that this unusual situation will occur again, so we can proceed with confidence.
6. Because he is being transferred, Rowan plans to buy a new car.
7. I think Alison is pretending to be sick so she won't have to go to work.
8. I prefer contemporary furniture to antiques.
9. Close friends usually share tastes and opinions.
10. I doubt that this innovation will succeed.

Exercise 1.10
On our recent trip to Montreal, just outside Dorval, we saw storm clouds ahead and realized that rain was likely. Within minutes, it began to rain so heavily that we couldn't see. When the rain turned to snow, we pulled into a nearby motel to wait for the storm to pass.

Exercise 1.11
For each item in this exercise, we have italicized the clichés and then provided a suggested revision.
1. The financial adviser told us there was *a window of opportunity* open to investors who could *think outside the box.* Then she gave us an *eye-popping ballpark-figure* of what our *bottom line* would look like *five years out* if we *put our money in her capable hands.*

    The financial adviser told us there was a good opportunity for creative investors. Then she gave us an impressive estimate of the gains we could expect over five years if we entrusted our money to her.

2. While you may want *cutting-edge* stereo and television equipment and a *state-of-the-art* computer and car, you need to understand that your *lifestyle choices* must depend on your income, not your desires. *At the end of the day,* your *take-home pay doesn't make the grade.*

While you may want the very best stereo and television equipment and the latest model of computer and car, you need to understand that your choices must depend on your income, not your desires. Your salary is not sufficient to pay for your dreams.

3. Kayla knew that she *was in over her head* when the meeting *ground to a halt* because she had not *done her homework*. When she became office manager, she thought it would be *child's play* to get everyone *on the same page*, but she soon learned that careful preparation is *a must*.

   Kayla knew that she had underestimated the demands of the job when the meeting ended because she had not prepared for it. When she became office manager, she thought it would be easy to get everyone to agree, but she soon learned that careful preparation is vital.

4. *Experts agree* that *meaningful relationships* are important to mental health, even as divorce rates have *reached epidemic proportions* and loneliness has become *a fact of life*.

   Psychologists agree that close relationships are important to mental health, even as divorce rates have greatly increased and loneliness has become commonplace.

5. *Last but not least,* I want to thank George and Navika, my *tried and true friends* who have *stood by me through thick and thin*, even when there was *no light at the end of the tunnel*. The list of times when they have *lent me a hand* is endless.

   Finally, I want to thank George and Navika, my faithful friends who have been supportive in all circumstances, even when there seemed to be no hope. The list of their many kindnesses to me is endless.

Exercise 1.12 (suggested answers)
1. I would be happy to meet **you** any time, **anywhere**.
2. You should not be discouraged that Jessa's father **can't stand** you; he's **prejudiced** against many of her friends.
3. Television is probably the best example of a **medium** that remains popular, **regardless** of the quality of the programming.
4. This course was supposed to be *** easy, but I could not **have** passed it without *** help.
5. Between you and **me**, the reason our group got a C+ on our project is **that** Chris **did nothing** to contribute to it. (*Or:* . . . **contributed nothing to it**.)

Answers for Chapter 2: Hazardous Homonyms (pages 26 to 40)
Exercise 2.1
1. Your, conscience
2. fourth, passed
3. principle, principal
4. Whether, lose, we're
5. It's, woman

Exercise 2.2
1. quite, minor
2. course, forth
3. know, your
4. whose, advice
5. past, their, led

Exercise 2.3

1. two, it's
2. conscious, dessert
3. lose, then, your
4. our, illusions
5. it's, whose

Exercise 2.4

1. Does, here
2. coarse, new
3. your, then
4. dinner, led
5. woman, choose, choose

Exercise 2.5

1. who's, effects, complement
2. accepts, many
3. stationery, your
4. Where, desert
5. were, dose, lead

Exercise 2.6

1. We certainly won't **choose** any candidate **whose** application was late.
2. Please check with the **Personnel** Department before you hire legal **counsel**.
3. I bruise easily, and **besides**, I faint at the **sight** of blood.
4. **Who's** the idiot who told us that our **principal** purpose in life was to serve as a warning to others?
5. You may think this is a **minor** point, but I think **it's** important to **choose** a **moral course** of action rather **than** an **unprincipled** one.

Exercise 2.7

Nothing causes more arguments between men and **women than** money. Recently, my husband and I were driving **through** the countryside and became involved in a **minor** disagreement about **whether** to treat ourselves to a vacation or buy a new refrigerator. I argued that if we bought the appliance, this would be the **fourth** year in which we had not had a holiday. He countered that our fridge had **passed its** useful life, and a functioning refrigerator took **precedence*** over having fun. What began as a spat quickly **led** to a battle. Before we **knew** it, our good sense **deserted** us, and we were having a serious fight. At this point, we **passed** a farmyard containing several goats and pigs. Pointing to them, my husband asked if they were relatives of mine. "Of **course**," I replied. "**They're** my in-laws."

*Did you find this error? If so, good for you! If not, be aware that our list of hazardous homonyms includes only the most commonly confused word pairs. There are dozens more that can trip you up—another reason you need to own and use a good dictionary.

Exercise 2.8

Many people today are **choosing** a quieter way of life, hoping to live longer and more happily by following the "slower is better" **principle**. Some, on the **advice** of **their** doctors, have been forced to slow down. One heart surgeon, for example, directs his patients to drive only in the slow lane rather **than** use the passing lane. They may arrive a few minutes later, but their blood pressure will not be **affected**. Others don't need to be prompted by their doctors. They **accept** that living at a slower pace doesn't mean **losing** out in any way. In fact, the opposite is true: choosing a healthy lifestyle benefits everyone. The **effect** of increased **peace** and **quiet** in your **personal** life leads to increased productivity, higher **morale**, and greater job satisfaction. Sometimes the improvements are **minor**, but as anyone who has **consciously** tried to slow the pace of life can tell you, the slow lane is the fast lane to longevity.

Exercise 2.10

These are examples only.

1. The wind was so strong that we couldn't wind the sail into position.
2. The supermarket will buy all of the produce your farm can produce.
3. The hawk dove from high above, targeting a dove.
4. She wound a long bandage around the wound on his arm.
5. They will present her birthday present at the end of the party.
6. The dump may refuse to take refuse from another municipality.
7. How can we object when the object that hit our house is from outer space?
8. Lead poisoning can lead to severe illness.
9. There was a row when two people were caught smoking in row seven.
10. Does this mean that does are more numerous than bucks?

Answers for Chapter 3: The Apostrophe (pages 41 to 54)

Exercise 3.1

1. can't	5. let's	8. won't
2. she'd	6. hasn't	9. she'll
3. he'll	7. you're	10. we'll
4. we'd		

Exercise 3.2

1. they're	5. everyone's	8. you're
2. I'll	6. couldn't	9. we'd
3. it's	7. who's	10. won't
4. wouldn't		

Exercise 3.3

1. I'm sure **she'd** help us if we asked her..
2. There **won't** be any problem if **you've** got an invitation.
3. **I'm** positive that contractions **shouldn't** be used in formal writing.
4. We **can't** leave until the **show's** over.
5. **Don't** worry about your heart; **it'll** last as long as you do.
6. **It's** best to get started on your paper early unless **you're** sure you can get an extension.
7. If you **can't** be a good example, maybe **you'll** be able to serve as a horrible warning.
8. **Wouldn't** it be great if everyone **who's** celebrating a birthday today could get together for a big party?
9. **I'd** support the idea only if the party **wasn't** held anywhere near my apartment.
10. A **man's** got to do what a **man's** got to do. A **woman's** got to do what he **can't**.

Exercise 3.4

   I am writing to apply for the position of webmaster for BrilloVision.com that **you have** advertised in the *Daily News*. I have the talent and background **you are** looking for. Currently, I work as a web designer for an online publication, Vexed.com, where

they are very pleased with my work. If you click on their website, I think **you will** like what you see. **There is** little in the way of web design and application that I **have not** been involved in during the past two years. But **it is** time for me to move on to a new challenge, and BrilloVision.com promises the kind of opportunity **I am** looking for. I guarantee you **will not** be disappointed if I join your team!

Exercise 3.5

1. Cass's voice
2. heaven's gate
3. families' budgets
4. crew's mutiny
5. soldiers' uniforms
6. everyone's choice
7. the all-candidate's debate
8. Britney Spears'(s) children
9. teacher's attitude
10. Marge Simpson's blue hair

Exercise 3.6

1. Bikers', Larry's
2. Whose, their
3. dogs', city's
4. month's, son's
5. Texas'(or Texas's), United States'
6. week's, men's, women's
7. whose, company's
8. consumers', WD-40's
9. its, your
10. their, cows'

Exercise 3.7

1. The **festival's** opening act was my little **brother's** punk band.
2. Who says **nobody's** perfect? In my **mother's** opinion, I am.
3. Most **mothers'** beliefs about their **children's** characters are unrealistically positive.
4. Most **fathers'** opinions are negative when they first meet their **daughters'** boyfriends.
5. Did you ever notice that when you blow in a **dog's** face, he gets mad at you, but when you take him on a car ride, he **sticks** his head out the window?

Exercise 3.8

1. This **year's** hockey schedule puts the Stanley Cup **finals** halfway through baseball season.
2. The **candidates'** debate was deadly boring until the **hecklers** in the audience started a fistfight.
3. **Today's** styles and **tomorrow's** trends are featured in every issue of our magazine.
4. My **in-laws'** home is about **four hours'** drive north of Red Lake.
5. Have you noticed that since **everyone's** got a cellphone camera or a hand-held camcorder, **there's** been a drop in the number of UFO sightings?

Exercise 3.9

1. Instead of a cake, Caro made both chocolate and vanilla **cupcakes** for the **children's** party.
2. My **iPod's** playlists need editing; they're full of **songs** I no longer want to listen to.
3. Golf requires different **clubs** for different shots: woods for long shots, irons for short **ones**, and a putter for character development.
4. Good writing **skills** may not guarantee success in **your** career, but their lack will certainly contribute to failure.
5. Forming plural nouns by using **apostrophes** is one way to ensure that your writing **attracts** attention.

Exercise 3.10

1. When your **car's** warranty expires, prepare yourself for some major **repairs**.
2. **I've** posted a sign on my front lawn: "**Salespeople's** visits are always welcome. Dog **food's** expensive."
3. Won't our **employees** be disappointed to hear that **you're** cancelling the **company's** annual picnic?
4. In Canada, as soon as **it's** warm enough to take off **your** shirt, you know it's mosquito season.

Exercise 3.11

1. One of Ogden **Nash's** most famous poems is both short and sweet: "Candy is dandy, but **liquor's** quicker."
2. We very much appreciated the **flowers** you sent for our **mother's** memorial service.
3. Four **months'** work was wasted by a few **minutes'** carelessness.
4. We will need **everybody's** maximum effort if we are to meet **tomorrow's** deadline.
5. Geoff devoted his two **years** at **Queen's** University to hard partying.

Exercise 3.12

1. Brain **cells** come and brain **cells** go, but fat **cells** live forever.
2. One of our **college's** objectives is to meet our **students'** social needs as well as their academic goals.
3. Anyone **who's** able to swallow **pills** at a drinking fountain deserves to get well.
4. The three **tenors'** most spectacular concert was held in **Rome's** ancient Coliseum.
5. The health of **Canada's** economy depends not only on its abundant natural **resources,** but also on its pool of skilled **labourers** and well-educated **professionals.**
6. What do I think of computer dating? **It's** terrific if **you're** a computer.

Answers for Chapter 4: Capital Letters (pages 55 to 63)

Exercise 4.1

1. **T**ime is nature's way of keeping everything from happening at once.
2. Dana called, "**Y**ou left the light on in the garage."
3. On the first day of term, our teacher told us, "**L**earning Standard English is, for many people, like learning another **l**anguage."
4. Richard Harkness summed up my feeling about committees when he wrote, "**A** committee is a group of the unwilling, picked from the unfit, to do the unnecessary."
5. **I**n conclusion, I want you to consider the words of Wendell Johnson: "*Always* and *never* are two words you should always remember never to use."

Exercise 4.2

1. After a brief stay in the **M**aritimes, **C**aptain **T**allman and his crew sailed west up the **S**t. Lawrence.
2. The **B**roadcast **D**epartment of **N**iagara **C**ollege has ordered six **S**ony cameras for their studios in **W**elland, **O**ntario.
3. Do you find that **V**isa is more popular than American **E**xpress when you travel to faraway places such as **M**exico, **F**rance, or **J**upiter?

4. Our stay at the **S**eaview **H**otel, overlooking the **P**acific **O**cean, certainly beat our last vacation at the **B**ates **M**otel, where we faced west, overlooking the city dump.

5. As a member of the **A**lumni **A**ssociation I am trying to raise funds from companies like **D**isney, **G**eneral **M**otors, **B**ell Canada, and the **CBC**, where our graduates have positions.

Exercise 4.3

1. Many of the celebrations we think of as originating in the last 2000 years have much older roots; **H**alloween and **E**aster are two such festivals.

2. The celebration of **C**hristmas has its origins in ancient **B**abylon, where the birth of the son of **I**sis was marked by feasting and gift-giving.

3. The **R**omans, too, had a traditional celebration called **S**aturnalia, held at the end of December. The tradition of seasonal songs, known to us as carols, began in **R**oman times.

4. The Christmas tree and mistletoe date from pagan celebrations called **Y**ule, which were held in northern **E**urope on the shortest day of the year.

5. The observance of **R**amadan is one of the five pillars of the **I**slamic faith and is a month when **M**uslims show obedience and submission by fasting.

6. At the end of **R**amadan, a huge feast called **E**id lasts the entire night.

7. In the Jewish faith, the festival of **H**anukkah often occurs at the same time that **C**hristians are observing **C**hristmas.

8. The celebration of **H**anukkah involves the lighting of one candle each day on a seven-branched candelabrum.

Exercise 4.4

1. My favourite months are **J**anuary and **F**ebruary because I love all **w**inter sports.

2. This **M**onday is **V**alentine's **D**ay, when messages of love are exchanged.

3. In the summer, big meals seem to be too much trouble; however, after **T**hanksgiving, we need lots of food to survive the winter cold.

4. In **C**uraçao, people celebrate **N**ew **Y**ear's **D**ay with elaborate firework displays.

5. By **T**hursday, I'll have finished my **St**. **P**atrick's **D**ay costume.

Exercise 4.5

1. I agreed to go out and see the movie *Basic Instinct 2*, but I should have stayed home, made some popcorn, and watched TV.

2. The 2007 movie with the longest title was *The Assassination of Jesse James by the Coward Robert Ford*.

3. Botticelli's famous painting, *Birth of Venus*, was the inspiration for my poem "**W**oman on the Half-**S**hell."

4. *All the King's Men* was a great film when it was made in 1949, but the 2006 remake was one of the year's worst movies.

5. Most reviewers found Conrad Black's memoir, *A Life in Progress*, to be well written but wordy.

6. Did you know that the great Francis Ford Coppola film, *Apocalypse Now*, was based on Joseph Conrad's novel, *Heart of Darkness*?

7. The Cowboy Junkies have issued a new CD that is a remake of their most famous album, *The Trinity Sessions*.

Exercise 4.6

1. We began our study of **s**ociology with the concept of relationships.
2. After studying geography for two years, I began taking courses in **S**panish and **E**uropean modern history.
3. Math is her strong subject, but Laurie struggles with **E**nglish and conversational **F**rench.
4. By taking Professor Subden's non-credit course, **I**ntroduction to Wine, I qualified to register for **W**inemaking 101 the next semester.
5. The prerequisite for **B**uddhism through the **A**ges. is Introduction to **W**orld **R**eligions.

Exercise 4.7

1. You must take some **s**cience courses, or you'll never get into the program you want at **M**alaspina **C**ollege in the **f**all.
2. Gore Vidal, author of *The Best Man*, once said, "**I**t is not enough to succeed; others must fail."
3. After the **g**ame, we went to the **B**urger **P**alace for a late snack and then went home to watch *This Hour Has 22 Minutes* on televison.
4. Next **T**hursday evening, the **A**nglican church on **B**irch **A**venue will hold a fund-raising dinner to support peace in **D**arfur.
5. We've been assigned to read *The Englishman's Boy,* a novel about life among the settlers of the **A**merican and **C**anadian west, by the end of **M**arch **B**reak.

Exercise 4.8

1. I wonder how our **c**ollege gets away with requiring students to take **E**nglish and **m**athematics courses in addition to our **m**ajor subjects.
2. Leonard Cohen first became famous as a novelist when he published *The Favourite Game* and *Beautiful Losers*.
3. Years later, **C**ohen's career was spectacularly revived with the release of albums such as *I'm Your Man* in 1988 and *The Future* in 1992.
4. Marg Delahunty's campaign to be elected mayor ran into trouble on **F**riday when she was quoted as saying, "**O**ur political system is nothing but mob rule with taxes."
5. I was raised a **B**aptist, but since taking **P**rofessor Chan's course, **I**ntroduction to **W**orld **R**eligions, I've been interested in **H**induism and **B**uddhism.
6. I plan to travel to **A**sia next **s**ummer to learn more about these religions.

Answers for Chapter 5: Numbers (pages 64 to 71)

Exercise 5.1

1. After listening to **four** of the songs on your demo tape, I urge you not to give up your day job.
2. **T**his is the **third** time you have been late this week.
3. The **first** six of the twenty contestants were simply awful, and the next **six** were awfully simple, as the *Idol* show limped along to its dreadful conclusion.
4. Did you know that with **one** ostrich egg you can make **nine** omelettes?
5. Third, and most important, always have a backup plan in case your **first** and **second** plans don't work out.
6. It takes **43** muscles to frown, but only **17** muscles to smile.

7. Jenn's grade was in the top **one-third** of her class, an excellent result, considering that almost **one-half** of the students failed.
8. When I was between **five** and **twelve** years old, my parents home-schooled me.
9. If we order a large pizza with **four** toppings, we get **two** bottles of cola and **nine** chicken wings for **half**-price.
10. On the **fifth** day, she received **five** gold rings, but by then she was pretty fed up with the mess made by the **four** calling birds, **three** French hens, **two** turtledoves, and the partridge in the pear tree.

Exercise 5.2

1. I was born on August **15**, 1983, and my horoscope for the day predicted a happy and eventful life. So far, so good. (Or **15 August 1983**)
2. The power went off in my building at **4:15** a.m., causing my clock radio to fail, which is why I slept through my **8:30** exam.
3. A fire at **610** East **44th** Street brought traffic to a standstill until firefighters put it out **four** hours later.
4. While **7 percent** of men suffer from colour blindness, only **1 percent** of women have it. Isn't that discriminatory?
5. After spending **$30** for a bottle of wine and **$26** for flowers, I didn't expect my date to spend the evening complaining that I was cheap!
6. If your skin gets dry in the winter, it may be because the humidity in the average Canadian home during the winter months is **13** percent. The Sahara Desert, by comparison, has a humidity level of 25 **percent**.
7. At **8** a.m., I was awakened by my roommate zooming up the driveway at **30** km/h on her motorcycle.
8. Driving a car at **90** km/h uses about **20** percent less fuel than driving it at 105 km/h.
9. My salary was raised on May **15** by 7 percent; however, I calculate that my expenses have risen at least **11 percent** over the past year.
10. To prepare prospective mothers for the effect having a baby might have on their bodies, a creative doctor urged his patients to strap a **4** kg beanbag to their stomachs, wear it for **nine** months, and then remove about **one-third** of the beans.

Exercise 5.3

1. We need three cases of **twelve** 1.5-L bottles.
2. A blue whale weighs as much as **30** elephants and is as long as three Greyhound buses.
3. The budget surplus of **5** billion dollars was more than expected and allowed the government to pay off a tiny fraction (less than 1 **percent**) of the national debt.
4. Almost 60 **percent** of students in my survey say they would rather be teachers, but more than **90** percent of teachers would rather be students.
5. I've told you **a million** times not to exaggerate! (*or*: 1 million)
6. In the **14th** century, the Black Plague killed **half** the population of Europe.
7. The Earth now supports more than **6** billion people, and two countries, India and China, account for more than **1 billion** each.
8. Although I was travelling at **80** km/h, which is what I thought the speed limit to be, the officer told me that I was **2** km inside the city limits, so the speed limit was 50 km/h. My fine was **$108.**

9. **One** 8-cylinder SUV puts more pollution into the atmosphere than two **4**-cylinder diesel Volkswagens or **three** Toyota gas-electric hybrids.

10. The total population of Earth in **5000** B.C. is estimated to have been about **5 million** people, about **one-sixth** the number who now live in Canada.

Answers for Unit 1 Rapid Review (page 72)

Note: Triple asterisks (***) indicate that a word or words have been deleted. Each set of triple asterisks counts as one error. The "Answer Key" following the answers identifies errors by sentence number and indicates the chapter or part of a chapter you should review if you missed an error.

¹**R**egardless of any negative attitudes *** you may have about working in retail sales, this kind of work does *** provide **employees** with **many** amusing moments. ²During our last **Boxing Day** sale, for example, I was serving a **woman** who wanted to buy **three** pairs of shoes to **complement** the *** new outfits she had just purchased. ³As she opened her **large ***** designer purse, she asked if we **accepted American Express**. I assured her that her credit card would be fine. ⁴She rummaged around for her wallet, then turned her purse upside down, dumping its contents all over the counter ***** beside the cash register. ⁵I could not help noticing a television remote control among the items scattered over our counter. ⁶Curious, I asked if **there** was a reason she carried a remote control when she went **shopping**. ⁷Her answer gave me one of the best laughs I've had in my job. ⁸She told me that her husband said he wanted to watch football rather than go shopping with her. ⁹She was so **angry** that she took the remote control because she thought that was the most evil thing she could legally do to him.

Answer Key

If you missed the error(s) in sentence. . .		See Chapter. . .	
1	*Irregardless*	1	Abusages
	attitudes, feelings, or thoughts	1	Wordiness
	does, in fact,	1	Wordiness
	actually provide	1	Wordiness
	employee's	3	The Apostrophe
	alot of	1	Abusages
2	*boxing day*	4	Capital Letters
	women	2	Hazardous Homonyms
	3 pairs	5	Numbers
	compliment	2	Hazardous Homonyms
	brand-new	1	Wordiness
3	*humongous*	1	Slang
	real leather	1	Wordiness
	accepted	1	Abusages
	american express	4	Capital Letters
4	*right beside*	1	Wordiness
6	*their*	2	Hazardous Homonyms
	on a purchasing expedition	1	Wordiness
9	*ticked off*	1	Slang

Answers for Unit 2 Quick Quiz (page 74)

[1]The 100-kilometre diet is not a way to lose weight. [2]**It is** a plan to encourage consumers to buy and **appreciate** locally grown food. [3]The idea is to buy **only** those meats and vegetables that have been produced within 100 km of where we live. [4]**It's a way for us consumers** to spend our dollars and at the same time help ourselves, our community, **and our planet.** [5/6]By insisting that we want to buy only meats and vegetables that have been grown in our region, **we support** local farmers, *** put pressure on merchants to stock local products, and minimize the amount of petroleum used to transport foods from producer to market, **a** distance that is often half a continent or more. [7(a)]Besides, when we buy fruits and vegetables fresh from the farm, we get better **food.** [7(b)]**Produce** that was harvested green and allowed to ripen during the **often** long journey to our stores has less colour, **less flavour,** and fewer nutrients.

[8(a)]Of course, not all foods can be found year-round in every **locality.** [8(b)]**Sometimes,** if we simply must have a certain fruit or vegetable to satisfy a craving or **to prepare** a special meal, we have no choice but to buy from outside our region. [9]With new growing and preserving techniques, however, it is becoming increasingly possible to stock up on local produce in season and enjoy it year-round. [10/11]Healthier consumers, decreased pollution, and profitable farms **make** the 100-kilometre diet a wise consumer choice.

Answer Key

If you missed the error(s) in sentence. . .	See Chapter. . .
2 Sentence fragment	7 "Missing Piece" Fragments
have an appreciation of	10 The Parallelism Principle
3 *to only buy*	9 Misplaced Modifiers
4 *As consumers,*	9 Dangling Modifiers
is good for the planet	10 The Parallelism Principle
5/6 *By insisting that . . .*	9 Dangling Modifiers
local farmers are supported	
we put pressure on	10 The Parallelism Principle
Sentence fragment	7 "Missing Piece" Fragments
7(b) Run-on sentence	8 Comma Splices
to ripen often during the	
long journey	9 Misplaced Modifiers
is not as flavourful	10 The Parallelism Principle
8(b) Run-on sentence	8 Fused Sentence
for the preparation of	10 The Parallelism Principle
10/11 Sentence fragment	7 "Missing Piece" Fragments

Answers for Chapter 6: Cracking the Sentence Code (pages 76 to 93)
Exercise 6.1
1. <u>Canadians</u> <u>love</u> doughnuts.
2. <u>They</u> <u>eat</u> more doughnuts than any other nation.
3. Most <u>malls</u> <u>contain</u> a doughnut shop.
4. <u>Doughnuts</u> <u>taste</u> sweet.
5. Glazed <u>doughnuts</u> <u>are</u> my favourite.
6. Hot <u>chocolate</u> <u>is</u> good with doughnuts.
7. [<u>You</u>] <u>Try</u> a bran doughnut for breakfast.

8. It is good for your health.
9. Doughnut jokes are common on television.
10. Dentists like doughnuts too, but for different reasons.

Exercise 6.2

1. I hate cellphones.
2. Today, however, cellphones are practically a necessity.
3. [You] Turn your cellphone off, please.
4. My cellphone takes pictures.
5. Alissa's cellphone is an expensive model.
6. She is on a very strict diet.
7. The cellphone's memory contains information about her diet.
8. Now she checks her cellphone before every meal.
9. Alissa is happy about her weight loss.
10. Her telephone bills, though, infuriate her.

Exercise 6.3

1. Whose homework is missing?
2. [You] Drive carefully.
3. Slowly down the spiral staircase came the bride.
4. Have you no heart?
5. [You] Then give me a kilogram of liver and a couple of kidneys instead.
6. Into the pool leaped the terrified cat.
7. There are two electives to choose from.
8. Which one is more interesting?
9. Here is just the person to answer your question.
10. Were you happy with the answer?

Exercise 6.4

1. We are finding most of the verbs.
2. Someday my prince will come.
3. Have you planned a party to celebrate his arrival?
4. This book must have been written by a genius.
5. The verbs must be underlined twice.
6. Keith will have another coffee and a doughnut.
7. Do you know anything about grammar?
8. We have knocked on the door several times.
9. I will be looking for verbs in my sleep.
10. We must have practised enough by now.

Exercise 6.5

1. I am making a nutritious breakfast.
2. It does not include pop.
3. You can add fresh fruit to the cereal.
4. The toast should be ready now.
5. My doctor has often recommended yogurt for breakfast.
6. I could never eat yogurt without fruit.
7. With breakfast, I will drink at least two cups of coffee.
8. I don't like tea.

9. I simply cannot begin my day without coffee.
10. I should probably switch to decaf.

Exercise 6.6

1. The security guard is sleeping again.
2. The security guard is often found asleep.
3. Have you ever been lonely?
4. There has never been a better time to invest.
5. Marie is carefully considering her options.
6. Where and when are we meeting?
7. Teenagers are sometimes embarrassed by their parents' behaviour.
8. Could you please explain one more time.
9. "Ladies are requested not to have children in the bar."
10. "The manager has personally passed all our water."

Exercise 6.7

1. A couple of hamburgers should be enough for each of us.
2. Only a few of us save money in an RRSP.
3. One-seventh of your life is spent on Mondays.
4. Exaggeration in your writing is a million times worse than understatement.
5. Your flu, despite your precautions, has infected everyone in the office.
6. In their secret dreams, many grown men would still like to own a train set.
7. Nothing in the known universe travels faster than a bad cheque.
8. During the trial, before the decision, you must have been nervous.
9. Ninety-eight percent of all statistics are made up.
10. A day without sunshine is, in most respects, just like night.

Exercise 6.8

1. According to my financial adviser, my earliest possible retirement date is 2052.
2. By waiting on tables, (by) baby-sitting, and (by) borrowing from friends, I manage to make ends meet.
3. Except for me, everyone understands prepositions.
4. With the permission of the professor, I will demonstrate my mastery of verb identification.
5. No book of Canadian humour would be complete without some shots at American tourists.
6. Despite its strong taste, espresso contains no more caffeine than regular coffee.
7. A daily intake of more than 600 mg of caffeine can result in headaches, (in) insomnia, and (in) heart palpitations.
8. Six to ten cups of coffee will usually contain about 600 mg of caffeine.
9. One of the network's foreign correspondents will speak at noon in the auditorium about her experiences in Afghanistan.
10. Our teacher's uncertainty about the date of the War of 1812 made us curious about his knowledge of Canadian history.

Exercise 6.9

1. In my opinion, fear of flying is entirely justifiable.
2. In our basement are stacks of magazines dating from the 1950s.
3. The rats in our building have written letters of complaint to the Board of Health.

4. When <u>did</u> the <u>president</u> of your company <u>decide</u> on this policy?
5. For reasons of privacy, <u>I</u> <u>am listed</u> in the telephone book under my dog's name.
6. Into the classroom and up to the front <u>marched</u> a tall, grey-haired <u>woman</u> with a determined look in her eyes.
7. After eight hours of classes, the <u>thought</u> of collapsing in front of the TV <u>is</u> very appealing.
8. In future, [you] <u>be</u> sure to read through your notes before the exam.
9. In your brochure, <u>you</u> <u>advertise</u> a "semiannual after-Christmas sale" of quality items.
10. According to my dictionary, the <u>word</u> "semiannual" <u>means</u> twice a year.

Exercise 6.10

1. <u>Maple sugar</u> and <u>wild rice</u> <u>are</u> native Canadian products.
2. <u>Professor Dasgupta</u> <u>handed out</u> the tests and <u>wished</u> us luck.
3. The <u>screen</u> <u>blinked</u> twice and then <u>went</u> blank.
4. <u>Elgar</u> and <u>Grieg</u> <u>are</u> the names of my two unfortunate nephews.
5. My weird <u>brother</u> and his equally weird <u>wife</u> <u>chose</u> the names in honour of their favourite composers.
6. <u>They</u> <u>could have done</u> worse and <u>chosen</u> Humperdinck and Shostakovich.
7. A good sermon <u>writer</u> <u>creates</u> a brilliant opening, <u>develops</u> a stirring conclusion, and <u>puts</u> the two as close together as possible.
8. Today my <u>neighbour</u> and <u>I</u> <u>raked</u> the leaves, <u>dug up</u> our gardens, and <u>put away</u> the lawn furniture.
9. <u>Students</u> with good time management skills <u>can research</u>, <u>organize</u>, <u>draft</u>, and <u>revise</u> a first-class paper by the deadline.
10. <u>Those</u> with excellent time-management skills <u>can keep</u> on top of their schoolwork, <u>hold</u> a part-time job, <u>volunteer</u> at a local charity, and still <u>find</u> time for a social life.

Exercise 6.11

1. <u>Food</u> and <u>drink</u> <u>are</u> the most reliable sources of pleasure.
2. According to Angelo, Werner, and Vijay, <u>Italy</u>, <u>Germany</u>, and <u>India</u> <u>produce</u> and <u>eat</u> the best food in the world.
3. [You] <u>Question</u>, <u>disagree</u>, and <u>argue</u> with them at your own risk!
4. When <u>can</u> the three <u>chefs</u> and their <u>guests</u> <u>gather</u> for a demonstration?
5. <u>Angelo</u>, <u>Werner</u>, and <u>Vijay</u> <u>discussed</u> and <u>debated</u> recipes all night.
6. During the following week, each <u>one</u> <u>chose</u> and <u>prepared</u> a meal for the other two.
7. Werner's <u>sauerbraten</u> with rösti and Black Forest <u>cake</u> <u>amazed</u> and <u>delighted</u> his friends.
8. <u>Angelo</u> <u>chopped</u>, <u>sliced</u>, <u>simmered</u>, and <u>baked</u> a magnificent Italian four-course meal.
9. <u>Vijay</u> and his <u>sister</u> <u>worked</u> in the kitchen for two days and <u>prepared</u> a delicious Indian feast.
10. By the end of the week, <u>Vijay</u>, <u>Angelo</u>, and <u>Werner</u> <u>were</u> ready for a fast.

Exercise 6.12

    <u>I</u> <u>have</u> news for all you short people out there. <u>Being</u> tall <u>is</u> not an enviable condition. First of all, tall people <u>are</u> the butt of constant jokes: "How' [i]s the <u>weather</u> up there?" "What great kneecaps <u>you</u> <u>have</u>!" The <u>humour</u> <u>is</u> pretty lame. Next, there <u>is</u> the <u>risk</u> of serious head injury. <u>I</u> <u>have been bashed</u> by cupboard doors and <u>concussed</u>

by signboards. On one memorable occasion, I was knocked senseless by a chandelier. Clothes present another problem. Finding anything to fit is a challenge. Finding anything remotely fashionable is next to impossible. Clerks in men's clothing departments are apparently hired for their ability to humiliate outsized men. They seem to be genuinely surprised at one's reluctance to appear in public wearing pants that end at mid-calf. And finally, there is basketball. Like many tall people, I detest the game. Despite popular belief, not all people more than 2 m tall have been blessed with the natural ability to dribble, jump-shoot, and slam-dunk. Many of us would rather join a chain gang than a basketball team. To be honest, though, for the most part, I do like being tall. But I wouldn't mind fewer jokes, more sympathy, and less basketball.

Answers for Chapter 7: Solving Sentence-Fragment Problems (pages 94 to 105)
Exercise 7.1
1. F   According to the government, our water is safe to drink.
2. S   Exhausted, I slept.
3. F   We are happy to help.
4. F   I am hoping to hear from you soon.
5. S   [You] Take another.
6. F   In case you were wondering, it is a wig.
7. F   Sentence fragments such as these make a poor impression on the reader.
8. S   [You] Close the door quietly on your way out.
9. F   The mayor is pausing to think of an appropriate reply.
10. S   Working as a server in a cheap restaurant is not rewarding.

Exercise 7.2

1. F	5. F	8. S
2. F	6. S	9. F
3. F	7. F	10. F
4. F		

Exercise 7.3 (suggested answers)
1. I wanted to stay home, but my girlfriend wanted to go to the movies to see the new Coen brothers' film.
2. In volleyball, our college is well respected. Our team won the provincial championship last year, placing three players on the All-Star team.
3. Whenever I go fishing, the fish aren't biting, but the mosquitoes are. Maybe I should give up fishing and start collecting insects instead.
4. My son is a genius. On his last birthday, he was given a toy that was guaranteed to be unbreakable. Guess what? He used it to break all his other toys. (*Note:* "Guess what?" is a complete sentence because it is a command: *guess* is the verb and [*You*] is the subject.)
5. We weren't lost, but we certainly were confused. I realized this when we drove past City Hall for the third time.
6. Correct
7. My friends and I often go to the hockey arena during the winter, not to watch sports, but to hear concerts by some of the best local bands. These concerts give new meaning to the word "cool."
8. Correct

9. I enjoy reading travel blogs **a**bout faraway places that I have never visited and will probably never get to see. The fun is in the dreaming, not the doing.

10. Spending my days skiing and boarding and my nights dancing and clubbing **is** how I plan to spend my retirement.

Exercise 7.4

1. S	5. F	8. S
2. F	6. S	9. F
3. F	7. F	10. S
4. S		

Exercise 7.5

Ed forgot his wife's birthday. **He knew** he was in trouble from the moment he got home from work and saw her angry face. **He apologized** and **asked** how he could make it up to her. She replied that she wanted to find something in the driveway that would go from zero to 100 in less than five seconds, **n**o later than tomorrow morning. The next day, Ed left for work early, **l**eaving a colourful package tied with a large bow in the middle of the driveway. Ed's wife eagerly tore the paper and ribbon off the package **and discovered** a new bathroom scale. Ed is still missing.

Exercise 7.6

1. F   When we left the party.
2. F   If you don't approve.
3. F   Although there is another side to the story.
4. S   Unless you cheat, I win.
5. F   Soon, when you have completed your education.
6. F   Even though you thought your effort was enough to win.
7. F   All of those who finish before the time is up.
8. S   If he were any dumber, he'd have to be watered twice a week.
9. F   Repulsive, although my sister seems to be genuinely in love with him.
10. F   When you decide to begin, whether or not the other team is ready.

Exercise 7.7

1. When we left the party, we could hardly stand up.
2. If you don't approve, then perhaps you could suggest another solution.
3. Although there is another side to the story, I am inclined to believe the defendant's version.
5. Soon, when you have completed your education, you will be able to support yourself.
6. Even though you thought your effort was enough to win, your competitor's talent earned the prize.
7. All of those who finish before the time is up can give me their papers and leave the room.
9. To me, Biff is repulsive, although my sister seems to be genuinely in love with him.
10. When you decide to begin, whether or not the other team is ready, [you] throw the Frisbee onto the field.

Exercise 7.8

1. Walking is probably the best form of exercise there is. Unless you're in the water. Then, swimming is preferable.
2. The modern world is confusing for all of us. If you can keep your head when all about you are losing theirs. Perhaps you just don't understand the situation.
3. The world is divided into good and bad people. The good ones sleep better. While the bad ones seem to enjoy their waking hours much more.
4. Doing the job right the first time gets the job done. While doing the job wrong again and again gives you job security. This principle explains how my uncle stays employed.
5. You know you have been teaching too long. When capital punishment seems a reasonable response to sentence fragments. Now is the time to think about early retirement.

Exercise 7.9

1. Because bear attacks are so well publicized in the media. Most people do not know that their chances of being killed by a bear are far lower than their chances of being killed by lightning. Bears seldom bother humans. Unless the humans are foolish enough to take food into their tents, approach a bear cub, or get close to a grizzly.
2. While getting lost in a country inhabited by cannibals would be a terrifying experience for most people. I know that my long career as a standup comic will keep me safe from harm. All cannibals know that comics taste funny.
3. The names of many Canadian landmarks have been changed over the years. Until the residents of Lethbridge, for example, petitioned for a change to a more dignified name. The Oldman River used to be called the Belly River.
4. After hearing the same song about 30 times in one week and liking it less each time. I finally took action. I reset all the buttons on my car radio. So that I could avoid any station that plays the top 10. I now listen only to talk radio and the CBC.
5. Superglue is a remarkable product. It can bond almost anything to almost anything else. Nevertheless, all parents of toddlers know there is another substance. That is much harder and stronger than Superglue. The glue that outperforms all others is mashed banana. Especially after it has dried in an infant's hair.

Exercise 7.10
Corrections to fragments in Exercise 7.8

1. Walking is probably the best form of exercise there is **u**nless you're in the water. Then, swimming is preferable.
2. The modern world is confusing for all of us. If you can keep your head when all about you are losing theirs**, p**erhaps you just don't understand the situation.
3. The world is divided into good and bad people. The good ones sleep better **w**hile the bad ones seem to enjoy their waking hours much more.
4. Doing the job right the first time gets the job done **w**hile doing the job wrong again and again gives you job security. This principle explains how my uncle stays employed.
5. You know you have been teaching too long **w**hen capital punishment seems a reasonable response to sentence fragments. Now is the time to think about early retirement.

Corrections to fragments in Exercise 7.9

1. Because bear attacks are so well publicized in the media, **m**ost people do not know that their chances of being killed by a bear are far lower than their chances of being killed by lightning. Bears seldom bother humans **u**nless the humans are foolish enough to take food into their tents, approach a bear cub, or get close to a grizzly.

2. While getting lost in a country inhabited by cannibals would be a terrifying experience for most people, I know that my long career as a standup comic will keep me safe from harm. All cannibals know that comics taste funny.

3. The names of many Canadian landmarks have been changed over the years. Until the residents of Lethbridge, for example, petitioned for a change to a more dignified name, **t**he Oldman River used to be called the Belly River.

4. After hearing the same song about 30 times in a week and liking it less each time, I finally took action. I reset all the buttons on my car radio **so** that I could avoid any station that plays the top 10. I now listen only to talk radio and the CBC.

5. Superglue is a remarkable product. It can bond almost anything to almost anything else. Nevertheless, all parents of toddlers know there is another substance **e**ven stronger than Superglue. The glue that outperforms all others is mashed banana, **e**specially after it has dried in an infant's hair.

Exercise 7.11

Because the chances of winning are so small, **l**otteries have been called a tax on people with poor math skills. Buying a lottery ticket will gain you about as much as betting that the next U.S. president will come from Moose Jaw, **o**r that the parrot in the pet store speaks Inuktitut. While winning a lottery is not impossible, **it** is so unlikely that you'd do better to use your money to light a nice warm fire. Although the winners are highly publicized, **n**o one hears about the huge numbers of losers **w**hose money has gone to pay the winners. In order for the lottery corporation to make its enormous profits, **m**illions of dollars must be lost whenever a lucky winner is declared.

Answers for Chapter 8: Solving Run-On Sentence Problems (pages 106 to 113)

Exercise 8.1 (suggested answers)

1. A fine mess this is. I'll never forgive you for getting me into this situation.
2. Let's take the shortcut; we need to get there as quickly as possible.
3. No one in the department supports her **because** she's arrogant and lazy.
4. I want to play the banjo; unfortunately, I have no musical talent.
5. We do not tear your clothing with machinery. **We** do it carefully by hand.
6. I'd rather be lucky than good; on the other hand, I'd rather be good than unlucky. (*Or* use a period)
7. I am busy right now, **so** you'll have to wait.
8. I don't want to achieve immortality through my work. I want to achieve it through not dying.
9. There are many factors to consider when you are looking for a new car, **and** the most important is price. (*Or* use a semicolon without "and")
10. Many good films are made in Canada. I just wish I could tell which ones they were before buying a ticket. (*Or* use a semicolon)

Exercise 8.2

1. I hate computers; they're always making mistakes.
2. Our company wants to hire a telepath. **T**he right person for the job will know where to apply.
3. Stop me if you've heard this one. **T**here was this cab driver on her first day at work.
4. Coffee is Ruth's weakness; she goes to Starbucks at least once a day.
5. Jason offered to take me to a movie, **so** I'll probably be going out tonight.
6. Time is the best teacher; unfortunately, it kills all its students.
7. Price and reliability are what I look for in a new car; performance is a long way down the list.
8. I'd love to teach you to play solitaire **as soon as** I have finished my assignment. (*Or* **,** **but** I have an assignment to finish first)
9. The English language makes no sense. **P**eople recite at a play and play at a recital.
10. We have not inherited the Earth from our ancestors; we are borrowing it from our children.

Exercise 8.3 (suggested answers)

1. In Canada, winter is more than a season. **I**t's a bad joke.
2. The largest dog in the world is the Irish wolfhound; the strongest dog in the world is the Newfoundland; the stupidest dog in the world is my mutt. **H**e's also the best loved.
3. Twice a week, my wife and I go to a nice restaurant for some good food, a little wine, and pleasant conversation. **S**he goes Tuesdays, and I go Fridays.
4. **When** Jessica backed her car out of the driveway, she forgot to check her rear-view mirror. **A**s a result, she produced a significant alteration to the front end of a passing Honda.
5. We understand his feelings of rejection **after** he discovered that his family had moved to another city while he was out getting a pizza.
6. Fast food is generally less nutritious than home-cooked meals, **but** this is not true of my mother's cooking. **H**ers rates below cardboard in nutritional value as well as taste.
7. Correct
8. There are two students in this class named Xan. **O**ne is from China; the other is from Russia. **T**he latter's name is a nickname, a short form of Alexandra.
9. The first sign of adulthood is the discovery that the volume knob also turns to the left. **T**his realization does not happen overnight; for some people, the process takes years.
10. Evaluating Frank's progress is difficult when you realize that he has submitted none of the assignments, written none of the tests, and attended less than a third of the classes. **Y**ou can see why I despair. (*Alternative revision:* Evaluating Frank's progress is difficult. **When** you realize that he has submitted none of the assignments, written none of the tests, and attended less than a third of the classes, you can see why I despair.)

Exercise 8.4 (suggested revision)

Last year, an exchange student from the south of France came to live with us. **H**er name was Simone**, and** she came to Canada to practise her English and learn something about our culture. Simone was amazed by ice hockey; she had never seen the game before and thought it was very exciting. In her first months here, Simone was surprised by what she perceived as Canadians' devotion to everything American, from television shows to sports events, to music, to fast food. **She** confessed that she couldn't see much that was uniquely Canadian. **S**he was disappointed by our lack of a distinct culture**, but** after she made a week's trip to Chicago, she began to understand some of the differences between the two countries. **T**he relative cleanliness of Canada's cities, our support of multiculturalism, and our respect for law and order impressed her. **T**he vast size of our country, with its huge expanses of untouched wilderness, intimidated her a little. Although she was homesick, especially in the first few weeks, Simone enjoyed her year in Canada. **W**hen she was packing to return to Provence, she was already planning her next visit. **S**he wants to go camping on Prince Edward Island.

Exercise 8.5 (suggested answers)

1. In answer to your letter, I have given birth to a boy weighing five kilos. I hope this is satisfactory.
2. That isn't food**;** that's what food eats.
3. A <u>cup</u> of coffee in the middle of the afternoon <u>helps</u> to keep me alert. **T**he caffeine chases away my after-lunch slump.
4. CRNC is the home of the million-dollar guarantee. **I**f you give us a million dollars, we guarantee to play any song you want.
5. It's far too hot**;** no one feels like working**, n**ot even people who claim to like summer temperatures.
6. A fine <u>wine</u> during a special meal **is** my only vice**;** otherwise**, I**'m perfect.
7. Eat sensibly. **E**xercise regularly. **D**ie anyway.
8. People who do not turn off their cellphones in movie theatres are inconsiderate**, and** they should be ejected without a refund.
9. When a football or hockey game is on TV**, m**y husband becomes deaf. **H**e doesn't hear a word I say.
10. Our dog loves children**, e**specially when they are eating French fries or hot dogs. In her excitement, she has sometimes frightened a child**, but** she has never bitten anyone.

Answers for Chapter 9: Solving Modifier Problems (pages 114 to 124)

Exercise 9.1

1. I watched the Leafs lose almost every night.
2. We were practically run over by every car that passed.
3. This recipe can be made in about an hour by anyone who has mastered basic cooking skills.
4. Walking through Wonderland, Alice discovered a magic mushroom.
5. She ate just one bite and found herself growing larger.
6. The rabid dog was captured by the Canine Control officer before anyone was bitten.
7. For less than a dollar, the online classified page lists the names of people who want to buy used cars.

8. We were told (only) |at the end of the test| that it was worth 10 percent of our grade.

(Or: We were told at the end of the test that it was worth (only) |10 percent of our grade.)|

9. In the ruins of Minoan Crete, there are wall paintings of |boys| (with no clothes on) jumping over bulls.

10. (Proud of his new tattoo—a python around his neck—) |Wayne| was told by his father to grow a long beard before he even thought of applying for a job.

Exercise 9.2

1. George has insulted (almost) |everyone| he's gone out with.

2. (After my performance review,) the company |offered| me a raise of nearly $50 a week.

3. Employees who are (frequently) |late| are dismissed without notice.

4. I will ask you (just) |once more| if you were present when your picture was taken.

5. Each year, (nearly) |500,000 Canadian men| have vasectomies.

6. Most pet owners don't bother having their dogs professionally groomed (unless) |they are poodles or terriers.|

7. I hate parties where food |is served| (on tiny paper plates) to guests who have no place to sit.

8. (On Monday,) |our instructor reminded us| we would have a test. (*Or*: Our instructor reminded us |we would have a test| (on Monday.))

9. Catalina turned the (badly bruised) |avocados| into great guacamole.

10. |A rare 1991 Saab convertible| (with only 50,000 km and a recent tune-up) is being offered for sale by an elderly lady.

Exercise 9.3

1. As a college English teacher, I am annoyed by dangling modifiers.
2. When you are writing, a dictionary is your best friend.
3. Lifting the lid carefully and quietly, I discovered the cookie jar was empty.
4. Before you apply the varnish, the surface must be sanded smooth.
5. While he attempted to hot-wire a '99 Jeep Cherokee, a suspect was arrested by the police.
6. As an advocate of healthy eating, I believe fast-food restaurants are purveyors of poison.

7. Because she was driving recklessly, Tara was stopped at a roadblock by the police.
8. When we arrived at the meeting room 20 minutes late, we found everyone had left.
9. In cold weather, [you should] warm up the engine thoroughly before attempting to drive.
10. Travelling abroad, you can learn much from the sights you see and the people you meet.

Exercise 9.4

1. After you change the tire, release the jack.
2. Having decided on pizza, we should decide next whether to order beer or soft drinks.
3. After I waited for you for an hour, the evening was ruined.
4. Jogging through Stanley Park, I saw a cluster of totem poles.
5. After four days on the trail, we agreed that a hot shower and a cold drink were necessities rather than luxuries.
6. After I set the microwave on "Automatic," the turkey cooked to perfection.
7. After you have completed the beginning, the ending is the second most-important part of an essay.
8. Convicted of aggravated assault, she was sentenced to two years in the penitentiary.
9. After scoring the goal in overtime, the team led a huge victory parade through the city.
10. After I had lived with the same roommate for two years, my parents suggested that I try living alone.

Exercise 9.5

1. If you are looking for style, economy, and performance, a Honda Fit or a Toyota Yaris might be worth a look.
2. Everyone stared as, in a sequin-spangled bikini, she rode into the ring on a white horse.
3. Looking out the window on a lovely fall day, I saw a squirrel raiding the bird feeder.
4. Ruth took the seagull, which had a broken wing and was unable to fly, to the Humane Society.
5. My guests were amazed by how tender the beef was after it was slow-cooked in red wine for two hours.
6. Gnawing his stolen steak and growling, Henry's dog could not be coaxed to come out from under the table.
7. My clumsy friends cannot be trusted with my wine glasses, which are made of delicate crystal.
8. Since they are used to drinking from jam jars, my crystal glasses would be wasted on them, anyway.
9. Our neighbours bought a Cornish Rex cat because this breed does not shed hair.
10. Having skipped class for most of the term and not having bothered to buy the textbook, I think a pass is probably too much for me to hope for.

Exercise 9.6

1. In our program, the women outnumber the men by almost a two-to-one ratio.
2. While I was sleeping, the blankets became tangled and ended up on the floor.
3. The sign on the door says that only students are admitted to the pub.
4. Having ruled out the other items on the menu, we chose the fully loaded pizza.
5. Swimming in the bay is not a good idea if the water is polluted.

6. With your textbook closed, please summarize what you have read.
7. Having been to Monte Carlo and visited its magnificent casino, I think Las Vegas seems trashy and cheap by comparison.
8. Our team's best player was rescued by his girlfriend from being thrown out of college in his third term.
9. I can recommend almost any of the restaurants in this town because I have eaten in nearly all of them.
10. After being convicted on drug charges, a 53-year-old truck driver, who has lived in Canada since he was a baby, has been deported to England, where he was born.

Answers for Chapter 10: The Parallelism Principle (pages 125 to 134)

Exercise 10.1

1. My new keyboard is ergonomic, functional, and attractive.
2. The three main kinds of speech are demonstrative, informative, and persuasive.
3. Wielding his knife swiftly and skilfully, the chef turned a tomato into a centrepiece that looked just like a rose.
4. I am overworked and underpaid.
5. You need to develop skill, strategy, and agility to be a competitive skateboarder.
6. On our trip to Finland, we sailed, explored, and hiked. (*Or* . . . we went sailing, exploring, and hiking.)
7. My doctor advised me to take two aspirins and call her in the morning.
8. After winning a hard-fought election campaign, our party leader spoke forcefully and confidently. (*Or* . . . with force and confidence.)
9. To make your court appearance as painless as possible, prepare your case thoroughly and maintain a pleasant, positive attitude.
10. We are looking for a car that is reliable, safe, and economical (*or* inexpensive).

Exercise 10.2

1. We're seeking a roommate who is responsible, flexible, enthusiastic, and reliable.
2. I'm considering a Smart car because they're cheap to run, easy to park, and fun to drive.
3. Tonight's program has all the ingredients of a successful reality show: ambition, greed, jealousy, violence, and sex.
4. The Internet provides us with unlimited possibilities for research, convenient access to shopping, and endless ways to waste time.
5. Olympic athletes in the modern era can be classified as able-bodied, physically challenged, and chemically enhanced.
6. Travel teaches us to be tolerant, patient, resourceful, and independent.
7. Digital cameras are now the standard because they are well made, inexpensive, and almost foolproof.
8. The cafeteria now offers a number of healthful menu items, including veggie burgers, homemade soups, and low-cholesterol French fries.
9. Why is it that so many movie stars, pop singers, talk-show hosts, and other television performers behave badly in public?
10. We are offering this once-in-a-lifetime opportunity for the discriminating buyer to purchase a unique home that is superbly constructed, thoughtfully designed, beautifully landscaped, and competitively priced.

Exercise 10.3 (suggested answers)

1. mechanically	manually	
2. security	value	safety
3. achieve her goals	find true happiness	
4. humorous	wealthy	intelligent
5. daily exercise	wholesome food	regular checkups
6. being a nurse nursing	being an engineer *or* engineering	
7. speed	comfort	manoeuvrability
8. look for bargains	choose quality	shop for value
9. a good cigar	a glass of brandy	conversation with friends
10. tanned golden-brown	clothed in a skimpy bathing suit	accompanied by a big boyfriend

Exercise 10.5 (suggested answers)

1. • Install nameplates on all office doors
    • Upgrade computers in all offices
    • Replace damaged furniture
    • Institute weekly office meetings
    • Provide flexible hours where practical
2. • Improve food at stadium concession stands
    • Lower prices for general admission
    • Increase the advertising budget by 20 percent
    • Acquire high-profile players
    • Update team logo and uniforms
3. • Be in bed by 10:00 p.m. on weekdays
    • Attend all classes and labs
    • Reduce entertainment spending by 50 percent
    • Submit assignments on time
    • Restrict hours for Internet surfing and computer gaming
    • Replace current crowd of friends
4. • A conference room for 150 people
    • A nearby 18-hole golf course
    • Full exercise facilities, including pool
    • A separate dining room
    • Wireless Internet access in each room
5. • Ability to work independently
    • College diploma in Business Administration, Hotel and Restaurant Administration, or related program
    • Experience in the travel/tourism industry
    • High-level computer skills
    • Fluency in at least one of French, German, Spanish, or Italian

Exercise 10.6

There can no longer be any question about the fact that our planet is getting warmer. The melting glaciers, **shorter winters**, record-breaking temperatures, and expanding deserts all point to a rapid warming trend. Many of us shrug our shoulders and leave solutions to this complex problem in the hands of governments, business leaders, **scientists**, and activists. We think, "How can one person do anything to make a difference?" We forget that if we all acted together, we could bring about a significant change for the better.

Buying more fuel-efficient cars, using our automobiles less, and even **doing** without them altogether would be a start, and imagine the impact if a million city dwellers decided to switch to public transit! We can turn our thermostats down in the winter and up in the summer—even a couple of degrees means a huge energy saving—and **change** to energy-efficient light bulbs. Would it be such a hardship to wear an extra sweater in the winter, **turn off** the air conditioning in the summer when we're out, or **switch** off the lights when we leave a room? Individual actions like these, if undertaken by enough of us, will not only save energy and reduce pollution, but also will demonstrate to business and government that we're serious, and **motivate** them to do more.

On a larger scale, we need to put more resources into research that will enable us to exploit wind power, capture solar energy, and **harness tidal forces**. We must insist on intelligently designed, energy-efficient buildings. Every project, whether large or small, will require the support and encouragement of individuals who buy thoughtfully, consume wisely, and **vote strategically**. All of us—individuals, corporations, and governments—need to dedicate ourselves to reducing, reusing, and recycling. Our comfort, our children's health, and our **grandchildren's lives** depend on it.

Answers for Chapter 11: Refining by Combining (pages 135 to 144)
Exercise 11.1 (suggested answers)
1. This is the car that I bought with my lottery jackpot.
2. Never worry about your heart, for it will last as long as you live.
3. The preacher, who talked for over an hour, didn't seem to take a single breath the whole time.
4. This punch bowl contains alcohol, while that one contains only fruit juice and ginger ale. (*Or* While this punch bowl contains alcohol, that one contains only fruit juice and ginger ale.)
5. The bank has added new service charges that I think are unjustified.
6. Even though football can be a violent game, Canadians love it.
7. I don't like Fords, nor do I like Chevrolets.
8. Office morale improved when she changed jobs.
9. Many people are not aware of the fact that "reality" television shows are, in fact, scripted.
10. While ancient scientists looked to the stars for guidance, and modern scientists look forward to travelling to the stars, Amanda looks for stars in dance clubs.

Exercise 11.2 (suggested answers)
1. Keep practising your singing, but don't give up your day job.
2. English muffins were not invented in England, nor were French fries invented in France.
3. I have a new laptop computer that I am going to use while sitting by the pool.
4. The gates are down and the lights are flashing, yet the train isn't coming.
5. Some people enjoy hockey, and others prefer soccer, the world's most popular spectator sport.

6. You are polite and considerate of the feelings of others, but you should be more assertive.
7. I want to leave class now and go home to lie down because my brain is full.
8. I was born in Sidney, British Columbia, but I have not lived there since I was 10.
9. This car has many of the features that I want and is the right price, but it is the wrong colour.
10. This restaurant is expensive, but it offers good food and excellent service, so I don't mind paying the price.

Exercise 11.3 (suggested answers)

1. Whereas most of my friends hate to cook, I love to create special dishes whenever I can. I am taking a college chef program that will enable me to do what I love as a career.
2. I have almost no ambition, so I never move quickly except to avoid work. I believe that all deadlines are unreasonable and that it is always possible that no one will notice I am late or that my work is unfinished. I begin a task when I get around to it, and I never put off until tomorrow what I can avoid altogether.
3. China is a country with a population of more than a billion people. It is not easy to be an individual in China, for even if you think of yourself as "one in a million," there are a thousand other people just like you!
4. Lawyers, doctors, and businesspeople are professionals who, although they make up less than 10 percent of the Canadian work force, occupy almost three-quarters of the seats in the House of Commons.
5. Blue-collar workers make up nearly 50 percent of the population, but they hold less than 10 percent of the positions in Parliament. Moreover, women, First Nations people, and minorities are also underrepresented in government, a fact that calls into question Canada's commitment to democracy.

Answers for Unit 2 Rapid Review (page 145)

Whenever we do something so stupid that we think no one could be as foolish as we are**, i**t is comforting to know that there are people who are even more foolish. The Stupid Awards were created to celebrate those who have committed outstandingly brainless or clumsy acts. Forgetting why we came into a room, or tripping over our own feet, or **spilling** a cup of coffee on our host's white wool carpet **are merely** minor embarrassments when compared to some of the truly awesome actions of past Stupid Award winners.

Take, for example, the gunman who aimed his .38-calibre handgun at a victim during a holdup in California. When the gun didn't go off, he shook the pistol, peered down the barrel, and pulled the trigger again. **I**t worked. Then there was the would-be thief in Arkansas who threw a cinder block at a liquor store window. The heavy block bounced back off the window**, which was made of Plexiglas,** and knocked him unconscious. **The store was protected** by a security camera, and the stunned thief was picked up by police before he regained consciousness. Another thief gave a store clerk a $20 bill and asked for change. **W**hen the clerk opened the cash register, the thief pulled out a gun and demanded all the money. Afraid for his life, the clerk handed over everything in the till**, a total of** less than $15.

The best of the Stupid Awards, in my opinion, took place in Zimbabwe, where a bus driver was hired to transfer 20 mentally ill patients from one asylum to another. Stopping at a bar for a well-earned drink on the way, **the driver** returned to find the bus was empty. Not wanting to admit his incompetence, he paused at a nearby bus stop **and offered** a free ride to everyone. The driver then delivered the passengers to the hospital, **where he** told the staff that the patients were highly delusional, and **drove** off home as fast as he could go. The deception wasn't discovered for three days.

Answer Key

(*Note:* The sentence numbers refer to the corresponding sentence numbers in the Unit 2 Rapid Review on page 145.)

If you missed the error(s) in sentence. . .	See Chapter. . .
1 Sentence fragment	7 Dependent Clause Fragments
4 Sentence fragment	7 Dependent Clause Fragments
a cup of coffee spilled	10 The Parallelism Principle
5 Sentence fragment	7 "Missing Piece" Fragments
merely are	9 Misplaced Modifiers
6 Sentence fragment	7 "Missing Piece" Fragments
7 Run-on sentence	8 Comma Splice
9 *Made of Plexiglas*	9 Dangling Modifiers
10 *Protected by a security camera,*	9 Dangling Modifiers
11 Run-on sentence	8 Fused Sentences
13 Sentence fragment	7 "Missing Piece" Fragments
15 *Stopping at a bar*	9 Dangling Modifiers
16 *a free ride was offered*	10 The Parallelism Principle
18 *Told the staff*	7 "Missing Piece" Fragments
driving off home	10 The Parallelism Principle

Answers for Unit 3 Quick Quiz (page 148)

[1]Every generation **has** one or two defining moments **that** are so significant that everyone remembers precisely where **he or she was** when the event occurred. [2]Most of the events that have **become** part of our consciousness were tragic, but there **are** exceptions. [3]Nobody **who** was alive when the Allied victory that ended World War II was declared **is** likely to forget the mingled joy and relief of that occasion. [4]**All** Canadian hockey **fans**, even if they were not watching the game at the time, remember The Goal: Paul Henderson's winner in the 1972 series against the Soviet Union. [5]Neither of these glorious moments **is** going to fade from the memories of those who experienced them. [6]Memorable tragic moments, however, are more common than joyful ones, and somehow they **seem** more important to us as we look back. [7]My contemporaries and **I** all remember exactly where we were when President John F. Kennedy was shot, while those who were born after 1980 will never forget the destruction of the World Trade Center in New York City in 2001. [8]No one **who** saw the televised images of the twin towers as they collapsed and crumbled **is** ever likely to forget the horror of those moments.

Answer Key

If you missed the error(s) in sentence. . .	See Chapter. . .
1 *generation have*	13 Singular and Plural
moments which	16 Relative Pronouns
everyone . . . they	16 Pronouns Ending in -*one,* -*body, -thing*
everyone . . . were	13 Singular and Plural
2 *have became*	12 Principal Parts of Irregular Verbs and
	14 Keeping Tenses Consistent
there's	13 Singular and Plural
3 *Nobody that*	16 Pronouns Ending in -*one,* -*body, thing*
Nobody . . . are	13 Singular and Plural
4 *Every . . . fan . . . they*	16 Pronoun–Antecedent Agreement
5 *Neither . . . are*	13 Five Special Cases
6 *are . . . seemed*	14 Keeping Tenses Consistent
7 *contemporaries and me . . . while them*	15 Subject and Object Pronouns
	15 Subject and Object Pronouns
8 *No one that*	16 Relative Pronouns
No one . . . are	13 Five Special Cases

Answers for Chapter 12: Choosing the Correct Verb Form (pages 150 to 163)

Exercise 12.1

1. ridden, rode
2. tore, torn
3. lay, lain
4. shaken, shook
5. grew, grown
6. knew, known
7. lay, laid
8. lent, lent
9. took, taken
10. went, gone

Exercise 12.2

1. The final scene in the play **shook** the audience so badly that they have **gone** to a bar to argue over the ending.
2. After **lying** around all day watching TV, Emma had no time to write her essay, so I **lent** her mine.
3. "Strike three!" called the umpire as I **swung** the bat, but I **ran** around the bases anyway.
4. While some of us have **swum** in the fountain of knowledge, and others have **drunk** from it, Grover just gargles.
5. Lisa should have **known** better than to challenge me at Trivial Pursuit because I have never been **beaten**.
6. I don't mind so much that James has **stolen** my girlfriend and **driven** off in my car, but he should not have **taken** my coffee mug.
7. All the team's players **shone** during the game, except for one defenceman who got into a fight and was **thrown** out in the first period.
8. Near the end of term we were **stricken** to think that if we had **gone** to class and had **done** the homework, we would have **passed** the course.

9. Television is nature's way of telling us we should have **gone** out and **done** something enjoyable this evening.
10. The lake had **frozen** solid, so after we had **eaten** supper, we **brought** our skates out and **spent** a couple of hours skating.

Exercise 12.3

1.   A   [You] <u>Do</u> not <u>number</u> your pages.
2.   P   Your meal <u>is being prepared</u> by an apprentice chef.
3.   P   Each year, Mount Washington <u>is visited</u> by thousands of tourists.
4.   A   "Some weasel <u>took</u> the cork out of my lunch!"
5.   P   Your essay <u>has</u> not been properly <u>formatted.</u>
6.   P   This computer <u>is connected</u> to the Internet.
7.   P   *The English Patient* <u>was written</u> by Canadian author Michael Ondaatje.
8.   A   Hollywood <u>made</u> Ondaatje's novel into a successful movie.
9.   P   Mandarin <u>is</u> the language <u>spoken</u> by most of China's 1.3 billion people.
10.   P   "Children <u>should</u> neither <u>be seen</u> nor <u>heard</u>—ever again."

Exercise 12.4

1. Your pages should not be numbered by you.
*2. An apprentice chef is preparing your meal.
3. Each year, thousands of tourists visit Mount Washington.
4. The cork has been taken out of my lunch by some weasel!
5. You have not formatted your essay properly.
6. A technician connected this computer to the Internet.
7. Canadian author Michael Ondaatje wrote *The English Patient.*
*8. Ondaatje's novel was made into a successful movie by Hollywood.
9. Most of China's 1.3 billion people speak Mandarin.
*10. One should neither see nor hear children—ever again.

Exercise 12.5

1. Mission Control contacted the astronauts.
2. In preparation for the long trip, we topped up the tank.
3. My sister is trying a new recipe.
4. After a slow start, the Mounties scored three runs in the fourth inning.
5. A new band will play a cover of their hit song.
6. My brother downloaded my screen saver, which is a picture of a peaceful scene in Tuscany.
7. In English, one can pronounce the sound "ough" eight different ways.
8. Someone must do something about the unreasonable popularity of SUVs.
9. To eat in the dining room, guests require shoes.
10. Historians think this piece of music was written by Mozart.

Exercise 12.6

1. One calls the white part of the fingernail the "lunula." (Passive voice is more effective; it is a scientific term, and we don't know who named it.)

---

*Passive voice is preferable in items 2, 8, and 10.

2. Somebody organized a parade to mark the team's arrival home after the Olympics. (Passive voice is more effective because it places emphasis on the parade rather than on its organizers who, in this sentence, are unknown.)

3. The Payroll Department will send a memo to explain why our cheques were late. (Active voice is more effective.)

4. The police cannot determine the person who is responsible. (Active voice is more effective.)

5. One of the paper's senior journalists covered the story. (Passive voice is more effective because it places emphasis on the story rather than on the journalist.)

6. I ate more food than necessary when I came off my diet. (Active voice is more effective.)

7. When she couldn't watch her favourite show, Bonnie broke the remote in a fit of anger. (Active voice is more effective.)

8. The neighbour's dog barked at the letter carrier until she was too terrified to deliver the mail. (Active voice is more effective.)

9. We know the two lines that connect your upper lip to the bottom of your nose as the "philtrum." (Passive voice is more effective to express a scientific or technical fact; furthermore, we don't know who gave the philtrum its name.)

10. Shakespeare created the word "assassination." (Choose active voice if you wish to emphasize the creator of the word; choose passive voice if you wish to place the emphasis on the word itself.)

Answers for Chapter 13: Mastering Subject–Verb Agreement (pages 164 to 177)
Exercise 13.1

1. has
2. has
3. succeeds
4. shows
5. is

6. makes
7. overhears
8. was
9. disposes
10. visits

Exercise 13.2

1. A <u>girl</u> just <u>wants</u> to have fun.
2. An <u>article</u> on the Internet <u>does</u> not always <u>contain</u> reliable information.
3. <u>Has</u> the lucky <u>winner</u> <u>collected</u> the lottery money?
4. A <u>student</u> often <u>prefers</u> to attend college away from home.
5. A college <u>student</u> often <u>complains</u> that she (or he) didn't learn anything in high school.

Exercise 13.3

1. A primary source of Earth's oxygen **is** trees.
2. British Columbia wine regularly **wins** international awards.
3. A good manager **consults** with **his or her** subordinates before making decisions.
4. She **insists** on doing whatever **she pleases**.
5. **We** do our best work when **we are** unsupervised.

Exercise 13.4

1. is
2. sleep

3. is
4. are

5. are
6. suggest
7. causes

8. seems
9. interest
10. sounds

Exercise 13.5

1. has
2. writes
3. is
4. has
5. is

6. wants
7. is
8. is
9. is
10. remains

Exercise 13.6

1. deserves
2. is
3. thinks
4. is
5. scores

6. has
7. is
8. has
9. is
10. works

Exercise 13.7

1. is
2. are
3. prides
4. fight
5. Has

6. was
7. gives
8. find
9. is
10. waits

Exercise 13.8

1. is
2. seems
3. is
4. sounds
5. doesn't

6. is
7. was
8. makes
9. seems
10. takes

Exercise 13.9

1. A group of unbiased students and faculty **has** been asked . . .
2. Anybody who really **wants** to succeed . . .
3. Correct
4. The lack of these four nutrients **is** thought . . .
5. You'll find that not only ragweed but also cat hairs **make** . . .
6. If there **are** . . .
7. Neither the twins nor their mother **was** willing . . .
8. The lack of things to write about **causes** . . .
9. Nicole, together with her agent, her stylist, two bodyguards, and three Chihuahuas, **was** seen . . .
10. The amount of money generated by rock bands on tour **is** . . .

Exercise 13.10

There **are** many good reasons for staying fit. The diminished strength, flexibility, and endurance that **result** from lack of exercise are compelling factors, but everyone who joins the many health clubs in this city **has** individual reasons as well. The people I talked with **say** appearance or weight loss **is** their main motivation for working out.

No one among the 200 patrons of a local health club **was** there for the social life, according to my poll. Either weight-lifting or daily aerobic workouts **were** what they wanted from the club, and the intensity of the workouts **was** clear evidence that they were serious. The manager of the club, along with all the members of the staff, **was** careful to point out that supervised exercise is essential for best results, but neither she nor her staff **were** in favour of fad diets or sweat programs.

Exercise 13.11

The rewards of obtaining a good summer or part-time job **go** well beyond the money you earn from your labour. Contacts that may be valuable in the future and experience in the working world **are** an important part of school-time employment. Even if the jobs you get while attending school **have** nothing to do with your future ambitions, they **offer** many benefits. For example, when scanning your résumé, an employer always **likes** to see that you know what working for other people **requires**: arriving at the work site on time, getting along with co-workers, following directions. Neither instinct nor instruction **takes** the place of experience in teaching these basic facts of working life. These long-term considerations, in addition to the money that is the immediate reward, **are** what make part-time work so valuable. Everyone who **has** gone to school and worked part-time or during vacations **is** able to confirm these observations.

Exercise 13.12

1. singular
2. singular
3. plural
4. singular
5. singular
6. singular
7. singular
8. plural
9. singular
10. singular

Answers for Chapter 14: Keeping Your Tenses Consistent (pages 178 to 182)

Exercise 14.1

1. I met Dana and **told** her what happened after she left.
2. After supper, even though he was tired from his long day at work, Rico **played** with the twins.
3. I enjoy my work, but I **am** not going to let it take over my life.
4. The abdominal cavity contains the bowels, of which there **are** five: a, e, i, o, and u.
5. There will be a parade on Canada Day and the mayor **will be** the grand marshal.
6. Correct
7. When the server went down, no one in the office **was** able to work.
8. The umpire stands there, unable to believe what he **is** seeing.
9. She goes to the fridge, gets a cold can of pop, and **proceeds** to drink it without offering me anything.
10. "I keep liquor on hand just in case I **see** a snake, which I also **keep** on hand."

Exercise 14.2

1. First, he backcombed his hair into spikes, and then he **coated** it with glue.
2. The lights dimmed and the crowd held its breath; Ricky **kept** them waiting for another minute or so before he **exploded** onto the stage.
3. The couple next door had a boa constrictor that **kept** getting loose and terrorizing the neighbourhood.

4. Typewriters were a vital piece of technology in the first two-thirds of the 20th century, but the advent of the personal computer **made** them obsolete within a decade.

5. Just as time ran out, Emil **launched** a three-point attempt from mid-court, but it **missed** the basket and the Chiefs lost their final home game.

6. The Peter Principle states that every employee **rises** to his or her level of incompetence.

7. I will have a first draft of my essay done by Thursday so the tutor **can** examine it for structural errors.

8. You will live a happy, healthy life until your forties, when you **will meet** a beautiful dark-haired woman who **will make** you miserable, **[will] break** your heart, **[will] ruin** your health, and **[will] leave** you for another man.

9. I used to smoke, drink, and eat poutine whenever I could until I **had** a case of indigestion that I **thought was** a heart attack and scared myself into eating a healthier diet.

10. The opposing coach was quoted in the paper as saying that Shack **was** too dumb to spell "goal," but after scoring the winning goal that night, Shack **skated** up to the coach and **snarled**, "Goal. G-O-A-L!"

Exercise 14.3

My most embarrassing moment occurred just last month when I **met** an old friend whom I **had not** seen in years. We **greeted** each other and **began** to chat, and I **told** her that I **had** been reading her daughter's columns in the newspaper. I **congratulated** her on her daughter's talent. I **told** her that she must be very proud to see her offspring's name in print. My friend **looked** puzzled for a minute, then she **laughed** and **told** me that the writer I **was** praising so highly **wasn't** her daughter. My friend had divorced long ago; her former husband **had remarried**, and the columnist **was** her ex-husband's new wife.

Answers for Chapter 15: Choosing the Correct Pronoun Form (pages 183 to 189)

Exercise 15.1

1. Computers and **I** are incompatible.
2. The photographer and **I** agree that you look better out of focus.
3. With **us** away skiing, the dogs will relax at the Pooch Parlour Spa.
4. **He** and **I** disagree about practically everything.
5. Neither they nor **we** deserve to be treated this way.
6. The agreement between your company and **us** will not be renewed.
7. It would be better for **them** to come here rather than for **us** to go there.
8. **Britney and I** wrote, shot, and edited the film over the weekend.
9. If I have to choose between you and **him**, it is **he** who will get the job.
10. Mainlanders might have more respect for **us** Newfoundlanders if **we** got to know each other better.

Exercise 15.2

1. **She** and her family are strict vegetarians; they don't eat honey, use leather products, or even wear wool.
2. From time to time, my boyfriend and **I** have gone skinny dipping in moonlight.
3. **He** and **I** agree, however, that no sane person would go bungee jumping in the dark, with or without clothes.

4. Amanda returned the videos before my boyfriend **and I** had a chance to see them.
5. It is not up to you or **me** to discipline your brother's children; that responsibility belongs to **him** and his partner.
6. Ted seems to be quite comfortable living with his mother; do you think **he** and Terry will ever get married?
7. The contract was not signed by the deadline, so Alex **and I** will have to negotiate it all over again.
8. Just as Kate and **I** approached it, the geyser erupted, and we got soaked.

Exercise 15.3

1. Nobody likes old movies more than **I** [do].
2. Andrea is more afraid of being alone than **he** [is].
3. At last, I have met someone who enjoys barbecued eel as much as **I** [do]!
4. While they have more talent than **we** [do], our team is in better condition.
5. You seem to have even more trouble with English than **I** [do].
6. No one in the world eats more doughnuts per capita than **we** Canadians.
7. Everyone wanted to watch the game except Max and **me**.
8. Gary drafts and revises on the computer more than **I** [do].
9. He doesn't write as well as **I** [do], but he does write faster.
10. Not many rock groups have sold as many albums as **they** [have].

Answers for Chapter 16: Mastering Pronoun–Antecedent Agreement (pages 190 to 201)

Exercise 16.1

1. It seemed that everybody in the mall was talking on **a** cellphone.
2. Anything found in the locker room will be returned to **its** owner, if possible.
3. A bandleader is someone who is not afraid to face **the** music.
4. According to the reviews, not one of the movies at the mall is worth **the** admission price.
5. Everyone is expected to pay **a** share of the expenses.
6. Would someone kindly lend **a** copy of the text to Mel?
7. Is there anybody here who can bring **her** own car?
8. Our hockey team is superstitious, so everyone has agreed not to wash **his** sweater until after the playoffs.
9. Bores are people who persist in **their** own opinions even after we have enlightened **them** with ours.
10. Anyone who wants an A for **this** essay should see me after class and give me **a** cheque.

Exercise 16.2 (deleted words are indicated by ***)

1. Everyone is a product of *** environment as well as heredity.
2. Nobody who is as smart as you needs to have help with*** (or **this**) homework.
3. Each car in all categories will be judged on **its** bodywork, engine, and interior.
4. Everybody who really tried should be satisfied with **his** or **her** performance.
5. Every movie-, theatre-, and concert-goer knows how annoying it is to have **an** evening's enjoyment spoiled by a ringing cellphone.
6. Put the sign at the curb so anyone looking for our yard sale won't have to waste *** time driving around the neighbourhood.

7. Everyone who pays **the** membership fee in advance will receive a free session with a personal trainer.

8. A true geek is somebody who has trouble deciding between buying flowers for **his** girlfriend and upgrading **his** RAM.

9. The accident could not have been avoided, and fortunately no one was hurt, so no one should have to **apologize**.

10. Ultimate is a game in which **all those who participate enjoy** themselves, whether their team finishes first or last.

Exercise 16.3 (suggested answers)

1. Our college strictly enforces the "no smoking" policy, so you can't even have **a cigarette** outside on campus.

2. Fishing is fun even when I don't catch **anything** (*or* **a fish**).

3. Every time David looked at the dog, **the dog** barked.

4. In a rage, Max hurled his cellphone at the computer and broke **the phone**.

5. When the baby has finished drinking, **the bottle** should be rinsed in cool water.

6. If the baby does not thrive on fresh milk, **the milk** should be boiled.

7. When I learned that reading for at least an hour a day reduces the threat of Alzheimer's, I went to the library and took out three **books** to read over the weekend.

8. The forest is spectacular at this time of year, especially **the trees** with red and gold leaves.

9. My boyfriend and I took a sailing course last summer, and now we're saving every dollar we can so that eventually we'll be able to afford to buy **a boat**.

10. **Three minutes into overtime, Nell's son scored the winning goal,** which Nell missed because she was arguing with another parent.

Exercise 16.4

1. A grouch is a person **who** knows himself and isn't happy about it.

2. The salesclerk **who** sold me my DVD player didn't know what he was talking about.

3. Everyone **who** was at the party had a good time, although a few had more punch than was good for them.

4. The open-office concept sounds good to anyone **who** has worked in a stuffy little cubicle all day.

5. The open-office concept, **which** many corporations have experimented with over the years, contributes to cooperative problem solving among workers **who** feel part of a community.

6. Is this the dog **that** attacked the mail carrier **who** carries a squirt gun?

7. Thanks to the computer, I regularly order supplies from companies **that** are located in cities all across the country.

8. The tests **that** we wrote today were designed to discourage anyone **who** didn't have the knowledge, preparation, and stamina to endure them.

9. Sales staff **who** want to earn promotion must have good people skills as well as a thorough knowledge of the products [**that**] they are selling.

10. WestJet, **which** offers discount fares across the country, encourages its employees to communicate in a friendly fashion with all customers **who** board its planes.

Exercise 16.5

Everyone **who** has been to Newfoundland knows that an outport is a small fishing community along the coast of that vast island province. Ladle Cove, for example, is a tiny outport with fewer than 200 residents who live there all year. Despite its small population, Ladle Cove is a village **that** enjoyed a nation-wide moment of fame when a man **who** lives there met the Queen. Fred had left Ladle Cove, as just about every man does when **he needs** to find work, and gone to St. John's. Fred wanted to work, but he had few marketable skills to help him get **a job**. Fortunately, he had relatives in St. John's **who** helped him find a place to stay and eventually found him a job at Purity Foods, a company famous for **its** baked goods—and for Newfoundland's favourite treat, Jam Jam cookies.

During Queen Elizabeth's visit to St. John's, the officials **who** organized her tour decided it would be a good idea for her to visit a local industry **that** had a national reputation. Purity Foods was the logical choice. While touring the plant, the Queen stopped to talk to a few of the men and women **who** were on the production line. Near the end of the tour, **which** was being filmed by the national media, the Queen stopped by one of the workers **who** were making the famous Jam Jams: Fred. As the television lights glared and **the reporters** held **their pencils** poised over **their note-books**, the Queen leaned toward Fred and asked, "And what are we making here?" With a courteous bow in Her Majesty's direction, Fred replied, "Ten-fifty an hour, Ma'am. Ten-fifty an hour."

Answers for Chapter 17: Maintaining Person Agreement (pages 202 to 209)

Exercise 17.1

1. one wants
2. you
3. he
4. You
5. we, our
6. we, us
7. we, were
8. we
9. us, our
10. us, we

Exercise 17.2

1. A speed limit is the speed you go as soon as **you see** a police car.
2. People who don't learn from history are doomed to find **themselves** back in Grade 9 for a second try.
3. If we think we can't learn these rules, then **we're** not really trying to grasp them.
4. If you are convicted on that charge, a fine is the least of **your** worries.
5. After we had driven almost four hours, it became difficult to keep **our** eyes open.
6. One cannot lead any farther than **one has** gone already.
7. The penalties for plagiarism are severe, but most of us don't think about the consequences of **our** actions until **we've** been caught.
8. Middle age is that time of life when you've met so many people that everyone **you meet** reminds **you** of somebody else.
9. Never try to impress a woman, because if **you do**, she'll expect you to keep up that standard for the rest of **your** life.
10. Many people are happy to ride with **you** in the limo, but what you want is someone who will take the bus with **you** when the limo breaks down.

Exercise 17.3

1. It has taken Canadians far too long to acknowledge the seriousness of **their** environmental problems.
2. (a) No one tests the depth of a river with both ***** feet**.
   (b) No one tests the depth of a river with both of **his** feet.
3. If you can't cope with the pressure, **you** must expect to be replaced by someone who can.
4. If any of you are planning to attend the class party next Friday, **your** tickets are now available in the Student Association office.
5. Some people are like Slinkies: they have no useful purpose, but you can't help but smile when **you see** them tumble down the stairs. (*Or* . . . one can't help but smile when one sees them tumble down the stairs.)
6. When they feel frustrated or angry, it can sometimes be difficult for **teenagers** to control **their** temper.
7. "Good health" is nothing more than the slowest rate at which **one** can die.
8. In the 60s, some people took acid to make the world seem weird; now the world *is* weird, and **they** take Prozac to make it seem normal.
9. When taking multiple-choice tests, don't stop and think about questions you aren't sure of. Finish the test and then go back to the questions that stumped **you**.
10. When you're gardening, the best way to make sure **you are** removing a weed and not a valuable plant is to grasp it firmly at the base of the stem and pull. If it comes out easily, it is a valuable plant.

Exercise 17.4

Second-person pronouns:

How can **you** fight the common cold? If **you** had the energy to research the subject, **you** would find books, videos, and thousands of articles in newspapers and magazines advising **you** how to cope with a cold. A cold cannot be prevented or cured since it is not known what organism actually causes it. However, **your** research will not be wasted: **you** will find no shortage of folk remedies and "personally guaranteed" cures, most of which do nothing more than make **you** feel better while **you wait** for the cold to go away. Advertisements for pharmaceutical companies promise their pills, syrups, lozenges, and capsules will relieve **your** symptoms, but no one claims to offer a cure.

There is something strangely comforting in this fact. Since the only thing **you** can do for a cold is wait for it to go away, **you** need not waste time visiting a doctor or seeking a miraculous remedy. **You** might as well relax, spend a day or two indulging **yourself** snuggled up in bed, and enjoy whatever restorative **you find** most to **your** liking. **You** might discover, for example, that chicken soup is **your** treatment of choice. Or **you** might prefer hot tea, with brown sugar and lemon.

Whatever **your** preferred treatment, **you** should indulge and enjoy **yourself**! This is one of the few times in **your** life when **you** can pamper **yourself** not just without guilt but also in the knowledge that self-indulgence is good for **you**.

Exercise 17.5

Third-person pronouns:

How can **people** fight the common cold? If **they** had the energy to research the subject, **they** would find books, videos, and thousands of articles in newspapers and magazines advising **them** how to cope with a cold. A cold cannot be prevented or cured since it is not known what organism actually causes it. However, **their** research will not be wasted: **readers** will find no shortage of folk remedies and "personally guaranteed" cures, most of which do nothing more than make **sufferers** feel better while **they wait** for the cold to go away. Pharmaceutical companies promise their pills, syrups, lozenges, and capsules will relieve **the** symptoms, but no one claims to offer a cure.

There is something strangely comforting in this fact. Since the only thing **sufferers** can do is wait for **the cold** to go away, **they** need not waste time visiting a doctor or seeking a miraculous remedy. **They** might as well relax, spend a day or two indulging **themselves** snuggled up in bed, and enjoy whatever restorative **they find** most to **their** liking. **Some** might discover, for example, that chicken soup is **their** treatment of choice. **Others** might prefer hot tea with brown sugar and lemon.

Whatever **their** preferred treatment, **cold sufferers** should indulge and enjoy **themselves**! This is one of the few times in life when **people** can pamper **themselves** not just without guilt but also in the knowledge that self-indulgence is good for **them.**

Exercise 17.6

(1) Second-person pronouns:

If **you are** a sports fan, you are already familiar with the astronomical salaries major players make. **You** sometimes lose sight of the fact that **your** favourite players live in the real world, and their salaries are sometimes out of touch with real life, at least as most people live it. You may be aware, for example, that all-time favourite basketball player Michael Jordan made nearly $200,000 per day in the last year of his contract. If **you** compare Jordan's salary with the incomes of other famous persons, however, **you find** some interesting numbers. For instance, you learn that, in his last year in professional basketball, Jordan earned 200 percent more than the total income of all the presidents of the United States, from George Washington to George W. Bush, *combined*. If **you** do a little more research, **you** also discover that, if Jordan were to save and invest all of his income for 250 years, he would accumulate less money than Bill Gates has now.

(2) Third-person pronouns:

If one is a sports fan, **one is** already familiar with the astronomical salaries major players make. **Fans** sometimes lose sight of the fact that **their** favourite players live in the real world, and their salaries are sometimes out of touch with real life, at least as most people live it. **One** may be aware, for example, that all-time favourite basketball player Michael Jordan made nearly $200,000 per day in the last year of his contract. If **one compares** Jordan's salary with the incomes of other famous persons, however, one finds some interesting numbers. For instance, **one learns** that, in his last year in professional basketball, Jordan earned 200 percent more than the total income of all the presidents of the United States, from George Washington to George W. Bush, *combined*. If **one does** a little more research, **one** also **discovers** that, if Jordan were to save and invest all of his income for 250 years, he would accumulate less money than Bill Gates has now.

Answers for Unit 3 Rapid Review (page 210)

[1]A professor at our college **began** the last week of term by giving a demonstration to her Business Administration students. [2]For 15 weeks, she had **spoken** about the need for balance in life, but she felt that she had not yet gotten her message across. [3]She suspected that most of the students **who** sat before her **were** still primarily focused on money and career advancement. [4]"People in business," she began, "sometimes have a hard time remembering **their** true priorities." [5]She placed a large glass jar on the desk and **filled** it with golf balls and asked the students if the jar was full. [6]**All** of the students nodded their heads. [7]She then **poured** pebbles into the jar, **filling** up the spaces around the golf balls. [8]"Is it full now?" she asked. [9]**The students** all laughed and said that they thought it was full. [10]**The professor then poured sand** into the jar, filling it to the brim. [11]Everyone **who** was watching agreed that the jar was now full. [12]Then the professor poured two cups of coffee into the jar. [13]She brought the demonstration to a close with this explanation. [14]"The golf balls **represent** the important things in your life: health, family, and relationships. [15]The pebbles are the less important things such as jobs, hobbies, cars, and houses. [16]And the sand is the small, unimportant stuff. [17]If I had filled the jar with sand, there wouldn't have been room for anything else. [18]The same thing is true in life: if you fill your life with small stuff, **you'll** have no room for the important things. [19]Take care of the important things first; there is always room for the small stuff."

[20]One student asked what the coffee **represented**. [21]"No matter how full your life may seem," the professor replied with a smile, "there's always room for a cup of coffee with a friend!"

Answer Key

If you missed the error(s) in sentence. . .	See Chapter. . .
1 *begun*	12 The Principal Parts of Irregular Verbs
2 spoke	12 The Principal Parts of Irregular Verbs
3 *students that*	16 Relative Pronouns
most . . . was	13 Singular and Plural
4 *People . . . one's*	17 Maintaining Person Agreement
5 *placed . . . fills*	14 Keeping Your Tenses Consistent
6 *Each . . . their*	16 Pronoun–Antecedent Agreement
	See also:
	13 Five Special Cases
7 *pours*	14 Keeping Your Tenses Consistent
which	16 Vague Reference
9 *Everyone . . . they*	16 Pronouns Ending in *-one, -body, -thing*
10 *Then sand was poured . . .*	12 Active and Passive Voice
11 *Everyone that . . .*	16 Relative Pronouns
14 *golf balls . . . represents*	13 Singular and Plural
18 *you . . . we'll*	17 Maintaining Person Agreement
20 *asked . . . represents*	14 Keeping Your Tenses Consistent

Answers for Unit 4 Quick Quiz (page 214)

[1]As a woman was leaving a convenience store, a man grabbed her purse and ran. [2]"Help!" she cried. [3]The store clerk, thinking quickly, called 911; the police arrived in minutes. [4]The woman was able to give a clear description of the thief: a small man with bleached blond hair, wearing a green leather jacket, baggy denims, and old canvas running shoes. [5]Within minutes, the police captured a man answering this description. [6]Could there be any doubt? [7]He was asked to stand in front of the woman for a positive identification. [8]"Yes, officer," said the young man, "that's her. [9]That's the lady I stole the purse from."

Answer Key

If you missed the error(s) in sentence. . .	See Chapter. . .
1 *store a man*	18 The Comma (Rule 3)
2 *Help she cried.*	21 Quotation Marks
	22 The Exclamation Mark
3 *clerk thinking*	18 The Comma (Rule 4)
called 911,	19 The Semicolon (Rule 1)
4 *of the thief,*	20 The Colon
hair wearing	
jacket baggy	
and red	18 The Comma (Rule 1)
5 *minutes the police*	18 The Comma (Rule 3)
6 *any doubt.*	22 The Question Mark
8 *Yes, officer*	21 Quotation Marks
officer said	18 The Comma (Rule 3)
that's her.	21 Quotation Marks
9 *That's the lady . . . from.*	21 Quotation Marks

Answers for Chapter 18: The Comma (pages 215 to 226)

Exercise 18.1

1. Does anyone remember Scary, Baby, Ginger, Posh, and Sporty?
2. Correct
3. In the typical Hollywood B Western, the villain rides into town and eats, shoots, and leaves.
4. Macdonald, Laurier, Borden, and Pearson were four dissimilar men who had one thing in common.
5. Arnold is an all-round athlete; he enjoys skiing, cycling, swimming, and showering.
6. Nicole has strong ambition, a cool head, good health, and an inquiring mind; everyone hates her.
7. Chicken Kiev, pork tenderloin with prune stuffing, rack of lamb with rosemary and garlic, and baked tofu au gratin were our choices for the banquet menu.
8. A good education, long-range planning, and pure luck led him to wealth, acclaim, and happiness.
9. Much of the world sees Canada as a land where French is spoken, ice and snow are year-round hazards, and violent hockey is a favourite pastime.
10. In fluent English and Italian, our tour guide described the construction of Notre Dame Cathedral, explained the causes of the French Revolution, and listed the ingredients in bouillabaisse.

Exercise 18.2

1. Pierre and I are good friends, yet we often disagree.
2. Correct
3. Noah had the last two of every creature on his ark, yet he didn't swat those mosquitoes.
4. Money can't buy happiness, but it makes misery easier to live with.
5. *Con* is the opposite of *pro*, so Congress must be the opposite of progress.
6. Correct
7. Flying may be the safest form of transportation, but why is the place where planes land called a "terminal"?
8. Pack an extra jacket or sweater, for evenings in September can be cold.
9. The phone hasn't worked for days, and the television has been broken for a month, but I haven't missed either of them.
10. Please pay close attention, for the instructions are a little complicated, and failure to follow the process precisely can result in disaster.

Exercise 18.3

1. First, we need to understand what an independent clause is.
2. In the end, we will be judged by how much happiness we have given others.
3. Unless I get my husband's money pretty soon, I will be forced to live an immortal life.
4. According to company policy, you may not personally collect Air Mile points accumulated on business-related travel.
5. If you live by the calendar, your days are numbered.
6. According to my stomach, lunch time came and went about an hour ago.
7. In most newspaper and magazine advertisements, the time shown on a watch is 10:10.
8. Even if a mixed metaphor sings, it should be stifled.
9. As her 40th birthday approached, Stella met the challenge by trading in her minivan for a sports car and one boyfriend for another who is 20 years her junior.
10. When the first robin heralds the return of spring, I begin to dream of lazy summer days beside the pool, with a cool drink in my hand and a ball game on the radio.

Exercise 18.4

1. Commas, like capitals, are clues to meaning.
2. Our hope, of course, is that the thieves will be caught and punished.
3. Our adventure began in Barcelona, which is the site of a famous unfinished cathedral designed by Gaudi.
4. Gaudi, who was killed by a bus in his 50s, began the cathedral as an atonement for the sins of mankind.
5. Correct
6. A compliment, like a good perfume, should be pleasing but not overpowering.
7. Trevor's job requires largely, but not exclusively, that he be available 24 hours a day to clean up any of senior management's mistakes.
8. Correct
9. One of our most experienced salespeople suggested, to our surprise, that we concentrate on making a better product instead of spending millions to persuade people to buy our current line.

10. The new office manager, now in her second month at the job, has made many changes to our procedures, not all of them welcome.

Exercise 18.5

1. All power corrupts, but we need electricity.
2. In January, the birds compete with the chipmunks over control of our backyard feeder.
3. No words in the English language rhyme with month, orange, silver, and purple.
4. My scanner, which is less than a year old, cannot reproduce a 20 dollar bill.
5. Our Superstore is unrivalled in size, unmatched in variety, and unparalleled in convenience.
6. The train would not get us to Saskatoon until after 8:00 p.m., so we decided to take the bus.
7. Unless the union intervenes, tomorrow will be her last day on the job.
8. Early diagnosis, often the key to successful treatment, is responsible for his recovery.
9. Yield to temptation, for it may not pass your way again.
10. Cleverly disguised as a fountain pen, the camera recorded the entire conversation.

Exercise 18.6

1. There is something wrong with this proposal, but I haven't yet figured out what it is. (Rule 2)
2. George Washington, the first president of the United States, was an officer in the British army before the American Revolution. (Rule 4)
3. While I respect your opinion and your right to express it, I disagree with everything you say. (Rule 3)
4. Politics is the art of looking for trouble, finding it, misdiagnosing it, and then misapplying the wrong remedies. (Rule 1)
5. Did you know that, pound for pound, the amoeba is the most vicious animal on earth? (Rule 4)
6. This department cannot support your proposal, nor can we recommend that any other department provide funding. (Rule 2)
7. The word *allegro*, thought by some to be a type of leg fertilizer, is actually a musical notation meaning "lively" or "quick." (Rule 4)
8. Further to your letter of last week, our Personnel Director will be pleased to meet with you on Thursday, but she can spare only 10 minutes for the meeting. (Rule 3, Rule 2)
9. The best feature of this book, a compact, concise, and clever guide to grammar, is its convenient spiral binding. (Rule 4, Rule 1)
10. Charlottetown, Quebec, and Kingston were the sites of the conferences that eventually led to Confederation, the birth of our nation, in 1867. (Rule 1, Rule 4)

Exercise 18.7

John Robert Colombo tells this story about Conrad Black, the discredited media tycoon, and his wife, columnist Barbara Amiel. Long before Black was disgraced, tried, and convicted for defrauding investors, the couple was invited for dinner by Cardinal Carter, the Roman Catholic Archbishop of Toronto. Unfortunately, they were late in arriving, and Cardinal Carter expressed his displeasure. He told them that when he dined with Pope John Paul II, the pope never kept him waiting. Black, who was well known for his haughty demeanour, refusal to accept blame, and quick wit, replied instantly. "Your Eminence, that is because he does not have a wife."

Exercise 18.8

As long as you are prepared and confident, you'll find that an employment interview need not be a terrifying experience. Some people, believe it or not, actually enjoy employment interviews and attend them with enthusiasm. Most of us, however, are intimidated by the prospect of being interrogated by an interviewer or, even worse, a team of interviewers. To prepare for an interview, the first thing you should do is to find out as much as you can about the company. Among the things you need to know are the title of the job you are applying for, approximately how much it pays, the name of the person or persons who will conduct the interview, the address of the company, and the location of the washrooms. Employment consultants usually recommend that you make an advance visit to the firm to which you've applied in order to confirm how long it takes to get there and where the interview room is. While on your scouting mission, you can learn valuable information about the company's working conditions, employee attitudes, and even dress code. On the day of the interview, be sure to show up 10 or 15 minutes in advance of your scheduled appointment. When the interviewer greets you, you should do three things: memorize his or her name, identify yourself, and extend your hand. Your handshake should be brief and firm, not limply passive or bone-crushingly aggressive. Practise! Now all you have to do is relax and enjoy the interview.

Answers for Chapter 19: The Semicolon (pages 227 to 235)

Exercise 19.1

Sentences 1, 4, 6, and 9 are correct.

Exercise 19.2

2. I need to replace my computer because it continually freezes.
3. It's a beautiful day, perfect for a long walk.
5. I do not approve of political jokes because I've seen too many of them get elected.
7. The lawn, a little ragged after all the rain, needs to be cut; the hedge, shrubs, and ivy need to be trimmed; the roses need to be pruned; and, most important, the gardener needs to be paid.
8. The label on the bag of potato chips proclaimed, "You could be a winner! No purchase is necessary; details are inside."
10. Here are the twins, looking adorable; their parents, who look in need of a good night's sleep; their baby-sitter, who appears to be on the verge of a nervous breakdown; and the family's four pet Schnauzers.

Exercise 19.3

Sentences 3, 5, 8, and 10 are correct.

Exercise 19.4

1. If life deals you a handful of lemons, make lemonade.
2. Sadly, the swimming pool was closed; however, the hot tub was working just fine.
4. Our vacation in Europe was a huge success, except for Euro-Disney, which was a major disappointment.
6. She made herself feel better by shopping for new shoes, a guaranteed strategy for chasing the blues.

7. Cookie pieces have no calories because all the calories leak out when the cookie is broken.

9. The weather is terrible, as it has been all month; I have a head cold that is making me miserable; the power has been out for several hours, so I can't cook; and, to top it all off, my in-laws are arriving for dinner in about an hour.

Exercise 19.5

1. I can't afford a Porsche; therefore, I drive a Focus.

2. Sometimes I stare at the blank page in front of me for hours, waiting for inspiration; it's very discouraging.

3. On my shopping list are carrots and onions for the stew; rhubarb and strawberries for the pie; Parmesan cheese, which Paula likes to grate over the salad; and espresso coffee to have after the meal.

4. I'm reading a fascinating book on levitation; I just can't seem to put it down.

5. The fact is I already have a boyfriend; however, don't let that stop you from worshipping me from afar.

6. Please turn off your cellphone; you will be asked to leave the room if it rings during class.

7. Newfoundland and Labrador is Canada's newest province; actually, it was known as Newfoundland until 2004, when the full name was officially recognized.

8. I love Michael Moore's films; however, I recognize that he presents a one-sided view of political issues.

9. When it comes to office politics, it's best to avoid being distracted by unproductive or irrelevant conflicts; I find that reading the comic strip *Dilbert* is a great help.

10. "For the physics section of your exam, explain the nature of matter; include in your answer an evaluation of the impact of the development of mathematics on the study of science."

Exercise 19.6

1. Turn left when you come to the fork in the road; otherwise, you will end up at the nuclear waste-disposal site and come out all aglow.

2. Watch your pennies; the government will take care of your dollars.

3. As gasoline prices continue to rise, hybrid cars make more and more sense; the problem is their high initial purchase price.

4. If you can afford one, however, it will pay for itself in gas savings over the life of the vehicle; in fact, my calculations indicate that a hybrid will save me money after only three years.

5. The Lord's Prayer is 66 words long; the Gettysburg address is 286 words; the Declaration of Independence is 1,322 words; but U.S. government regulations on the sale of cabbage total 26,911 words.

6. When I am tired, I listen to classic rock 'n' roll because it energizes me; however, when I am working at home, nothing stimulates my creativity like Mozart.

7. I am nobody, and nobody is perfect; therefore, I must be perfect.

8. From the moment I picked up your book until I put it down, I was convulsed with laughter; someday I intend to read it.

9. Buying a house involves enormous responsibilities, not to mention enormous debt; consequently, I plan to live with my parents until I find a wealthy woman with her own home.

10. I'm sure you understand that I would like nothing better than for you to pass this course; however, there may be a small fee involved.

Exercise 19.7

1. I saw Elvis; he sat right between the Sasquatch and me on the UFO.
2. There are only 190 shopping days left until my next birthday; that's barely enough time to plan the enormous party and select an appropriate gift.
3. My new office chair was supposed to have been custom-fitted; however, when I sat down, I quickly discovered that it had been custom-fitted for someone else.
4. When we skied silently through the north woods, we saw the tracks of a lynx that was stalking a snowshoe rabbit; we heard the cracking, groaning, and sighing of the river as ice solidified on its surface; and we felt the minus 40-degree-temperatures nipping at our noses and fingers.
5. One movie reviewer loved this movie, another hated it, and a third thought it was so-so; however, audiences flocked to it and made the producers very rich. Apparently, critics do not have as much influence as they like to think.
6. My pager beeped just as I was answering my cellphone. The pager message was my computer reminding me not to forget my girlfriend's birthday; the phone call was from my answering service, telling me I had a message from my mother.
7. We're unhappy about our instructor's evaluation process; in fact, we believe it is irrational, arbitrary, and unfair.
8. One of the products of the computer age was supposed to be increased leisure; however, most of us are working longer hours and even taking our work into our cars, homes, and gardens.
9. I read a lot of books; consequently, I rarely watch television, which is why I assumed my friends were talking about the evening news when they mentioned a "reality show."
10. Every year at tax time, I am faced with the same problem: assembling my bills and receipts; figuring out my gas consumption; trying to recall which expenses were business-related and which were personal; finding my T-4s, T-5s, and other T-forms; and organizing this mess so my accountant can attempt to keep me out of jail for another year.

Exercise 19.8

A friend of mine had not been feeling very well for some time, so he finally went to the doctor for a complete physical examination. After many tests and two more visits, he was told to come back once more; he was also asked to bring his wife. When they arrived at the doctor's office, the doctor asked the wife to wait outside while he examined her husband. After several minutes, the husband emerged from the office and told his wife to go in; the doctor wanted to see her alone. The doctor asked the wife to sit down, and then he told her that her husband was seriously ill. While she listened attentively, the doctor outlined what she must do to save her husband. The doctor revealed that stress was the cause of the husband's illness; stress must be eliminated from his life. He must stop working immediately and stay at home. She would have to make sure he sat quietly in a comfortable chair while she brought him whatever he wanted. Even driving would be too stressful; she would have to take him wherever he wanted to go. She would have to cook his favourite meals, screen his telephone calls, bring him snacks while he watched TV, keep the children away from him, and cater to his every wish. The wife listened to these instructions with concern; she left the office deep in thought. On the way home, the husband finally asked her, "What did the doctor say, dear?"

She replied, "My dear, I'm so sorry; unfortunately, nothing can be done."

Answers for Chapter 20: The Colon (pages 236 to 241)

Exercise 20.1

Sentences 1, 4, and 6 are technically correct.

Exercise 20.2

2. We cannot write the report until we are given accurate data.
3. Our weekly grocery shopping always includes pizza, pretzels, and pastries.
5. The essential characteristics of a good manager are decisive leadership, clear communication, and meaningful consultation.
7. A shin is a device for finding furniture in the dark.
8. We are looking for a computer firm that can supply several important components: reliable hardware, adaptable software, and timely support.
9. Let me give you an example: Joey Smallwood.
10. In an effort to encourage me, my parents gave me a book for my birthday: *The Dog Ate My Résumé: Survival Tips for Life After College.*

Exercise 20.3

1. The only ways to get rich quickly are to win the lottery or marry money.
2. According to Samantha, men are like Kleenex: soft, strong, and disposable.
3. The pioneers made their own candles, soap, butter, and beer.
4. Correct
5. Correct
6. My roommate, who loves horror movies, persuaded me to go with her to see *Nosferatu: The Vampire* and *Evil Dead 2: Dead by Dawn.*
7. There are two sides to every divorce: yours and the idiot's.
8. My parents think I am lazy, selfish, ignorant, and inconsiderate, but what do they know?
9. Your paper lacks three essential features: a title page, a Works Cited list, and some original content in between.
10. Every time I walk into a singles bar, I can hear my mother's warning: "Don't pick that up! You don't know where it's been."

Exercise 20.4

Imagine, if you can, Oscar's surprise on being told that he had won a big prize in the lottery: one million dollars. At first, he didn't believe it; it was simply too good to be true. Once the reality had sunk in, however, he began to make plans for his fortune. As he thought about how to spend the money, he kept one goal in mind: "I want to help others as well as myself." He talked to the counsellors at the college, who advised him that setting up a scholarship would be a good use of his funds. Every year, five thousand dollars would go to three students who were doing well in school, but who couldn't afford to continue their education without assistance. It was a perfect way for Oscar to share his good fortune with others. Of course, he also bought himself the car of his dreams: a sleek, silver Porsche.

Answers for Chapter 21: Quotation Marks (pages 242 to 251)

Exercise 21.1

1. There are not many quotations that everyone who speaks English knows, but Shakespeare's "To be or not to be, that is the question" must be one of the most familiar.
2. Correct
3. "It is good to obey the rules when you are young," wrote Mark Twain, "so that you'll have the strength to break them when you're old."
4. A dedicated non-athlete, Twain also observed, "I take my exercise acting as pall-bearer at the funerals of those who exercised regularly."
5. Will and Ian Ferguson describe Canadian cuisine in simple terms: "If you let a Canadian anywhere near a piece of food [he or she is] sure to fling it into a deep fryer. Or cover it with sugar. Or fling it into a deep fryer and *then* cover it with sugar."

Exercise 21.3

1. While *Casablanca* is on most lists of the best movies of all time, and *Citizen Kane* is on all of them, *The Spy Who Shagged Me* is on none.
2. Mel Gibson's *The Passion of the Christ* caused as much controversy and discussion as Michael Moore's *Sicko*, but among very different audiences.
3. Canada's national anthem, "O Canada," was written by Calixa Lavallée.
4. In her best-selling book, *Eats, Shoots & Leaves*, Lynne Truss devotes a chapter entitled "Airs and Graces" to colons and semicolons.
5. In his book *Open Secrets*, John Robert Colombo warns, "Do not confuse citizenship with nationality. One does not have to be a Canadian to be Canadian."
6. Today's headline in the *Newark Times* made me smile: "New Jersey Judge to Rule on Nude Beach."
7. Pierre Elliott Trudeau made many memorable statements during his years in Parliament, but he is probably best known for two: "Just watch me!" and "Fuddle-duddle."
8. In an article entitled "Family: You Can't Live With It and You Can't Live Without It," Dana writes, "My mother is the world's top travel agent for guilt trips."
9. The latest issue of *Consumer Universe* magazine features an article about shopping on board a cruise ship. The article is entitled "Veni, Vidi, Visa," which can be roughly translated as "I Came, I Saw, I Shopped."
10. Dawn Hanna begins her essay "Hooked on Trek" by confessing that she is a *Star Trek* junkie: "My heart beats just a little faster when I hear William Shatner intone, 'Space . . . The final frontier. . . .'"

Answers for Chapter 22: Question Marks, Exclamation Marks, and Punctuation Review (pages 252 to 259)

Exercise 22.1

1. If we succeed, who will know?
2. I wonder who won the game last night.
3. Does the name Pavlov ring any bells?
4. Wouldn't it be great if, whenever we messed up our lives, we could simply press "Ctrl Alt Delete" and start all over?
5. Who could have predicted that a game like Trivial Pursuit would enrich so many lives, especially the lives of those who developed it?

6. I am curious about what the new chief financial officer plans to do about our chronic deficit.

7. Please have a look at these exams and tell me if you agree that some of the students may have been cheating.

8. Our manager queried the vice president about the likelihood of completing this project on time or on budget.

9. If we continue to make a profit, I question whether the new owners would close us down or move our operation offshore.

10. I do not understand why the Americans don't adopt a health care system like ours instead of leaving millions of people with no coverage for medical problems or emergencies.

Exercise 22.2 (suggested answers)

1. Row faster! It's gaining on us!
2. Never introduce a quotation with a semicolon.
3. Don't even think about it!
4. Just imagine! She actually got a job!
5. Turn the heat up. I'm freezing!
6. She's here at last. Let the celebrations begin!
7. Try it! You'll like it!
8. The fans were on their feet, screaming "Skate!"
9. "Lights, camera, action!"
10. Go for it! You'll never know unless you try.

Exercise 22.4

The symbol *** means a punctuation mark has been deleted.

1. Did you know that in English the word "karate" means empty hands?
2. If your goal is to be a millionaire before you are 35, you will have to *** make work the focus of your life and be uncommonly lucky.
3. The question of whether evolution is fact or myth doesn't worry most of the people in my biology class; they're more concerned about whether there's a dance on Friday night.
4. Do you think Sara has any idea how lucky she is that her supervisor did not find out she took the day off to go to the casino?
5. The cure is readily at hand: drink plenty of liquids, take an aspirin with each meal, get lots of rest, and take three grams of Vitamin C daily.
6. When her grandfather told her how large computers used to be, the wide-eyed child exclaimed, "Gosh! How big was the mouse?"
7. I think it was Mark Twain who once said, "Clothes make the man; naked people have little or no influence in society."
8. This is the first entry in my new book, *Words of Wisdom*: "If at first you don't succeed, skydiving is not the sport for you."
9. Your résumé is the second piece of writing that an employer will see; the first is the cover letter, which is one of the most important documents you will write in your career.
10. Today's passenger jets are so fast and the airlines so efficient that when you land in Amsterdam, it only takes them a couple of days to locate your luggage and fly it in from Brazil. (*Or:* !)

Exercise 22.5

All too often, it seems that the Canadian national pastime is complaining about the weather. Our summers are criticized because they're too hot, while our springs are too wet, our autumns too cool, and our winters too long. If the climate is so bad here, why does anyone live north of the U.S. border? Perhaps the answer is not that Canadians don't like living in Canada, but that they love to complain.

Two of the most popular sports teams in Canada were at one time those with the worst records: the Argonauts and the Maple Leafs. Could their popularity have been due to the ample opportunity and scope they gave to their fans for complaint? Not only do we moan about the records of such teams when they lose, but, when they win, we dwell with glee on the possibilities of disaster for next year.

The same syndrome can be seen in our attitude toward Canadian heroes. It has often been said that we are a nation without heroes, but I suspect that we have plenty of candidates. It's just that we enjoy complaining so much, we try to find fault wherever we can, and prefer to focus on failure rather than success. One cannot help but wonder how Canadians fare in heaven, where everything is perfect. I suspect they must be desperately unhappy!

Exercise 22.6

When most of us think of Chinese food, we think of the dozen or so dishes offered on Chinese restaurant menus in towns and villages across Canada. In China, however, the cuisine, like the nation itself, is remarkably diverse. Each province in China has a unique cuisine. Some of these regional specialties are available in Canada, particularly in communities where immigrants have settled to create a demand for regional dishes. In addition to Cantonese cooking, which is what most of us think of as "Chinese food," we can now choose among Szechwan, Hunan, Beijing, Guangdong, and Shanghai cuisine. Szechwan and Hunan provinces are famous for spicy food; it is highly seasoned with locally grown hot peppers. Be careful when tasting this food! The most famous dish from Beijing is Peking duck, but Bejing is also home to many other delicious dishes, including Mongolian hot pot and Beggar's Chicken. Each region of China not only boasts its own culinary specialties, but also influences the cuisine of its neighbours. The result is a gourmet's dream: *(or ,)* a delectable patchwork of diverse and delicious foods. Given its astonishing variety, how can we define Chinese food? To attempt such a definition is like trying to describe the Chinese people themselves: infinitely variable, often surprising, and always interesting. Whoever said, "Variety is the spice of life" might well have been describing Chinese cuisine.

Answers for Unit 4 Rapid Review (page 260)

[1]At a meeting of the college faculty, an angel suddenly appears and tells the head of the philosophy department, "I will grant you whichever of three blessings you choose: wisdom, beauty, or 10 million dollars." [2]Immediately, the professor chooses wisdom. [3]Lightning flashes, and a tremendous clap of thunder reverberates throughout the room. [4]The professor appears to be transformed, but he just sits there, staring down at the table. [5]One of his colleagues whispers, "Say something!" [6]The professor says, "I should have taken the money."

Answer Key

If you missed the error(s) in sentence. . .	See Chapter. . .
1 *college faculty an angel*	18 The Comma (Rule 3)
department I will (2 errors)	21 Quotation Marks
you choose wisdom	18 The Colon (Rule 2)
wisdom beauty or 10 million dollars (2 errors)	18 The Comma (Rule 1)
2 *Immediately*	18 The Comma (Rule 3)
3 *flashes and*	18 The Comma (Rule 2)
4 *transformed but*	18 The Comma (Rule 2)
there staring	18 The Comma (Rule 4)
5 *whispers Say* (2 errors)	21 Quotation Marks
Say something	22 Exclamation Marks
6 *professor says I* (2 errors)	21 Quotation Marks

Answers for Chapter 23: Finding Something to Write About (pages 262 to 278)

Exercise 23.1

1. Not single or specific
2. Not significant. (Even children know what they are.)
3. Not significant
4. Not single
5. Not significant
6. Not single
7. Not specific (summer? winter?) or supportable (not known where they will be held)
8. Not supportable (How can we know?)
9. Not single
10. Not specific or supportable (unless you're an expert in the field).

Exercise 23.2

1. Not specific. If limited, the subject could yield several possibilities: e.g., "Bottled water is an environmental catastrophe"; "Bottled water is a waste of money"; "The water bottling industry is depleting Canada's limited sources of pure water."
2. Too broad. You could limit it in several ways so that it passes the 4S test: e.g., "What makes a male/female attractive to Canadian teenagers?" or "How the notion of physical attractiveness has changed since my parents' generation."
3. Not significant. This could be useful if revised to instruct dishwasher users how to conserve water or energy. If your dishwasher is a human being, the topic has humorous potential.
4. Not specific and not supportable without a great deal of research. Apply one or more limiting factors to it: e.g., "Effects on the elderly of Russia's transition to a market economy."
5. Not specific. What about them? How do they work? What are their advantages? What are the possibilities we'll see them at a dealership soon?
6. Not significant.
7. Not specific or supportable. It needs limiting: e.g., "Weather forecasting is becoming more precise" or "Basic palm-reading techniques."
8. Not single. Choose one hero from one war.

9. Not specific. What about them? How to use them? Why are they useful? What are they used for?
10. Not specific. Limit the discussion to one kind of Internet piracy: e.g., "The impact of Internet piracy on the gaming software industry."

Exercise 23.6

1. Oromocto Blues is not relevant. They may be wildly popular in New Brunswick, but they can't be called a popular Canadian team.
2. "Better looks" and "improved appearance" are the same point.
3. Shovelling snow is not significant when compared to the other problems, and it overlaps with "adjusting to climate."
4. *Oprah* is an example of a talk show, not a separate category.
5. The "great white" is a species of shark; this description does not relate to all sharks.
6. Eyestrain from video screens is not an advantage, so the point is not relevant to the subject.
7. Coal is not related to the subject. It has been a mainstream source of energy for many years, so it cannot be considered to be an "alternative" source.
8. The last point listed, "Government has less to spend on social services," does not support the subject.

Exercise 23.8

Subject	Order	Main Points	
1. How to prepare for a job interview	chronological	1	Visit the company's website.
		4	Dress appropriately.
		2	Prepare answers to standard interview questions.
		3	Ask a friend to role-play the interview with you.
2. Differences between spoken and written language	climactic	3	Speech is transitory; writing is permanent.
		1	Speech is spontaneous; writing isn't.
		2	Speech can't be revised; writing can.
3. How to write a research paper	chronological	3	Read and take notes on selected research sources.
		4	Draft the paper.
		2	Compile a working bibliography of research sources.
		1	Define the subject.
		7	Type and proofread final draft.
		5	Insert source citations and reference list.
		6	Revise the paper.

Subject	Order	Main Points	
4. How colleges benefit society	logical	_2_	They provide the individual with a higher level of general education.
		_3_	They contribute to increased national productivity.
		_1_	They provide students with job skills.
5. Effects of malnutrition	logical	_3_	Malnutrition affects the productivity and prosperity of nations as a whole.
		_1_	Malnutrition impedes the mental and physical development of children.
		_2_	Undernourished children become sickly adults unable to participate fully in their society.
6. Why pornography should be banned	chronological	_1_	It degrades those who make it.
		_3_	It brutalizes society as a whole.
		_2_	It desensitizes those who view it.

7. and 8. Decide on your own climactic arrangements for these questions. Be sure you can explain your reasoning.

Answers for Chapter 24: The Thesis Statement (pages 279 to 290)

Exercise 24.1

1. Three essential components of a strong and lasting relationship are good communication, sexual compatibility, and mutual respect.
2. Don Cherry simultaneously amuses and provokes viewers with his opinions about hockey violence, his taste in clothing, and his perspective on international hockey.
3. If I were you, I would avoid eating in the cafeteria because the food is expensive, tasteless, and unhealthy.
4. The responsibilities of a modern union include protecting jobs, increasing wages, improving working conditions, and enhancing pensions and benefits.
5. If we are to compete internationally, our company needs a strong board of directors, creative executives, and dynamic middle managers.
6. The original Volkswagen Beetle, the Citroen CV, and the Morris Minor are three cars that will be remembered for their endearing oddness.
7. Fad diets are not the quick and easy fixes to weight problems that they may seem to be; in fact, they are often costly, ineffective, and even dangerous.
8. Taking the time and trouble to buy locally grown foods is better not only for you, but also for the local economy and the environment.

9. <u>Do you lack basic skills</u>, <u>study skills</u>, <u>or motivation?</u> (If so,) you are at high risk of failing your first year of college.

10. What makes a great movie? Not top stars or a huge budget. Great movies—those that are destined to be viewed generations from now—(are based on) a fortuitous combination of <u>memorable stories</u>, <u>unforgettable characters</u>, and <u>brilliant direction</u>.

Exercise 24.2

1. parallel
2. not parallel
3. not parallel
4. not parallel
5. not parallel

Exercise 24.3

1. Correct
2. Good writing involves applying the principles of organization, sentence structure, spelling, and punctuation.
3. Our company requires employees to be knowledgeable, honest, disciplined, and reliable.
4. Hobbies are important because they provide us with recreation, stimulation, and relaxation.
5. Some of the negative effects of caffeine are nervousness, sleeplessness, and heart palpitations.

Exercise 24.4

1. The four kinds of essay writing are description, narration, exposition, and argumentation. (parallelism)
2. To survive, this corporation needs improved products, increased sales, and a smaller work force. (parallelism)
3. Increasingly, scientists are finding links between the weather and diseases such as colds, cancer, and arthritis. (parallelism and relevance—aging isn't a disease)
4. The most prolific producers of pretentious language are politicians, educators, advertising copywriters, and sports writers. (overlap between *teachers* and *educators*; parallelism)
5. There are three categories of students whom teachers find difficult: those who skip class, those who sleep through class, and those who disrupt class. (parallelism—and wordiness! *Better* … skippers, sleepers, and disrupters)

Exercise 24.5 (suggested answers)

1. violent video games? No, a different topic
   There are three reasons why watching television is a valuable way to spend time: it teaches us many things, it provides relaxation, and it supplies us with topics to discuss with others.

2. A 30-hour work week would increase our company's productivity.
   • Employees will be more focused: Good point, but note overlap between "less tired," "more focused," and "more productive."
   • It would allow employees to get part-time jobs: No, doesn't support the thesis.
   • "Family time" and "leisure time" overlap. "Free time" would cover both. Try "More free time improves employee satisfaction."
   • Work hours will not be in sync with those of suppliers and clients: No, doesn't support the thesis; the lack of compatible work schedules may well decrease productivity.

- Reduction in work hours will be compensated for by reduction in absenteeism: This point should be provable, but you will need hard evidence to support it; note that sick leave is a form of absenteeism.

  A. Three reasons why our company should reduce the work week to 30 hours (are that) workers would be more productive, employee satisfaction would increase, and absenteeism would decline.

  B. Our company should reduce the work week to 30 hours (because) workers would be more productive, employees would be more satisfied, and absenteeism would be decreased.

3. Immigration is a good policy for Canada.
   - Immigrants offer new skills: Yes, good point.
   - Immigrants may find it difficult to adjust to life in Canada: No, doesn't support thesis.
   - Immigrants may bring investment dollars: Yes.
   - Immigrants must often learn a new language: No, doesn't support thesis
   - Immigrants enrich Canadian culture: Yes, supports thesis.

   A. Immigration is a good policy for Canada (because) immigrants offer new skills, often bring investment dollars, and enrich Canadian culture.

   B. Immigration is a good policy for Canada: immigrants offer new skills, investment, and cultural enrichment.

4. Most of us look forward to vacations, but the kind of vacation we enjoy depends on the kind of people we are.
   - beach resorts: Yes, a kind of vacation
   - gambling trips: Yes, a kind of vacation
   - Cancun, Mexico: No, example of a beach resort
   - adventure vacations: Yes, a kind of vacation
   - Buckingham Palace: No, an example of a cultural attraction in London
   - too much sun: No, doesn't support thesis
   - mountain climbing: No, an example of an adventure vacation
   - touring cultural attractions: Yes, a kind of vacation

   A. Different people like different kinds of vacation (; for example,) some people like to relax at a beach resort, some people like to gamble, some people like to have adventures, and other people like to tour cultural attractions.

   B. Some of the kinds of vacations that different people like to take (are) relaxing at a beach resort, playing games of chance, enjoying adventure travel, or touring cultural attractions.

5. A satisfying career
   - interesting: Yes, but an overused word; "stimulating" expresses the idea more originally and more accurately, and is the word the author chose when he came to draft the paper
   - well-paid: Yes
   - respected: Yes, but could be combined with "well-paid" under "rewarding" (a more comprehensive main point)

- provides opportunities for advancement: Yes, but overlaps with "rewarding" and "makes employee feel appreciated"
- makes employee feel needed and appreciated: Yes, but rephrase as "productive" to maintain parallel phrasing and avoid overlap with "provides opportunities for advancement"

A. To enjoy a satisfying career, an employee (must be) interested, rewarded, and productive.

B. To be truly satisfying, a career (should be) interesting, rewarding, and productive.

Now compare these thesis statements to the one the author used in his final draft, on page 336.

Answers for Chapter 26: Paragraphs (pages 298 to 314)

Exercise 26.1

Paragraph 4:

Topic sentence — Although I am usually able to decipher the gist of quickspeak, I'm never sure that I have translated the message accurately. In many cases, this failure stems from the fact that the writer didn't provide complete or accurate information.

Supporting sentences — Take the example that introduces this essay. I know there will be a meeting (about what?) on Tuesday (which week?) at 9:00 (a.m. or p.m.?). Where is this meeting? Who will be present? What documents am I expected to bring? Without the answers to these questions, how can I prepare? Far from saving time, quickspeak actually wastes it. Now I have to respond to the e-mail sender to find out the answers to these questions. At least

Conclusion — three messages will be needed where one would have done. If only the writer had recognized this basic rule of writing: to be brief takes time!

Paragraph 5:

Topic sentence — E-mail is no different from any other business correspondence: it must be clear and concise. Achieving clarity and conciseness is not difficult, but it does require planning. Begin with an introduction that briefly explains the purpose of your message. Next, outline how you are going to develop that message. Use numbered or bulleted points to guide the reader from your position statement through your reasoning to your conclusion.

Supporting sentences — Reinforce your message with a conclusion that states any follow-up actions you require and that confirms the time, place, and responsibilities of those who are contributing to the project. Next, re-read your message as if you were reading it for the first time. Revise to be sure that you have included all the necessary details: dates, reference numbers, times and places of meetings, and whatever other information is needed to get the right people together in the right places, on the right days, at the right times, with the right information in their briefcases. Use a spell-checker, but don't rely on it to catch all your errors

Conclusion — and typos. Remember: A clear message, clearly delivered, is the essence of effective communication.

Paragraph 6:

People who write in quickspeak ignore the reason that rules for correct writing evolved in the first place. Writing that communicates accurately depends upon precise thinking.

Topic sentence

Supporting sentences

A message with a statement of purpose, logically arranged points, and a confirming summary is the work of a writer whose message has been thought through and can be trusted. In contrast, quickspeak, which can be bashed out in no time, reflects no planning, little coherent thought, and no sense of order or priority.

Conclusion

The message, the reader, and, ultimately, the writer all suffer as a result.

Exercise 26.7

1. process
2. definitions + question
3. specific details + contrast
4. examples
5. definition + contrast

6. examples
7. examples + numerical details
8. descriptive details + examples
9. quotations
10. quotation and contrast

Exercise 26.10

(We have italicized the words and phrases that need to be revised to change the tone of this paragraph from tactless to tactful. We've given some suggestions in square brackets following the offensive phrases.)

I'm from the city, so I may not know much about the subject, but [delete] it seems to me that we urban-dwellers have lost touch with the food we eat. By this I mean, *obviously,* [delete] that we no longer appreciate the farmers and farm workers who supply the food that we enjoy every day. *Anyone with half a brain should realize that* [delete] Most of the food we buy is prepackaged in Styrofoam, wrapped in plastic, or precooked and frozen by huge corporations *whose goal is to make humongous profits by selling us the packaging, not the contents.* [who put at least as much effort into designing attractive packaging as they do into preparing food.] *Do any urban consumers understand that* [How many urban consumers think about the fact that] their ketchup is made from farm-grown tomatoes? Do *any advertising-driven* [delete] supermarket shoppers *really think about the fact* [stop to consider] that those *over-* [delete] packaged frozen pork chops, so irresistible with their sprig of parsley, were once a pig, raised by a farmer? *Not only are we ignorant, but also we couldn't care less* [Let's face the facts: Do many of us know or even care] about the journey our food makes from farm to fridge[?] My guess is that if you asked most *city kids* [urban children] where their food comes from, they'd say, "the food factory."

Here is how a final draft of this revision might read. (Note that we've added a conclusion to the paragraph.)

It seems to me that we urban-dwellers have lost touch with the food we eat. By this I mean that we no longer appreciate the farmers and farm workers who supply the food that we enjoy every day. Most of the food we buy is prepackaged in Styrofoam, wrapped in plastic, or precooked and frozen by huge corporations who put at least as much effort into designing attractive packaging as they do into preparing food. How many urban consumers think about the fact that ketchup is made from farm-grown tomatoes? Do supermarket shoppers stop to consider that those packaged frozen pork chops, so irresistible with their sprig of parsley, were once a pig, raised by a farmer? Let's face facts: How many of us know or even care about the journey our food makes from farm to fridge? My guess is that if you asked most urban children where their food comes from, they'd say, "The food factory." But the correct answer is, "Canadian farmers." They deserve our attention and support.

Answers for Chapter 27: Revising Your Paper (pages 315 to 327)
Exercise 27.1
Attention-getter: As the recipient of approximately 1,000 business-related e-mail messages every month, I am something of an expert on what is effective and what is not in e-mail correspondence.

Thesis statement: The three areas that need attention in most e-mail messages are the subject line, the content and format of the message, and the use of attachments.

Main points:

I. Subject line
   A. Never leave the subject line blank (*or* Always include a subject line).
   B. Make sure the subject line states clearly what the message is about.

II. Message
   A. Content
      1. Be concise and to the point.
      2. Tell the reader what action is needed, by whom, and when.
      3. Use plain English, not "cyberspeak."
      4. Use an appropriate level of language in your message as well as in your salutation and signature.
   B. Format
      1. Use bullets to identify points you want to emphasize.
      2. Leave white space between points.
      3. Avoid sending your message in upper case letters (shouting).
      4. Avoid smilies and other "cute" computer shorthand symbols.

III. Attachments
   A. Use only if necessary:
      1. may carry viruses
      2. take time to transfer and to open
   B. Attach text-only files, unless a graphic is absolutely necessary.

Summary: If you follow my recommendations on these three points whenever you write an e-mail, you will make the recipient of your message very happy.

Memorable statement: Especially if you're writing to me.

Exercise 27.2 (suggested answer)
In the following answer, we have corrected only the errors in paragraph structure, sentence structure, and grammar. The passage still contains errors in spelling, punctuation, and usage. We will correct those errors at Step 3.

1   As the recipient of almost 1,000 business-related e-mail messages every month, I am something of an expert on what is effective in e-mail correspondence and what is not. The three areas that need attention in most e-mail messages are the subject line, the **content and format** of the message, and the use of attachments.

2   Some people leave the subject line blank**. T**his is a mistake. I want to know what the message is about before I open it so I can decide if it needs my immediate attention **or** can wait until later. A message with no subject line or with a line that **doesn't** tell me **anything** about the content of the e-mail **gets** sent to the bottom of my "to-do" list. There are lots of readers like me—busy people who receive tons of e-mail, much of it unsolicited advertising that **clutters** up **our** inboxes. For this reason the subject line should always clearly state the subject of the message and should never be vague or cute**,** like "hello," or "message," or "are you there?"

3   As for the message itself, it's function should be to tell the reader what action **you want. Y**ou need to be clear about this and be as brief as possible. What is it that you want the recipient to do. Who else needs to be involved. By when does the action need to take place. Communicate your message in plain English, not in "cyberspeak." Not everyone knows Net lingo, and even some who are famliar with it find it irritating not charming. Use an appropriate level of language (general-level Standard English **is** always appropriate) to convey you're message. Use the same level of language in you're salutation and closing or "signature." **Never** sign off a message to your client or your boss with "love and kisses."

4   **(New Paragraph)** Format you're message so that the recipient **can read it quickly and understand** it easily. Use bullets to identify points you want to emphasize**, and** separate the bullets with white space so **that your points** can be read at a glance and reviewed individually if neccessary.

5   **(New Paragraph)** There are some important points of e-mail etiquette that you should observe. Don't type you're message in uppercase letters. **This is** considered "shouting." Do avoid "smilies" and other "cute" computer shorthand symbols. Some of you're readers won't understand them. **O**thers will have seen them so often they will be turned off.

6   Attachments should be included only if they are really necessary. **One reason is that** attachments can carry virruses, so some people won't open them. Another disadvantage is that **attachments** take time to send download and open. Unless I am sure that an attachment is both urgent and vitally important—the agenda of tomorrow's meeting, for example—I don't bother to open it. **F**or all I know, it might contain not only a virus but also footage of the sender's toddler doing her latest photogenic trick. As a general rule **you should** attach only what you must and attach text-only files. Try to include everything you need to say in the message itself**;** use attachments only as a last resort. Think of them as equivalent to footnotes, supplementary to the message**,** not an essential part of it.

7   If you follow my recommendations on these three points whenever you write an e-mail, you will make the recipient of your message very happy, **especially** if you're writing to me.

Exercise 27.3 (suggested answer)
(Words that have been omitted are indicated by ***.)

1   As the recipient of approximately 1,000 business-related e-mail messages every month, I am something of an expert on what is effective in e-mail correspondence and what is not. The three areas that need attention in most e-mail messages are the subject line, the content and format of the message**,** and the use of attachments.

2   Some people leave the subject line blank. This is a mistake. I want to know what the message is about before I open it, so I can decide if it needs my immediate attention or can wait until later. A message with no subject line, or with a line that doesn't tell me anything about the content of the e-mail, gets sent to the bottom of my "to-do" list. There are lots of readers like me: busy people who receive tons of e-mail, much of which is unsolicited advertising that clutters up our inboxes. For this reason, the subject line should always clearly state the subject of the message and should never be vague or cute. **Some examples of inappropriate subject lines include** "Hello," *** "**M**essage," **and** "**A**re you there?"

3   As for the message itself, **its** function should be to tell the reader what action you want **taken**. *** Be clear about this, and be as brief as possible. What *** do you want the recipient to do**?** Who else needs to be involved**?** By when does the action need to **be completed?** Communicate your message in plain English, not in "cyberspeak." Not everyone knows Net lingo, and even some who are **familiar** with it find it irritating, not charming. Use an appropriate level of language (general-level Standard English is always appropriate) to convey **your** message. Use the same level of language in **your** salutation and closing or "signature." Never sign off a message to your client or your boss with "love and kisses."

4   Format **your** message so that the recipient can read it quickly and understand it easily. Use bullets to identify points you want to emphasize, and separate the bullets with white space so that your points can be read at a glance and reviewed individually, if **necessary**.

5   There are some important points of e-mail etiquette that you should observe. Don't type your message in uppercase letters. This is considered "shouting." Do avoid "smilies" and other "cute" computer shorthand symbols. Some of **your** readers won't understand them. Others will have seen them so often **that** they will be turned off.

6   Attachments should be included only if they are really necessary. One reason is that attachments can carry **viruses,** so some people won't open them. Another disadvantage is that attachments take time to send, download, and open. Unless I am sure that an attachment is both urgent and vitally important—the agenda of tomorrow's meeting, for example—I don't bother to open it. For all I know, it might contain not only a virus but also footage of the sender's toddler doing her latest photogenic trick. As a general rule, you should attach only what you must, and attach text-only files. Try to include everything you need to say in the message itself; use attachments only as a last resort. Think of them as equivalent to footnotes: supplementary to the message, not an essential part of it.

7   If you follow my recommendations on these three points whenever you write an e-mail, you will make the recipient of your message very happy, especially if you're writing to me.

Exercise 27.4 (suggested answers)

Do you find it a struggle to pay the bills every month**?** When **you live** beyond your means, even a small shortfall at the end of each month can quickly add up to a **significant** debt. To **overcome** this problem, you can choose to spend less or **earn** more. At first, the former may seem the more **difficult** choice. **C**utting back on what you spend may mean giving up some of the things you "need," such as eating out, **going to** movies, or **buying** the latest fashions. Doing without such expensive pleasures, however, often **produces** significant savings. **Y**ou may even save enough to balance the monthly books.

Earning more money and *** continuing to spend at your present pace may seem like a more attractive **option**, but is it realistic**? First,** there is the challenge of finding another job that pays better **or** adding part-time work to the job you already have. **E**ither way**,** you're going to **lose** even more of your already scarce study and leisure time. **Second, it is a** fact that most people continue to spend at the same rate**,** regardless of how much money **they** make. **S**o it's likely that, even with additional income, you'll still be **overdrawn** at the end of the month. **Perhaps** the best solution to the end-of-month budget blues is a combination of cutting costs where practical and adding to income where possible.

Answers for Chapter 28: Using Research Resources Responsibly (pages 328 to 334)
Exercise 28.1
1. This "paraphrase" is plagiarism. The writer has made little attempt to rethink or rewrite the author's original. Many of the phrases in this attempt at paraphrasing have been taken word for word from the original source.
2. This paragraph is an acceptable paraphrase. The writer has made the idea her own by expressing the gist of Green's paragraph in her own words.
3. Good try, but this paragraph is closer to plagiarism than it is to paraphrase. While the writer has made an effort to express the author's ideas in her own words, she hasn't been entirely successful. Her paragraph begins well, but after a strong start, she drifts into repeating the original author's words (e. g., *a positive and healthy image of femininity* and *beauty, success, and thinness*). The second sentence begins with Rys's words (*Young women . . . must realize*) and even uses the author's "not . . . but" sentence construction.

INDEX

Note: A page reference followed by *n* (for example, 191n) refers to a footnote at the bottom of that page.

1.1) CBABC
1.2) ABBBA

CREDITS